D1398707

ORGANIZATIONAL
CLIMATE
AND
CULTURE

Benjamin Schneider,
Editor

ORGANIZATIONAL CLIMATE AND CULTURE

 Jossey-Bass Publishers
San Francisco • Oxford • 1990

ORGANIZATIONAL CLIMATE AND CULTURE
by Benjamin Schneider, Editor

Copyright © 1990 by: Jossey-Bass Inc., Publishers
350 Sansome Street
San Francisco, California 94104
&
Jossey-Bass Limited
Headington Hill Hall
Oxford OX3 0BW

Copyright under International, Pan American, and
Universal Copyright Conventions. All rights
reserved. No part of this book may be reproduced
in any form—except for brief quotation (not to
exceed 1,000 words) in a review or professional
work—without permission in writing from the publishers.

Library of Congress Cataloging-in-Publication Data

Organizational climate and culture / Benjamin Schneider, editor.—
1st ed.
    p.   cm. — (Jossey-Bass management series) (Jossey-Bass
social and behavioral science series) (Frontiers of industrial and
organizational psychology)
    Includes bibliographical references and index.
    ISBN 1-55542-287-X
    1. Corporate culture.   I. Schneider, Benjamin, date.
II. Series.   III. Series: Jossey-Bass social and behavioral science
series.   IV. Series: Frontiers of industrial and organizational
psychology.
HD58.7.07355   1990
658.4—dc20   90-41779
                                                                  CIP

Manufactured in the United States of America

The paper in this book meets the guidelines for
permanence and durability of the Committee on
Production Guidelines for Book Longevity of the
Council on Library Resources.

JACKET DESIGN BY WILLI BAUM

FIRST EDITION

Code 9089

A joint publication in
The Jossey-Bass Management Series
and
The Jossey-Bass
Social and Behavioral Science Series

Frontiers of Industrial and Organizational Psychology

Series Editor

Irwin L. Goldstein
University of Maryland

Editorial Board

Richard J. Campbell
New York University

Edwin A. Fleishman
George Mason University

J. Richard Hackman
Harvard University

Douglas T. Hall
Boston University

Lyman W. Porter
University of California, Irvine

Patricia C. Smith
Bowling Green State University

Contents

Preface

This volume in the Frontiers Series presents cutting-edge chapters that advance thinking about some of the conceptual, methodological, and applications issues existing in the organizational climate and organizational culture literatures. While climate has a longer history of research than does culture in organizational psychology and organizational behavior, the two constructs have developed rather independently and have typically been presented as relatively isolated from each other. A purpose, then, of *Organizational Climate and Culture* is to bring together in one place some of the thinking going on in each camp so that future scholars and practitioners might build on these related constructs. As will become clear to readers, climate and culture are clearly complementary topics, with each having much to contribute to the other. These contributions are in conceptual richness, methodological sophistication, and applications questions and procedures.

A theme running through the volume is that all that goes on in organizations is somehow interpreted by members, this interpretation having implications for member thoughts and behavior and, possibly, organizational performance. The focus of the chapters is on the ways by which members interpret what happens to and around them and the implications of those interpretations for behavior.

Overview of the Book

Organizational Climate and Culture is organized around three major topics: conceptual issues, methodological issues, and applications. In addition, an integrating conclusion presents a holistic overview of the current state of climate and culture research and applications. Part One, "Conceptual Issues," presents both a historical overview of climate and culture research (Chapter One) and a series of chapters that summarize contemporary thinking about how climate and culture are learned, interpreted, and caused. The chapters range from a detailed conceptual analysis of the psychology of the meaning of organization (Chapter Two), to the ways by which newcomers to organizations become acculturated (Chapter Three), to the influence of an organization's strategic environment on that organization's climate (Chapter Four). The chapters included in this section suggest the multiple levels at which the climate and culture constructs exist in work settings and at which they may be usefully conceptualized and studied.

Part Two, "Methodological Issues," outlines considerations in the collection and analysis of organizational climate and culture data. The problem of data collection is shown to be one of choosing the *most appropriate* method, not the *best* method; this conclusion follows from a review of the strengths and weaknesses of both qualitative and survey research approaches to data collection, which is offered in Chapter Five. With respect to the analysis of data, the problem addressed in Chapter Six concerns the legitimation of the use of data collected from individuals for analyses at other levels of aggregation, such as teams or organizations. The chapters in Part Two provide a comprehensive picture of the possibilities that exist for the reliable, valid collection and analysis of climate and culture data.

Part Three, "Applying Climate and Culture Constructs," presents a series of chapters that demonstrate the usefulness of climate and culture as constructs and approaches to understanding the behavior in and of organizations. The chapters include an insightful exploration of why culture may not be reflected in an organization's financial performance (Chapter Seven), a detailed analysis of relationships among culture, climate, human resources practices, and organizational productivity (Chapter Eight), an examination of behavioral approaches to creating and maintaining climate and culture (Chapter Nine), a rich description of the clash of cultures during an acquisition (Chapter Ten), and the usefulness of the climate construct for the diagnosis and change of organizations to a service climate (Chapter Eleven).

Each of the three main parts of the volume is preceded by an introduction and overview. Readers will find it informative to contrast the issues raised by the different authors in each part. It will be the melding of the diverse perspectives that is most likely to push along future understanding of the ways by which organizational activity gets interpreted by organizational members and the implications those interpretations have for individual behavior and organizational functioning. To facilitate this integration, *Organizational Climate and Culture* concludes with an overview chapter that integrates the various issues raised in the prior chapters and proposes the study of organizations as political and cultural systems vis-à-vis organizational competitiveness and strategic change.

Audience for the Book

There is a very real need for understanding how the activities of organization get translated into the reality of organization for organization members. The desperate need is caused by the seeming failure of both business educators (in finance, economics, and marketing, as well as in human resources management) and business managers to appreciate the fact that organization members interpret all that happens to and around them. Business managers must begin to view their functions and actions as messages and communications that have implications for member behavior and organizational functioning. Financial plans, marketing programs, economic decisions, training programs, and so forth do not stand alone—they are the cues used by members as messages about the climate and culture of the organization. *How* this interpretation occurs, how to *measure* what the interpretations are, how to *create* particular kinds of climate and culture, and the *relationships* of climate and culture to organizational performance constitute the content of this volume. These issues should spark both manager/practitioner and scholar interest. The former group will find new ways to think about the many ways by which organizations, in their multilevel and multifaceted ways, influence behavior in the workplace. In addition, managers and practitioners will find insights into ways by which they may begin to change the meaning of an organization to the employees in that organization. Scholars will be challenged by the opportunities, some might say insurmountable opportunities, suggested in these chapters for both conceptual and methodological progress as well as research issues suggested by the application of the climate and culture constructs.

Acknowledgments

Preparation of *Organizational Climate and Culture* has been greatly helped by the Frontiers Series editors, Raymond Katzell and Irwin Goldstein. Ray first contacted me about the possibility of editing a volume on these topics and, after I agreed to do it, let Irv become the series editor so that Irv would have to work with me. Actually Irv was very helpful, providing authors feedback on their chapters in a timely fashion while steering the academic (and basketball!) fortunes of the College Park campus of the University of Maryland.

At Maryland I have been fortunate to have the kinds of terrific colleagues who facilitate ideas and writing as well as the kind of secretarial help that facilitates finished products. In no special order, these people have been Jenny Ireland, Katherine Klein, Paul Hanges, Richard Guzzo, and Irwin Goldstein. In addition, students in my various climate and culture seminars have been sources of both amazing insight and boundless enthusiasm.

The authors of the chapters deserve special praise. They not only volunteered to write the chapters as a service to the Society for Industrial and Organizational Psychology (SIOP), but they produced superb scholarship. And they did this despite my sometimes extended comments and suggestions.

Finally I want to thank SIOP for the opportunity to work

on this book. Over the years my membership in SIOP has been a constant source of friendships as well as stimulation for both my research and my practice as an industrial and organizational psychologist. My hope is that this volume will provide the same kinds of stimulation for its readers.

College Park, Maryland   Benjamin Schneider
September 1990

For Lee and Rhody

The Editor

Benjamin Schneider is currently professor of psychology and of business management at the University of Maryland, College Park, where he received his Ph.D. degree (1967) in industrial and social psychology. His professional experience includes a position at Yale University, a Fulbright to Israel, and a chaired professorship at Michigan State University. Schneider has been president of both the Organizational Behavior Division of the Academy of Management and the Society for Industrial and Organizational Psychology. He has consulted on long-term projects with Chase Manhattan Bank, AT&T, and GEICO. His work has three main foci: service climate and culture organizational diagnosis and change, personnel selection, and work facilitation. He has published more than seventy articles and book chapters as well as five books on these topics. His most recent work has been on the assessment of service climate and culture, the design of human resources systems to enhance service organization effectiveness, and research on how "the people make the place."

Schneider serves on the editorial board of the *Journal of Applied Psychology* and, along with Arthur P. Brief, he edits Lexington Books' Series on Organization and Management. He is vice president of Organizational and Personnel Research, Inc., a consulting firm that specializes in the design and implementation of human resources approaches to organizational effectiveness.

The Contributors

Joseph A. Alutto is professor of organization and human resources in the School of Management, State University of New York, Buffalo, where he is also dean of the School of Management. He is the coauthor of two books and over 100 articles and papers. He received his Ph.D. degree (1968) from Cornell University in labor and industrial relations.

Donna K. Ashe is a graduate student at the Georgia Institute of Technology. She is pursuing a degree in industrial and organizational psychology. Her research interests include psychological climate, organizational culture, and quantitative methods.

Arthur P. Brief received his Ph.D. degree (1974) from the University of Wisconsin, Madison and is currently professor of organizational behavior at Tulane's A. B. Freeman School of Business. He also holds an appointment in Tulane's Department of Psychology. Brief's research focuses on how the economic instrumentality of work in people's lives affects their psychological well-being and motivation to work. With Walter Nord, he is completing a book on the topic, which will be his seventh.

Fred Dansereau is associate professor of organization and human resources in the School of Management, State University of New York, Buffalo. He is the coauthor of four books and over forty articles and papers, and he serves on the editorial review board of *Leadership Quarterly*. He received his Ph.D. degree (1972) from the University of Illinois in psychology and labor and industrial relations.

Richard A. Guzzo is associate professor of psychology and management at the University of Maryland, College Park. Since receiving his Ph.D. degree (1979) from Yale University in administrative sciences, he has also served on the faculties of McGill University and New York University. His research primarily concerns effective performance by individuals and teams at work, and he has published several papers and two books on these topics.

Lawrence R. James is Pilot Oil Professor of Management and Industrial-Organizational Psychology at the University of Tennessee, Knoxville. He serves on the editorial boards of *Human Performance*, the *Journal of Applied Psychology*, and *Organizational Behavior and Human Decision Processes*. He received his Ph.D. degree (1970) from the University of Utah in industrial psychology.

Lois A. James is visiting assistant professor of psychology at the Georgia Institute of Technology. She received her Ph.D. degree (1987) from the Georgia Institute of Technology in industrial-organizational psychology.

William F. Joyce is professor of strategy and organization theory at the Amos Tuck School of Business of Dartmouth College and is currently serving as the director of research there. Joyce came to Tuck from the Wharton School of the University of Pennsylvania where, in addition to teaching, he was director of the doctoral programs in management. His most recent books include *Implementing Strategy* (with L. G. Hrebiniak, 1984), *Perspectives on Organizational Design and Behavior* (ed., with A. H. Van de Nen, 1981), and *Organization Design* (with J. Galbraith, 1977). He has consulted or presented programs for a large number of organizations, including Digital Equipment Corporation, TRW

Systems, General Electric, Bell Laboratories, S. C. Johnson Corporation, Los Alamos Scientific Laboratories, McNeil Pharmaceuticals, and CIBA-GEIGY Pharmaceuticals.

Richard E. Kopelman is professor of management at Baruch College and director of the Baruch/Cornell Master of Science in Industrial and Labor Relations (MSILR) program. He received his D.B.A. degree (1974) from Harvard University with a concentration in organizational behavior. Kopelman has written numerous articles in academic and professional journals and is an editorial review board member for three journals. His research and writing have focused on organizational reward systems, motivation theories, productivity management, and professional career development. He wrote *Managing Productivity in Organizations* (1986) and is currently president of the Metropolitan New York Association for Applied Psychology (METRO).

Meryl Reis Louis is an associate professor of organizational behavior at Boston University's School of Management and a research associate at the Center for Applied Social Science. Before returning to UCLA's Graduate School of Management for a doctorate, she served on the consulting staff of Arthur Andersen & Co. and worked as a counselor in a community mental health center. Her research interests have centered on cognitive processes in work settings, career transitions, and workplace cultures. For the past twelve years, she has been studying "life after M.B.A. school" with a panel of graduates from four major M.B.A. programs. Louis has been a member of the editorial boards of *Administrative Science Quarterly*, the *Academy of Management Review*, the *Organizational Behavior Teaching Review*, *Organizational Dynamics*, and *Human Resource Planning*.

Fred Luthans is the George Holmes University Distinguished Professor of Management at the University of Nebraska, Lincoln, where he teaches and does research in organizational behavior and management. He served as president of the Academy of Management during 1986. He is a fellow of both the

Academy of Management and the Decision Sciences Institute. Luthans has published about a dozen books and 100 articles. The consulting editor for the McGraw-Hill Management Series, he also serves on a number of editorial boards. He is currently an associate editor of *Decision Sciences* and editor of *Organizational Dynamics*. In addition, he is a consultant to both private- and public-sector organizations and conducts workshops on behavioral management in the United States and abroad. His current major work is with Wal-Mart Corporation.

Joanne Martin is an associate professor of organizational behavior at the Graduate School of Business and is, by courtesy, also in the Department of Sociology at Stanford University. She received her Ph.D. degree (1977) from Harvard University in psychology and social relations. She has published two books and numerous articles on organizational culture and distributive injustice. She is currently writing a book, tentatively titled *Harmony, Conflict, and Ambiguity in Organizational Culture*.

Philip H. Mirvis is a private researcher and consultant in Sandy Spring, Maryland. He has an active practice focused on large-scale organizational change involving the human aspects of mergers and acquisitions, the introduction of new technology, and the development of labor-management cooperation. Mirvis has written extensively about organizational development, including an edited book (with D. N. Berg, 1977) titled *Failures in Organization Development and Change*.

His broader interests in social change and its consequences are reflected in a "map" and guidebook to *Work in the 20th Century* and (with D. Kanter, 1989) *The Cynical Americans*. Mirvis received his Ph.D. degree (1980) from the University of Michigan in organizational psychology and is a member of the American Psychological Association.

Andrew M. Pettigrew is director of the Centre for Corporate Strategy and Change at the University of Warwick. He is also professor of organizational behavior in Warwick Business School. He received his Ph.D. degree from Manchester University in 1970 and was awarded an honorary doctorate by Linkoping University in Sweden in 1989.

Pettigrew is a member of the Economic and Social Research Council and of the joint committee of the Science and Engineering and Economic and Social Research Councils in the United Kingdom. He is also chairman of the British Academy of Management.

Arnon E. Reichers received her Ph.D. degree (1983) from Michigan State University in business administration. Since then she has been on the faculty in the Department of Management and Human Resources at the Ohio State University. Her research interests focus on organizational commitment and newcomer socialization. Reichers teaches undergraduate courses in supervision and graduate courses in organizational behavior. She has received teaching awards for her work with M.B.A. students and is currently the academic director of Ohio State University's M.B.A. programs.

Denise M. Rousseau is professor of organization behavior at Northwestern University's Kellogg School of Management. She obtained her Ph.D. degree (1977) in industrial-organizational psychology from the University of California, Berkeley. She has previously been on the faculties of the University of Michigan, the Naval Postgraduate School at Monterey, and Chulalongkorn University (Thailand). Her research interests include the effects of organizational technology and culture on employee motivation and well-being, the impact of managerial style and personality on stress and quality of work life, and the management of high-reliability organizations. Her consulting work includes organizational culture assessment and change in American and European corporations, and management development and team building in profit and nonprofit organizations. She is the author of numerous articles, including publications in the *Journal of Applied Psychology*, *Administrative Science Quarterly*, and the *Academy of Management Review*; her work on effective organizational problem solving in schools won the William A. Davis award for research in educational administration. Rousseau is coauthor (with K. H. Roberts and C. L. Hulin, 1978) of *Developing an Interdisciplinary Science of Organizations* and is currently conducting research on the cultures of high-reliability organizations and intensive care units.

Amy L. Sales received her Ph.D. degree (1984) from Boston University in social psychology. Her dissertation was on the social adjustment of Soviet émigrés in Boston. She is now assistant professor in the Department of Psychology at Boston University and research associate at the Center for Applied Social Science. Her research has two foci. One is cross-cultural adjustment, as seen in the experience of immigrants coming to the United States. The other is the assessment of the quality of work life and the examination of how organizational change — the advent of new technology or a corporate takeover — is perceived by workers on the job. Her cross-cultural perspective, derived from her work with immigrants and foreign students, has been key to her framing of the "cultural" issues involved in a corporate acquisition.

Caren Siehl received her Ph.D. degree (1984) from Stanford University in business (organizational behavior). She is an associate professor of organizational behavior at INSEAD, the European Institute of Business Administration. Her research focuses on the study of organizational cultures and related issues, such as the influence of subcultures on the implementation of cooperative organizational linkages. Her work has been published in the *Academy of Management Review, Organizational Dynamics*, and the *Academy of Management Executive*. She is currently on leave from the School of Business, Arizona State University, West Campus.

John W. Slocum, Jr., holds the O. Paul Corley Professorship in Organizational Behavior at the Edwin L. Cox School of Business, Southern Methodist University. He received his Ph.D. degree (1967) from the University of Washington in organizational behavior. He is past president of the Academy of Management and has held major editorial positions with the

Academy of Management Journal, Organization Science, Decision Sciences, and the *Academy of Management Executive*. He is the author or coauthor of more than eighty-five articles and six books. His current research focuses on the origins of climates in organizations and the career paths of executives.

Kenneth R. Thompson is department chair and associate professor of management at DePaul University. He received his Ph.D. degree (1977) from the University of Nebraska in business administration. He has written several articles in the area of organizational behavior, management, and social responsibilities of business. He has coauthored three books and does consulting in the application of behavioral principles in the work setting. Thompson is active in the Midwest Division of the National Academy of Management.

ORGANIZATIONAL
CLIMATE
AND
CULTURE

PART ONE

CONCEPTUAL ISSUES

The chapters in Part One focus on historical, definitional, and conceptual issues that underly climate and culture constructs. I have sometimes heard people refer to the problem of defining climate and culture as trying to nail Jell-O to the wall! The authors of the chapters in Part One, however, show that a definition may be useful for explicating the insight that climate and culture can provide into the ways organizations have meaning for their members. These ways include the psychology of individuals, the acculturation of individuals to settings, and the effects of the environment of the setting on the climate of the setting.

Reichers and Schneider first present a framework in which to explore the evolution of research and thinking about the two constructs. This framework suggests that scientific constructs have a predictable evolution and that one facet of that evolution is to ignore similar competing constructs. In describing the parallel developments of climate and culture, they present an overview of the ways by which the definitions, implicit or explicit, of climate and culture have evolved over time. In addition, they suggest ways in which the two constructs might be used to complement each other conceptually, methodologically, and in practice.

In the second chapter, James, James, and Ashe present an insightful and informative analysis of the cognitive issues associated with the attachment of meaning to organizations. They make it very clear that individuals, not organizations, cognize but that individuals' cognitions may be aggregated to study units of analysis beyond the individual. A fundamental issue around which they build their understanding of meaning concerns the concept of values. For James, James, and Ashe, individuals have values that influence their cognitions of organizations, thus yielding climate perceptions. Simultaneously, individuals' cognitions of organizational (system) values constitute culture of organizations for individuals. James, James, and Ashe present a comprehensive review of the climate literature that they summarize in a unique hierarchical framework. On the basis of this hierarchical framework they present a persuasive argument for the idea that climate for individuals in organizations is the extent to which the organization provides for the well-being of its members.

In Chapter Three, Louis fills in an interesting matrix of the kinds of cultural learnings people have when they enter a new work setting and discusses the sources or agents of those learnings. She proposes that newcomers to organizations learn insiders' views (of, for example, the appropriate way to display affect) as a function of themselves as agents as well as a function of peers, supervisors, and mentors as agents. In addition, she shows how each of these agents may be differentially effective as a source of relevant information depending on the particular cultural learning of interest.

In Chapter Four, Joyce and Slocum move us outside the organization, to an organization's strategic environment, for implications about the climate and culture of organizations. They propose that the strategic environment of the organization has powerful influences on the nature of the practices and procedures of the organization and, thus, on the climate of the organization. It follows from their very interesting argument that organizations that function in similar strategic environments will have similar climates and cultures.

Chapters Two through Four move us from the cognitive psychology of individuals, to the acculturation agents of organizations, to the larger environment of organizations, each having implications for the climate and/or culture of a setting. These chapters, combined with the historical overview presented in Chapter One, indicate the multiple levels and kinds of conceptual issues underlying a complete understanding of the meaning of organizations to their members.

Chapter 1

Arnon E. Reichers
Benjamin Schneider

Climate and Culture:
An Evolution of Constructs

The purpose of this chapter is to discuss the idea that concepts in the organizational sciences exhibit a predictable, developmental sequence characterized by a series of definable stages. This idea is related to Kuhn's (1970) beliefs about the evolution of scientific paradigms, but it is more particular in its focus. That is, Kuhn's emphasis is on major shifts of perspective that usher in new theories and explanations for scientific phenomena. The views expressed in this chapter relate more to what Kuhn terms *normal science.* Our belief is that the conduct of normal science produces a patterned evolution of ideas. This pattern of development can be accurately understood as a three-stage evolution that begins with the introduction of a "new" concept and concludes with the concept's acceptance into mainstream literatures, such as textbooks.

Our three-stage model of the evolution of constructs was developed inductively based on our thinking, research, and teaching. We believe the three stages apply to the evolution of many constructs, although the model is presented here with respect only to the evolution of climate and culture. In what follows, we first present an overview of the evolutionary model. The model is then explicated with reference to some of the

Note: We appreciate the comments of Eric Braverman, Irwin Goldstein, and Jodi Schneider on earlier versions of this chapter.

historical and contemporary literature in climate and culture. This is followed by exploration of some conceptual, methodological, and practical issues we feel require attention for the continued evolution and acceptance of climate and culture. Finally, a concluding section addresses the paradox of the parallel, but generally nonoverlapping, evolution of similar constructs.

The Evolution of Constructs

The first stage in a concept's development is termed *introduction and elaboration*. This occurs when a concept is invented, discovered, or borrowed from another field. Morey and Luthans (1985) refer to this borrowing as *displacement* and cite Schön's (1963) model of the displacement process. Displacement, according to Schön, involves transposing an "old" idea into a "new" field, where it is interpreted and modified to suit its new context. Stage 1 of our model includes, but is not limited to, concepts originating in other fields. Ideas are also "born" within a field; they are indigenous to it.

In general, the introduction and elaboration stage is characterized by attempts to legitimize the new (or newly borrowed) concept. These attempts take the form of articles that educate a largely naive readership with respect to the concept's definition, its importance, and its utility for integrating and/or understanding previously vague ideas or disparate findings. Articles in stage 1 also elaborate on the earliest definitions of the new concept and present preliminary data to "prove" that the concept describes a phenomenon that really exists. During the introduction and elaboration stage, authors of articles develop and apply particular methods of operationalization and treat the concept primarily as an independent or dependent variable.

The second stage of concept development is called *evaluation and augmentation*. During this stage, the first (though by no means the last) critical reviews of the concept and the early literature appear. These critiques address issues such as faulty conceptualization, inadequate operationalization, and equivocal empirical results. Authors begin to suggest moderating and mediating variables as explanations for conflicting findings. There are general and specific exhortations to improve measurement techniques. In response to and in tandem with these critiques, articles appear that attempt to overcome some of the major criticisms and augment preliminary findings. Researchers present data that support the uniqueness of the concept and demonstrate its distinctiveness from other, similar concepts. Limitations of the earlier conceptual and empirical work are acknowledged while authors offer "new and improved" conceptualizations and empirical studies. Reconceptualizations of the construct appear, and it is applied to a variety of theoretical and/or practical problems.

The third and final stage of concept development is termed *consolidation and accommodation*. During this stage, controversies wane and reviews of the literature state matter of factly what is and is not known. One or two definitions of the construct become generally accepted, and relatively few operationalizations or operationalization procedures predominate. The antecedents and consequences of the concept are well known, and boundary conditions are specified. Books and/or meta-analyses appear and consolidate previous findings. Sometimes a concept—like climate, for example—is so well accepted that it is deemed dead (Schneider, 1985). However, in most cases concept acceptance is signaled by its inclusion in general models of individual and/or organizational behavior. Typically, a well-accepted concept appears as a moderator, mediator, or contextual variable in models of more general interest.

It is at this point in concept development that many researchers move on to "younger" concepts, and the overall quantity of research devoted to the topic declines. A few persistent individuals, however, continue to chip away at the remaining mysteries inherent in the mature concept. Occasionally, some aspects of a concept's history will be revived and recycled by a particular researcher, leading to further explication and retort.

The foregoing stage model is subject to the same weaknesses as other developmental models (Reichers, 1987). For example, stages are not defined purely in a chronological sense, but also by the type of research activity being conducted. There-fore, it is possible that an article published in 1986 is appropri-ately categorized as being in stage 2 (evaluation and augmenta-tion), while a piece published in 1980 is illustrative of the third stage (consolidation and accommodation). This phenomenon contributes to the "fuzziness" of stage boundaries and the in-ability to specify precisely at what point in time an idea makes the transition from one stage to another.

In addition, it is particularly difficult to place critical review pieces in a particular stage. That is, our field is such that reviews appear periodically throughout a concept's develop-ment, summarizing literatures in approximately five-year blocks. While we have placed *critical* reviews in stage 2 of the model, it is important to recognize that reviews can occur at any time in a concept's development.

Despite the imprecision just discussed, the life cycle stage model is useful in a number of ways. First, it helps organize the massive amounts of literature generated about a particular topic. In the absence of this (or some other) organizing scheme, the literature on a topic is an unmanageable morass of only loosely connected ideas and empirical findings. The develop-mental model presented here suggests that there is a pattern in the evolution of concepts, and the apprehension of this pattern adds meaning beyond that contained in any one piece of writing or research.

The model is also useful because it is general and can, therefore, be applied to any topic in organizational behavior and psychology. Though the degree of fit between the model and an idea may vary from topic to topic, the model fits most topics enough to provide the structure and meaning discussed earlier. And the failure of the model to fit a particular idea well provides an opportunity for further analysis and insight into the peculiar developmental histories exhibited by some concepts.

Finally, the model provides an interesting insight into the relationship between the development of a concept and the development of the careers of individual people in the field. That is, concepts develop because of the contributions of many individuals, and over time a pattern of development emerges that is not due to any one person. Individuals pursue their own interests within a topic area, and there is a great deal of variation with respect to how much subsequent research builds on or is affected by earlier work. Nevertheless, this more-or-less disjointed outpouring of individual effort results in a domain of scholarly interest that lurches and veers toward maturity.

Some of this lurching and veering can be attributed to development in the thinking of certain individual researchers who begin work early in the creation of an idea and who programmatically pursue it over a long period of time. These scholars may punctuate the development of the concept with influential pieces of research in every stage. These are the individuals whose names are readily associated with a particular topic and who come to be recognized as the leading scholars in that area. So, it is possible to see the developmental structure of an idea by examining most of the research conducted over the life of the concept. But it is also possible to see this structure within the life's work of a single scholar.

To provide an overview of the ways in which the climate and culture concepts have developed and evolved, Tables 1.1 and 1.2 have been compiled. Table 1.1 presents books and articles concerning the evolution of climate and Table 1.2 summarizes the same evolution for culture. We have attempted to present representative illustrations in Tables 1.1 and 1.2 rather than an exhaustive listing. The tables should, however, be sufficiently comprehensive to illuminate the nature of the three stages of development in these two literatures and the way individual scholars have made periodic contributions. Perhaps of special interest will be the column in each table labeled "Primary Emphasis." This column presents a brief summary of the focus of the piece cited. Examination of these summaries provides an informative "feel" for the issues explored by papers at different stages in the development of these constructs.

Explication of the Model: Evolution of Climate and Culture

As can be seen in Tables 1.1 and 1.2, climate has a long history in the fields of industrial and organizational psychology and orga-

Table 1.1. The Development of the Climate Concept.

Stage	Date	Author(s)	Title	Primary Emphasis
1	1939	Lewin, Lippitt, & White	Patterns of Aggressive Behavior in Experimentally Created "Social Climates"	Relationship between leadership style and climate.
1	1953	Fleishman	Leadership Climate, Human Relations Training, and Supervisory Behavior	Development of leader attitude and behavior scales.
1	1958	Argyris	Some Problems in Conceptualizing Organizational Climate: A Case Study of a Bank	Use of the climate/culture concept to diagnose group dynamics in a bank.
1	1960	McGregor	The Human Side of Enterprise	Chapter 10 focuses on the managerial climate; climates are primarily determined by the assumptions managers hold and enact in their relationships with subordinates.
1	1968	Litwin & Stringer	Motivation and Organizational Climate	Climate as a molar concept that describes the effect of the situation on individual motives for achievement, power, and affiliation.
1	1968	Tagiuri & Litwin	Organizational Climate: Explorations of a Concept	A collection of chapters by various authors that explores the nature of the concept and early research on climate.
1	1968	Schneider & Bartlett	Individual Differences and Organizational Climate I: The Research Plan and Questionnaire Development	Development of a measure of climate on managerial employees in life insurance agencies.
1	1970	Campbell, Dunnette, Lawler, & Weick	Managerial Behavior, Performance, and Effectiveness	Chapter 16 summarizes existing literature on "environmental variation," yielding four climate dimensions.
1	1970	Schneider & Bartlett	Individual Differences and Organizational Climate II: Measurement of Organizational Climate by the Multi-Trait, Multi-Rater Matrix	Perceptions of climate dimensions vary as a function of position in the organization.
1	1972	Schneider & Hall	Toward Specifying the Concept of Work Climate: A Study of Roman Catholic Diocesan Priests	Climate is a function of particular behaviors that people engage in as well as their work values and needs.
2	1972	Schneider	Organizational Climate: Individual Preferences and Organizational Realities	New employees' climate perceptions are similar to the perceptions of established employees; preferences are not congruent with reality.

2	1974	Waters, Roach, & Batlis	Organizational Climate Dimensions and Job-Related Attitudes	Factor analytic study of climate's relationship to similar constructs.
2	1971	Friedlander & Greenberg	Effect of Job Attitudes, Training, and Organization Climate on Performance of the Hard-Core Unemployed	The only correlate of the unemployed persons' performance was the supportiveness of the employing organization's climate.
2	1973	Pritchard & Karasick	The Effects of Organizational Climate on Managerial Performance and Job Satisfaction	Climate shown to be related to subunit performance and individual job satisfaction.
2	1973	Johannesson	Some Problems in the Measurement of Organizational Climate	Critical review of climate as redundant with work attitudes.
2	1973	Payne & Mansfield	Relationships of Perceptions of Organizational Climate to Organizational Structure, Context, and Hierarchical Position	Climate perceptions vary as a function of organizational level.
2	1973	Guion	A Note on Organizational Climate	Critique of climate as redundant with job satisfaction.
2	1974	James & Jones	Organizational Climate: A Review of Theory and Research	Organizes earlier work into three distinct approaches; offers a rationale for distinguishing between organizational and psychological climate.
2	1974	Hellriegel & Slocum	Organizational Climate: Measures, Research, and Contingencies	Critical review of climate research as an independent, intervening, and dependent variable.
2	1974	Lawler, Hall, & Oldham	Organizational Climate: Relationship to Organizational Structure, Process, and Performance	Climate shown to be significantly related to organizational performance and job satisfaction.
2	1975	LaFollette & Sims	Is Satisfaction Redundant with Organizational Climate?	Found no support for the satisfaction/climate redundancy hypothesis.
2	1975(a)	Schneider	Organizational Climate: Individual Preferences and Organizational Realities Revisited	The fit between expectations and reality for new agents was predictive of success in agencies with positive climates.
2	1975	Downey, Hellriegel, & Slocum	Congruence Between Individual Needs, Organizational Climate, Job Satisfaction and Performance	Satisfaction is a function of congruence between needs and climate.
2	1975	Gavin	Organizational Climate as a Function of Personal and Organizational Variables	Climate perceptions are influenced by personal and organizational variables; no significant interactions found.

Table 1.1. The Development of the Climate Concept, Cont'd.

Stage	Date	Author(s)	Title	Primary Emphasis
2	1975	Schneider & Snyder	Some Relationships Between Job Satisfaction and Organizational Climate	Distinguishes conceptually and empirically between satisfaction and climate.
2	1975(b)	Schneider	Organizational Climates: An Essay	Explores the etiology of climate; proposes a distinction between climate and satisfaction; specifies "climates for something."
2	1976	Payne, Fineman, & Wall	Organizational Climate and Job Satisfaction: A Conceptual Synthesis	Discusses similarities and differences in the ways climate and job satisfaction have been conceptualized and measured.
2	1976	Payne & Pugh	Organizational Structure and Climate	Focuses on the relationships among objective and perceptual measures of structure and climate.
2	1976	Johnston	A New Conceptualization of Source of Organizational Climate	Multiple climates exist in organizations and are a function of the individual/organization relationship.
2	1977	Drexler	Organizational Climate: Its Homogeneity Within Organizations	Climate perceptions vary as a function of organization and subgroup.
2	1977	Howe	Group Climate: An Exploratory Analysis of Construct Validity	Climate perceptions found to be more a function of group membership than person-type.
2	1978	Powell & Butterfield	The Case for Subsystem Climates in Organizations	Reviews literature that supports the idea that multiple climates exist in the same organization.
2	1978	James, Hater, Gent, & Bruni	Psychological Climate: Implications from Cognitive Social Learning Theory and Interactional Psychology	Climate is reexamined in light of social learning theory and interactional psychology; insights from these fields are used to suggest directions for future research.
2	1978	Woodman & King	Organizational Climate: Science or Folklore?	Reviews and critiques climate theory and research; focuses on measurement issues.
2	1982	Field & Abelson	Climate: A Reconceptualization and Proposed Model	Literature is reviewed; key measurement and conceptual issues are addressed through development of a new model of the climate construct and its relationship to work attitudes and behaviors.

	Year	Author	Title	Description
2	1983	Schneider & Reichers	On the Etiology of Climates	A symbolic interactionist perspective is offered as an explanation for the formation of climates in organizations.
2	1983	Schnake	An Empirical Assessment of the Effects of Affective Response in the Measurement of Organizational Climate	Climate measurement improves when job satisfaction is partialed out.
2	1985	Ashforth	Climate Formation: Issues and Extensions	The symbolic interactionist approach to climate formation is extended through consideration of corporate culture, symbolic management, and other issues.
2	1980	Zohar	Safety Climate in Industrial Organizations: Theoretical and Applied Implications	First empirical assessment of a climate "for something."
3	1982	Joyce & Slocum	Climate Discrepancy: Refining the Concepts of Psychological and Organizational Climate	Explores relationship between climate discrepancy and other outcomes; climates empirically defined by clustering similar scores.
3	1983	Abbey & Dickson	R&D Work Climate and Innovation in Semi-Conductors	The climate for innovation in the R&D subsystem of semiconductor companies is related to number of technological breakthroughs.
3	1984	Joyce & Slocum	Collective Climate: Agreement as a Basis for Defining Aggregate Climates in Organizations	Builds on their 1982 piece; solidifies idea that collective climates are defined by similarity of perceptions.
3	1985	Glick	Conceptualizing and Measuring Organizational and Psychological Climate: Pitfalls in Multi-level research	Critical review of climate theory and measurement; addresses issue of correct level of analysis.
3	1985	Schneider	Organizational Behavior	Concludes that interest in climate has waned due to its acceptance; acknowledges that some advances remain to be made.
3	1987	Kozlowski & Hults	An Exploration of Climates for Technical Updating and Performance	Assessment of the climate for updating; indicates that performance is associated with climate for updating.

nizational behavior. As such, it has experienced several reconceptualizations and empirical breakthroughs that are not yet
characteristic of culture's development. In particular, the climate construct got off to a relatively quick empirical start. At the
time of its major introduction in the late 1960s, climate researchers did not devote many years or many articles to haggling
over definitions or elaborating all the possible nuances of climate. Rather, applied psychologists began gathering data and
assessing the validity of the concept right from the start. Thus
the early studies of climate considered climate to be a correlate
of work motivation and productivity (Litwin & Stringer, 1968) or
salesperson success (Schneider & Bartlett, 1968, 1970). This
yielded for climate a relatively meager number of articles in
stage 1 and a great many articles in stage 2.

More specifically, most would agree that the earliest explicit reference to the concept occurred in Lewin, Lippitt, and
White's (1939) article on experimentally created social climates
in boys' groups. Yet these authors offered neither a definition
nor a measure of climate per se and used the term in quotation
marks ("social climates") in the title of their famous article. In a
1953 article, Fleishman discussed leadership climate as an explanatory construct for the failure of a training program to
transfer to a field setting but left climate, as a construct, un-
defined. In 1958 Argyris wrote a key paper on climate in a bank,
and he defined climate in a way that would look reasonably
familiar to present-day researchers (that is, in terms of formal
organization policies, and employee needs, values, and personalities that operate in a self-perpetuating system of "living complexity"). However, Argyris still had the term *climate* in quotation
marks and used it interchangeably with the term *informal culture*.

McGregor, in his famous 1960 book *The Human Side of
Enterprise*, devoted an entire chapter to what he called "the
managerial climate." He did not use climate in quotation marks,
conceptualizing it as the ". . . day-by-day behavior of the immediate superior and of other significant people in the managerial
organization. . ." (1960, p. 133). He identified these behaviors as
those that convince subordinates that they will receive a fair
break, that management has concern for the welfare of subordi-

Table 1.2. The Development of the Culture Concept.

Stage	Date	Author(s)	Title	Primary Emphasis
1	1979	Pettigrew	On Studying Organizational Cultures	Traces the emergence and development of an organization's culture over time.
1	1980	Dandridge, Mitroff, & Joyce	Organizational Symbolism: A Topic to Expand Organizational Analysis	Urges the study of myths and symbols as revealing the deep structure of organizations.
1	1982	Deal & Kennedy	*Corporate Cultures*	Extensive discussion of the nature of culture, types of culture, and managing culture.
1	1983		*Administrative Science Quarterly* special edition devoted to culture	Introduces and explains the concept from a variety of perspectives; promotes the study of culture in particular ways.
1	1983	Jelinek, Smircich, & Hirsch	Introduction: A Code of Many Colors	
1	1983	Smircich	Concepts of Culture and Organizational Analysis	
1	1983	Gregory	Native-View Paradigms: Multiple Cultures and Culture Conflicts in Organizations	
1	1983	Smith & Simmons	A Rumpelstiltskin Organization: Metaphors on Metaphors in Field Research	
1	1983	Barley	Semiotics and the Study of Occupational and Organizational Cultures	
1	1983	Riley	A Structurationist Account of Political Cultures	
1	1983	Martin, Feldman, Hatch, & Sitkin	The Uniqueness Paradox in Organizational Stories	
1	1983	Jones	Transaction Costs, Property Rights, and Organizational Culture: An Exchange Perspective	
1	1983	Broms & Gahmberg	Communication to Self in Organizations and Cultures	

Table 1.2. The Development of the Culture Concept, Cont'd.

Stage	Date	Author(s)	Title	Primary Emphasis
1	1983		*Organizational Dynamics* special issue devoted to culture	Urges managers to adopt the culture concept as a practical tool.
1	1983	Sathe	Implications of Corporate Culture: A Manager's Guide to Action	
1	1983	Wilkins	The Culture Audit: A Tool for Understanding Organizations	
1	1983	Koprowski	Cultural Myths: Clues to Effective Management	
1	1983	Schein	The Role of the Founder in Creating Organizational Culture	Extensive definition of culture; discussion of its etiology and transmission.
1	1983	Pondy, Frost, Morgan, & Dandridge	*Organizational Symbolism*	Series of chapters focuses on a cultural perspective on organizations and the role of language, myths, and symbols in that perspective.
1	1984	Schein	Coming to a New Awareness of Organizational Culture	Definition and exploration of the concept.
1	1984	Trice & Beyer	Studying Organizational Cultures Through Rites and Ceremonials	Definition of culture; advocates studying culture through rites and ceremonials.
1	1985	Frost, Moore, Louis, Lundberg, & Martin	*Organizational Culture*	A series of chapters focusing on definitions of culture and on issues of managing culture, studying culture, and linking organizational culture to the societal culture.
2	1983	Wilkins & Ouchi	Efficient Cultures: Exploring the Relationship Between Culture and Organizational Performance	Explores the conditions that give rise to strong cultures; delineates ways in which culture contributes to efficiency.
2	1983	Martin & Siehl	Organizational Culture and Counterculture: An Uneasy Symbiosis	Critiques assumptions underlying most culture research; offers a partial reconceptualization of the concept.

	Year	Author	Title	Description
2	1985	Morey & Luthans	Refining the Displacement of Culture and the Use of Scenes and Themes in Organizational Studies	Reviews and critiques the concept of culture as it has been used in organizational studies.
1–2	1985	Schein	*Organizational Culture and Leadership: A Dynamic View*	In-depth discussion of the nature of the concept, its etiology, and the role of the leader in cultural exchange.
2	1985	Sathe	*Culture and Related Corporate Realities*	Textbook; uses a cultural perspective on problems of organizational entry, establishment, and change.
2	1985	Nicholson & Johns	The Absence Culture and the Psychological Contract—Who's in Control of Absence?	Absence rates are a consequence of varying types of cultures in combination with varying psychological contracts.
2	1986	Barney	Organizational Culture: Can It Be a Source of Sustained Competitive Advantage?	Explores consequences of culture such as performance and economic profit.
2	1986	Harris & Sutton	Functions of Parting Ceremonies in Dying Organizations	Explores the consequences of one aspect of organizational culture.
2	1986	Kets De Vries & Miller	Personality, Culture, and Organization	Culture is the vehicle through which executives' personalities influence strategy.
2	1987	Schriber & Gutek	Some Time Dimensions of Work: Measurement of an Underlying Aspect of Organization Culture	Knowledge of norms about time facilitates rich descriptions of organizational cultures.
2	1988	Nahavandi & Malekzadeh	Acculturation in Mergers and Acquisitions	Successful implementation of a merger is a function of the degree of congruence between the two original organizations' cultures.
2	1989	Ott	*The Organizational Culture Perspective*	Exploration of various definitions and defining attributes of culture as well as culture formation, management, and change.

nates as well as for their morale and productivity, and that management has upward influence in the organization and is competent. In other words, McGregor's view of climate was that managers create the climate in which subordinates work by what they do, how they do it, how competent they are, and their ability to make things happen through upward influence in the organization. McGregor designed no quantitative measures of his climate conceptualization.

The first paper that relatively comprehensively conceptualized and operationalized climate as it is studied now was presented by Litwin and Stringer in 1966 at a conference on climate. This article presented a now familiar set of six climate dimensions—including structure, reward, and warmth and support—as reported by organization member perceptions. A version of this paper appears in the book of collected papers from the conference on climate that was edited by Tagiuri and Litwin and published in 1968. These papers explore the nature of the climate construct, its definition, and early empirical findings.

Another book, by Litwin and Stringer, also published in 1968, was entitled *Motivation and Organizational Climate*. This book focuses on the concept of climate as it affects human motives for power, achievement, and affiliation. It reports the results of several experimental and field studies, attempts to operationalize climate through assessment of members' perceptions, and addresses the practical implications of the research. This book, along with the one edited by Tagiuri and Litwin, marks the beginning of the construct's more contemporary history in our field. Thus, even though the word *climate* appeared in much earlier articles (Lewin, Lippitt, & White, 1939, for example), the concept of climate as we now know it was not fully explicated until thirty years later.

In contrast, the culture construct has a great many articles in stage 1 and relatively few in stage 2. Culture researchers have devoted numerous articles and books to explorations of the nature of the concept, to its definition, and to discussion of what is and is not "in" the concept of culture (for example, norms, values, shared meanings and/or rituals, myths, artifacts, language, assumptions, and so on).

n addition, empirical research on culture is just begin-
appear. Note that the point being made here is not the
ion between qualitative and quantitative research (to be
ed later). Rather, there is a paucity of *any kind* of empirical
h on culture.

This historical/evolutionary overview of the development
climate and culture literatures yields some interesting
. For example, we now see the emphasis in climate on
h activities and application compared to a focus on
tual issues in culture. In what follows we explore in more
he conceptual, methodological, and applications sim-
and differences in the climate and culture literatures.

Conceptual Considerations

researchers make a distinction in the definition of
between culture as something an organization *is* versus
as something an organization *has* (Smircich, 1983). The
inition promotes the study of organizational culture qua
and uses a native-view paradigm (Gregory, 1983). This
h is for the most part exploratory and descriptive in
yielding thick descriptions of the deep structure of
ations.

he second definition of culture, as something an organi-
as, promotes an examination of organizational cultures
ms of shared meanings, assumptions, and underlying
Schein, 1985). This approach encourages the investiga-
he causes (that is, the founder; the societal context) and
that is, organizational performance; problematic merg-
rganizational culture. This second approach to culture
ne distinct similarities to the concept of climate
der, 1985).

limate is widely defined as the shared perception of "the
ngs are around here." More precisely, climate is shared
ions of organizational policies, practices, and pro-
, both formal and informal. Climate is a molar concept
ndicative of the organization's goals and appropriate
o goal attainment. It is also a more specific construct

Differences in the relative emphasis in stage 1 versus stage
2 may be due to the displaced nature of culture in the fields of
industrial and organizational psychology and organizational
behavior. Whereas climate, as an indigenous concept, seemed to
be a natural outgrowth of the desire to specify environmental
influences on motivation and behavior, culture is a borrowed
concept that may require more careful introduction and elaboration. Indeed, early climate researchers were so at ease with
the concept that some—such as Lewin, Lippitt, and White
(1939) and Fleishman (1953)—did not even bother to define or
measure it at all. Culture, on the other hand, seems indigenous
to anthropology, not psychology. As such, the displacement
process (Schön, 1963) may require the more careful education
of a largely naive readership. This results in a greater attention
to matters of definition and elaboration, which explains the
numerous stage 1 pieces in the culture literature.

The beginnings of formal writing on the concept of organizational culture are thus somewhat easy to identify. Pettigrew
published an article on culture in *Administrative Science Quarterly*
in 1979. In that article, he introduced the anthropological concept of culture to a naive organizational science readership and
showed how related concepts (symbolism, myth, ritual, and so
on) could be used in organizational analysis. Deal and Kennedy's 1982 book *Corporate Cultures: The Rites and Rituals of Organizational Life* elaborated and popularized similar ideas to a very
broad readership, and in 1983 *Administrative Science Quarterly*
devoted a special issue to the concept of culture. This issue,
edited by Jelinek, Smircich, and Hirsch, explored and attempted to define the culture construct. In the same year, *Organizational Dynamics* also devoted a special issue to the culture
concept, focusing on its implications for managers. Together,
these two special issues mark the beginning of the scholarly
explication and study of culture in work organizations. In a very
brief period of time, then, the concepts and methods of culture
research were fairly well explicated. These efforts regarding
culture represented much more of a displacement of a concept
than was true for climate, the latter being more indigenous to
organizational psychology and thus comfortable for the organi-

zational psychologists and organizational behaviorists who pursued its study.

Perhaps another difference between climate and culture development concerns the ways of science in applied psychology compared to anthropology. Research from a climate perspective comes almost linearly from Kurt Lewin's influence, and Lewin believed there was nothing so practical as a good theory. Lewin's protégés included Argyris (for example, 1957, 1960), McGregor (1960), and the entire University of Michigan school of thought on group and organizational functioning (for instance, Cartwright & Zander, 1968; Seashore, 1981). All of these researchers appear to have been more concerned with organizational effectiveness than with climate, climate being a construct to help understand *why* some organizations experienced more effective functioning than others.

In contrast, effectiveness is not an important concept in anthropology, especially in comparative or cultural anthropology; *description* is the issue. That is, the goal of the study of culture is comparison with no implicit or explicit value judgments about which culture is more effective. Comparisons of cultures are made along fairly standardized dimensions such as the nature of laws, handicrafts, economic life, clothing and dwellings, social organization, and spiritual life (for example, Birket-Smith, 1965). This predilection for describing one culture compared to another yields considerable discussion of what the elements of culture *are* and produces case studies of one culture at a time (for an exception, see Denison, 1990). However, in contrast to academics, practitioners have attempted to make culture an effectiveness issue; we discuss this topic in more detail later.

A second difference in the developmental history of the two constructs, then, concerns the relative dearth of empirical research and critical reviews in stage 2 for the culture construct.

The 1970s produced numerous literature reviews and critiques of the climate construct and its measurement. For example, in a book by Campbell, Dunnette, Lawler, and Weick (1970), climate was subsumed under a broader heading of "environmental variation." They found the early research deficient

on two counts: (1) that the climate environmental variation still unco dency for researchers to cull items fi (1970, p. 394) yields incomplete op Hellriegel and Slocum (1974), Jai Payne and Pugh (1976) are also climate as early critical reviews of garding the conceptualization and in climate research. In addition, Gu (1973) wrote particularly pointed c and conceptualization of climate, whether climate offered any theore to the already existing literature o

Consistent with stage 2 act response to these critical pieces. Jol Sims (1975), Powell and Butterf Snyder (1975), and Schneider (19 tualizations of the construct or c criticism. For instance, the contro measurement of climate has con emplified in the work of Glick (198 and Slocum (1988), Joyce and S Schneider, Schoorman, and Bern

The concept of organizatio therefore few reviews and critiqu written. Indeed, we could find onl (Martin & Siehl, 1983), even thou have been published on the topi Louis, Lundberg, & Martin, 19 Schein, 1985). Rather, the articles appear in stage 2 tend to elabor plication to other organizational mains rather than evaluating or c For instance, the similarity of th construct of strategy is explored (aspects of organizational decline mergers and acquisitions (Nahav studied.

that has a particular referent, as in the climate *for* service or the climate *for* safety (Schneider & Rentsch, 1988). Multiple climates are thought to exist in organizations, and these climates have recently been specified by identifying clusters of persons who share common perceptions (Joyce & Slocum, 1984; Rentsch, 1988).

No single accepted definition of culture exists, but culture as something an organization *has* is defined by Schein (1985) as learned responses to the group's problems of survival and internal integration. These responses are subconscious, taken for granted, and shared by members of the social unit. Schein maintains that the existence of multiple cultures in organizations is an empirical question, but he believes that multiple organizational cultures can and do exist. According to Schein, norms, values, rituals, and climate are all manifestations of culture. Culture itself is an interpretive scheme or way of perceiving, thinking, and feeling in relation to the group's problems. Louis (1985) echoes this view when she defines culture as a commonly held set of understandings for organizing action. Gregory (1983) and Martin and Siehl (1983) explicitly hold the view that organizations are multicultural.

The preceding definitions cannot be neatly collapsed into a composite. However, running through all definitions of culture as something an organization has is the idea that culture is a common set of shared meanings or understandings about the group/organization and its problems, goals, and practices.

We believe that climate and culture are very similar concepts. Climate focuses on organization members' perceptions of the way things are, but perception includes the idea that meaning is attached to the perceived event or thing (Bruner, 1964). In addition, climate researchers have acknowledged the importance of *shared* perceptions (meanings) for some time and have wrestled extensively with the operationalization of the shared aspect of the perception. For example, Schneider (1972) suggested that shared perceptions are indicated by mean responses to questionnaire items that have low variance. Joyce and Slocum (1984) have used a clustering technique to define subgroup climates based on shared perceptions. We see these definitions and measurement approaches to climate as conceptually very similar to concepts of organizational culture as something the organization has, albeit the possession in climate research is through the perceivers of it (James, Joyce, & Slocum, 1988).

Yet, we stop short of asserting that climate and culture are identical or almost identical. We agree with Schein (1985) that climate can most accurately be understood as a manifestation of culture. Culture is probably a deeper, less consciously held set of meanings than most of what has been called organizational climate. However, at a general level, there is substantial overlap between the two concepts. This is especially true when climate and culture are viewed as reciprocal processes, the one causing the other in an endless cycle over time. In this manner, climate (for example, the reward policies of an organization) is both the manifestation of culture (for instance, assumptions about worker motivation) and the data on which culture comes to be inferred and understood (Schneider & Gunnarson, in press). This high degree of conceptual overlap raises a question regarding why research and writing on climate and culture have proceeded in parallel rather than in tandem. We return to this question after a discussion of methodological and practical considerations in climate and culture research.

Methodological Considerations

Culture researchers and climate researchers come from different scientific traditions, as noted earlier. These traditions concern both theoretical and methodological issues, with the latter being the focus here. A key methodological distinction in science concerns the familiar oppositions between subjectivist/objectivist approaches and qualitative/quantitative methods. These differences are also reflected in the type of research conducted on climate and culture. Climate researchers have been content, for the most part, to use the nomothetic, quantitative procedures that encompass an etic perspective. The *etic* perspective imposes meaning on a set of data rather than letting the meaning emerge from the members of the group under study. This latter approach is termed *emic* (Barley, 1983).

Within each "camp" of researchers, there has been sub-stantial agreement on the appropriateness of the overall (qualitative versus quantitative) research strategy. To be sure, climate researchers have vigorously debated issues concerning level of analysis, aggregation procedures, and the like (see James, Joyce, & Slocum, 1988; Roberts, Hulin, & Rousseau, 1978). But few, if any, have suggested that climate be studied qualitatively. Similarly, culture researchers have argued over the appropriate "stuff" for analysis. For example, Barley (1983) advocates an analysis of signs and codes of meaning, while Trice and Beyer (1984) promote the study of rites and ceremonials. But, culture researchers have rarely advocated or used a quantitative ap-proach to studying culture (see Schriber & Gutek, 1987, for an exception).

Some would argue that this lack of cross-fertilization of method is completely appropriate given (1) the etic/emic dis-tinction and (2) the conceptual differences between the two constructs discussed earlier. However, we believe that the study of organizational culture could be enhanced by the increased use of quantitative methods. We are not advocating the aban-donment of the interview, or observation or participation as methods in culture research. However, we believe that shared meanings and assumptions can be accurately assessed through questionnaire methodology. The use of questionnaires that are *both* developed for the particular organization or subgroup under study *and* derived from in-depth interviews with key actors makes it possible to compare the meanings different people attach to events (Rentsch, 1988) and to compare one culture with another. Thus, our proposal is to combine generic culture issues (for example, rites, rituals) with particularistic manifestations of those generic issues (how the rituals manifest themselves) in the same surveys. This kind of research also makes multivariate analyses of the antecedents and conse-quences of particular cultural forms possible. In addition, it would advance knowledge about organizational culture through stage 2 of the life cycle and contribute to the concept's maturity.

This lack of empirical research on culture may be a func-tion of culture's relative youth compared to the maturity of climate. If the development of culture research adheres to the evolutionary stage model, we would predict an upsurge in empirical research in the near future followed rather quickly by critical reviews. Critical reviews will not appear, however, until there is a sufficient mass of research to be critiqued; it is the gathering of data that provides the grist for debating and refuting the proliferation of conceptualization.

The lack of empirical research on culture may also be explained by the difficulty of doing such research and/or of getting it published. Culture research calls for in-depth case studies . . . the kind of research that may require multiple organizations as the units of analysis to do the kind of comparative work suggested by an anthropological heritage. This kind of research requires the use of research teams to conduct interviews, make observations, examine archival data, and so on, and the research is more time consuming to conduct than paper-and-pencil surveys of employees. In addition, organizations may be more reticent about participating in large-scale, in-depth investigations.

Finally, qualitatively oriented culture research is still viewed with suspicion by many mainstream, quantitatively oriented academics. There is the halfhearted (or in some cases whole-hearted) belief that qualitative methods and "mushy" topics like culture may not really constitute appropriate scientific endeavors. Until such prejudices wane, the number of researchers investigating culture will remain small and the opportunities to publish culture research will be restricted. The popularity of books like Peters and Waterman's *In Search of Excellence* (1982) contributes to the suspicions of more quantitatively oriented researchers about culture because of the inappropriateness of (1) the sample studied (only "excellent" companies) and (2) a failure to rigorously pursue such fundamental research issues as the reliability of data and the validity of conclusions.

We believe, however, that the increased use of qualitative methods in the study of organizational climate may result in richer, more useful descriptions of organizations. Our advice to organizational psychologists against the willy-nilly use of canned climate questionnaires across varied settings is not something that originated with us. However, we wish to reiterate the notion that qualitative methods such as interviews, observation, and the analysis of archival data can substantially enrich traditional quantitative research. Even so, climate researchers have probably been more willing to augment their primarily quantitative approach with qualitative methods than culture researchers have been willing to attempt quantitative analysis. While culture as something an organization *is* does not easily lend itself to quantitative methods, the study of culture as something an organization *has* is amenable to their use. If organizational culture as a construct is to gain and maintain significance among researchers and practitioners, then the pattern of relationships that exists between culture and other variables of interest must be determined. Only rigorous, well-done research will establish these relationships with sufficient clarity to warrant an important niche for the culture construct in the field of organizational psychology.

Conversely, the typical off-the-shelf climate survey that yields perhaps eight or ten climate dimension scores as the data, is an insufficient source of information about the inner workings of an organization. Thus, canned climate surveys may paradoxically be more useful for comparative organizational studies than as a source of information for promoting change toward, for example, safety or service. This is true because these types of climate surveys provide limited information about the actual activities in an organization that yield employee perceptions of warmth, reward, or support. To change an organization requires data about *that* organization as well as data about how that organization compares to others. In sum, it appears that for both theory testing and practicality, the method of choice for climate and culture research is an integrated emic/etic strategy.

Practical Considerations

In fact, both climate and culture have had a decidedly practitioner orientation — the former from researchers and the latter from practitioners. For example, Argyris (1958) explored the climate construct using a case study of a bank and discovered that hiring only the "right types" was yielding a noncompetitive bureaucratic climate. Litwin and Stringer (1968) included a lengthy chapter in their book on the implications of climate for management practices, especially with respect to the creation and maintenance of a climate in which achievement motivation would be displayed.

The concept of cultures for organizational effectiveness has had wide popular appeal almost since its inception. The popular books by Deal and Kennedy (1982), Peters and Waterman (1982), and others certainly have influenced management thinking, although the influence on actual practice is not so clear, and only recently have more research-oriented people begun to grapple with managing and changing culture. For example, Schein (1983, 1984, 1985) links culture to the values and beliefs of an organization's founder and devotes considerable attention to the management of cultural change. Similarly, Frost, Moore, Louis, Lundberg, and Martin (1985) devote six chapters of their book *Organizational Culture* to questions concerning the management of culture. Indeed, as Weick (1985) noted, it is becoming increasingly difficult to differentiate contemporary writings on culture change from those on strategy and strategic change (see Pennings, 1985). Even Pettigrew, who may be said to have begun the academic exploration of organizational culture (1979), is now writing on *The Management of Strategic Change* (1987).

We believe both concepts could benefit from a continued focus on practical application. It seems to us that both climate and culture are important concepts because in combination they can specify, fairly precisely, the context of human behavior in organizations. An analysis of the context allows researchers to describe, explain, and perhaps predict behavior in a variety of circumstances. If culture is the next attempt to explain the E in Lewin's famous $B = f(P, E)$ equation, then the culture concept must add something beyond climate's previous contribution. We believe culture can do that because it focuses on the assumptions and values that underlie the policies and procedures that are indicative of climate. That is, culture is at the next higher level of abstraction, and so captures additional influences (direct and indirect) on behavior and on lower-level context variables, such as climate. Culture's real value as a "new" variable in the field may lie in its face validity and the degree to which it seems to capture previously seemingly ineffable organizational attributes that researchers and practitioners alike agree are there. If culture retains its "real-world" quality and succeeds in establishing empirical linkages to important "real-world" outcomes (see Denison, 1990), it may surpass the contributions made by the climate construct.

Climate and Culture: Parallel or Overlapping Constructs?

One puzzling question remains to be answered, and it concerns the relationship between climate and culture. Specifically, why have two concepts that share so many conceptual similarities proceeded to develop in parallel rather than in tandem? Put another way, why has there not been more collaborative research between culture and climate writers, and why have the lessons learned in one tradition failed to enlighten the work of the other school?

Before we answer this question, it may be helpful to reiterate and summarize the similarities between the two concepts. Both climate and culture deal with the ways by which organization members make sense of their environment. These sense-making attempts manifest themselves as shared meanings that form the basis for action. Both climate and culture are learned, largely through the socialization process and through symbolic interaction among group members. Climate and culture are at the same time both monolithic constructs and multidimensional ones. Thus, we can correctly speak of organizational climates, cultures, and subcultures. Culture and climate are both attempts to identify the environment that affects the behavior of people in organizations. Culture exists at a higher level of abstraction than climate, and climate is a manifestation of culture.

Despite the similarities just mentioned, culture research has developed apart from any real connection with climate research or history. Interestingly, few if any articles appear in the culture literature that even use the term *climate* or cite climate researchers. For example, the book of readings on culture edited by Frost, Moore, Louis, Lundberg, and Martin (1985) has no contributions by climate researchers and does not cite some of the more prolific climate researchers (for example, James, Slocum, or Schneider). Similarly, a recent comprehensive treatment of culture concludes that "organizational climate is not an element of organizational culture. It is a related but separate phenomenon" (Ott, 1989, p. 47). This book allots one paragraph to climate and also fails to cite climate researchers. We believe there are three reasons that account for this nonoverlap of literatures.

First, there exists a very real pressure in science to differentiate one idea or concept from another. Collectively and individually, we are at pains to differentiate our work from the work of others and thereby justify it. Thus, concepts proliferate and obvious similarities are downplayed in favor of dubious distinctiveness (Morrow, 1983). Through this process of differentiation, individuals gain prominence as their names are associated with "new" ideas. Research careers are enhanced by developing a new idea, even if the idea is very similar to others that have gone before it. In the most cynical case, the game is to get others to use your "new" idea or label; in the most optimistic case the challenge is to derive an idea that others find truly useful and interesting (Davis, 1971). Thus, the differentiation of similar constructs is not only the result of career-minded self-interest. To some extent, the practice of any scientific discipline demands precision in the nature of concepts and the terminology that is associated with them. Thus, even a small distinction between an established concept and a potential new idea may be deserving of a separate concept, term for the concept, and developmental evolution.

Second, as noted earlier, we believe that the different scientific backgrounds and traditions associated with researchers in the climate and culture camps have made the work of one school somewhat inaccessible to the other. Mutual lack of familiarity and experience with alternative methods leads to mutual accusations of wrongheadedness. The innate feelings of superiority that each camp experiences prevents real collaboration. Thus, the lessons that each school could teach to and learn from the other are largely lost.

Finally, we believe that the separation of climate from culture research may be an artifact of time that will diminish in the future (see Ashforth, 1985). Climate and culture have overlapped in their evolution in the field of organizational psychology only for about ten years. Ten years is not a very long time in the development of a concept, and there is some evidence just beginning to appear that culture and climate are drawing closer together. For example, Nicholson and Johns (1985) published an article on "absence culture" in organizations in which they acknowledge that the "climate for absence" is also an appropriate term for the phenomenon they discuss. Similarly, Schriber and Gutek (1987) published an article in the *Journal of Applied Psychology* on the time dimensions of organizational culture that uses questionnaire data and a principal-components analysis to develop measuring instruments for the temporal aspects of culture. In an *Annual Review of Psychology* article, Schneider (1985) reviewed both literatures, suggesting ways in which they complement each other. These recent articles may indicate a trend in the development of both concepts toward a marriage of methods and terminology. If so, we would expect that the next ten years in the evolution of both concepts would yield an amalgamated climate/culture concept that exhibits many of the conceptual, methodological, and practical characteristics that are presently unique to one concept or the other.

References

Abbey, A., & Dickson, J. W. (1983). R&D work climate and innovation in semi-conductors. *Academy of Management Journal, 26*, 362–368.

Argyris, C. (1957). *Personality and organization.* New York: Harper & Row.

Argyris, C. (1958). Some problems in conceptualizing organizational climate: A case study of a bank. *Administrative Science Quarterly, 2,* 501–520.

Argyris, C. (1960). *Understanding organizational behavior.* Homewood, IL: Dorsey.

Ashforth, B. E. (1985). Climate formation: Issues and extensions. *Academy of Management Review, 10*(4), 837–847.

Barley, S. R. (1983). Semiotics and the study of occupational and organizational cultures. *Administrative Science Quarterly, 28,* 393–413.

Barney, J. B. (1986). Organizational culture: Can it be a source of sustained competitive advantage? *Academy of Management Review, 11,* 656–665.

Birket-Smith, K. (1965). *The paths of culture.* Madison: University of Wisconsin Press.

Broms, H., & Gahmberg, H. (1983). Communication to self in organizations and cultures. *Administrative Science Quarterly, 28,* 482–495.

Bruner, J. S. (1964). The course of cognitive growth. *American Psychologist, 19,* 1–15.

Campbell, J. P., Dunnette, M. D., Lawler, E. E., III, & Weick, K. E. (1970). *Managerial behavior, performance, and effectiveness.* New York: McGraw-Hill.

Cartwright, D., & Zander, A. (Eds.). (1968). *Group dynamics: Research and theory* (3rd ed.). New York: Harper & Row.

Dandridge, T. C., Mitroff, I., & Joyce, W. F. (1980). Organizational symbolism: A topic to expand organizational analysis. *Academy of Management Review, 5,* 77–82.

Davis, M. S. (1971). That's interesting. *Philosophical Social Science, 1,* 309–344.

Deal, T. E., & Kennedy, A. A. (1982). *Corporate cultures: The rites and rituals of organizational life.* Reading, MA: Addison-Wesley.

Denison, D. R. (1990). *Corporate culture and organizational effectiveness.* New York: Wiley.

Downey, H. K., Hellriegel, D., & Slocum, J. W. (1975). Congruence between individual needs, organizational climate, job satisfaction and performance. *Academy of Management Journal, 18,* 149–155.

Drexler, J. A. (1977). Organizational climate: Its homogeneity within organizations. *Journal of Applied Psychology, 62,* 38–42.

Field, R.H.G., & Abelson, M. A. (1982). Climate: A reconceptualization and proposed model. *Human Relations, 35,* 181–201.

Fleishman, E. A. (1953). Leadership climate, human relations training, and supervisory behavior. *Personnel Psychology, 6,* 205–222.

Friedlander, F., & Greenberg, S. (1971). Effect of job attitudes, training, and organization climate on performance of the hard-core unemployed. *Journal of Applied Psychology, 55,* 287–295.

Frost, P. J., Moore, L., Louis, M. R., Lundberg, C. C., & Martin, J. (Eds.). (1985). *Organizational culture.* Newbury Park, CA: Sage.

Gavin J. F. (1975). Organizational climate as a function of personal and organizational variables. *Journal of Applied Psychology, 60,* 135–139.

Glick, W. H. (1985). Conceptualizing and measuring organizational and psychological climate: Pitfalls in multilevel research. *Academy of Management Review, 10*(3), 601–616.

Gregory, K. L. (1983). Native-view paradigms: Multiple cultures and culture conflicts in organizations. *Administrative Science Quarterly, 28,* 359–376.

Guion, R. M. (1973). A note on organizational climate. *Organizational Behavior and Human Performance, 9,* 120–125.

Harris, S. G., & Sutton, R. I. (1986). Functions of parting ceremonies in dying organizations. *Academy of Management Journal, 29,* 5–30.

Hellriegel, D., & Slocum, J. W., Jr. (1974). Organizational climate: Measures, research, and contingencies. *Academy of Management Journal, 17,* 255–280.

Howe, J. G. (1977). Group climate: An exploratory analysis of construct validity. *Organizational Behavior and Human Performance, 19,* 106–125.

James, L. R. (1982). Aggregation bias in estimates of perceptual agreement. *Journal of Applied Psychology, 67,* 219–229.

James, L. R., Hater, J. J., Gent, M. J., & Bruni, J. R. (1978).

Psychological climate: Implications from cognitive social learning theory and interactional psychology. *Personnel Psychology, 31,* 781–813.

James, L. R., & Jones, A. P. (1974). Organizational climate: A review of theory and research. *Psychological Bulletin, 81,* 1096–1112.

James, L. R., Joyce, W. F., & Slocum, J. W., Jr. (1988). Comment: Organizations do not cognize. *Academy of Management Review, 13*(1), 129–132.

Jelinek, M., Smircich, L., & Hirsch, P. (1983). Introduction: A code of many colors. *Administrative Science Quarterly, 28,* 331–338.

Johannesson, R. E. (1973). Some problems in the measurement of organizational climate. *Organizational Behavior and Human Performance, 10,* 118–144.

Johnston, H. R. (1976). A new conceptualization of source of organizational climate. *Administrative Science Quarterly, 21,* 95–103.

Jones, G. R. (1983). Transaction costs, property rights, and organizational culture: An exchange perspective. *Administrative Science Quarterly, 28,* 454–467.

Joyce, W. F., & Slocum, J. W., Jr. (1982). Climate discrepancy: Refining the concepts of psychological and organizational climate. *Human Relations, 35,* 951–972.

Joyce, W. F., & Slocum, J. W., Jr. (1984). Collective climate: Agreement as a basis for defining aggregate climates in organizations. *Academy of Management Journal, 27,* 721–742.

Kets De Vries, M.F.R., & Miller, D. (1986). Personality, culture, and organization. *Academy of Management Review, 11,* 266–279.

Koprowski, E. J. (1983). Cultural myths: Clues to effective management. *Organizational Dynamics, 12,* 39–51.

Kozlowski, S.W.J., & Hults, B. M. (1987). An exploration of climates for technical updating and performance. *Personnel Psychology, 40,* 539–563.

Kuhn, T. S. (1970). *The structure of scientific revolutions* (2nd ed.). Chicago: University of Chicago Press.

LaFollette, W. R., & Sims, H. (1975). Is satisfaction redundant with organizational climate? *Organizational Behavior and Human Performance, 13*, 257–278.

Lawler, E. E., Hall, D. T., & Oldham, G. R. (1974). Organizational climate: Relationship to organizational structure, process, and performance. *Organizational Behavior and Human Performance, 11*, 139–155.

Lewin, K., Lippitt, R., & White, R. K. (1939). Patterns of aggressive behavior in experimentally created "social climates." *Journal of Social Psychology, 10*, 271–299.

Litwin, G. H., & Stringer, R. A. (1968). *Motivation and organizational climate.* Cambridge, MA: Harvard Business School, Division of Research.

Louis, M. R. (1985). An investigator's guide to workplace culture. In P. J. Frost, L. F. Moore, M. R. Louis, C. C. Lundberg, & J. Martin (Eds.), *Organizational culture.* Newbury Park, CA: Sage.

McGregor, D. M. (1960). *The human side of enterprise.* New York: McGraw-Hill.

Martin, J., Feldman, M. S., Hatch, M. J., & Sitkin, S. B. (1983). The uniqueness paradox in organizational stories. *Administrative Science Quarterly, 28*, 438–453.

Martin, J., & Siehl, C. (1983). Organizational culture and counterculture: An uneasy symbiosis. *Organizational Dynamics, 12*(2), 52–64.

Moeller, A., Schneider, B., Schoorman, F. D., & Berney, E. (1988). Development of the work-facilitation diagnostic. In F. D. Schoorman & B. Schneider (Eds.), *Facilitating work effectiveness.* Lexington, MA: Lexington.

Morey, N. C., & Luthans, F. (1985). Refining the displacement of culture and the use of scenes and themes in organizational studies. *Academy of Management Review, 10*, 219–229.

Morrow, P. C. (1983). Concept redundancy in organizational research: The case of work commitment. *Academy of Management Review, 8*, 486–500.

Nahavandi, A., & Malekzadeh, A. R. (1988). Acculturation in mergers and acquisitions. *Academy of Management Review, 13*, 79–90.

Nicholson, N., & Johns, G. (1985). The absence culture and the psychological contract—who's in control of absence? *Academy of Management Review, 10,* 397–407.

Ott, J. S. (1989). *The organizational culture perspective.* Pacific Grove, CA: Brooks/Cole.

Payne, R. L., Fineman, S., & Wall, T. D. (1976). Organizational climate and job satisfaction: A conceptual synthesis. *Organizational Behavior and Human Performance, 16,* 45–62.

Payne, R. L., & Mansfield, R. (1973). Relationships of perceptions of organizational climate to organizational structure, context, and hierarchical position. *Administrative Science Quarterly, 18,* 515–526.

Payne, R. L., & Pugh, D. S. (1976). Organizational structure and climate. In M. D. Dunnette (Ed.), *Handbook of industrial and organizational psychology* (pp. 1125–1173). Chicago: Rand McNally.

Pennings, J. M. (Ed.). (1985). *Organizational strategy and change: New views on formulating and implementing strategic decisions.* San Francisco: Jossey-Bass.

Peters, T. J., & Waterman, R. H. (1982). *In search of excellence.* New York: Harper & Row.

Pettigrew, A. M. (1979). On studying organizational cultures. *Administrative Science Quarterly, 24,* 570–581.

Pettigrew, A. M. (Ed.). (1987). *The management of strategic change.* Oxford: Blackwell.

Pondy, L. R. (1982). The role of metaphors and myths in organization and the facilitation of change. In L. R. Pondy, P. J. Frost, G. Morgan, & T. C. Dandridge (Eds.), *Organizational symbolism.* Greenwich, CT: JAI Press.

Pondy, L. R., Frost, P. J., Morgan, G., & Dandridge, T. C. (Eds.). (1982). *Organizational symbolism.* Greenwich, CT: JAI Press.

Powell, G. N., & Butterfield, D. A. (1978). The case for subsystem climates in organizations. *Academy of Management Review, 3,* 151–157.

Pritchard, R. D., & Karasick, B. W. (1973). The effects of organizational climate on managerial job performance and job satisfaction. *Organizational Behavior and Human Performance, 9,* 126–146.

Reichers, A. E. (1987). An interactionist perspective on newcomer socialization rates. *Academy of Management Review, 12,* 278–287.

Rentsch, J. R. (1988). *An action theory perspective on climate and culture.* Unpublished doctoral dissertation, University of Maryland, Department of Psychology, College Park, MD.

Riley, P. (1983). A structurationist account of political cultures. *Administrative Science Quarterly, 28,* 414–437.

Roberts, K. H., Hulin, C. L., & Rousseau, D. M. (1978). *Developing an interdisciplinary science of organizations.* San Francisco: Jossey-Bass.

Sathe, V. (1983). Implications of corporate culture: A manager's guide to action. *Organizational Dynamics, 12,* 5–23.

Sathe, V. (1985). *Culture and related corporate realities.* Homewood, IL: Irwin.

Schein, E. (1983). The role of the founder in creating organizational culture. *Organizational Dynamics, 12,* 13–28.

Schein, E. (1984). Coming to a new awareness of organizational culture. *Sloan Management Review, 25,* 3–16.

Schein, E. (1985). *Organizational culture and leadership: A dynamic view.* San Francisco: Jossey-Bass.

Schnake, M. E. (1983). An empirical assessment of the effects of affective response in the measurement of organizational climate. *Personnel Psychology, 36,* 791–807.

Schneider, B. (1972). Organizational climate: Individual preferences and organizational realities. *Journal of Applied Psychology, 56,* 211–217.

Schneider, B. (1975a). Organizational climate: Individual preferences and organizational realities revisited. *Journal of Applied Psychology, 60,* 459–465.

Schneider, B. (1975b). Organizational climates: An essay. *Personnel Psychology, 28,* 447–479.

Schneider, B. (1985). Organizational behavior. *Annual Review of Psychology, 36,* 573–611.

Schneider, B., & Bartlett, J. (1968). Individual differences and organizational climate I: The research plan and questionnaire development. *Personnel Psychology, 21,* 323–333.

Schneider, B., & Bartlett, J. (1970). Individual differences and organizational climate II: Measurement of organizational climate by the multitrait-multirater matrix. *Personnel Psychology*, *23*, 493–512.

Schneider, B., & Gunnarson, S. (in press). Organizational climate and culture: The psychology of the work place. In J. Jones, B. D. Steffy, & D. Bray (Eds.), *Applying psychology in business: The manager's handbook*. Lexington, MA: Lexington.

Schneider, B., & Hall, D. T. (1972). Toward specifying the concept of work climate: A study of Roman Catholic diocesan priests. *Journal of Applied Psychology, 56*, 447–455.

Schneider, B., & Reichers, A. E. (1983). On the etiology of climates. *Personnel Psychology, 36*, 19–39.

Schneider, B., & Rentsch, J. (1988). Managing climates and cultures: A futures perspective. In J. Hage (Ed.), *Futures of organizations*. Lexington, MA: Lexington Books.

Schneider, B., & Snyder, R. A. (1975). Some relationships between job satisfaction and organizational climate. *Journal of Applied Psychology, 60*, 318–328.

Schön, D. A. (1963). *Displacement of concepts*. London: Tavistock.

Schriber, J. B., & Gutek, B. A. (1987). Some time dimensions of work: Measurement of an underlying aspect of organization culture. *Journal of Applied Psychology, 72*, 642–650.

Seashore, S. E. (1981). The Michigan quality of work program: Issues in measurement, assessment and outcome evaluation. In A. Van de Ven & W. F. Joyce (Eds.), *Perspectives on organization design and behavior*. New York: Wiley.

Smircich, L. (1983). Concepts of culture and organizational analysis. *Administrative Science Quarterly, 28*, 339–358.

Smith, K. K., & Simmons, V. M. (1983). A rumpelstiltskin organization: Metaphors on metaphors in field research. *Administrative Science Quarterly, 28*, 377–392.

Tagiuri, R., & Litwin, G. H. (Eds.). (1968). *Organizational climate: Explorations of a concept*. Cambridge, MA: Division of Research, Graduate School of Business Administration, Harvard University.

Trice, H. M., & Beyer, J. M. (1984). Studying organizational cultures through rites and ceremonials. *Academy of Management Review, 9*(4), 653–669.

Waters, L. K., Roach, D., & Batlis, N. (1974). Organizational climate dimensions and job-related attitudes. *Personnel Psychology, 27*, 465–476.

Weick, K. E. (1985). The significance of corporate culture. In P. Frost, L. F. Moore, M. R. Louis, C. C. Lundberg, & J. Martin (Eds.), *Organizational culture*. Newbury Park, CA: Sage.

Wilkins, A. (1983). The culture audit: A tool for understanding organizations. *Organizational Dynamics, 12*, 24–38.

Wilkins, A. L., & Ouchi, W. (1983). Efficient cultures: Exploring the relationship between culture and organizational performance. *Administrative Science Quarterly, 28*, 468–481.

Woodman, R. W., & King, D. C. (1978). Organizational climate: Science or folklore? *Academy of Management Review, 3*, 816–826.

Zohar, D. (1980). Safety climate in industrial organizations: Theoretical and applied implications. *Journal of Applied Psychology, 65*, 96–102.

Chapter 2

Lawrence R. James
Lois A. James
Donna K. Ashe

The Meaning of Organizations: The Role of Cognition and Values

It is often stated that individuals respond to situations in terms of the meaning that the situations have for them. This intuitively appealing and empirically defensible statement is not without ambiguity, inasmuch as the term *meaning* is subject to several interpretations. For example, meaning may refer to a descriptive cognition of an actual stimulus such as group size, or it may refer to a subjective interpretation that reflects the significance of the stimulus to the individual (for instance, crowding). Meaning may also connote primarily nonaffective cognitive interpretations, but the most widely cited study of meaning in psychology (Osgood, Suci, & Tannenbaum, 1957) defines meaning in affective/evaluative terms for affectively loaded objects. Or, as a number of psychologists have stated, meaning is a phenomenological experience. Yet other psychologists, in concert with some anthropologists and sociologists, regard meaning as a social or collective event that cannot be defined or explained in terms of the phenomenological experiences of individual members of the collective.

Manifestations of the alternative interpretations of meaning are evident in past and current controversies in the climate literature (for example, is climate descriptive or affective, is it an attribute of individuals or situations). Similar controversies are brewing in the culture literature. Our intention here is to explore the concept of meaning in the context of climate and culture. We hope to clarify what is meant by *meaning*, what is meant by *climate* (both psychological and organizational), and what is meant by *culture*. We also hope to convince organizational researchers that a more psychologically based approach to the study of culture — one based on group dynamics — may be fruitful.

It is noteworthy that we have taken positions in regard to most of the controversies, as will become evident in the section titled "An Informal Overview of Meaning." We will attempt to solidify these positions with more formal treatments of the issues in the remaining sections of this essay. Our thesis is that climate is a product of personal values and remains a property of individuals irrespective of the empirical level of analysis, whereas culture is engendered by system values (and involves system norms) and is a property of the collective. We suggest that many of the recent criticisms of climate reflect inappropriate attempts to force a collective, culture model onto an individual, climate construct. We recommend that the constructs be distinguished, and that both constructs may provide fruitful areas for research.

An Informal Overview of Meaning

The attribution of meaning to external stimuli refers to the process of using previously stored mental representations to interpret — that is, to make sense of — sensory information (see Shaver, 1987). We will refer to this interpretation process as a *meaning analysis* (Mandler, 1982). Our interest is limited to work-related stimuli representing environmental events, processes, structures, and the like, for which we will use the term *work environment attribute(s)*. A key to understanding meaning is to attain knowledge of the content and organization of the stored mental representations used to make sense of incoming information. These stored mental representations reflect beliefs about work environment attributes that are learned through

processes involving actual interactions with environments, social influences, vicarious learning experiences, self-reflection,
and insight (see James, Hater, Gent, & Bruni, 1978; Stotland &
Canon, 1972). The stored mental representations are referred to
as cognitive categories, percepts, prototypes, referent bins, sche-
mata, and schemas. We will employ the terms *schema* and *schemas*.

The emphasis on mental operations in meaning analysis
underscores the assumption that the attribution of meaning is a
phenomenological experience. This means that the world that people know is the world they have cognitively constructed via
internal representations of environmental information (see Rotter, 1981; Shaver, 1987). Unfortunate opinions extrapolated
from this phenomenological perspective are that (1) there is no
real or objective world because the only world that exists is that
provided by (each individual's) phenomenological experience,
and (2) phenomenological experience is synonymous with nonveridical perceptions of real-world events. However, to say that
an environmental attribute appears to an individual as it is
phenomenologically experienced should *not* connote that the
attribute fails to exist objectively (although there may be some
problem in defining *objective*) (Magnusson, 1981; Shaver, 1987).
In our view, phenomenology coexists with a real or objective
world, and many phenomenological experiences are veridical
representatives of real-world objects and events.

On the other hand, the schemas employed to impute
meaning to environmental attributes often involve abstract and
generalized beliefs. These beliefs are generated by individuals'
subjective attempts to reduce the sheer number of stimuli to
manageable levels by first clustering a large number of stimuli
into a much reduced number of interpretive, yet often descriptive, categories. Awareness of relationships among these categories (for example, recurring patterns and configurations in the
occurrences of selected categories) and cognitive associations
between occurrences of categories and experienced mental
events (for instance, mental challenge, self-determination) allow
for higher-order processing and the development of abstract
and generalized schemas (see James, Hater, Gent, & Bruni, 1978;
James & Jones, 1980; Stotland & Canon, 1972). These are re-

ferred to as *higher-order schemas* (HOSs) and are reflected in general and abstract beliefs about relationships among environmental attributes and/or among environmental attributes and internal events. In the terms of scientific models, HOSs are the higher-order latent variables—that is, constructs—in a nomological net designed to explain the occurrences of perceptions of environmental attributes (see James & Jones, 1976).

The introduction of subjectivity, abstraction, and schemas in the form of latent variables or constructs to a meaning analysis increases the probability that individuals may differ in regard to how a uniform stimulus, or set of stimuli, are phenomenologically experienced. This need not be the case inasmuch as the use of schemas or latent variables to impute meaning does *not* constitute prima facie evidence for differences in interpretations. However, it is also possible that individuals may differ in regard to such things as (1) the cognitive schema(s) used to interpret a stimulus, which constitutes *qualitative* differences in meaning, or (2) the conceptual score on a common latent cognitive variable or schema—for example, a common factor—assigned to the stimulus, which represents *quantitative* differences in meaning. Qualitative or quantitative differences in phenomenological experiences, especially in regard to the more general and abstract schemas deep in the nomological net, are often described in terms of differences in "acquired meaning" (see Mischel, 1968). Differences in acquired meanings may reflect the influence of such things as differences in the individual attributes of perceivers (for example, cognitive structures, personality), interactions between the stimulus and the individual, and the social context in which perception takes place. A scenario based on Rommetveit's (1981) and Menzel's (1978) discussions of meaning potentials is used to illustrate several of these points.

Meaning Potentials

The term *meaning potential* refers to alternative acquired meanings that could be imputed to the same environmental attribute(s). For example, suppose members of a university department observe that a member of their unit, say an assistant professor named Henry, is staying to work late. The initial phenomenological experience is both veridical and shared by departmental members; Henry is staying late. But there are a variety of acquired meanings that might be attributed to the agreed-on observation that Henry is staying late. These meaning potentials might include:

1. Henry wants to be promoted and tenured, and is staying late to work on research, articles, and papers.
2. Henry appears to have had some marital problems and uses working after hours as an excuse to avoid his spouse.
3. Henry works after hours on consulting projects to enhance his income.
4. Henry is trying to ingratiate himself with the department head by being seen putting in extra hours.
5. Henry is a workaholic and seems not to know when to quit.
6. Henry's research is challenging and requires many hours of concentration and effort.

These meaning potentials are neither exhaustive nor independent, merely plausible. The plausibility of one or more of the meaning potentials may be a function of the social context in which Henry's behavior occurred. Consider, for example, the system norm (Katz & Kahn, 1966, 1978) in this department that assistant professors should publish three to five articles a year. This system norm is supported by the collectively agreed on (or at least collective public compliance with the) ideology or system value (Katz & Kahn, 1966, 1978) that the professional reputation of this department should be maintained through demonstrations of scholarly contributions. Given that this system norm and this system value are collectively shared by all or most members of this department, we might surmise that a strong emphasis on "professional productivity" is a key aspect of this department's "culture." Moreover, if we have reason to believe that Henry has internalized, identifies with, or at least is willing to comply with (see Kelman, 1961) the prevailing culture of professional productivity, then meaning potential 1 assumes high probability. Other meaning potentials remain possible as alternative or collateral explanations. Nevertheless, the culture may furnish a contextual force for all or most members of the department to perceive that Henry is working late to produce articles and papers. (Latent or expressive consequences [Trice & Beyer, 1984] that support system norms and values, such as that publications attract research funding which in turn furnishes overhead to the school and department, suggest further that professional productivity is a salient aspect of this department's culture.)

Of course, Henry may choose to eschew the prevailing departmental culture. If other members of the department are aware of Henry's failure to comply (independence?, deviance?), then attributions for staying late may vary as a function of knowledge of Henry and/or the predispositions of the perceiver. For example, one of Henry's close friends might be aware that financial burdens have motivated Henry to take on consulting efforts. If this were the case, this perceiver might veridically impute meaning potential 3 to Henry's behavior. On the other hand, another departmental member, who has less knowledge of Henry, might just have had an argument with his or her spouse, rendering this explanation more accessible (see Wyer & Srull, 1986). Like himself or herself, Henry is perceived to be staying late to avoid another domestic confrontation. It might also be that a highly job-involved department member, who truly subscribes to living and breathing one's job, believes that Henry is a workaholic.

The preceding discussion suggests that the presence of a strong contextual influence, namely a departmental culture characterized by a normative influence (Rousseau, 1988; Sproull, 1981) *and* a supporting system value for professional productivity, increases the probability that a specific meaning potential will be used to make sense of an environmental occurrence. And, given collective internalization of, or identification with, the system norm and value, incumbents of the system will tend to share the meaning imputed to the event. However, the illustration also demonstrates that (1) lack of consensus (Henry's possible lack of commitment to the departmental culture) promotes dispositional attributions (see Green & Mitchell, 1979), and (2) the dispositional attributions may reflect knowledge and veridicality, or be products of nonveridical cognitive biases that reflect the perceiver's predispositions. The latter condition is a form of person-by-situation (P × S) interaction (see James, Hater, Gent, & Bruni, 1978).

Variation in the meanings assigned to the same environmental attribute may reflect more than a simple lack of consensus. Indeed, such variation may suggest the lack of a collective (common, shared) culture, or perhaps the existence of subcultures and countercultures (see Martin & Siehl, 1983). In any event, this discussion suggests the need to be sensitive both to similarities and to variations in phenomenological experiences or meanings imputed to the same or similar environmental attributes, especially the higher-order or acquired meanings that depict potential explanations for the occurrences of environmental events. This is because (1) the (higher-order) meanings employed by an individual may tell us a great deal about the cognitive structure and belief system of that individual (see Mischel, 1973), (2) individuals tend to react to environments as a function of the meaning and significance that those environments have for them (see Endler & Magnusson, 1976; Lewin, 1938, 1951; Murray, 1938), and (3) the assignment of similar acquired meanings to an environment by different individuals may be indicative of "shared psychological fields" (Asch, 1951; Katz & Kahn, 1978) or "temporarily shared social realities" (Rommetveit, 1981), which in today's jargon refers to collective social realities, organizational cultures, and perhaps even organizational climates (see Schneider & Reichers, 1983).

To close this informal overview, it would be interesting to ask Henry why he is working late. It is unlikely that Henry will be able to furnish ultimate truth in this regard (see Nisbett & Wilson, 1977). For example, automaticity of some cognitive factors—such as a personal norm for working hard—may limit the accessibility of these factors, and subconscious motivations to avoid failure and/or to ingratiate oneself with powerful others may be protected by defense mechanisms. Conversely, Henry may be aware that he is staying late to work on research and manuscripts in the interest of future tenure and promotion decisions, especially in a culture that promotes professional productivity. However, this self-serving meaning potential may be tempered with the belief that the research is challenging and difficult. Unlike the first five dispositionally oriented meaning potentials, the perception that the work is challenging portrays an interpretation of an environmental attribute (work) in psychological terms, which is to say in terms of HOSs that reflect the subjective, acquired meaning and significance of the environment to the individual. This is psychological climate (see James & Jones, 1974; James & Sells, 1981; Jones & James, 1979).

Like the dispositional meaning potentials, psychological climate is a phenomenological experience that is subject to contextual and social influences, as well as to P x S interactions. For example, a socially constructed and common belief shared by many professors in Henry's department, including Henry himself, may be that their research is challenging. If so, then we may indeed have a shared assignment of meaning and thus what some consider an organizational climate (see James, 1982; Joyce & Slocum, 1979; Schneider, 1983). Yet, while the members of Henry's department may agree that, as a matter of general principle, their research is challenging, the *specific* research that Henry believes is challenging might be perceived as rather unimaginative and a little pedestrian by a more intellectually gifted member of the department, or as unfathomably complex by a less gifted colleague. (Presumably, all members of the department are not identical in regard to intelligence and creativity.) The latter perceptions are components of P x S interactions and connote that agreement among department members is less than perfect and that variations in perceptions of challenge reflect reliable individual differences and not just error variance (James, Hater, Gent, & Bruni, 1978).

In summary, meaning refers to attempts to make sense out of what is occurring in an environment; it is the interpretative aspect of cognition and perception. And, by definition, it is phenomenological. In many cases, meaning is reflected in purely descriptive, and often veridical, interpretations of actual environmental stimuli, such as that Henry is staying late (or that one is now reading a book). Of greater interest to many is what we have referred to as acquired meanings or interpretations based on HOSs, which describe the "acquired significance or meaning of the environment to the individual" (Rotter, 1981, p. 170). The meaning potentials for Henry's behavior reflected possible acquired meanings and HOSs and involved much more than a simple description of Henry's behavior. They reflected attributions, environmental contexts, explanations, predispositions, socially constructed realities, shared generalities, and P × S interactions. Thus, what it is that is significant about environments to individuals is the attribution of meaning they give to the stimuli they encounter.

The next section presents a more formal view of the role of meaning in psychology and the relevance of meaning for understanding the development and use of schemas for attributing meaning to stimuli in work settings. The role of meaning in psychology is explored more fully since the historically strong emphasis on the affective-evaluative elements of acquired meanings may have resulted in an underestimation of the salience of the cognitive elements of acquired meanings. Then the role of schemas, especially HOSs, is discussed in some detail because we believe that it is possible to integrate a significant portion of the work environment perception literature. The integration is achieved via relating various perceptual variables to a higher-order factor that reflects the degree to which work environments are perceived as being beneficial versus harmful to the well-being of the individual. A recent attempt to test the hypothesis of a higher-order factor of meaning in climate is then reviewed. Discussion proceeds to causal models for climate and culture, where an examination is made of potential relations among the two constructs. These discussions include an interpretation of the most perplexing issue for climate, and, perhaps, for culture as well (see Rousseau, 1988). This is the unit-of-analysis problem in the context of aggregation (see Roberts, Hulin, & Rousseau, 1978).

The Study of Meaning in Psychology

The term *meaning* in psychology invokes the now classic text by Osgood, Suci, and Tannenbaum (1957) entitled *The Measurement of Meaning.* These authors identified concepts that individuals used naturally and spontaneously to describe environmental objects in relation to themselves. Exploratory factor analyses of responses to items used to measure meaning produced the three well-known dimensions of evaluation, potency, and activity. These three dimensions collapsed into the single dimension of evaluation for affectively loaded objects (Osgood, Suci, & Tannenbaum, 1957), which are the type of objects often encountered in research on work environment perceptions. The defining characteristic of evaluation is the judged "goodness" versus "badness" of an object.

Whereas Osgood, Suci, and Tannenbaum (1957) focused on affective-evaluative elements to describe meaning, we have chosen to focus on cognitive elements to describe meaning. That is, in the present paper we emphasize interpretative constructs such as ambiguity, challenge, loyalty, cooperation, equity, rationality, stress, and support to interpret environmental objects and events rather than evaluations of the goodness or badness of these objects and events. Both cognitive and affective-evaluative approaches are needed for a full understanding of meaning and, as will be discussed, these approaches to understanding meaning are presumed to be functionally and reciprocally related.

It was noted earlier that, from a cognitive perspective, meaning analysis refers to the use of schemas (stored mental representations that depict beliefs) to interpret (to make sense of) work environment attributes (for example, events, objects, processes, structures) (see Mandler, 1982; Jones & Gerard, 1967; Shaver, 1987; Stotland & Canon, 1972). The meanings imputed to the environmental attributes are phenomenological experiences, which is to say they are cognitive constructions designed to interpret information sensed from the environment. Many meaning analyses have an "out there" quality (Mandler, 1982). The individual employs schemas (internal semantic meanings, semantic networks, prototypes, cognitive categories) to describe environmental attributes, such as discerning the presence or absence of features and structures of environmental objects. Terms such as *descriptive cognition* and *descriptive meaning* (Mandler, 1982), *cold cognition* (Zajonc, 1980), *lower-order* or *descriptive schemas* (James & Sells, 1981; Stotland & Canon, 1972), and *denotative meaning* (Osgood, Suci, & Tannenbaum, 1957) emphasize the orientation of this type of meaning analysis toward the description of environmental attributes.

Much of the contemporary work in cognitive science and experimental social psychology is designed to examine the content of, and processes associated with, descriptive meaning (see Wyer & Srull, 1986). In effect, models are being developed to explain the cognitive processes by which stimuli are, or are not, represented in short-term memory. Much of the environmental perception work in organizational studies is also oriented toward measures of descriptive meaning. Included here are measures of physical environmental attributes, such as group size and the temperature of working spaces, as well as less seemingly objective variables that nevertheless are operationally defined in terms of real-world objects and events and that have an "out there" quality (for example, centralization of decision making, functional specialization, formality of rules and regulations, technological complexity). The fact that measures of these variables involve perception in one way or another is viewed as an issue of measurement and is not intrinsic to the definition of the variable (for example, group size should be the same irrespective of who does the counting; see Magnusson, 1981). However, the fact that perception is involved may open the door to various information processing functions, and thus the role of perception is not necessarily benign (see Feldman & Lynch, 1988).

But, as noted earlier, we are concerned with the significance that perceived environmental attributes have for individuals—the interpretation of such attributes in terms of their acquired meaning to individuals. In this regard, Mandler (1982) suggested that information processing of environmental attributes may proceed beyond descriptions of what is "out there" to *valuations* of environmental attributes. A "valuation" is a judgment or cognitive appraisal of the degree to which a value is represented in or by a (perceived) environmental attribute. We will elaborate on the concept of valuation by drawing on a recent discussion by James and James (1989) that viewed psychological climate perceptions—that is, perceptions that assess the significance and meaning of work environments to individuals—as partial functions of personal value systems.

Psychological Climate as a Function of Valuation

A personal value has been defined as "that which a person wants, or seeks to obtain . . ." because it is "that which one regards as conducive to ones' welfare" (Locke, 1976, p. 1304). Personal values serve as latent indicators of what it is about environments that is significant to individuals because it is the attainment of what is personally valued that determines one's welfare in a work environment, or one's sense of organizational well-being (James & James, 1989). James and James employed this rationale to propose that (1) latent psychological values (such as desires for clarity, harmony, and justice—see Locke, 1976) will (2) engender the psychological schemas (for instance, cognitive scales or standards for judging role clarity, role conflict, and equity) used (3) to impute meaning to environmental attributes (for example, to assess the amount of clarity present in job descriptions, the conflict represented in interactions between members of different departments, the equity represented in recent pay raises) because (4) it is these value-engendered or value-based schemas that reflect what it is that is significant and meaningful to individuals in regard to work environments.

In sum, personal values produce the schemas employed to cognitively appraise work environment attributes in terms of their significance to the individual. The cognitive appraisal itself, namely the judgment of the degree to which a value is represented in or by an environmental attribute, is the *valuation.* Valuation thus provides assessments of the *meaningful environment* considered so important by authors such as Rotter (1981), Ekehammer (1974), and Endler and Magnusson (1976). James and James (1989) suggested further that valuations of work environments are provided directly by measures of psychological climate (PC—see Jones & James, 1979; James & Sells, 1981). In part, this suggestion was definitional inasmuch as the concept of PC was developed expressly to refer to work environ-

Table 2.1. Perceptual Measures of the Meaning of Work Environments
Clustered by First-Order Factor.

Role Stress and Lack of Harmony	*Leadership Facilitation and Support*
Role ambiguity	Leader trust and support
Role conflict	Leader goal facilitation
Role overload	Leader interaction facilitation
Subunit conflict	Psychological influence
Lack of organization identification	Hierarchical influence
Lack of management concern and awareness	*Work Group Cooperation, Friendliness, and Warmth*
Job Challenge and Autonomy	Work group cooperation
Job challenge and variety	Work group friendliness and warmth
Job autonomy	Responsibility for effectiveness
Job importance	

ments as they are "cognitively represented in terms of their psychological meaning and significance to the individual" (James, 1982, p. 219). The emphasis on higher-order, subjective interpretations of environmental attributes is portrayed by designations given to the PC variables listed in Table 2.1.

The PC variables are clustered within the following four factors: (1) Role Stress and Lack of Harmony; (2) Job Challenge and Autonomy; (3) Leadership Facilitation and Support; and (4) Work Group Cooperation, Friendliness, and Warmth. These four PC factors have been shown to be invariant over a number of diverse work environments (see James & James, 1989; James & Sells, 1981). If, as proposed, the PC variables and the factors underlying these variables are engendered by values, then we would expect a close correspondence between clusters of perceived work environment measures and clusters of personal values. This correspondence is evident if we compare the PC factors in Table 2.1 to four of the salient latent psychological values proposed by Locke (1976, p. 1329). These latent values are desires for (1) clarity, harmony, and justice; (2) challenge, independence, and responsibility; (3) work facilitation, support and recognition; and (4) warm and friendly social relations.

A Hierarchical Model of Climate. James and James continued their exploration of the meaning of work environments by noting that the subjective, value-based, acquired meanings provided by valuation are often given designations that reflect the key role played by valuation in emotion. These designations include evaluative meanings (Mandler, 1982), affective (connotative) meaning (Osgood, Suci, & Tannenbaum, 1957), and emotionally relevant, or emotional, cognitions (Reisenzein, 1983; Schachter & Singer, 1962). The rationale here is that individuals respond emotionally to environmental attributes as a function of the significance that such attributes are perceived to have for personal well-being. And, as discussed, it is the valuation process that furnishes individuals with interpretations of environmental attributes in terms that are significant to them, which denotes significance in terms of having influence on their sense of organizational well-being. Thus, for example, we could view Henry's perception that his research is challenging as an emotional cognition because (1) the perceived challenge suggests that the desire (value) for challenge has in part been satisfied, which (2) in combination with perceived physiological arousal (Reisenzein, 1983), should (3) be efficacious in promoting a positive sense of organizational well-being for Henry.

The purpose of the James and James attempts to tie PC to valuation, and then both PC and valuation to emotionally relevant cognitions, was to build a case that a single, higher-order factor underlies measurements of PC. This objective was based on a theoretical perspective presented by Lazarus (1982, 1984) and Lazarus and Folkman (1984) that all emotionally relevant cognitions share a single latent component—a *general factor (g-factor)*—that furnishes them with the facility to cognitively assess significance for well-being. This g-factor is a higher-order schema for judging the degree to which *the environment is personally beneficial versus personally detrimental (damaging, painful) to one's sense of well-being.*

This perspective suggests that a single, higher-order g-factor underlies the emotionally relevant climates represented by PC perceptions. This factor may be defined as *a cognitive appraisal of the degree to which the work environment is personally beneficial versus personally detrimental to the organizational well-being of the individual*. A hierarchical model for PC is presented in Figure 2.1; the proposed g-factor of meaning is designated *psychological climate–general*, or simply *PC-g*. As discussed, each of the PC variables and each of the four first-order PC factors represents a valuation of environmental attributes. The causal arrows from PC-g to the first-order PC factors, and, indirectly, the PC variables, signify that the acquired meanings reflected in these valuations are a function of a deeper, more pervasive judgment of the degree to which the environment is personally beneficial versus personally detrimental to the well-being of the individual.

James and James used confirmatory factor analysis on four different samples from diverse organizations to test the hierarchical model in Figure 2.1. The model was confirmed in each case. Moreover, alternative models based on a pervasive method factor were disconfirmed. Thus, initial, but by no means conclusive, tests support the model in Figure 2.1 and the theory used to develop that model. While we are aware that other theories and models may explain the data equally well (James, Mulaik, & Brett, 1982), we will proceed on the assumption that the theory and model of meaning for climate that we have proposed here is useful for explanatory purposes. In summary form, the key aspects of this theory are as follows:

1.   Psychological climate (PC) represents valuations of environ-mental events, objects, processes, and structures, which is to say cognitive appraisals of environmental attributes in terms of their acquired meaning and significance to the individual.

2.   The higher-order schemas that comprise the measurement model or domain of PC — that is, the higher-order schemas (HOSs) used to impute acquired meaning — are engendered by personal values that represent what it is in the work environment that is significant or desired for enhancing, maintaining, or protecting one's sense of organizational well-being.

3.   The key determinant of organizational well-being is an over-all, abstract, and pervasive appraisal of the degree to which

Figure 2.1. A Hierarchical Model of Meaning.

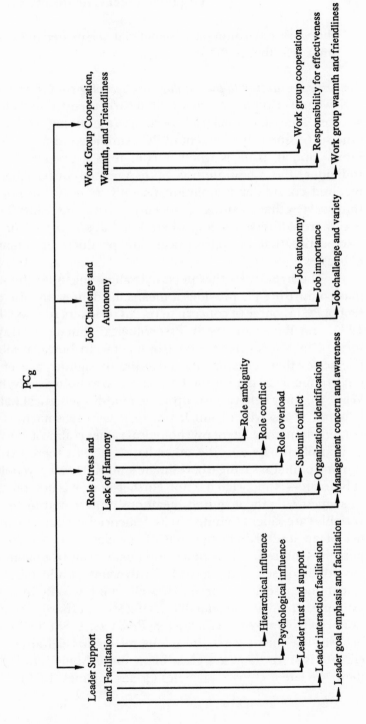

the work environment is beneficial versus detrimental to one's self (that is, PC-g).

Concerns Pertaining to the Etiology of Psychological Climate. The reviews and critiques of climate cited earlier tended to focus on selected issues that collectively pertain to the etiology of climate. One such issue is the content of PC. Another, and perhaps the most popular, issue is whether climate is a property of the individual, the organization, or both. A related concern that has received considerable attention recently is the social interactionists' view that meaning is a socially constructed reality. These issues are addressed below, where emphasis is placed on the perspective that PC perceptions are products of valuation processes.

The hypothesis that personal values engender the schemas comprising PC provides a means for delineating the content of PC (a source of concern to recent reviewers such as Glick, 1985, and Rousseau, 1988). Psychological climate portrays a form of "as is" assessment of environmental attributes on subjective scales that represent the meaning or significance of the environment as determined by latent psychological values. While this may help to clear up some muddy theoretical waters, it is not necessarily of much practical help inasmuch as the content domain of latent psychological values is almost as vague as that of climate. On the other hand, at least there exists a starting point for saying what climate — at least what psychological climate — is and what it is not. Furthermore, it is now possible to suggest why the acquired meanings represented in the PC variables are salient to individuals. Salience is in part the product of an underlying appraisal of the degree to which one perceives himself or herself as being okay or in trouble in this environment (see Lazarus, 1984). Furthermore, while it is useful to conduct research in terms of a climate for something (for example, creativity, productivity, safety, or perhaps organizational well-being; see Schneider & Reichers, 1983), we do not believe that this is a parsimonious means for defining what climate is since there are great many more "somethings" than there are latent climate variables (Jones & James, 1979). Thus, redundancies will exist over the set of climates for things, which in turn will stimulate a search for underlying explanatory constructs that apply to multiple things. But then, we already have a reasonable idea as to the domain of these explanatory constructs (see also Insel & Moos, 1974).

The emphasis on psychological climate reflects a tradition in psychological studies of meaning to focus on individual differences in phenomenological experiences pertaining to valuations, acquired meanings, and affect (see Lewin, 1938; Mandler, 1982; Mischel, 1973; Osgood, Suci, & Tannenbaum, 1957; Rotter, 1981). The principal hypothesis is that individuals with different learning experiences, cognitive construction competencies, encoding abilities, self-regulatory systems, needs, values, expectancies, and self-concepts will be predisposed to differ in what they regard as personally beneficial versus personally harmful and what they perceive as ambiguous, challenging, loyal, fair, supportive, and warm. What little empirical research exists in climate supports the position that person (P) variables, situational (S) variables, and $P \times S$ interactions are all related significantly to PC perceptions (James, 1988; James, Gent, Hater, & Coray, 1979; James, Hartman, Stebbins, & Jones, 1977; James, Hater, & Jones, 1981; James & Jones, 1980; James & Tetrick, 1986; Jones & James, 1979).

A salient implication of individual differences in PC perceptions is that the acquired meanings attributed to a particular work environment at a particular point in time have a historical component that transcends both that particular environment and that specific point in time (James, Hater, Gent, & Bruni, 1978; Jones, 1983). Consider that the individual brings with him or her to the organization a set of cognitive processing skills, a set of values, and a set of higher-order schemas engendered by these values for imputing meaning to work environment attributes. The actual valuations of environmental attributes (for instance, an appraisal of the degree to which pay is equitable) is the product of an interaction between the perceived environmental attribute (pay) and the internal schemas (for example, standards for equity) used "to valuate" the attribute. It is this internal interaction between the pay perceived to exist and the standards for equity that lies at the heart of cognitive appraisals, cognitive constructions, and phenomenological experiences. And, by definition, the interaction occurs at the individual level of explanation, since it is only individuals that valuate.

Now, if the value-engendered schemas used to valuate environmental events are learned early in childhood and are set in concrete thereafter, one might argue that much of the variance in acquired meanings in current environments is individually based. However, as noted previously (James, Hater, Gent, & Bruni, 1978), our position is that values and value-engendered schemas *may* change — that is, accommodate — as a function of experiences in a new work environment. In general, however, we assume that individuals first attempt to assimilate information into acquired belief systems (see Jones & Gerard, 1967). Assimilation connotes that the underlying structure of value-engendered schemas — that is, the beliefs or standards used to make valuations — is stable even though contemporaneous perceptions (valuations) of environmental attributes vary as the environmental attributes vary. The stability of the belief structure derives from the rationale that higher-order schemas (1) are abstract and generalized and thus not highly influenced by specific events in a particular situation, (2) are familiar to the individual and indeed may be used automatically (Shiffrin & Schneider, 1977), and (3) are salient to the individual in the sense that they are the product of values (James, Hater, Gent, & Bruni, 1978).

The underlying belief system may nevertheless accommodate, especially in the interest of achieving an adaptive fit with an organization (Dieterly & Schneider, 1974; Jones, 1983; Schneider, 1975). Social influence processes, such as early socialization in the organization (Schneider & Reichers, 1983), are believed to be important causal factors for this accommodation.

To illuminate this idea, consider the literatures on the related concepts of social influence, shared meanings and shared psychological fields (see Asch, 1951; Katz & Kahn, 1978; Rommetveit, 1981). The basic idea is that members of a social unit communicate with one another and discuss their perceptions. In some cases, these perceptions reflect acquired meanings and the communication process serves to inform and perhaps to compare and contrast acquired meanings (valuations). A consensus may exist or develop among these valuations, which in part may reflect prior similarities in beliefs among the members of the social unit. Or, differences in acquired meanings may stimulate the need among individual members to reevaluate their valuations and perhaps to change them. A change in a valuation does not necessarily suggest an accommodation in the underlying belief system, although it might. The point here is that the sharing of information, particularly with others that one trusts and respects, may result in causal influences to change not only contemporaneous valuations, but also the value-engendered schemas that provided the valuations.

The preceding discussion allows for both a historical component in belief systems that produces assimilation and a contemporaneous component that may stimulate accommodation. It implicitly assumes that valuation is a phenomenological experience. The historical component and forces for assimilation will be reduced in situations where incoming information is novel and/or ambiguous. If the information is novel and/or ambiguous for all members of a social collective, then interactions among the members may focus on collectively constructing (creating, enacting, evolving) a higher-order, acquired meaning to make sense of the novel/ambiguous environmental attribute(s) (see Ashforth, 1985; Glick, 1985, 1988; Schneider & Reichers, 1983; Weick, 1979). The resulting meaning, which is usually assumed to be shared, is said to be socially constructed (Berger & Luckmann, 1966), which also reflects the rationale of symbolic interactionism (see Blumer, 1969, as well as the reviews by Ashforth, 1985; Glick, 1985; Schneider & Reichers, 1983).

A set of socially constructed meanings may be developed for various novel/ambiguous environmental stimuli. This set of meanings may then be referred to as a socially constructed reality (see Ashforth, 1985). The members of the social collective may choose to internalize these socially developed schemas and thus to employ them to valuate the novel/ambiguous environmental events that stimulated social interaction in the first place. Or, socially constructed meanings that have been developed previously may be communicated to newcomers as part of the socialization process (see Ashforth, 1985; Jones, 1983; Schneider & Reichers, 1983). This process is not necessarily unidirectional; over time the newcomer may introduce new information that causes revisions in acquired meanings and accommodation in the socially constructed schemas. Thus, this "social interactionist" perspective is dynamic and allows for revision and emergence of new bases for interpreting environmental attributes.

The social interactionist model espoused by Ashforth (1985), Glick (1985, 1988), and Schneider and Reichers (1983) for climate is useful for pointing out that the belief systems underlying valuations of an environment may have a contemporaneous social construction component. The problem is that the social interactionists are proposing an *ahistorical* model in which all, or almost all, construction of belief systems takes place in the current work environment. Some contemporaneous social construction, and some contemporaneous social influence, will likely occur. But to assume that valuations of the current work environment are predicated on higher-order schemas developed via social construction processes in that environment is to disregard the historical component of perception. Consider that much of the information to be interpreted by the individual in a work environment is neither novel nor ambiguous (especially for individuals with previous work experience). Consider next that perception has a historical component in which individuals attempt first to preserve familiar and valued belief systems prior to subjecting them to the changes likely required by contemporaneous social construction processes. Finally, consider that even if novel or ambiguous information stimulates social interactions, such interactions do not guarantee consensus or agreement on the ensuing "meanings." Individual differences may stimulate differences in such meanings in much the same manner that they do for any other socially constructed meaning.

In sum, social influence and social construction processes in the current work environment likely have causal roles in influencing both belief systems and contemporaneous valuations. We do not believe, however, that meaning analysis is ahistorical and based exclusively on social construction processes in current environment. Moreover, we particularly disagree with an additional point suggested by the social interactionist school. This point is that meaning—that is, the social reality enacted by and shared by the social collective—resides at the level of the social collective (Glick, 1985), or is a joint property of both the individual and the organization (Ashforth, 1985), or "does not exist merely in the experience of a single individual, but...exists in the behavioral transaction itself" (Schneider & Reichers, 1983, pp. 29–30). In short, meaning is not, as we have proposed, strictly a phenomenological experience, since meaning resides at least in part *outside* the individual—namely in the social collective, the object of perception (that is, the organization), or the social interaction process.

Our critique of this perspective begins with the proposal that meaning partially resides in the object of perception, namely the organization (Ashforth, 1985). Stated simply, we know of no credible theory of cognition or perception that allows the acquired meaning attributed to an environmental object to reside in the object itself (Mandler, 1982). Acquired meanings reside in the cognitive systems of individuals because, as we have discussed, the attribution of meaning is a valuation that rests on $P \times S$ interactions within each individual. The possibility that the higher-order schemas used in valuation are a function of social influence or social construction processes does not alter the fact that the attribution of meaning is a phenomenological event. When this rationale is applied to the positions that meaning at least partially resides in social collectives (Glick, 1985) or in transactions (Schneider & Reichers, 1983), we submit that to equate the processes (behavioral transactions) or the sources (social collectives) that influenced the event (development of internal schemas) with the event itself (the schemas themselves) is to confuse cause with effect (James, Joyce, & Slocum, 1988). Moreover, and as a general point, to suggest that meaning resides in environmental objects, collectives, or communication processes disregards not only the human intellectual component and free agency, in which individuals reflect on social influences and perhaps develop their own unique meanings, but also the possibility of individual differences in acquired meanings that ensue irrespective of the immediate social construction processes.

Finally, the position that meaning resides outside the individual, in either organizational objects or in social collectives, rests on the assumption that acquired meanings are shared among perceivers, at least those within the social collective. All of our social interactionists–climate theorists assert that individuals within a common social unit share perceptions (Ashforth, 1985; Glick, 1985; Schneider & Reichers, 1983). The evidence, when based on legitimate statistics and legitimate empirical data, suggests that agreement is possible but not as prevalent as asserted by the social interactionists (see James, 1982; James, Demaree, & Wolf, 1984; James, Joyce, & Slocum, 1988). At the present time, the empirical evidence furnishes no basis for unequivocal statements regarding general levels of agreement.

Lest this position be construed to mean that no agreement occurs on PC perceptions, allow us to hasten to add that it is quite possible for individuals to concur in regard to acquired meanings. The forces for agreement include strong situational influences exerted by the targets of perception, strong contextual effects that guide the search for meaning potentials, restriction in range on individualistic factors that engender individual differences in perception (a possible product of attraction, selection, and attrition; see Schneider & Reichers, 1983; Schneider, 1987), social influences from other members of a work unit, and social construction processes. As noted by James (1982) and James, Joyce, and Slocum (1988), agreement on a PC variable or variables indicates a shared psychological environment (in other words, shared phenomenological experiences and acquired meanings), and provides the opportunity *to describe an environment in psychological terms*—that is, in terms of the shared acquired meanings of the perceivers.

However, as observed by James (1982) and James, Joyce, and Slocum (1988), one must first demonstrate that the acquired meanings are indeed shared among members of a social unit or a collective (see Joyce & Slocum, 1984). Some form of interrater reliability analysis is required in which the individual is the unit of analysis (see James, Demaree, & Wolf, 1984; Kozlowski & Hults, 1987; Schneider & Bowen, 1985). If the interrater reliability analysis suggests that sufficient agreement exists on a PC variable to infer a shared assignment of (acquired) meaning, then it is possible to aggregate the climate scores to a higher level of analysis, such as the group, subsystem, or organization level of analysis. It is the shared assignment of meaning that provides the composition theory (Roberts, Hulin, & Rousseau, 1978) that links a construct defined and operationalized at the individual level of analysis (PC) to another form of that same construct at a higher level of analysis (for example, group, subsystem, or organizational climate) (see James, 1982; James, Joyce, & Slocum, 1988).

Summary: It is hoped that the proposal that PC perceptions are products of valuation processes will assist in defining more closely the content of the PC domain in future research. In this regard, viewing PC perceptions as valuations suggests that PC perceptions are (1) phenomenological, and (2) multiply determined, which is to say functions of various individual, situational, and social influences, and interactions among these influences. Situational influences generally involve the environmental attributes that are the subjects of perception, whereas individual attributes refer to the factors that give perception a historical component and render such perceptions as phenomenological (for instance, learning experiences, cognitive construction competencies, values). Social influences include factors that shape PC perceptions in the contemporaneous social environment—for example, socialization processes, socially constructed meanings to interpret novel information. One might expect a continuing antimony between the forces for assimilation, stimulated by the desire to protect the existing cognitive structure, and forces for accommodation, stimulated by the desire to obtain an adaptive fit in a particular organization. The interaction of these two forces must be considered since new information requires continuous analysis by the collective to infer meaning, whereas it is quite possible that certain personal values (such as beliefs in freedom, equity, and justice) are immutable for large sections of the work force.

Relations Among Acquired Meanings, Emotions, and Evaluations. Periodically we again hear the question of how one differentiates between (psychological) climate and affect, or climate and evaluation. The objectives of this section are (1) to differentiate among the emotionally relevant cognitions comprising PC, emotion itself, and evaluation, and yet (2) to demonstrate why these constructs should be related. As part of this process we will also attempt to integrate the cognitively oriented approach to meaning adopted here with the more emotionally toned, evaluation-oriented approach of Osgood, Suci, and Tannenbaum (1957). The principal hypothesis guiding this discussion is that emotionally relevant cognitions (for example, PC), emotions, and evaluations of goodness and badness are components of reciprocally interacting, interdependent, nonrecursive, fused processes (see James & Jones, 1974, 1980; James & Tetrick, 1986; Lazarus, 1982, 1984; Park, Sims, & Motowidlo, 1986). We will present our thoughts via illustration.

Suppose Henry, the untenured assistant professor, receives information that a manuscript on which he invested considerable effort has been rejected by a prestigious journal. Henry immediately interprets the rejection as detrimental to his organizational (and professional) well-being. Information that acceptances in prestigious journals are prerequisite to tenure has already been well-learned by Henry and is not consciously processed. What does enter short-term memory and awareness is that the rejection is threatening— that is, detrimental— to his career. The perception of threat is a manifestation of PC-g and is an emotionally relevant cognition because it, in combination with perceived physiological arousal (readers may wish to consider the physiological arousal experienced just prior to, during, and just after reading a review), is instrumental not only in labeling the emotion but also in determining the direction and intensity of the emotion experienced (Lazarus, 1982, 1984; Reisenzein, 1983; Schachter & Singer, 1962). Indeed, it is not the rejection letter itself that directly generates emotion. It is the meaning that the letter has for organizational well-being—that is, threat—that directly generates emotion (Lazarus, 1982).

Given that the letter is interpreted as threatening to organizational well-being, we may surmise that the ensuing emotion(s) is a form of negative affect such as fear, distress, and/or anxiety (see Watson & Clark, 1984). We may also surmise that emotions such as fear, distress, and anxiety will result in a feeling of dislike for the letter and an evaluation that the letter is "bad." Note that the evaluation of bad is a product of emotion, which in turn is a product of the perception of threat. Stated simply, we tend to evaluate as "bad" those things that are detrimental to our well-being and generate negative affect. Conversely, we tend to evaluate as "good" those things that are beneficial to our well-being and produce positive affect (Stotland & Canon, 1972). This scenario connotes strong relations between cognitive appraisals reflecting significance to well-being, emotions, and evaluations. It does not, however, suggest that cognitions, emotions, and evaluations are one and the same construct, semantic or otherwise (see Lazarus, 1982, 1984).

If, over time, Henry receives acceptances on other manuscripts as well as positive feedback on other criteria for tenure, the single case of rejection should not determine Henry's overall perceptions. The summary perception regarding all instances may, in fact, produce primarily a positive affect and a positive sense of professional and organizational well-being. The overall job itself could be thus evaluated as "good."

The immediately preceding discussion may be summarized by the following model: Emotionally relevant cognition (for example, PC-g) affects evaluation. But this recursive model is incomplete. One major, missing component is reciprocal causal arrows from evaluation to affect, and from affect to psychological climate. It is proposed that, once affect and evaluation have stabilized—that is, reached a stage of temporary equilibrium (see Heise, 1975)—they are highly fused and interdependent. This appears to be why few theorists attempt to differentiate between affect and evaluation. This fusing of affect and evaluation will be adopted here in discussing the reciprocal portion of the model, which involves the reciprocal effect of affect (evaluation) on cognition.

The main ingredients in this proposed reciprocal effect are that affect (evaluation) may cause individuals to (1) be attentive primarily to those environmental cues that engender existing or desired levels of affect; (2) impute desirable or undesirable attributes to a work environment for which an individual has positive/negative affect; (3) cognitively redefine environmental cues so as to increase the likelihood that they will be responded to positively/negatively; and (4) cognitively restructure acquired meanings so as to make them consistent with expectations regarding whether this type of work environment should promote positive/negative reactions (see James & Jones, 1980; James & Tetrick, 1986).

To summarize, emotions and evaluation have a strong cognitive component inasmuch as individuals are believed to respond emotionally to environments in terms of how they perceive them. The key aspect of perception in this regard is the acquired meaning of the degree to which the work environment is personally beneficial versus damaging to one's welfare. Such a perception indicates the extent to which one believes that the work environment is efficacious in promoting one's sense of organizational well-being (James & James, 1989). This belief is likely to be influenced not only by feedback loops from actual or experienced affect (for example, the experienced feeling of well-being), but also by various cognitive processes that make some aspects of the work environment more accessible to perception than other aspects. The ensuing reciprocal causation between perception and affect suggests that the acquired meanings represented by PC perceptions have a potentially strong affective component. This provides yet another reason to regard the acquired meanings underlying climate perceptions as phenomenological experiences that exist at the individual level of explanation. The reciprocal relation between affect and acquired meaning has only begun to be investigated theoretically and empirically (see prior references). Early research on the acquired meanings of jobs, a salient component of PC, suggests that (1) job satisfaction has a strong influence on valuations of jobs, and (2) affect is postcognitive (James & Tetrick, 1986). But this research is neither conclusive nor exhaustive.

It would be interesting to pursue the reciprocal causation argument and extend it to a more general systems model in which climate is encapsulated in a general organizational behavior paradigm. Theoretically, this has already been attempted (James & Jones, 1976). Moreover, implications of reciprocal causation for models of organizational behavior in general, and climate in particular, have also been addressed. For example, based on Endler (1975), James, Hater, Gent, and Bruni (1978) asserted that reciprocal causation between persons and environments precludes attempts to partition variance in climate perceptions and attitudes into situational versus personalistic factors. Working from the same person-situation model, Schneider (1987) and Schneider and Reichers (1983), based on Bowers (1973), argued for the Attraction-Selection-Attrition (ASA) model in which factors such as self-selection reduce the variance on individual difference variables in (sub) organizational units. (Recent research by James, 1988, suggests that the ASA process reduces variance on personality variables by about 50 percent. This figure is based on a comparison of a sample that was selected in part based on scores on the personality variables and comparison to the normative population used in the development of the personality inventory.)

However, this area awaits serious attempts at empirical research designed to explicitly test reciprocal causation hypotheses. We suggest that it is time to back up the theory with empirical data. Until we have these data, we will refrain from further theorizing, at least in regard to climate.

Summary and conclusions. James and Sells (1981) referred to psychological climate as the psychological environment of the workplace. The term *psychological environment* refers specifically to perceptions that reflect the psychological meaning and significance of work environmental attributes to individuals. Heretofore, we have elaborated on and extended the James and Sells position by describing PC in terms of meaning analyses and acquired meanings, and by defining PC in terms of valuation. A strong emphasis on a phenomenological, perceptual construct was evident throughout this presentation. This emphasis was reinforced by portraying PC as being influenced by both affect and a multitude of reasonably stable individual (difference) characteristics. The latter variables furnish PC with a historical component that transcends a particular organization. On the other hand, it was noted that cognitive structures are subject to accommodation, especially as part of socialization processes and in work environments subject to ambiguous and/or novel stimuli. Social influences among members of a system resulting in socially constructed meanings are quite likely with ambiguous/novel stimuli. The extent to which recent or contemporaneous socially constructed meanings are themselves products of prior belief systems, are shared among members of a collective, and/or stimulate changes in prior belief systems remain subjects for empirical research.

The discussions of meaning, psychological environments, and social influences were based largely on extant theories and debates from psychology. The novel aspect of the current essay is the proposal of, and empirical support for, a single, higher-order latent variable (factor) for PC. Inspection of the manifest indicators of PC in Table 2.1 demonstrates that many popular perceptual measures of roles, jobs, leaders, groups, and subsystems/organizations are represented. The possibility exists that all of these measures relate to a common construct that reflects perceived benefit versus harm to personal welfare in the perceived organization. If this possibility is valid, then it follows that (1) it may be possible *to integrate* the diffuse field of the perceived work environment, and (2) the portion of the perceptual system pertaining to the meaning of work environments to individuals may be rather simple and straightforward (see James & James, 1988).

Climate and Culture

One final objective for this chapter is to compare and contrast psychological and organizational climate with organizational culture. This section opens with the perspective that "Culture is a fuzzy construct" and that "Clearly, the picture [regarding culture] is very complex, and it will take decades of research to unravel it" (Triandis, Bontempo, Villareal, Asai, & Lucca, 1988, pp. 323, 329). These statements were applied to societies or civilizations, but they probably apply equally well to organizations. These points are not offered as criticism, because climate is hardly less fuzzy than culture. They are offered only to suggest that major or novel insights into culture are unlikely in the near future, and that we have no pretensions in this regard. On the other hand, the position is taken here that the study of organizational culture could benefit from a "psychological perspective" in addition to the anthropological and sociological themes that have thus far influenced this subject. One such benefit pertains to methodological rigor. As psychologists like Triandis have demonstrated, it is quite possible to conduct nomothetic, psychometrically and statistically rigorous studies of culture (see Triandis, Bontempo, Villareal, Asai, & Lucca, 1988).

Another benefit is substantive. As intimated earlier, we will address organizational (subsystem, group) culture from the perspective of system or group norms and values (Katz & Kahn, 1966, 1978). This opens the door to a vast domain of social psychological research on subjects such as group norms, group values, social influence, conformity, compliance, identification, socialization, individual-group conflict, intergroup conflict, conflict resolution, groupthink, and so forth — in short, the field of group dynamics (see Shaw, 1976). In this section, we will only touch on selected concepts from dynamics that pertain to system norms and values. Our principle concerns are to underscore the need to adopt a psychological perspective on organizational culture and to attempt to clarify the similarities and differences between the concepts of culture and climate.

Climate Versus Culture: A Question of Personal Values Versus Group Values and Norms

Psychological climate has been described as a product of an interaction between information sensed from the environment and higher-order schemas engendered by latent personal values. The frame of reference for the products of this interaction — the

acquired meanings or valuations of environmental attributes —
is thus the individual. To illustrate, a desire or personal value for
independence and autonomy in work-related decision making
connotes that independence and autonomy comprise salient
standards (schemas) that the individual will use to valuate (cognitively appraise) his or her work environment in terms of its
significance and meaning to him or her. Moreover, a strong
desire for independence and autonomy in the current environment may be a function of social influence and/or contemporaneous organizational sense-making activities, such as socialization processes in which the individual is informed what
he or she may realistically expect in regard to independence in
this work environment. However, it is also probable that this
individual had already developed not only a desire, or a lack of
such, for independence and autonomy prior to entering the
current work environment, but also a set of cognitive standards
for evaluating what is and what is not conducive to independence and autonomy in social situations in general. While the
desire and standards may partially accommodate to the specif-
ics of a particular work environment, they are also products of
basic personality development and, as such, are unlikely to be
quickly or completely overhauled simply by entering a new work
environment or continuing to work in that environment.

Now, suppose that all or most individuals in a work environment (social unit, in-group) agree that their work provides
many opportunities for personal independence and autonomy
(for example, the scores on the PC variables for Job Autonomy
and Psychological Influence are high). We could then say that
these individuals share the perception (acquired meaning, valuation) that their work provides many opportunities for personal
autonomy and influence. This sharing would reflect an organizational climate (OC). (We will use the term *organizational climate*
in the generic sense to refer to aggregates of PC scores, whatever
the level of aggregation.) Note that the frame of reference for OC
is still the individual — that is, individuals in the work unit share
the perception that work provides opportunities for individuals
there to experience personal independence and autonomy.

Similar arguments may be constructed for the remaining

PC variables and factors, and for interpretations of aggregate PC, or OC. The orientation rests on personal, value-based schemas, where the basic frame of reference is always the individual. This point is represented most clearly by PC-g, which is defined as the degree to which the work environment is believed to be *personally* beneficial versus detrimental to one's [own] sense of organizational well-being. Note, however, that an OC analogue would exist for PC-g if many or most people in a work setting shared valuations regarding the extent to which this setting was personally beneficial versus detrimental to their well-being.

It is this personal orientation and frame of reference for PC, which carries over into OC, that, in our opinion, separates climate from culture. That is, whereas PC and OC have a personal frame of reference, organizational (again in a generic sense) culture appears to employ the system (for instance, group, division, department, organization, type of organization, type of profession, and so on) as the frame of reference. This rationale can be developed by continuing with the illustration for independence and autonomy.

Note that an individual's personal desire for independence and autonomy does not connote that he or she believes that all members of the social unit (collective) should possess the same degree of independence or autonomy that he or she values (Katz & Kahn, 1966, 1978). An individual who desires a high degree of independence and autonomy may realize that, in this work unit, coordination and reliability would suffer if *all* work unit members worked independently. Conditional on requirements for coordination and reliability, this individual may perceive that only some individuals, preferably himself or herself, may function independently. Or, he or she may see that personally the desired level of independence is inconsistent with the goals of the overall work unit. Thus, while a personal desire may be thwarted, the individual realizes that personal values must be subordinated to the needs — the system values — of the collective.

Individuals may thus differentiate between personal desires supported by a personal frame of reference and the needs or desires of a collective, which has a system (group) frame of reference (Katz & Kahn, 1966, 1978). And, there is no need to have agreement on personal values or the valuations engendered by personal values (that is, PC) to have a system value. Note, then, that the same constructs—independence and autonomy—are being addressed, but from different frames of reference. It is not the content of variables per se that differentiates climate from culture. Rather, it is the frame of reference, personal versus group, that is the key to differentiating between climate and culture. Stated alternatively, individuals may have quite different expectations and goals for (1) personal independence and autonomy, versus (2) the levels or distributions of independence and autonomy they regard as beneficial for the productive functioning and survival of the system (group, culture) (Katz & Kahn, 1966, 1978).

It is the latter type of value—what is desired as beneficial for the productive functioning and survival of the system or the collective—that we believe is the frame of reference for culture. Specifically, it is *system values* that engender the schemas (standards) for evaluating environmental attributes in terms of culture. It may be reasonable to assume that many if not most of the constructs addressed as personal values in Table 2.1 could also function at the level of system value. For example, it would seem that harmony, clarity, justice, responsibility, support, friendliness, and cooperation could all serve as desirable states for system functioning and survival.

However, it is improbable that the system values underlying culture are limited to system-level analogies of the personal values associated with climate. Additional system values reviewed by Katz and Kahn (1966, 1978) and James and Jones (1974, 1976) include conformity, rationality, predictability, impersonality, loyalty, reciprocity, adherence to chain of command, local versus cosmopolitan orientation, and programmed versus unprogrammed approaches to problem solving. The intent here is not to be exhaustive but to suggest that some qualitative differences in the domains of constructs may separate climate and culture, as well as differences in frames in reference.

System Norms

An additional means for differentiating culture from climate is that normative beliefs (Rousseau, 1988; Sproull, 1981), also called system norms (Katz & Kahn, 1966, 1978), are associated with culture. System norms refer to explicit, system-sanctioned behaviors that are expected in the sense of being considered appropriate for members of the system (Katz & Kahn, 1966). System values, in addition to furnishing desires for maintaining and/or enhancing the viability of the system, furnish justifications for the normative behaviors and for the system activities that derive from these behaviors. The system values may be quite abstract, elaborate, and generalized, encompassing transcendental, moral, or sacred values (for example, loyalty) with accompanying symbols, myths, legends, and the like (Katz & Kahn, 1966; Trice & Beyer, 1984). The associated normative behaviors may, accordingly, take on ritualistic qualities (Katz & Kahn, 1966). However, when all is said and done, Katz and Kahn (1966, 1978) suggested that organizations tend toward pragmatic norms and values, particularly in today's technologically oriented, data-based society.

The combination of expected behaviors (system norms) and an ideology to justify those behaviors (system values) provide the individual with a basis for selecting a particular course of action over alternative courses of action, for defending why a particular action (thought) is more desirable than other actions (thoughts), and, in general, for choosing a frame of reference for making sense of things and explaining reality at the system level of analysis. The system-level values, expected behaviors, and supporting ideologies and justifications are often viewed as the products of group dynamics, namely interactions among system members designed to collectively develop (create, enact, evolve) a set of socially constructed schemas for making sense out of the functions of the system (see Katz & Kahn, 1966, 1978; Rousseau, 1988; Weick, 1979). Somewhat like psychological climate, these socially constructed schemas about system functioning furnish a basis for identifying what it is that is significant about the system, especially if the socially constructed schemas delve into presumed causes of system functioning. Unlike those related to psychological climate, however, beliefs pertaining to system functioning are not designed to reflect individuals' personal valuations. The schemas employed to make sense of the environment at the system level are a product of contemporaneous group dynamics (Katz & Kahn, 1966), and the objective is to describe an attribute of the system (that is, its culture — see Morey & Luthans, 1985) rather than to describe an attribute of the individual (that is, each individual's personal belief system).

The system frame of reference suggests that culture has the "out there" quality discussed by Mandler (1982). Nevertheless the constructs underlying culture are often vague and abstract, and perception is involved in both the awareness by individuals of culture and in the measurement of culture. But the constructs germane to culture apply to organizational systems and not to the personal belief systems of each individual. Phenomenology is involved in the sense that development of a construct such as system-level autonomy and independence involve cognitive constructions, subjectivity, and higher-order processing on the part of each individual. However, each person's cognitions of system autonomy and independence are components in a (presumably) shared psychological field in which personal phenomenological experiences (that is, personal beliefs about system autonomy and independence) may, if divergent from other members of the group, give way to a common, mutually agreed-on set of system-level standards for autonomy and independence (that is, system norms) and system-level explanations and justifications for those standards (that is, system values).

It is important to recall here the distinction between personal values for autonomy and independence and system values for autonomy and independence. Perhaps what is needed is new jargon to distinguish between the personally oriented climate concepts and the system-oriented culture concepts. Also, following the lead of Triandis and colleagues, we might pursue studies of the possible reciprocal effects of climate on culture and culture on climate. For example, how do beliefs regarding personal loyalty influence the development of system norms and values for system loyalty in social enactment processes, and, once developed, what influences do system norms and values have on accommodation of personal beliefs about loyalty? Or, what happens when poor person-environment fits occur, such as when an individual with a high need for independence is placed in an organizational culture that places high value on coordination, cooperation, and harmony? These questions are meant to be illustrative and to indicate the many interesting avenues of research pertaining to culture-climate interfaces.

Of course, one has first to establish that a culture, or perhaps a set of subcultures, exist in an organization (see Rousseau, 1988). And here we must again confront the issue of agreement among individuals in an in-group, social unit, or collective. However, this is not a new issue in psychology in regard to establishing the presence, or lack of such, of group norms (see Jackson, 1965; Shaver, 1987; Shaw, 1976). To state the matter simply, the existence of a group (system) norm requires that most members of a group share or agree on expected behaviors, whereas the existence of a group (system) value requires that most members of a group share or agree on the ideology for the norm (see Katz & Kahn, 1966, 1978; Jackson, 1965; Shaw, 1976). The level of analysis for assessing agreement is the individual because the question being asked is whether *individual members of the group share beliefs regarding system norms and system values*. Arguments presented by Glick (1985, 1988) that the unit of analysis for socially constructed, group-based meanings is the group apply no more here than they did for climate (see James, Joyce, & Slocum, 1988). And, it is critically important that all, or a representative sample of all, members of the group be consulted in attempting to estimate agreement among group members (James, Joyce, & Slocum, 1988). But, then, these are points already well established in the social psychological literature.

Final Thoughts on Climate and Culture

A bifurcation of theory and research approaches has characterized climate research from the beginning. Whereas Forehand

and Gilmer (1964) described climate primarily in terms of environmental attributes such as structure and actual reward/ punishment processes, Payne and Pheysey (1971) conceptualized and measured climate in terms of a "beta" press, which is to say in terms of the acquired meanings and valuations associated with the environmental attributes rather than in terms of the attributes per se. James, Jones, and colleagues' psychological climate approach is consistent with the Payne and Pheysey orientation, and, as reviewed by James (1982), most current climate researchers have adopted the use of acquired meanings or valuations as the basic unit of analysis for climate.

What must be realized is that once one has focused on valuations, one is addressing primarily personal values. Thus, the acquired meanings that are engendered by these personal values are the subjects of interest. It follows that aggregates of psychological climate, which most current climate researchers refer to as organizational climate, describe the mean (median, mode) of a set of personal valuations. There is nothing magical in the aggregation process that transforms a personal valuation into a system-level variable (James & Jones, 1974). The mean, for example, of a set of personal valuations describes nothing more than the central tendency in the distribution of these valuations (for example, the average of how people perceive the degree to which a work environment is personally beneficial versus detrimental to their well-being).

Culture is a different story because the frame of reference for the culture construct is the system and the basic question is what is beneficial to the functioning of the system (rather than being oriented toward the functioning of the individual). Culture is a group-level construct, a product of social interactions among group members. It appears to us that some recent critiques of climate (Ashforth, 1985; Glick, 1985, 1988; Schneider & Reichers, 1983) have confused the system-oriented culture concept with the person-oriented climate concept. Much of what these authors discussed in regard to climate applies better to culture. Perhaps the distinctions offered (as hypotheses) in this paper will serve to clarify what climate is and what it is not.

As data accumulate, it may be seen that the distinction between climate and culture is more a matter of emphasis or degree than a true qualitative difference in frames of reference. Consider, for example, the possibility that personal values may accommodate to system values so extensively that one could say that an individual has internalized the system values (see O'Reilly & Chatman, 1986). In this instance the personal values and system values would be one and the same. Processes such as internalization may be partial products of the fact that individuals self-selected organizations whose systems values were consonant with their personal values. Of course, these personal and system values need not converge and thus we could consider various degrees of convergence or divergence of beliefs regarding system values and personal values, the causes of convergence/divergence, and the effects of convergence/divergence. These issues relate to the prior recommendation that reciprocal relations between climate and culture appear to be a fruitful area of research.

Climate and culture may also be related in other ways. Earlier in this essay it was noted that system norms and values could produce a context that influenced the probability that one or a few meaning potentials would take precedence over other meaning potentials. The example given was that the system norm for professional productivity and the supporting system value for maintenance of the departmental reputation via scholarly contributions enhanced the attractiveness of the meaning potential that Henry is staying late so that he can work on research articles and papers. An infinite number of alternative examples, of organizational contexts posed as hypotheses, could be developed. Indeed, psychology has a long history of proposing, and intermittently empirically supporting, theories in which system norms and values influence perceptions of behavior in environments (see Bronfenbrenner, 1977). Thus, a large, potentially rich domain of research possibilities are available. We also have the interesting instance in which the culture variables become the subjects of a climate analysis. For example, we might ask each organizational incumbent whether system norms and values are "equitable," "ambiguous," or "facilitating."

In conclusion, we believe that one of the key benefits of adding culture to the general research domain of perceived work environments will be the clarification of what it is that climate measures, or should measure. It has been proposed that climate reflects a personal orientation, being a function of personal values, whereas culture reflects an organizational orientation, being a product of system values and norms. Perhaps the key problem in the climate literature has been the inability of climate investigators to reach a consensus regarding the basic unit of analysis for climate (that is, is climate an individual variable or an organizational variable). As noted, it seems that many of the arguments advanced by those who wish to give climate an organizational frame of reference apply better to culture than to climate. Thus, if we can agree that culture is the macro, organizational, or systems construct whereas climate is the micro, individual, or phenomenological construct, then we can proceed to address new and salient issues such as those illustrated earlier. We may also draw on the accumulated knowledge of the climate literature in regard to such things as techniques for estimating interrater agreement. Most important, however, is the opportunity to initiate empirical research in areas in which problems are still being identified and defined. This vastness of opportunity is made even more salient when one realizes that both the general public and managerial folklore have described climate and culture as being critical to the success of organizations and individuals. Such opinions suggest that extensive resources will be available for research in climate and culture.

References

Asch, S. E. (1951). Effects of group pressure upon the modification and distortion of judgements. In H. Guetzkow (Ed.), *Groups, leadership, and men* (pp. 177–190). Pittsburgh: Carnegie Press.

Ashforth, B. E. (1985). Climate formation: Issues and extensions. *Academy of Management Review, 10*(4), 837–847.

Berger, P. L., & Luckmann, T. (1966). *The social construction of reality: A treatise in the sociology of knowledge.* Garden City, NY: Doubleday.

Blumer, H. (1969). *Symbolic interactionism: Perspective and method.* Englewood Cliffs, NJ: Prentice-Hall.

Bowers, K. S. (1973). Situationism in psychology: An analysis and a critique. *Psychological Review, 80,* 307–336.

Bronfenbrenner, U. (1977). Toward an experimental ecology of human development. *American Psychologist, 32,* 513–531.

Dieterly, D. L., & Schneider, B. (1974). The effect of organizational environment on perceived power and climate: A laboratory study. *Organizational Behavior and Human Performance, 11,* 316–337.

Ekehammer, B. (1974). Interactionism in personality from a historical perspective. *Psychological Bulletin, 81,* 1026–1048.

Endler, N. S. (1975). The case for person-situation interactions. *Canadian Psychological Review, 16,* 12–21.

Endler, N. S., & Magnusson, D. (1976). Toward an interactional psychology of personality. *Psychological Bulletin, 83,* 956–974.

Feldman, J. M., & Lynch, J. G., Jr. (1988). Self-generated validity and other effects of measurement on belief, attitude, intention, and behavior. *Journal of Applied Psychology, 73*(3), 421–435.

Forehand, G., & Gilmer, B.V.H. (1964). Environmental variation in studies of organizational behavior. *Psychological Bulletin, 62,* 361–382.

Glick, W. H. (1985). Conceptualizing and measuring organizational and psychological climate: Pitfalls in multilevel research. *Academy of Management Review, 10*(3), 601–616.

Glick, W. H. (1988). Response: Organizations are not central tendencies: Shadowboxing in the dark, round 2. *Academy of Management Review, 13*(1), 133–137.

Green, S. G., & Mitchell, T. R. (1979). Attributional processes of leaders in leader-member interactions. *Organizational Behavior and Human Performance, 23,* 429–458.

Heise, D. R. (1975). *Causal analysis.* New York: Wiley.

Insel, P. M., & Moos, R. H. (1974). Psychological environments: Expanding the scope of human ecology. *American Psychologist, 29,* 179–188.

Jackson, J. (1965). Social stratification, social norms, and roles.

In I. Steiner & M. Fishbein (Eds.), *Current studies in social psychology* (pp. 301–309). New York: Holt, Rinehart & Winston.

James, L. A., & James, L. R. (1989). Integrating work environment perceptions: Explorations into the measurement of meaning. *Journal of Applied Psychology, 74,* 739–751.

James, L. R. (1982). Aggregation bias in estimates of perceptual agreement. *Journal of Applied Psychology, 67*(2), 219–229.

James, L. R. (1988). The psychological environments of the workplace: Issues in psychological and organizational climate. In S. G. Cole & R. G. Demaree (Eds.), *Applications of interactionist psychology: Essays in honor of S. B. Sells.* Hillsdale, NJ: Erlbaum, pp. 253–282.

James, L. R., Demaree, R. G., & Wolf, G. (1984). Estimating within-group interrater reliability with and without response bias. *Journal of Applied Psychology, 69,* 85–98.

James, L. R., Gent, M. J., Hater, J. J., & Coray, K. E. (1979). Correlates of psychological influence: An illustration of the psychological climate approach to work environment perceptions. *Personnel Psychology, 32,* 563–588.

James, L. R., Hartman, E. A., Stebbins, M. W., & Jones, A. P. (1977). Relationships between psychological climate and a VIE model for work motivation. *Personnel Psychology, 30,* 229–254.

James, L. R., Hater, J. J., Gent, M. J., & Bruni, J. R. (1978). Psychological climate: Implications from cognitive social learning theory and interactional psychology. *Personnel Psychology, 31,* 781–813.

James, L. R., Hater, J. J., & Jones, A. (1981). Perceptions of psychological influence: A cognitive information processing approach for explaining moderated relationships. *Personnel Psychology, 34,* 453–477.

James, L. R., & Jones, A. P. (1974). Organizational climate: A review of theory and research. *Psychological Bulletin, 81,* 1096–1112.

James, L. R., & Jones, A. P. (1976). Organizational structure: A review of structural dimensions and their conceptual relationship with individual attitudes and behavior. *Organizational Behavior and Human Performance, 16,* 74–113.

James, L. R., & Jones, A. P. (1980). Perceived job characteristics and job satisfaction: An examination of reciprocal causation. *Personnel Psychology, 33*, 97–135.

James, L. R., Joyce, W. F., & Slocum, J. W., Jr. (1988). Comment: Organizations do not cognize. *Academy of Management Review, 13*(1), 129–132.

James, L. R., Mulaik, S. A., & Brett, J. M. (1982). *Causal analysis: Assumptions, models and data.* Newbury Park, CA: Sage.

James, L. R., & Sells, S. B. (1981). Psychological climate: Theoretical perspectives and empirical research. In D. Magnusson (Ed.), *Toward a psychology of situations: An interactional perspective* (pp. 275–295). Hillsdale, NJ: Erlbaum.

James, L. R., & Tetrick, L. E. (1986). Confirmatory analytic tests of three causal models relating job perceptions to job satisfaction. *Journal of Applied Psychology, 71*(1), 77–82.

Jones, A. P., & James, L. R. (1979). Psychological climate: Dimensions and relationships of individual and aggregated work environment perceptions. *Organizational Behavior and Human Performance, 23*, 201–250.

Jones, E. E., & Gerard, H. B. (1967). *Foundations of social psychology.* New York: Wiley.

Jones, G. R. (1983). Psychological orientation and the process of organizational socialization: An interactionist perspective. *Academy of Management Review, 8*(3), 464–474.

Joyce, W. F., & Slocum, J. W., Jr. (1979). Climates in organizations. In S. Kerr (Ed.), *Organizational behavior* (pp. 317–333). Columbus, OH: Grid.

Joyce, W. F., & Slocum, J. W., Jr. (1984). Collective climate: Agreement as a basis for defining aggregate climates in organizations. *Academy of Management Journal, 27*, 721–742.

Katz, D., & Kahn, R. L. (1966). *The social psychology of organizations* (1st ed.). New York: Wiley.

Katz, D., & Kahn, R. L. (1978). *The social psychology of organizations* (2nd ed.). New York: Wiley.

Kelman, H. C. (1961). Processes of opinion change. *Public Opinion Quarterly, 25*, 57–78.

Kozlowski, S.W.J., & Hults, B. M. (1987). An exploration of climates for technical updating and performance. *Personnel Psychology, 40*, 539–563.

Lazarus, R. S. (1982). Thoughts on the relations between emotion and cognition. *American Psychologist, 37*, 1019–1024.

Lazarus, R. S. (1984). On the primacy of cognition. *American Psychologist, 39*, 124–129.

Lazarus, R. S., & Folkman, S. (1984). *Stress, appraisal, and coping.* New York: Springer-Verlag.

Lewin, K. (1938). *The conceptual representation of the measurement of psychological forces.* Durham, NC: Duke University Press.

Lewin, K. (1951). Behavior and development as a function of the total situation. In D. Cartwright (Ed.), *Field theory in social science.* New York: Harper & Row.

Locke, E. A. (1976). The nature and causes of job satisfaction. In M. D. Dunnette (Ed.), *Handbook of industrial and organizational psychology* (pp. 1297–1350). Chicago: Rand McNally.

Magnusson, D. (1981). Wanted: A psychology of situations. In D. Magnusson (Ed.), *Toward a psychology of situations: An interactional perspective* (pp. 9–32). Hillsdale, NJ: Erlbaum.

Mandler, G. (1982). The structure of value: Accounting for taste. In M. S. Clark & S. T. Fiske (Eds.), *Affect and cognition: The Seventeenth Annual Carnegie Symposium on Cognition.* Hillsdale, NJ: Erlbaum.

Martin, J., & Siehl, C. (1983). Organizational culture and counterculture: An uneasy symbiosis. *Organizational Dynamics, 12*(2), 52–64.

Menzel, H. (1978). Meaning—who needs it? In M. Brenner, P. Marsh, & M. Brenner (Eds.), *The social contexts of method.* London: Croom Helm.

Mischel, W. (1968). *Personality and assessment.* New York: Wiley.

Mischel, W. (1973). Toward a cognitive social learning reconceptualization of personality. *Psychological Review, 80*, 252–283.

Morey, N. C., & Luthans, F. (1985). Refining the displacement of culture and the use of scenes and themes in organizational studies. *Academy of Management Review, 10*, 219–229.

Murray, H. A. (1938). *Explorations in personality.* New York: Oxford University Press.

Nisbett, R. E., & Wilson, T. D. (1977). Telling more than we can know: Verbal reports on mental processes. *Psychological Review, 84*, 231–259.

O'Reilly, C., & Chatman, J. (1986). Organizational commitment and psychological attachment: The effects of compliance, identification, and internalization on prosocial behavior. *Journal of Applied Psychology, 71*(3), 492–499.

Osgood, C. E., Suci, G. J., & Tannenbaum, P. H. (1957). *The measurement of meaning.* Urbana: University of Illinois Press.

Park, O. S., Sims, H. P., Jr., & Motowidlo, S. J. (1986). Affect in organizations. In H. P. Sims, Jr., D. A. Gioia, and Associates (Eds.), *The thinking organization: Dynamics of organizational social cognition.* San Francisco: Jossey-Bass.

Payne, R. L., & Pheysey, D. C. (1971). G. G. Stern's organizational climate index: A reconceptualization and application to business organizations. *Organizational Behavior and Human Performance, 6,* 77–98.

Reisenzein, R. (1983). The Schachter theory of emotion: Two decades later. *Psychological Bulletin, 94,* 239–264.

Roberts, K. H., Hulin, C. L., & Rousseau, D. M. (1978). *Developing an interdisciplinary science of organizations.* San Francisco: Jossey-Bass.

Rommetveit, R. (1981). On meanings of situations and social control of such meaning in human communication. In D. Magnusson (Ed.), *Toward a psychology of situations: An interactional perspective* (pp. 151–167). Hillsdale, NJ: Erlbaum.

Rotter, J. B. (1981). The psychological situation in social-learning theory. In D. Magnusson (Ed.), *Toward a psychology of situations: An interactional perspective* (pp. 169–178). Hillsdale, NJ: Erlbaum.

Rousseau, D. M. (1988). The construction of climate in organizational research. In C. L. Cooper & I. T. Robertson (Eds.), *International review of industrial and organizational psychology* (Vol. 3). New York: Wiley.

Schachter, S., & Singer, J. E. (1962). Cognitive, social, and physiological determinants of emotional state. *Psychological Review, 69,* 379–399.

Schneider, B. (1975). Organizational climates: An essay. *Personnel Psychology, 28,* 447–479.

Schneider, B. (1983). Work climates: An interactionist perspective. In N. W. Feimer & E. S. Geller (Eds.), *Environmental psychology: Directions and perspectives*. New York: Praeger.

Schneider, B. (1987). The people make the place. *Personnel Psychology, 40*, 437–453.

Schneider, B., & Bowen, D. E. (1985). Employee and customer perceptions of service in banks: Replication and extension. *Journal of Applied Psychology, 70*, 423–433.

Schneider, B., & Reichers, A. E. (1983). On the etiology of climates. *Personnel Psychology, 36*, 19–39.

Shaver, K. G. (1987). *Principles of social psychology*. Hillsdale, NJ: Erlbaum.

Shaw, M. E. (1976). *Group dynamics: The psychology of small group behavior*. New York: McGraw-Hill.

Shiffrin, R. M., & Schneider, W. (1977). Controlled and automatic human information processing: II. Perceptual learning, automatic attending, and a general theory. *Psychological Review, 84*, 127–190.

Sproull, L. S. (1981). Beliefs in organizations. In P. C. Nystrom & W. H. Starbuck (Eds.), *Handbook of organizational design* (Vol. 2, pp. 203–224). London: Oxford University Press.

Stotland, E., & Canon, L. K. (1972). *Social psychology: a cognitive approach*. Philadelphia: Sanders.

Triandis, H. C., Bontempo, R., Villareal, M. J., Asai, M., & Lucca, N. (1988). Individualism and collectivism: Cross-cultural perspectives on self-ingroup relationships. *Journal of Personality and Social Psychology, 54*(2), 323–338.

Trice, H. M., & Beyer, J. M. (1984). Studying organizational cultures through rites and ceremonials. *Academy of Management Review, 9*(4), 653–669.

Watson, D., & Clark, L. A. (1984). Negative affectivity: The disposition to experience aversive emotional states. *Psychological Bulletin, 96*, 465–490.

Weick, K. E. (1979). *The social psychology of organizing* (2nd ed.). Reading, MA: Addison-Wesley.

Wyer, R. S., & Srull, T. K. (1986). Human cognition in its social context. *Psychological Review, 93*, 322–359.

Zajonc, R. B. (1980). Feeling and thinking: Preferences need no inferences. *American Psychologist, 35*(2), 151–175.

Chapter 3

Meryl Reis Louis

Acculturation in the Workplace: Newcomers as Lay Ethnographers

This chapter focuses on the process by which new members come to appreciate cultures and climates indigenous to work settings and organizations. I refer to these processes as *acculturation*. Finding one's feet, becoming able to pass, learning the ropes, and getting up to speed are among the metaphors used by newcomers and anthropologists to describe what acculturation entails.

Individuals are commonly faced with the task of acculturation when they are entering unfamiliar settings, especially work settings, or when taking on new roles, especially occupational roles. Acculturation is an essential part of a variety of role transitions, whether they entail moves from one city to another or moves within or between work settings. Examples include the move from apprentice to craftsperson, intern to doctor, organizational newcomer to insider, technician to manager (Louis, 1980a).

Role transitions are occasions in which individuals must master the basic skills of a job, build relationships with coworkers and others, and learn the values and norms of relevant groups. These tasks among others comprise the agenda of organizational socialization (Brim, 1966; Schein, 1968; Feldman, 1981). Socialization tasks can be grouped by their focus — some tasks are job-related, others are interpersonal, and still others

85

are culture-related. I will use the term *acculturation* specifically to refer to the pursuit of culture-related socialization tasks.

In the past, researchers studying organizational socialization have not distinguished among different types of tasks. However, resources and strategies for pursuing one type of socialization task may not be particularly relevant in pursuing another. This chapter is about the occasions, resources, and strategies through which acculturation, as distinct from other socialization tasks, takes place. It develops a set of descriptive propositions about agents as resources of acculturation, about newcomers' strategies, and about classes of everyday situations as occasions in which newcomers and agents typically come together around acculturation agenda. The framework tries to capture the point of view of the newcomer and proceeds from a phenomenological tradition.

Socialization researchers have noted that newcomers experience a need to reduce uncertainty, make predictions, and otherwise gain control in the new environment (Falcione & Wilson, 1988, p. 156). Reduction of uncertainty, a common theme in writings on socialization (Lester, 1986), provides a link to the role that culture serves for organizational members.

A recognition of ways in which workplace cultures serve members is a first step in addressing the issue of how acculturation takes place. Social science scholars from Schutz (1964) to Festinger (1954) agree that much of our reality is socially rather than physically instantiated. Much of the time, a number of interpretations or meanings of situations and events are possible. Festinger observed that there are times when "physical evidence is unavailable and judgment is uncertain" (as reported in Salancik & Pfeffer, 1978, p. 228). In the organizational sciences, Weick (1979) echoes this theme in his discussions of equivocality—that is, the possibility of alternative interpretations of organizational experiences. When such situations occur, "validity is consensually judged" (Schein, 1979, p. 144). Members of a setting negotiate definitions of reality among themselves and arrive at agreed-on meanings (Berger & Luckmann, 1966). Patterns of attitudes emerge and workers come to interpret events and see their immediate work worlds in terms similar to those of their co-workers (Salancik & Pfeffer, 1978, p. 229). Once developed, such meanings remain largely tacit or unconscious until exceptions arise or meanings prove inadequate in particular situations. The meanings are renegotiated when problems arise with old interpretations. Sets of meanings, collective situational definitions (Thomas, 1951), or "trustworthy recipes" (Schutz, 1964) are the essence of organizational culture; they *are* the culture.

In a sense, members of a group have available to them the group's set of "trustworthy recipes." Drawing on the common views, members develop individualized definitions of the situation. In the face of uncertainty and equivocality or ambiguity, they rely on definitions of situations to help construct meaning in the immediate situation. A more extensive appreciation of how this happens will allow us to consider where and how acculturation may occur.

Situational definitions include cognitive structures organized around temporal frameworks, categorization devices, and interpretive procedures. They "provide us with the interactional savvy to perform appropriately in everyday life" (Van Maanen, 1979a, p. 26). In particular, situational definitions supply "an individual with a practical theory for 'what's going on' in concrete terms. Such a theory includes notions of what typically occurs in such situations (normality) and when it should occur (themes). . . . Situation definitions also include beliefs regarding why things occur as they do (causality) and the amount of control people believe they have over these things (ownership)" (Van Maanen, 1979b, p. 64).

These cognitive structures develop through experiences in the cultures in which we grow up—the national, ethnic, religious, political milieux of our early lives. They continue to develop in adulthood. Through membership in regularly occurring situations, such as weekly staff meetings, and regularly convening settings, such as the payables unit of the accounting department (Louis, 1983), we take in other interpretively oriented cognitive structures of a specialized, localized, and shared nature.

A group's set of "trustworthy recipes" serve "as a scheme of expression... [and] a scheme of interpretation.... It is the function of the cultural pattern to eliminate troublesome inquiries by offering ready-made directions for use, to replace truth hard to attain by comfortable truisms, and to substitute the self-explanatory for the questionable" (Schutz, 1964, p. 95).

The metaphor of negotiation can help convey how Schutz's "trustworthy recipes" or situational definitions serve organizational members in immediate situations. Members are endlessly negotiating meaning in settings. In one sense, negotiation represents navigation of an experiential landscape, controlling one's course or position. Through the navigational aspect of cultural processes, individuals develop and refine their personal definition in and of the situation. Features are identified and interpreted in light of one's present sociological position and destination. In the other sense, negotiation represents bargaining among alternative meanings possible and preferred by the various parties to an interaction (Louis, 1983). In an interaction, the person's individualized version of the set of shared meanings guides perception, interpretation, and action. For instance, consider how a person might determine whether a particular performance constitutes a job well done. First, a performance is identified from a continuous stream of experience. What is noticed in the stream of experience is, to a great extent, a function of the shared definition of the situation. Second, the individual attends to certain features of the performance considered worth assessing — those considered worth assessing may be derived from shared meanings about performance features that are appropriate to evaluate. Third, the individual evaluates those features of the performance, using shared rules of interpretation as yardsticks. Fourth, individuals choose actions through which to respond based on meanings made of the performance (Louis, 1983, p. 44). In other words, "human beings act toward things on the basis of the meanings that the things have for them..." (Blumer, 1969, p. 2). "If men define situations as real, they are real in their consequences" (Thomas, 1951, p. 584).

In part, then, competence as a member of a social group is based on being conversant in the set of meanings shared by group members. One may choose to respond to the shared meanings in a variety of ways—as advocate or devil's advocate, rebel or team player. But one must recognize those shared meanings in order to be effective in either role. Becoming a group member entails acquiring an appreciation of local meanings. A challenge for new group members, then, is to gain an appreciation of what is normal in the work setting, an appreciation of the shared though tacit meanings through which veteran members of the work group and organization interpret, express, and act in the setting. Armed with such knowledge, an individual can interpret what is going on, anticipate what is likely to happen, and otherwise manage the uncertainties, equivocalities, and exceptions normal in everyday life at work.

Cultural knowledge is tacit, contextual, informal, unofficial, shared, emergent. Together these characteristics make teaching or otherwise transmitting local cultures to newcomers problematic. For instance, since it is tacit knowledge, insiders cannot simply print up a sheet summarizing it. Since it is contextual, statements about it out of context may be meaningless, or at least very difficult to comprehend. Attempts to present cultural information may provide official views rather than a view of what really matters and what is really done by insiders in various circumstances. Since it is emergent, statements at a point in time lack a sense of historical development that may be important in applying the information. The nature of what is to be learned during acculturation and the location of the information about it makes transmission of it and, thus, the acquisition of it, problematic. Mastery of cultures of workplaces or groups is analogous to developing competence in a foreign language. Facility in a language consists of more than mastering vocabulary. One learns not only how to swear and write love letters, but when and how to deliver them. As Geertz (1973) relates, it is being able to tell when a wink is merely a wink and when it is a conspiratorial signal.

Although the task of coming to appreciate local workplace cultures appears challenging and elusive, evidence that newcomers do in fact alter their values, views, and interpretive schemes has been amassed by organizational researchers examining a variety of settings. For instance, in following a group of incoming doctoral students, Green and his colleagues (1988) have been able to document cognitive redefinition or shifts in the kinds and relative importance of values held by doctoral students after one year in graduate programs. Similar effects are emerging in a study currently in progress of the induction of corrections officers (Meglino, personal communication, September 1988; Meglino, Ravlin, & Adkins, 1989). Early results indicate that commitment is highest and turnover is lowest among those who internalize the value of fairness — found to be a core value among veteran officers in an early phase of the study. And Carlson (1988) found shifts in newcomers' values and views among recruits to People's Express. The effect of becoming acculturated is also evident in results such as those found in a study of production workers in a large industrial products manufacturing plant (Meglino, Ravlin, & Adkins, 1989). Workers whose values were congruent with the values of their supervisor were more satisfied and committed to the organization.

The remainder of the chapter focuses on how acculturation takes place in work settings. Resources, strategies, and occasions of acculturation are discussed. In terms of *resources*, the potential contribution of various organizational members or agents to the acculturation agenda is analyzed. Newcomers' information-seeking *strategies* are outlined, and patterns of use are discussed in terms of characteristics of newcomers, their transitions, and organizational contexts. The final section identifies natural, everyday *occasions* or situations in which newcomers and organizational agents come together around the task of acculturation.

Resources: Agents of Acculturation

Much has been written about socialization processes. The literature contains descriptions of stages through which newcomers pass, tasks they must accomplish en route to becoming insiders, and structures and people who help facilitate the processes (for recent reviews, see Feldman, 1988; Fisher, 1986; Rynes, in press;

Wanous & Colella, 1989). Researchers have long recognized that socialization is accomplished in large part through interactions between newcomers and others in the setting, or agents (Brim, 1966; Wheeler, 1966). Past work has developed a variety of explanations for the interpersonal processes through which socialization tasks are accomplished (see Mortimer & Simmons, 1978). However, almost no work on organizational entry or socialization has focused on how agents and interpersonal processes affect the acculturation aspect of socialization specifically. That, then, is an objective of this section.

In this section, the discussion focuses on agents who can aid newcomers in the specific task of acculturation—whether as a separate task or as a by-product of building a role or mastering the basics of the job. As types of agents are discussed, interpersonal processes through which their acculturation affects are facilitated will be identified. By way of introduction, the broad set of relevant interpersonal processes associated with socialization are reviewed first. Next, types of agents are compared in terms of the ways in which they may facilitate the acculturation component of socialization. As indicated in Figure 3.1, agents are to be contrasted in terms of: views of the organization, basis for interacting with newcomers, formality of and affect in their interactions with newcomers, time frame, locus and content of cultural material they make available, and metaphor capturing their relationships with newcomers.

A variety of interpersonal processes are at work during organizational entry and socialization as adults make transitions from being newcomers to being insiders. The processes affect various of the socialization tasks, from learning basics of the job, to building role relationships, to acculturation. Among processes identified by Mortimer and Simmons (1978, pp. 429–432) are role processes and reference group effects, identification, exchange processes, expectancy effects, symbolic interactionism, and generalization processes. In role processes, newcomers' interactions with reference groups are the vehicle through which they acquire "norms, attitudes, self-images, values, and role behaviors..." (Mortimer & Simmons, 1978, p. 429). In the identification processes operative during so-

Figure 3.1. Comparing Organizational Agents in Acculturation, Part 1.

	PEERS	SUPERVISOR	MENTOR
View of Organization			
Basis of Interacting			
Formality			
Affect			
Information: Time Frame			
Subject Matter			
Cultural Content			
Relationship Metaphor			

cialization, a strong emotional attachment forms between a model and the novice, and the novice emulates the model. Social learning theory has been applied to describe such modeling in terms of vicarious learning (Manz & Sims, 1981). In exchange processes, the newcomer is negotiating and bargaining with veteran members. In expectancy effects, the newcomers' expectations influence an actor's behaviors and motivations. In symbolic interactionism, there is an active creation of meaning among newcomers and others in ambiguous situations. Generalization processes operate as newcomers apply learnings from previous similar experiences to present situations. Interactionist processes reflect the mutual influence of the situation and the individual newcomer as socialization progresses (Jones, 1983; Schneider, 1983). Some of the processes operative during the transition from newcomer to insider are especially relevant to the task of acculturation, as we will see in the following discussion.

In addition, Schein's (1979) discussion of the process through which personal change takes place sheds light on part of the process by which newcomers come to adopt local "trustworthy recipes." Building beyond Lewin's work (1951), Schein (1979) describes how unfreezing, the first phase of personal change, requires that the individual experience three conditions: (1) disconfirmation; (2) "guilt-anxiety," or a sense of personal consequence of the disconfirmation; and (3) psychological safety. As we will see, agents may play a role in the unfreezing process. Following unfreezing, cognitive redefinition takes place. For instance, through cognitive redefinition, the newcomer might adopt the local, shared definition of the situation. Evidence of cognitive redefinition among newcomers has been gathered by Green and his colleagues (1988). They have documented that newcomers take in new categories, redefine old ones, and construct different interpretive maps out of the cognitive materials they have imported and have on hand. The result is a set of trustworthy recipes, a definition of the situation that can be used in negotiating social reality and situational uncertainties. As various agents of acculturation are discussed below, associated interpersonal processes will be identified.

Peers: In Groups. Veteran co-workers contribute to the acculturation of newcomers. They serve as day-to-day guides, providing help in sense making and problem solving. ". . . the primary group often is the main agency of socialization with these formal institutions" (Brim, 1966, p. 35). Groups of co-workers teach informal aspects of what and how things are done (Moreland & Levine, 1984). They help label and thus shape how members experience the work setting. As newcomers pay attention to their co-workers, their definitions of local situations are shaped. The social context that newcomers enter has a potent influence on the individual's emerging job attitudes and experiences (Salancik & Pfeffer, 1978).

The role of peers is more important when tasks are unclear or complex. For instance, workers may need to prioritize tasks when workloads exceed individuals' capacities. Rules for prioritizing may be informal and emergent. What senior co-workers indicate are high priority are likely to be given at least as much credence as more official statements by supervisors. Senior co-workers can discuss contingencies, answer questions off the record, and otherwise fill in nuances and shadings in newcomers' growing cognitive maps of the new territory that is the work environment. For instance, second-year M.B.A. students may pass on to entering students information about which of an instructor's major assignments have counted most even though the syllabus may indicate that they are to be given equal weight.

In terms of organizational perspective, peers look at very nearly the same hierarchical and functional slices of the organizational world as does the newcomer. Their perspectives are comparable in terms of time and space horizons. The interests of peers as roleholders should be approximately the same as the newcomers'. They look through the same window, so to speak. The basis for the relationships through which veterans and newcomers interact is likely to be a combination of physical proximity and task interdependence. Both characteristics afford the opportunity for interactions that are more casual, responsive, informal, and frequent than are interaction opportunities between newcomers and others such as supervisors. The subject matter of interactions between veteran co-workers and newcomers are likely to include the "here and now" work situation, through which uncertainties and surprises may emerge for the newcomer. The informational time frame will be immediate, the present; information can flow in response to newcomers' questions close to the time when questions arise. The locus and content of cultural material in interactions between veterans and newcomers would include norms, symbols, values-in-use, and other operational aspects of shared definitions of the situation.

Role theory is particularly relevant in accounting for effects on groups of co-workers during acculturation (Mortimer & Simmons, 1978, p. 429). New members seek to interact with and observe members of relevant groups or reference groups in order to gain acceptance into the group as well as competence in carrying out their roles. Through these interactions with reference group members, newcomers acquire understandings not only of their roles, but of the group's norms, values, and attitudes as well. Role theory is concerned with influence of a group or set of people rather than with one particular individual. The situation of a newcomer having a group of co-workers available facilitates scanning several sources for cues to understanding a situation (Schein, 1979). (See Figure 3.2.)

PROPOSITION 1. Interactions with groups of veteran peers will facilitate acculturation — in particular, appreciation of work group culture including group norms, values-in-use, shared attitudes toward work, and sense of self in work situations.

Peers: Individually. Not all newcomers enter work situations in which there is a natural work group. And even when they do, they may link up with one particular veteran instead of or in addition to the group. New members learn how a respected senior peer interprets and responds to situations. In contrast to the ways in which groups of peers contribute to acculturation through role theory and reference group effects, effects of individual peers on newcomers occur through identification and modeling. The veteran guides by example, imparting standards and values. It is not unusual for the newcomer to form an emotional attachment to the model. In modeling — a form of vicarious learning — an agent, in this case the veteran peer, influences the target or newcomer with the result being that the newcomer's behavior becomes more similar to the veteran's (Weiss, 1977, 1978). As Manz and Sims note, modeling can occur in day-to-day relationships or in training programs set up for the purpose of changing the newcomer's behavior and attitudes. Effects of successful modeling are traced through to enhanced self-efficacy expectations (which can also be understood in terms of altering one's effort-to-performance expectancy) and enhanced outcome expectations (akin to enhancing performance-to-reward expectancy) (Manz & Sims, 1981, p. 106).

Through day-to-day relationships with a respected senior co-worker, modeling effects may occur. Information passing through this channel may center on task procedures, at least initially. Over time and with greater exposure, emulation of a wider range of behaviors and attitudes can be expected, including normative behavior and symbol use.

In comparison with other possible sources of cues about

Figure 3.2. Comparing Organizational Agents in Acculturation, Part 2.

	PEERS	SUPERVISOR	MENTOR
View of the Organization	Narrow Similar	Official	Broad Unofficial
Basis of Interacting	Interdependence Proximity	Position power Involuntary	Voluntary Mutual selection
Formality	Informal	Formal	Informal
Affect	Low and high	Low	High
Information: Time Frame	In response Immediate	In advance Distant	Historical Future
Subject Matter	Present work context	Work role Reward contingencies	Larger organization Career
Cultural Content	Norms, symbols Interpretations Values-in-use Local culture	Exposused values	Ideology Organizational culture
Relationship Metaphor	Siblings	Parent	Aunt/uncle Grandparent

the work situation and culture, the newcomer sees the co-worker as similar in role and as a result considers the veteran more understandable than those who are less similar (Fisher, 1986; Schein, 1968; Weiss, 1977). How senior the peer is to the newcomer makes a difference. Greater seniority may enhance the newcomer's respect for the peer but will decrease the newcomer's sense of similarity to the agent. The co-worker is seen as more trustworthy than a supervisor because of the latter's position power (Schein, 1979). Where alternative sources of information are available to newcomers, they select sources during acculturation based on characteristics of availability and expertise (Fisher, 1986, p. 137). More effective models are seen by targets as credible; they are high in status, competent, and successful (Manz & Sims, 1981).

In summary, nearly all newcomers have at least one veteran co-worker available; newcomers report that daily interactions with peers are most helpful in aiding them in learning the ropes (Louis, Posner, & Powell, 1983). For some jobs, there are no real co-workers nor are there predecessors in the immediate vicinity. These are situations in which socialization experiences are disjunctive rather than serial (Wheeler, 1966; Van Maanen, 1976). Newcomers entering such situations are deprived of an important resource, a source of help in learning local cultures.

PROPOSITION 2. Interactions with individual veteran peers will facilitate acculturation—in particular, appreciation of local cultures and values-in-use.

Other Newcomers. Other newcomers, individually or in groups, are used as a source of help in acculturation. Newcomers usually are comfortable calling on other newcomers, especially in the absence of more senior co-workers or in situations in which there are norms restricting interactions among workers or between senior workers and new workers. Reliance on other newcomers, however, may not be a very good strategy. Newcomers are not well equipped to interpret uncertainties and surprises in the new situation; they are likely to disseminate inaccurate information since they are not well informed about the local culture. Newcomers do, however, provide social support for one another (Fisher, 1985); they are going through similar experiences, so can be "kindred spirits" to one another. Effects of social support on acculturation have not yet been identified. Social support may enhance the newcomer's sense of psychological safety or security, a condition necessary for personal change (Schein, 1979). However, in the absence of veterans who can provide reliable information about local cultures, the effects of newcomers on one another are likely to be mixed.

In a classic study of the effects of interaction with newcomer peers during socialization, Evan (1963) found that turnover was higher among those new employees who were located in departments with one other newcomer than it was among new employees located in departments with no other newcomers present. Although Evan refers to this latter group as isolates, it is clear that these new employees are in the proximity of veteran co-workers. Newcomers have more incentive to interact with veterans when no other newcomer is present. Thus the "isolates" are likely to gain an improved understanding of their new work worlds and to negotiate their transitions more easily than are those new employees who develop strong buddy relationships primarily with other newcomers — who are inferior sources of local information. Evan also found lowest turnover among newcomers who became members of peer groups, where three or more individuals were present. In these cases, group members were other newcomers. Evan explains this finding in terms of a greater chance of congeniality in the presence of more people. However, an additional explanation for this finding might be that group membership affords an opportunity for the newcomer to scan and thus consider several sources of information, whereas the presence of one other newcomer reinforces identification with an reliance on a single source (Schein, 1979). Further, although in the Evan study turnover was lowest for new employees who were members of larger new employee peer groups, it remains to be seen whether acculturation would be greatest among new employees fraternizing with other newcomers or with veteran co-workers.

PROPOSITION 3. Acculturation will be more difficult for newcomers who interact primarily with other newcomers. They may overlook important interpretive categories and rules, and/or they may take longer to appreciate local cultures.

PROPOSITION 4. Interaction with other newcomers can provide social support.

Supervisor. Supervisors interact with newcomers as official agents of the organization. Their formal positions, with power to reward and punish, make them less trustworthy as providers of information other than the official view, which may differ substantially from the real story (Schein, 1968; Fisher, 1986). Over time, newcomers may develop other relationships with supervisors and become able to see beyond the official role relationship. The distant, formal, and involuntary qualities of the superior-subordinate relationship make supervisors not very good sources of local cultural information. Even if they were willing and able to provide valid cultural information, it is unlikely that newcomers would turn to them for such information. The supervisor sees a different organizational world than does the newcomer.

With respect to time frame and locus and content of cultural material, supervisors are likely to focus more on the organization's espoused values, formal work role requirements, and task performance and to focus less on the interaction context in which cultural knowledge is employed. Information may come through initial orientation and periodic goal setting. This is in advance of newcomers' specific interpretational tasks in which cultural knowledge would be needed. Supervisors may also provide information after the need has passed—in periodic feedback and appraisal sessions.

Newcomers are not likely to see supervisors as available for impromptu input and help in deciphering surprises or uncertainties. Even when supervisors have made it clear that they are available and wish to be called on for such help, most newcomers will not be very comfortable "interrupting" parent-like supervisors, especially to expose their ignorance, confusion and need for help. In contrast, newcomers may be considerably more comfortable "dropping in" on a co-worker for support and information, especially if given a little encouragement for doing so. Exchange processes are at work between supervisor and newcomer (Mortimer & Simmons, 1978). Supervisors also influence newcomers' expectancies that effort leads to performance and that performance leads to desired outcomes (Falcione & Wilson, 1988).

Supervisors may be adopted by newcomers as models if they are seen as credible and are respected in their own right beyond formal position power. This is especially likely to occur in the absence of co-workers, or where co-workers differ significantly from the newcomer in role perspective and/or important background characteristics. For instance, where the supervisor has held the job the newcomer now holds and is viewed as more similar than co-workers in education or functional area expertise, the newcomer may look to the supervisor as a primary source of learning about the local culture. (See Figure 3.2.)

> PROPOSITION 5. Supervisors will contribute less to newcomers' acculturation than will veteran peers — both because they have less of the necessary information and because newcomers will turn to them less.

> PROPOSITION 6. When supervisors are effective in encouraging newcomers to call on them for sense-making help, they may contribute to acculturation — especially with respect to shared understandings about such things as relationships across boundaries (that is, among departments, between department and larger units).

Mentor/Adviser. In contrast to the newcomer's supervisor, a mentor does not necessarily have a formal organizational relationship with the newcomer. A few companies have instituted mentor programs in which senior personnel are assigned the job of being mentors to recruits. This section is concerned with the natural process through which mentor relationships develop in work settings. The mentor relationship is voluntary. It is based on mutual selection by mentor and newcomer as two individuals rather than as roleholders. The mentor is not charged with bearing an official organizational view to the newcomer.

Mentors are usually considerably senior to newcomers in terms of both their careers and their experience in the organization. Although they are thus dissimilar in organizational perspective, a mentor serves less to fill in cultural knowledge for immediate interpretation tasks and more to provide broader sweeps across the organization's past and future. Therefore, lack of similarity in role perspective and vantage on the organization does not necessarily make the mentor significantly less attractive. In fact, the newcomer may see the difference as useful in filling out a bigger picture of the organization.

The newcomer who develops a mentor gains a valuable source of interpretive information different from that which is available from either peers or one's supervisor. Mentors can tell the story of the company better than can co-workers. They have seen more of it across time and space. They can convey the historical view that shows ideological themes and core values, perhaps through legends or sagas. Mentors can also paint a picture of the company in a future context better than can peers.

So where peers can fill in cultural blank spots associated with the day-to-day flow of life in the department and work group, mentors can provide cultural information about the broader organization and its historical contexts. Ideally, both kinds of cultural information are gained during acculturation. In contrast to the supervisor's focus on the current task, discussions between newcomers and mentors are likely to cover the newcomer's longer-term career in the company.

Processes like those occurring between newcomers and senior co-workers operate with mentors. Through identification and modeling, newcomers learn from mentors how to interpret uncertainties and surprises; they come to recognize patterns in the environment, and to appreciate local ideals, meanings, modal behaviors, and deviance as well as acceptable responses.

Mentor relationships may develop between formal supervisor and newcomer or between newcomer and a very senior peer. However, mentor relationships are most likely to develop between newcomers and individuals at or above their supervisor's level (Kram, 1985). Since the mentor is unlikely to be someone the newcomer works with directly, the relationships will take more time to develop. Therefore, the cultural knowledge available through this source is not usually available initially. In addition, where relationships with peers developed on the basis of task interdependence or physical proximity, no organizational necessity or structural features of the newcomers' worlds fosters interactions with potential mentors. (See Figure 3.2.)

> PROPOSITION 7. Relationships with a mentor will facilitate acculturation—in particular, appreciation of broader organizational culture, historical perspective, ideologies, and organization-level values-in-use.

> PROPOSITION 8. A relationship with a mentor will facilitate acculturation—in particular the newcomer's acquisition of a view of him or herself in the culture.

Customers/Clients. New members or trainees also interact with customers, clients, patients, and others who are not members of the organization. Recent research has demonstrated that in certain ways, such roleholders can be considered quasi-employees. For instance, Schneider and Bowen (1985) have documented significant relationships between the perceptions of customers and those of employees about service in bank branches, among other things. By extension, clients and customers as quasi-employees may act as socializing agents (Mills & Morris, 1986). That is, interactions between newcomers and customers or patients can help to socialize new members. The role of patients in inculcating values in medical students has frequently been documented (Becker, Geer, Hughes, & Strauss, 1961; Klass, 1987). "... there is in every profession a kind of bootlegging, in which the student, unwittingly or not, acquires from non-official vendors the ideas, values, and ways of behaving and thinking that are attributed ... to the profession" (Olesen & Whittaker, 1977, p. 158).

> PROPOSITION 9. Interactions with clients will facilitate acculturation — in particular, acquisition of norms, values-in-use, and standard procedures for handling relationships across organizational boundaries.

This look at sources of assistance and information during acculturation indicates that newcomers have several sources of potential information about workplace cultures. Multiple sources allow for triangulation and convergence and reduce "bias" from one source. Different cultural information is available from different types of sources. Interaction with multiple types of sources facilitates acquisition of a broader array of cultural knowledge, about different aspects of the organization and its cultures. Sources similar to the newcomer and sources seen as more successful are more likely to be sought out by newcomers. When information is provided by these sources, they are more likely to be listened to. However, exclusive interaction with other newcomers, though similar to the newcomer, undermines acculturation; newcomers have little to offer one another in the way of cultural information about the new setting. Supervisors may have little information about the work group culture and/or they are required by role to convey official rather than actual descriptions of priorities, procedures, and practices.

Interventions should be considered to enhance effectiveness/presence of each agent. It is likely that natural interventions such as management training programs in which newcomers work in a number of departments facilitate the development of mentor relationships.

Strategies: Information Seeking by Newcomers

In the previous section, potential agents of acculturation were examined. This section considers actions newcomers take to seek out information, guide agents' actions, and otherwise affect the process and outcomes of their acculturation. The discussion here differs from past approaches to socialization by adopting an interactionist orientation. As Schneider (1983, p. 18), has observed, a situationist orientation ". . . has dominated studies of socialization to work." That is, in the past, researchers have examined how socialization settings affect newcomers, treating newcomers as passive recipients of organizational influence. Almost no studies have explored possible *reciprocal* influences of workers, especially newcomers, on work settings. The notable exceptions to the situationist perspective, such as the work of Kohn and Schooler (1978), have largely been overlooked by researchers of organizational socialization. Schneider (1983, p. 20) indicates that an exclusively situationist perspective to socialization is inadequate: ". . . specific types of organizations and occupational roles are likely to be characterized by individuals with particular characteristics yielding characteristic people-processing or socialization devices. Only when one entertains this natural selectivity of individuals for roles and organizations with concomitant differences in socialization programs will findings across studies be understandable." In contrast to previous work, this section develops an explicitly interactionist perspective. I propose that newcomers affect their own acculturation processes, in that differences in newcomers' entry situations draw out different resources and assistance from organizational agents. A theoretical rationale is developed here to support the efficacy of such interactions.

Although the premise of the passive or responsive newcomer was implicit in most past work, more recently some organizational researchers have taken the position that newcomers *are and should be active* in their own socialization. For instance, Reichers (1987, p. 279) proposed that the early socialization tasks of "establishing a situational identity" and "making sense of (attaching meaning to) organizational events, practices, and procedures" will be accomplished more rapidly if "both newcomers and insiders proact on each other by seeking out interactions." In essence, Reichers is proposing that by being proactive in initiating interactions, newcomers can affect job-related and culture-related socialization tasks. The result appears to be more an advocacy of newcomer proactivity than a true interactionist approach.

In a study of feedback-seeking behavior, Ashford (1986) found that the best predictor of the perceived value of feedback about performance was job tenure. Job tenure was negatively related to perceived value of feedback, which in turn was significantly and positively related to the frequency of seeking feedback through direct inquiry and monitoring or observation. These results provide support for the idea that newcomers seek information directly more frequently than do insiders to help them in developing the ability to gauge their own performance, a key job-related socialization task. In a study in progress, Laliberté is building on Ashford's work to compare patterns of newcomers' information seeking about cultural matters as well as about task performance (see Laliberté, 1988).

Although the advent of a more active view of the newcomer represents progress, recognition of culture-related socialization tasks suggests the need for a more fine-grained analysis of newcomer activity. In this section, I will propose that the efficacy of newcomer (pro)activity be considered in light of the type of socialization task (culture-, interpersonal-, and/or job-related) at hand, certain situational contingencies, and activity alternatives. Alternative indicators of efficacy need to be considered as well. For instance, whereas speed may be the most useful indicator of effectiveness in accomplishing job or interpersonal tasks, it may be less appropriate for assessing accomplishment of cultural tasks.

In building this view of newcomers' strategies, we will first examine activity alternatives and then consider contingencies. Among organizational researchers, Reichers (1987), for instance, talks in terms of seeking out interactions, and Ashford (1986) talks in terms of seeking feedback through direct inquiry and monitoring. A useful typology of information-seeking strategies has been developed by Miller and Jablin (1987), writing in organizational communications.

Miller and Jablin (1987, p. 3) identify seven kinds of activity through which newcomers obtain information about the work environments they have entered. Newcomers may use *overt* means or direct questioning to obtain information when they feel "comfortable" with the source, when they wish to be able to clarify ambiguities, and in order to build relationships to make future information seeking easier. Newcomers may *indirectly question* a particular source; the questions are asked but not in a direct fashion, allowing for face-saving by newcomers on subjects they think may be sensitive or in areas in which they do not feel well enough prepared for direct questioning. Newcomers may ask questions of a *third party*, substituting a secondary source such as a co-worker for a primary source such as a supervisor. Newcomers use third parties when primary sources are unavailable. They also use third parties to help interpret messages from primary sources (Miller & Jablin, 1987, p. 5), making use of multiple sources about particular issues. These first three strategies represent different ways in which newcomers inquire of insiders through interactions they themselves have initiated. These are the most direct information-gathering strategies.

In other strategies, newcomers *test limits*, confronting others by breaking rules or otherwise deviating in order to gain understandings of rules about work and relationships. Newcomers may engage in *disguised conversations* by putting others at ease and getting them to talk open-endedly about a subject. Joking, self-disclosure, establishing common ground, and use of verbal prompts are among the techniques used to start and get another person to continue talking. In testing limits and engaging in disguised conversations, newcomers deliberately create occasions designed to provide them with information that is then obtained more by observation than by direct questioning of the source.

In using an *observational* strategy, newcomers pay attention when specific issues of interest arise. They watch particular actions or events. In contrast to the previous strategies, they do not intervene but observe naturally occurring events. Through observation, they unobtrusively obtain information about others' values and attitudes as well as about task procedures. Individuals prefer to observe people interacting rather than a single person and prefer to observe informal settings rather than formal ones (Berger & Perkins, 1978). Finally, newcomers engage in *surveillance* or monitoring. They pay attention to whatever happens to be going on, scanning broadly. They note, for instance, which topics of conversation are discussed among incumbents over lunch as well as how people talk with one another, how members talk about members of a rival department, and so forth. In contrast to the strategy of observation, surveillance is casual and general rather than directed and particular.

Consider the situation of a newcomer who realizes that he will be leaving to attend his first national sales meeting in two days. He may inquire about appropriate dress directly from the boss; he may ask a co-worker (and learn that the boss regularly overdresses); he may seek out a co-worker returning today from a similar meeting and see what the co-worker is wearing. Additionally or alternatively, the newcomer may engage a co-worker in disguised conversation, perhaps telling a humorous story about the time in his last job when a new salesperson attended a meeting inappropriately dressed. These and other methods could be used to obtain information needed to guide his actions in line with the culture of the work organization.

Knowledge of the range of behavioral options used by newcomers does not help us predict what a particular newcomer might do or should do. The challenge is to develop a framework for describing efficacious behavior associated with types of situations newcomers face. In developing the framework, I draw a parallel between researchers and newcomers. That is, in doing field research, the researcher is like a newcomer, learning about an unfamiliar setting. This analogy yields the idea that newcomers, like field organizational researchers, develop the capacity for "inquiry from the inside" (Evered & Louis, 1981). Just as the objective for the researcher is to gain an appreciation of the setting from the point of view of an actor in that setting, newcomers are faced with the same challenge. Researchers, then, take on roles as participating observers and/ or observing participants, incorporating ethnographic and phenomenological approaches into their work. It may be possible to understand the newcomer as a researcher coming to appreciate the setting from the point of view of veteran members: a situation in which the newcomer behaves as a lay ethnographer. The newcomer's objective is almost identical to that of ethnographers—to see through an insider's eyes—although Schutz (1964) reminds us that gaining knowledge in order to act in the setting is the sole province of the newcomer.

If the analogy is accepted, it follows that patterns in the newcomer's use of information-seeking strategies will parallel those of field researchers. When researchers are beginning work in a new area, exploration precedes hypothesis testing; unstructured questioning precedes structured interviewing. Once investigators have pioneered a research domain, they become more focused in their data gathering. They have a better sense of what to ask. Initially, their efforts are open and exploratory. Similarly, we would expect the newcomer as lay ethnographer to employ information-seeking methods associated with his or her level of familiarity with the setting.

Experience with related settings, or the familiarity or novelty of the context (Brett, 1984; Nicholson, 1984), affects the level of information-seeking activities the newcomer employs. All else being equal, the complete novice has the "most" to learn, so to speak, and simultaneously must resort to the most basic, least directive, least active, and most exploratory information-seeking activities. For example, the newcomer moving from school to a first full-time job is likely to have little familiarity with basic characteristics of the work world. In such situations, exploratory tactics make more sense. The newcomer is capable of surveillance and observation initially. As the newcomer gains a better sense of what to ask and experiences psychological safety, disguised conversations can be used.

An individual entering a not entirely unfamiliar setting can start at a higher level in information gathering. For instance, someone moving from one commercial bank to another can work on appreciating distinctive features of this bank, because she has already appreciated some of the commercial banking culture. The situation is analogous to one in which researchers are learning a second word processing software package; they already know the kinds of questions to ask. They can be more active in structuring their own learning, and are usually more confident, having had prior experience relevant to the current situation. Overt questioning is more comfortable and safe; perhaps it is even a way to demonstrate one's competence.

Newcomers can be thought of as moving through a sequence of investigative roles as they move from novice to insider. When they are most unfamiliar with the setting, they begin as participating observers, graduate to being observing participants, and eventually retire from observational roles except under novel or disruptive conditions (Louis & Sutton, 1990), when any insider shifts into a conscious mode of observation and problem solving. Evidence in support of this perspective is found in a study by Feldman and Brett (1983) in which the behavioral strategies of new hires were compared with those of job changers who were remaining in the same company. For job changers, context novelty was by definition less than for new hires. In general, new hires employed strategies that "solicit the aid and social support of others" while "job changers favor[ed] strategies that involve higher activity levels for themselves and more control of others" (Feldman & Brett, 1983, p. 270). In addition, Pavelchak, Moreland, and Levine (1986) found that information-seeking or reconnaissance activities varied depending on prior experience in relevant groups. Among college freshmen exploring memberships in campus groups, those with prior experience with relevant groups during high school initiated interactions with the college groups more often than did those without such experience.

PROPOSITION 10. The less familiarity newcomers have with similar work environments—that is, the greater the context novelty—the more they will use observational information-seeking strat-

egies and the less they will use overt questioning
strategies as they pursue acculturation tasks.

A similar argument can be made about the effect of
experience with making role transitions, whether into familiar
or unfamiliar settings. Experience as a lay ethnographer — experience with reconnaissance — helps individuals develop a sense
of resources that are useful and the kinds of things they will need
to know in order to cope in a new setting. Consider the individual taking a job in a high-tech firm who has worked in
banking and manufacturing in previous jobs. This newcomer
has had a chance to develop a map of what it is to get up to
speed. And although context novelty is high because she has
little familiarity with the new setting, she is familiar with the
tasks of learning a culture.

> PROPOSITION 11. The less experience new-
> comers have with making role transitions, the more
> they will use observational strategies and the less
> they will use overt questioning strategies as they
> pursue acculturation tasks.

Thus far, we have considered how newcomers' relationships to the situation affects the information-seeking strategies
they employ. In addition, there are characteristics of newcomers
that are likely to lead them to adopt certain information-seeking
strategies rather than others during acculturation. Among the
more relevant individual characteristics are self-esteem and cognitive complexity.

In previous research, self-esteem has been associated with
successful adaptation to new role demands (Mortimer & Simmons, 1978). In particular, Hall (1971) has documented that
individuals with higher self-esteem engage in greater search for
information and more risk taking, which leads them to "more
confidently master occupational tasks," this fosters a cycle of
"spiraling success." There is no reason to think that this pattern
does not apply to acculturation as well as other socialization
activities.

PROPOSITION 12. Newcomers with higher self-esteem will use overt questioning strategies more than will newcomers with lower self-esteem as they pursue acculturation tasks.

Another individual characteristic with implications for newcomers' strategies during acculturation is cognitive complexity. Individuals with different patterns of cognitive complexity exhibit different patterns of information use. Of most relevance here is integrative complexity. Stabell (1978) found that more integratively complex individuals seek out and use a greater volume of information, use information more often, sample a greater number of sources of information, and more evenly sample across a variety of information sources than do less integratively complex individuals. Together these effects of integrative complexity are directly relevant to understanding newcomers' information-seeking behaviors.

PROPOSITION 13. More integratively complex newcomers will use overt questioning strategies more than will less integratively complex newcomers as they pursue acculturation tasks.

Although it is beyond the scope of this chapter, it would be useful to consider the broader pattern of relationships among individual characteristics and the set of socialization tasks. For instance, some characteristics may affect ways newcomers handle task-related and culture-related socialization tasks. While level of self-esteem is likely to be related to patterns of information-seeking for acculturation, level of self-efficacy—a related construct—has been linked to patterns in the role responses or role orientations newcomers build. In particular, Jones (1986) found that when high self-efficacy newcomers experienced an institutionalized socialization process they responded with a less "custodial" and more "individualized" orientation to the role than did their low self-efficacy counterparts. Future work on acculturation should incorporate relevant individual characteristics to reflect a more appropriately interactionist perspective.

In considering newcomers' strategies, the magnitude of the acculturation tasks they face is also relevant. The extensiveness of the acculturation task varies among transition situations and among settings. This section identifies situational characteristics hypothesized to affect the magnitude of the acculturation task. Just as the magnitude of the task of learning the basic skills necessary to do a job varies for different newcomers depending on both what the job requires and the newcomer's background experiences and skills, so too does the magnitude of the acculturation task vary depending on the complexity of the setting into which the newcomer is moving and the newcomer's experience in similar settings.

In an earlier discussion we considered the impact of a newcomer's prior experience on his or her *information-seeking strategies*. Here we consider the effect of prior experiences (or context novelty) on the *magnitude of the acculturation task*. A newcomer with experience in similar contexts will have less new cultural material to decipher and master than will a newcomer with little or no experience in similar contexts. The complete novice will have a great deal to learn. Experience in making other role transitions is not expected to affect the magnitude of the acculturation task.

> PROPOSITION 14. The greater the context novelty, the greater the magnitude of the acculturation task.

Workplaces differ in the extent to which they exhibit cultures. In some settings, there is very little in the way of informal organization or work group norms that differ from the explicit and formal organizational procedures. Symbols and symbolism are not used very much. Hall (1976) refers to such settings as low-context. In other settings, work groups, departments, and divisions may each have developed their own special symbols and "trustworthy recipes." In such cases, each represents a high-context environment. A single employee may participate in multiple nested and overlapping subcultures. The cultural landscape in such situations is complex. Consider the newcomer whose job is financial analyst for the cardiac supply division of National Hospital Supply Corporation's West Coast region. There may be cultural content associated with the corporation, region, division, department, and work group (Louis, 1985). The orientation meeting at headquarters attended by all professional newcomers from around the country may convey corporate values and history. Regional values may be conveyed with division values if totally nested. Or regional values may not be very relevant for this newcomer in performing the job or interacting with others in the organization. The extensiveness of cultures associated with newcomers' work environments as well as the multiplicity of cultures together influence the magnitude of the acculturation task.

> PROPOSITION 15. The more a work environment can be characterized as high versus low in context, the more extensive will be the newcomer's acculturation task.

> PROPOSITION 16. The more a newcomer's work setting is associated with multiple overlapping and nested subcultures, the more extensive will be the newcomer's acculturation task.

> PROPOSITION 17. The more conflict there is among cultures, the more difficult will be the newcomer's acculturation task.

We have now considered the potential of a variety of agents in facilitating acculturation as well as the role of newcomers' own strategies, backgrounds and situations in contributing to their acculturation. The third element in the argument is the specific impetus that brings the newcomer together with the agent around the agenda of "learning the ropes."

Occasions for Acculturation Activity

The immediate impetus for seeking information affects the potential of the interaction to yield cultural insights. The openness of the newcomer and the availability of relevant information are affected by the impetus or trigger for the interaction. Differences among situations in their capacity to enhance or inhibit the likelihood of newcomers gaining appreciation of a group's shared understandings is the subject of this section.

As a basis for identifying how the impetus for seeking and sharing cultural information affects acculturation potential, we return to the image of the newcomer as lay ethnographer. It is helpful to consider how newcomers have been linked to the ethnographic tradition, to an interpretive paradigm, rather than consider the newcomer as lay experimenter or lay survey researcher. The answer lies in the epistemological challenge of acculturation. If phenomena about which knowledge is sought are contextually embedded, then learning about them should capture the context and preferably occur in context. This is true whether the learner is a researcher or a newcomer. Learning about contextual phenomena out of context is a strain, if not impossible. In order to examine how acculturation actually takes place, researchers look at the naturally occurring situations in which cultural patterns are accessible — to the newcomer or researcher. Newcomers in their unconscious wisdom adopt ethnographic modes of learning, modes especially appropriate for contextual phenomena, to gain knowledge of the cultural patterns indigenous to the unfamiliar work settings they enter. Perhaps once acculturated, new members find tools of experimentation useful. But as a newcomer, the individual must come to appreciate phenomena embedded in social and events contexts.

As discussed earlier, sets of shared meanings help members negotiate the social landscape. They serve perceptual, interpretive, and expressive functions for members of regularly convening settings. They are displayed where there is a violation, when definitions are suddenly problematic, when several conflicting meanings are possible. As a result, cultural information may be available to newcomers in situations in which that information is needed by newcomers or by insiders, then and there, to help negotiate the immediate situation. In addition, efforts are often made to make cultural information available away from situations of direct usage. We will consider the effects of differences in situations on the quality, credibility, and relevance of such information to the newcomers.

Several types of impetus for display and exchange of cultural information will be discussed. This is not intended to represent comprehensive assessment of all situations, but rather to illustrate archetypal situations. Cultural information may be made available: (1) in situations where newcomers need information to help cope with their own surprises; (2) in situations in which insiders experience surprise; (3) in the presence of uncertainty or equivocality or when normal exceptions occur; or (4) in situations unrelated to those in which cultural information would need to be used.

One situation in which newcomers seek cultural information is that of surprise. The newcomer's experiences of crisis, failure, discrepancy, culture shock (Hughes, 1958), and other "upending" experiences (Schein, 1968) provoke the need to interpret problematic situations. Because actual experiences frequently differ from what newcomers anticipate, it is commonplace for newcomers to experience surprises—differences between what they anticipate in new situations and their actual experiences. In fact, surprise seems to be an inherent part of the process of negotiating role transitions, even when efforts are made to provide a realistic picture of what the new situation will be like (Premack & Wanous, 1985; Louis, 1980b). Newcomers may be surprised about aspects of the job, work unit, larger organization, or oneself. Surprises are a function of differences between actual experience and prior expectations or forecasts. Expectations may reflect promises made by recruiters, images and desires fostered by acquaintance with employees of the firm, public relations material, and so forth. Newcomers may be consciously aware of some of the expectations they hold while they may be largely unaware of others. Though some discrepancies between expectations and experience may be the source of delight, others provoke disappointment. In either case, surprises require explanation.

It is when coping with surprise that newcomers seek cultural information. Surprises trigger sense-making processes in which individuals rely on and revise their own definitions of the situation, as well as local sets of shared meanings. Individuals in transition into new settings are most lacking in such knowledge. In fact, the newcomers' lack of adequate cultural knowledge of the setting often precipitates surprises. As Van Maanen (1977, p. 20) has observed, newcomers seldom know that they do not know how things work in the new setting.

During sense making, individuals are involved in several tasks. Sense makers account for the source of surprise; that is, they try to develop an acceptable explanation for the discrepancy or error in forecasting the situation. They seek to provide a correct interpretation of the event or experience that was inaccurately forecast. Further, they select any behavioral responses needed to repair the present situation. Fourth, they adjust their forecasts to prevent future surprises; they incorporate refinements to capture local contingencies; and they update definitions of the situation (Louis, 1980b). Sense making represents problem-triggered interpretive work.

During sense making, individuals rely on several resources or aids. The two interpretive tasks of accounting for the surprise and providing a corrected description of the event are aided by recourse to one's own past experience, to others' interpretations, and to local interpretation schemes. However, newcomers are often lacking in access to veterans' interpretations, and their local interpretation schemes or appreciations of local cultures are inadequate. These differences in interpretive resources of insiders and newcomers and in particular newcomers' deficiencies further support their need for assistance from insiders (rather than other newcomers) when the need for sense-making or interpretive repair work arises. Thus when newcomers experience surprises and crises, they need to engage in interpretive repair work. At such times they are especially open to input about the local culture and especially able to seek such information.

A second impetus for display and exchange of cultural information is when insiders experience surprises. When other members of the work group or department experience discrepancy, crisis, or surprise, the newcomer is less threatened than when the crisis was his or her own. That is, the sense of psychological safety when observing another's surprise is likely to be greater than when grappling with one's own surprise. And we have seen that psychological safety is one of the three conditions necessary for unfreezing as part of personal change (Schein, 1968). Yet when the newcomer observes that dealing with the surprise is urgent and consequential for insiders, this situation will be compelling for the onlooking newcomer—another condition for unfreezing. The newcomer may sense "that could be me," "maybe it is and I just can't see it yet." The process of identification with the insider experiencing the surprise makes that surprise personally meaningful for the newcomer. Through a vicarious disconfirmation, the newcomer becomes open to change in a process similar to a remembered disconfirmation, as discussed by Schein (1968). Just as during the newcomer's own sense-making in response to surprise, during attempts by one or more insiders to cope with surprise and to do interpretive repair work on the normally tacit interpretive rules and shared meanings, newcomers can increase their learning. Thus, while normal interpretive work is real-time, tacit, and prospective, when surprise triggers sense-making, time-out is called, so to speak, as the "taken-for-granted" is violated. In sense-making, actors' "cognitive gears" shift from automatic to conscious (Louis & Sutton, 1990). The actor shifts from real-time engagement to reflection and retrospective interpretation. In this more aware state, individuals have access to their definitions of situations, their tacit knowledge of shared meanings. Newcomers who are present when veterans are grappling with sense-making tasks will see more of the local culture in brief periods of time than in many days of "business as usual."

In addition, newcomers have opportunities to interact with insiders as they negotiate everyday uncertainties, ambiguities, and normal exceptions. Interpretive work is carried out in order to manage such situations. This third impetus or situation

in which newcomers and agents join in pursuit of an acculturation agenda gives newcomers the opportunity to observe and
decipher interpretive rules for everyday general use. These situations are characterized by less personal stake and affect than
are situations in which newcomers or insiders are responding to
surprises, or failures of past interpretations, through sense-
making processes. Where there is greater uncertainty and equivocality associated with the task and task environment, there is
greater display of culture. During the frequent normal exceptions characteristic of uncertain environments, interpretive
rules are displayed or used more often than where there is less
uncertainty. (Although discussion of antecedents of workplace
cultures is beyond the scope of this chapter, it is likely that more
extensive cultures develop in settings characterized by more
uncertainty.)

Another impetus for acculturation activities is the formal
orientation and socialization activities initiated by organizations. One such strategy is the use of realistic job previews (RJPs),
which by definition pursue the objective of assisting newcomers
in gaining a realistic picture of life in the organization and on
the job in advance of or soon after entering the unfamiliar work
setting (Premack & Wanous, 1985; Wanous & Colella, 1989;
Rynes, in press). Although the procedures vary (from reliance
on video to printed materials), information is presented in
advance of the newcomers' entry. The aim is to have the RJP serve
as a kind of inoculation for newcomers against possibly inaccurate views and expectations of the job and organization. The
material RJPs attempt to convey often covers cultural content.
They may convey values, symbols, management style, climates of
support, or competition or cooperation, for instance. The objectives are certainly worthwhile. However, as the perspective
developed here suggests, it is unlikely that such contextually
embedded information can be communicated very effectively
out of context or that newcomers can be very responsive when
there is neither a sense of personal significance to the information—there is no consequential situation in which such information is needed—nor a credible source for it. So for a variety of
reasons, it is doubtful that RJPs can be an effective means of

communicating cultural information or otherwise facilitating acculturation of newcomers.

Similarly, other formal socialization structures and processes are unlikely to be very useful in facilitating acculturation. Orientation programs and formal off-site training sessions are abstracted from situations in which shared understandings are invoked or needed. In addition, when providing information during formal orientation and training sessions, insiders are "in role" as officials acting on behalf of the organization. They are required, for instance, to provide information about espoused values rather than values-in-use, and about official procedures rather than standard operating procedures. This "in-role" quality reduces the credibility they might otherwise have to newcomers. The useful and valid information is that which is "off the record."

Thus we see that impetus or occasion for newcomer information seeking and other aspects of acculturation matters. (Figure 3.3 provides a comparison of features of acculturation occasions.) The more removed the situation is from a particular live "need to know" situation, the less valid and relevant the information is likely to be and to seem. The information context is less motivating for the newcomer. The newcomer will have difficulty seeing the personal relevance of cultural information conveyed at a distance. It is difficult to grasp the utility of information presented out of context. In addition, the information is less valid when it is abstracted from situations in which it might serve as guide to interpretation or expression. Contingencies and conditions give social information or shared meanings practical significance.

PROPOSITION 18. The more real-time the context in which cultural material is conveyed, the more motivated will be the newcomer to appreciate it and the more valid the information will appear to the newcomer.

Figure 3.3. Occasions for Acculturation.

	Occasion			
	Newcomer Surpise	Insider Surprise	Uncertainty Ambiguity	In Advance of Need to Know
Is information about culture and local meanings available?				
Tacit knowledge is accessible	?	Yes	Yes	No
Tacit knowledge is provokable	Yes	Yes	Yes	?
Is there motivation for acculturation and openness to new meanings?				
Disconfirmation— personal or vicarious	Yes	Yes	Yes	No
Disconfirmation personally important	Yes	Yes	?	NA
Adequate psychological safety	?	Yes	?	Yes

Conclusion

In this chapter, we have examined how newcomers accomplish one of several socialization tasks associated with entering unfamiliar organizational settings. The focus has been on the task of acculturation. The aim was to propose a way of understanding how newcomers come to appreciate local workplace cultures—the sets of shared though tacit meanings and symbols that emerge in regularly convening groups and organizations.

An extensive literature on organizational entry and socialization has been amassed in the organizational sciences. However, little of it directly addresses the task of acculturation. Although past work on organizational socialization and entry was an essential resource in preparing this chapter, it was necessary to ask repeatedly whether and if so how that work related directly to acculturation. Socialization studies have moved into considering multiple tasks, including mastering basic skills required to do the job, building relationships, and building an orientation to the role. Recent work has begun to document the internalization of local values as a critical socialization task. It is clear that socialization researchers are moving toward studying the acculturation task of organizational entry. It is also clear that there is a need for a more comprehensive and grounded description to serve as a guide and foundation for future research. This chapter has attempted to provide the beginnings of such a description. One process used here has been to attempt to engender a sense of personal recognition, to facilitate the reader's recall of his or her own experiences as a newcomer and as a source of assistance to newcomers entering settings in which one is well entrenched. Analogies and other narrative devices have been instrumental in this effort. Although analogies may provoke experiential recognition, they do not constitute empirical evidence. For that, methodologically sound studies are needed.

In planning studies of acculturation, the researcher is encouraged to be cautious about making common assumptions underlying socialization studies. Some are particularly relevant to tasks of learning the culture of an organization or work group and ought to be treated either as questions or as explicit premises. It has been a common practice to proceed as if all work settings were characterized by local cultures to be mastered by new members. As indicated in this chapter, the magnitude of cultural patterns associated with a setting varies extensively. In some situations, what newcomers need to know may not be of a cultural nature at all.

A second assumption often made is that the aim of relevant organizational agents is to have newcomers accept what is already present in the local culture. In fact, newcomers may be hired at times because they are seen by insiders as likely to reject current common understandings. Further, researchers should not assume that the content of culture to which newcomers are exposed is "good," either in terms of local work group cultures supporting larger organizational objectives, or in terms of cultural participation benefiting the individual member. Thus far, researchers and managers have tended to think and write in terms of a one-way influence of the organization on the new-comer, making the assumption that the newcomer adjusts to the "way things are done here" or leaves. But there is increasing recognition that newcomers may affect the settings and groups they enter (Louis, 1981; Sutton & Louis, 1987). In particular, Jablin (1982)—writing in the area of organizational commu-nications—has proposed an assimilation model of organiza-tional entry to explicitly address the two-way nature of the process. Assumptions such as these may undermine efforts by researchers to appreciate how newcomers come to appreciate workplace cultures.

In this chapter, we argued that not all insiders are equal with respect to their potential for contributing to the accultura-tion of newcomers. Peers in groups and as individual agents, supervisors, mentors, and other newcomers differ in the kinds and validity of cultural information they can offer as well as the likelihood that newcomers will turn to them.

We also argued that not all newcomers are equal with respect to their information-seeking strategies. Their strategies depend on the extent to which they have some experience that is relevant to the transition—with similar kinds of transitions or with similar work settings. Initially, those who are complete novices with respect to the particular setting will adopt roles as observers and shift into more participative roles as they flesh out their understandings of the new situations. We argued that the process parallels that of the ethnographer who attempts to grasp what life is like in a particular setting from the point of view of someone who lives and functions there.

Further, we argued that the immediate impetus for shar-ing cultural information matters. Only in certain types of situa-tions will such information be available to insiders or new-comers. The basis for this point was epistemological. Shared meanings are tacit, emergent, and context-embedded. They are accessible or displayed only under certain conditions. Knowl-edge about them can be developed as they are accessible. Condi-tions for effectively accessing and conveying shared meanings include when newcomers are surprised, when insiders are surprised, and when normal exceptions occur. Attempts to convey information about local cultures under other circumstances are unlikely to be very fruitful.

References

Ashford, S. J. (1986). Feedback-seeking in individual adaptation: A resource perspective. *Academy of Management Journal, 29,* 465–487.

Becker, H. S., Geer, B., Hughes, E. C., & Strauss, A. L. (1961). *Boys in white: Student culture in medical school.* Chicago: University of Chicago Press.

Berger, P., & Luckmann, T. (1966). *The social construction of reality: A treatise in the sociology of knowledge.* Garden City, NY: Doubleday.

Berger, C. R., & Perkins, J. W. (1978). Studies in interpersonal epistemology I: Situational attributes in observational context selection. In B. Ruben (Ed.), *Communication yearbook 2.* New Brunswick, NJ: Transaction.

Berlew, D. E., & Hall, D. T. (1966). The socialization of managers: Effects of expectations on performance. *Administrative Science Quarterly, 11,* 207–223.

Blumer, H. (1969). *Symbolic interactionism: Perspective and method.* Englewood Cliffs, NJ: Prentice-Hall.

Brett, J. M. (1984). Job transitions and personal and role development. In K. M. Rowland & G. Ferris (Eds.), *Research in personnel and human resources management* (Vol. 2). Greenwich, CT: JAI Press.

Brim, O. G., Jr. (1966). Socialization through the life cycle. In O. G. Brim, Jr. & S. Wheeler (Eds.), *Socialization after childhood: Two essays.* New York: Wiley.

Brim, O. G., Jr. (1968). Adult socialization. In J. A. Clausen (Ed.), *Socialization and society.* Boston: Little, Brown.

Carlson, M. S. (1988). *Newcomer socialization in small groups: Collective sense-making before and after work begins.* Unpublished manuscript, University of Michigan, Department of Psychology.

Eisenberg, E. M., & Riley, P. (1988). Organizational symbols and sense-making. In G. M. Goldhaber & G. A. Barnett (Eds.), *Handbook of organizational communication*. Norwood, NJ: Ablex.

Evan, W. M. (1963). Peer group interaction and organizational socialization: A study of employee turnover. *American Sociological Review, 28*, 436–440.

Evered, R., & Louis, M. R. (1981). Alternative perspectives in the organizational sciences: 'Inquiry from the inside' and 'inquiry from the outside.' *Academy of Management Review, 6*, 385–395.

Falcione, R. L., & Wilson, C. E. (1988). Socialization processes in organizations. In G. M. Goldhaber & G. A. Barnett (Eds.), *Handbook of organizational communication*. Norwood, NJ: Ablex.

Feldman, D. C. (1981). The multiple socialization of organizational members. *Academy of Management Review, 6*, 309–318.

Feldman, D. C. (1988). *Managing careers in organizations*. Glenview, IL: Scott, Foresman.

Feldman, D. C., & Brett, J. M. (1983). Coping with new jobs: A comparative study of new hires and job changers. *Academy of Management Journal, 26*, 258–272.

Festinger, L. (1954). A theory of social comparison processes. *Human Relations, 7*, 114–140.

Fisher, C. D. (1985). Social support and adjustment to work: A longitudinal study. *Journal of Management, 11*, 34–53.

Fisher, C. D. (1986). Organizational socialization: An integrative review. *Personnel and Human Resource Management, 4*, 101–145.

Geertz, C. (1973). *Interpretation of culture*. New York: Basic Books.

Green, S. G., & Mosher, P. (1988, August). *Socializing pivotal values in professional newcomers*. Paper presented at the meeting of the National Academy of Management, Anaheim, CA.

Hall, D. T. (1971). A theoretical model of career subidentity development in organizational settings. *Organizational Behavior and Human Performance, 6*, 50–76.

Hall, E. T. (1976). *Beyond culture*. New York: Doubleday.

Hughes, E. C. (1958). *Men and their work*. New York: Free Press.

Jablin, F. M. (1982). Organizational communication: An assimilation approach. In M. Roloff & C. Berger (Eds.), *Communication and cognition*. Newbury Park, CA: Sage.

Jones, G. R. (1983). Psychological orientation and the process of organizational socialization: An interactionist perspective. *Academy of Management Review, 8*(3), 464–474.

Jones, G. R. (1986). Socialization tactics, self-efficacy, and newcomers' adjustment to organizations. *Academy of Management Journal, 29,* 262–279.

Klass, P. (1987). *A not entirely benign procedure: Four years as a medical student.* New York: Signet.

Kohn, M. L., & Schooler, C. (1978). The reciprocal effects of the substantive complexity of work and intellectual flexibility: A longitudinal assessment. *American Journal of Sociology, 84,* 24–52.

Kram, K. E. (1985). *Mentoring at work: Developmental relationships in organizational life.* Glenview, IL: Scott, Foresman.

Laliberté, M. M. (1988). *Proactive information seeking behavior as a predictor of the rate of organizational socialization.* Unpublished master's thesis, University of Maryland.

Lester, R. E. (1986). Organizational culture, uncertainty reduction, and the socialization of new organizational members. In S. Thomas (Ed.), *Communication and information science*: Vol. 3. *Studies in communication.* Norwood, NJ: Ablex.

Lewin, K. (1951). Behavior and development as a function of the total situation. In D. Cartwright (Ed.), *Field theory in social science.* New York: Harper & Row.

Louis, M. R. (1980a). Career transitions: Varieties and commonalities. *Academy of Management Review, 5,* 329–340.

Louis, M. R. (1980b). Surprise and sense making: What newcomers experience in entering unfamiliar organizational settings. *Administrative Science Quarterly, 25,* 226–251.

Louis, M. R. (1981, April). *The emperor has no clothes: The effect of newcomers on work group culture.* Paper presented at the meeting of the Western Academy of Management, Monterey, CA.

Louis, M. R. (1983). Organizations as culture-bearing milieux. In L. R. Pondy, P. J. Frost, G. Morgan, & T. C. Dandridge (Eds.), *Organizational symbolism.* Greenwich, CT: JAI Press.

Louis, M. R. (1985). An investigator's guide to workplace culture. In P. J. Frost, L. F. Moore, M. R. Louis, C. C. Lundberg, & J. Martin (Eds.), *Organizational culture.* Newbury Park, CA: Sage.

Louis, M. R., Posner, B. Z., & Powell, G. N. (1983). The availability and helpfulness of socialization practices. *Personnel Psychology*, *36*, 857–866.

Louis, M. R., & Sutton, R. I. (1990). Switching cognitive gears: From habits of mind to active thinking. *Human Relations*, *43*.

McShane, S. L. (1987). *The impact of perceived task characteristics on the socialization of new employees: A longitudinal study*. Paper presented at the Administrative Sciences Association of Canada (ASAC) conference, Toronto.

McShane, S. L. (1988). *The impact of orientation practices on the socialization of new employees: A longitudinal study*. Paper presented at the Administrative Sciences Association of Canada (ASAC) conference, Halifax, Nova Scotia.

Manz, C., & Sims, H. P., Jr. (1981). Vicarious learning: The influences of modeling on organizational behavior. *Academy of Management Review*, *6*, 105–113.

Meglino, B. M., Ravlin, E. C., & Adkins, C. L. (1989). A work values approach to corporate culture: A field test of the value congruence process and its relationship to individual outcomes. *Journal of Applied Psychology*, *74*, 424–432.

Meyerson, D. E. (1990). The social construction of ambiguity and burnout: A study of hospital social workers. *Dissertation Abstracts International*, *50*(7).

Miller, V. D., & Jablin, F. M. (1987, November). *Newcomers' information seeking behaviors during organizational encounter: A typology and model of the process*. Paper presented at the annual meeting of the Speech Communication Association, Organizational and Instrumental Communication Division.

Mills, P. K., & Morris, J. H. (1986). Clients as 'partial' employees of service organizations: Role development in client participation. *Academy of Management Review*, *11*, 726–735.

Moreland, R. L., & Levine, J. M. (1984). Role transitions in small groups. In V. L. Allen & E. Van de Vliert (Eds.), *Role transitions: Explorations and explanations*. New York: Plenum Press.

Mortimer, J. T., & Simmons, R. G. (1978). Adult socialization. *Annual Review of Sociology*, *4*, 421–454.

Nicholson, N. (1984). A theory of 'work role transitions.' *Administrative Science Quarterly*, *29*, 172.

Olesen, V. L., & Whittaker, E. W. (1977). Characteristics of professional socialization. In R. L. Blankenship (Ed.), *Colleagues in organizations: The social construction of professional work.* New York: Wiley.

Pavelchak, M. A., Moreland, R. L., & Levine, J. M. (1986). Effects of prior group memberships on subsequent reconnaissance activities. *Journal of Personality and Social Psychology, 50,* 56–66.

Premack, S. L., & Wanous, J. P. (1985). A meta-analysis of realistic job preview experiments. *Journal of Applied Social Psychology, 70,* 706–719.

Reichers, A. (1987). An interactionist perspective on newcomer socialization rates. *Academy of Management Review, 12,* 278–287.

Rynes, S. (in press). Recruitment, organizational entry, and early work adjustment. In M. D. Dunnette (Ed.), *Handbook of industrial and organizational psychology* (2nd ed.). Palo Alto, CA: Consulting Psychologists Press.

Salancik, G. R., & Pfeffer, J. (1978). A social information processing approach to job attitudes and tasks design. *Administrative Science Quarterly, 23,* 224–253.

Schaubreck, J., & Green, S. G. (1989). Confirmatory factor analytic procedures for assessing change during organizational entry. *Journal of Applied Psychology, 74,* 892–900.

Schein, E. H. (1968). Organizational socialization and the profession of management. *Industrial Management Review, 9,* 1–16.

Schein, E. H. (1979). Personal changes through interpersonal relationships. In W. Bennis, J. Van Maanen, E. H. Schein, & F. I. Steele (Eds.), *Essays in interpersonal dynamics.* Homewood, IL: Dorsey Press.

Schneider, B. (1983). Interactional psychology and organizational behavior. In L. L. Cummings & B. M. Staw (Eds.), *Research in organizational behavior* (Vol. 5). Greenwich, CT: JAI Press.

Schneider, B., & Bowen, D. E. (1985). Employee and customer perceptions of service in banks: Replication and extension. *Journal of Applied Psychology, 70,* 423–433.

Schutz, A. (1964). The stranger: An essay in social psychology. In

A. Brodersen (Ed.), *Collected papers II: Studies in social theory*. The Hague: Nijhoff.

Stabell, C. B. (1978). Integrative complexity of information environment perception and information use: An empirical investigation. *Organizational Behavior and Human Performance*, 22, 116–142.

Stohl, C. (1986). The role of memorable messages in the process of organizational socialization. *Communication Quarterly*, 34, 231–249.

Sutton, R. I., & Louis, M. R. (1987). How selecting and socializing newcomers influences insiders. *Human Resource Management*, 26, 347–361.

Taft, R. (1977). Coping with unfamiliar cultures. In N. Warren (Ed.), *Studies in cross-cultural psychology* (Vol. 1). London: Academic Press.

Tagiuri, R. (1968). Concepts of organizational climate. In R. Tagiuri & G. H. Litwin (Eds.), *Organizational climate: Explorations of a concept*. Cambridge, MA: Division of Research, Graduate School of Business Administration, Harvard University.

Thomas, W. I. (1951). *Social behavior and personality: Contribution of W. I. Thomas to theory and social research*. (E. H. Volkart, Ed.) New York: Social Science Research Council.

Van Maanen, J. (1976). Breaking in: Socialization to work. In R. Dubin (Ed.), *Handbook of work, organizations, and society*. Chicago: Rand McNally.

Van Maanen, J. (1977). Experiencing organization: Notes on the meaning of careers and socialization. In J. Van Maanen (Ed.), *Organizational careers: Some new perspectives*. New York: Wiley.

Van Maanen, J. (1979a). The self, the situation, and the rules of interpersonal relations. In W. Bennis, J. Van Maanen, E. H. Schein, & F. I. Steele (Eds.), *Essays in interpersonal dynamics*. Homewood, IL: Dorsey Press.

Van Maanen, J. (1979b). On the understanding of interpersonal relations. In W. Bennis, J. Van Maanen, E. H. Schein, & F. I. Steele (Eds.), *Essays in interpersonal dynamics*. Homewood, IL: Dorsey Press.

Wanous, J. P., & Colella, A. (1989). Organizational entry research: Current status and further directions. In K. Rowland & G.

Ferris (Eds.), *Research in personnel and human resource management*. Greenwich, CT: JAI Press.

Weick, K. E. (1979). *The social psychology of organizing*. (2nd ed.). Reading, MA: Addison-Wesley.

Weiss, H. M. (1977). Subordinate imitation of superior behavior: The role of modeling in organizational socialization. *Organizational Behavior and Human Performance, 19,* 89–105.

Weiss, H. M. (1978). Social learning of work values in organizations. *Journal of Applied Psychology, 63,* 711–718.

Wheeler, S. (1966). The structure of formally organized socialization settings. In O. G. Brim, Jr. & S. Wheeler (Eds.), *Socialization after childhood: Two essays*. New York: Wiley.

Chapter 4

William F. Joyce
John W. Slocum, Jr.

Strategic Context and Organizational Climate

The purpose of this chapter is to relate the characteristics of organizational climates to a typology of strategic contexts. Previous research and theory have demonstrated that both organizational and psychological climate have important consequences for work outcomes, such as job performance and work attitudes (see Joyce & Slocum, 1979, 1984; Schneider, 1975; Schneider & Reichers, 1983; James & Jones, 1974; Hellriegel & Slocum, 1974). Based in part on these findings, researchers have sought to identify the sources or antecedents of climate perceptions. Few of these studies have systematically considered the potential impact of the firm's strategic position and environment as a determinant of climate perceptions. This may be because climate research has confronted difficult problems in cross-level inference. For example, numerous debates concerning the appropriate level of analysis of the climate concept have occurred (Guion, 1973; Schneider, 1975) and persist, although to a somewhat lesser extent now (Glick, 1985; James, Joyce, & Slocum, 1988). Issues concerning appropriate units of analysis, theory, and observation have made organizing and appraising the existing literature difficult.

Note: Support for the second author was obtained from the Center for Enterprising, Cox School of Business, Southern Methodist University, Dallas, Texas. The authors acknowledge the suggestions of Ellen Jackofsky, Donald Hellriegel, Jeffrey Kerr, Joan Rentsch, and Benjamin Schneider on earlier drafts of this paper.

Some tentative conclusions, however, can be derived from our knowledge of the climate literature. First, most researchers have consistently recognized the basic unit of theory in climate research as the individual, regardless of the subsequent level of data analysis. Second, most empirical studies that have employed an aggregate unit of analysis (organizational, group, or collective climate, for example) have been based on individuals' observation of organizational practices and procedures. For example, individual-level psychological climate perceptions have been aggregated to represent the climates of work groups (Drexler, 1977) as well as specific levels (Schneider & Snyder, 1975) and divisions of the organization (James & Jones, 1974). While the unit of analysis in these studies varied (work group, level, division), the individual was consistently employed as the element of theory and the source of data. Because of these practices, there has been some terminological confusion in applying names to various climate concepts. Climates have always been based on perceptions of individuals. Virtually all concepts have been "psychological" in nature, regardless of the level of aggregation. Similarly, since all climate measures have been taken focusing on organizational practices and procedures as elements of analysis, all climate concepts have been organizational. This has proved confusing since researchers have generally relied on a simple distinction between "psychological" and "organizational" climates for purposes of theoretical discussion.

Regardless of the level of analysis being employed, climate perceptions represent a response to external stimuli that are intrinsically psychological in nature. These represent individuals' cognitive processing of those external stimuli and assignment of psychological meaning to them. Much of the confusion concerning whether climate is an individual or organizational property (see Glick, 1985; James, Joyce, & Slocum, 1988) can be traced directly to whether climate is assumed to be a stimulus or response. Glick (1985) obviously views climate as a stimulus; that is, climate is itself the external stimulus. Conversely, James, Joyce, and Slocum (1988) argue that climate is an internal representation of the external stimulus.

The current state of the art in climate research suggests that "psychological" and "organizational" climate labels are no longer adequate. A number of mid-range climate concepts based on groups, division, or some other basis for aggregation, such as consensus of perceptions (Joyce, 1977; Joyce & Slocum, 1982, 1984; James, 1982; James, Joyce, & Slocum, 1988), have emerged. All of these concepts are *both* psychological and organizational. Given richness of this emerging typology of climates, an important theoretical issue concerns the relationships among these various types of climates, and not simply between organizational and psychological climate in the traditional sense of these terms.

The basic premise of this paper is that research concerning climate would be enhanced by efforts to understand relationships among climate concepts across various levels of analysis. Thus far, attempts at developing such "composition" theories have used agglomerative methods seeking to validate mid-range climate concepts based on aggregation of individual level climates. An alternative and complementary perspective addresses this problem from the opposite direction by examining the effects of higher-order climate concepts on mid-range formulations of the concept. In this approach, we ask what are the consequences of strategic context and the resulting overall organizational climate (employing the term in its traditional and restrictive sense) for mid-range concepts of climate, such as group or collective climates. Pursuing the problem in this fashion will complement analyses based on individual-level climates, enhance our understanding of mid-range climate concepts, and contribute to a true composition theory of organizational climate.

Few (if any) researchers have addressed relationships between climate at the organizational level of analysis and other aggregate climate notions such as subunit, division, or work group climates. Groups, subunits, levels, and divisions reflect the basic horizontal and vertical division of labor within organizations. Perceptions of strategic context influence the choices management makes in designing the organization's division of labor and in prescribing acceptable practices and procedures.

These practices and procedures, in turn, would represent the stimuli for mid-range climate concepts, such as group or sub-unit climates that collectively comprise an organization's climate. The strategic context of organizations, then, may prescribe certain patterns of functioning that lead to identifiable patterns of relationships between an overall organization climate and mid-range versions of the concept that comprise it. Research exploring these relationships would be complementary to other research that seeks to link the formation of aggregate climates to individual-level processes. Some of these processes are selection, attraction and attrition (Jackofsky & Slocum, 1988), interaction patterns (Joyce & Slocum, 1984; Poole, 1985), or basic psychological processes, such as meaning creation (James, 1982; James, Joyce, & Slocum, 1988).

In order to pursue this line of inquiry, it is necessary to select a particular mid-range climate concept for study and then to systematically describe the characteristics of this type of climate in relation to the overall organization climate in various strategic contexts. The next section proposes and defends the use of collective climate (Joyce & Slocum, 1984) for this purpose. Following this, we introduce a typology of strategic context based on current research in organization theory. The characteristics of organizational and collective climates expected under each of these conditions are then discussed.

Collective Climates in Organizations

The previous discussions have indicated the desirability of relating mid-range climate theory and data to strategic context and organizational climate. Collective climate is a mid-range concept that is particularly attractive for this purpose (Joyce 1977; Joyce & Slocum, 1979, 1982, 1984). Collective climates are based upon the perceptions of individuals who share common multidimensional descriptions of their work environment. The composition rule for forming collective climates is consensus among individuals' perceptions of the work setting.

Consensus has been extensively discussed as an appropriate basis for the aggregation of perceptions. Consensus allows for aggregate units of analysis, while maintaining the individual as the basic unit of theory and data. This is regardless of the level to which data are aggregated. Collective climates have been studied in terms of the operations appropriate for aggregation from the individual level (James, 1982; James, Joyce, & Slocum, 1988), and also in terms of their hypothesized antecedents in technology, workforce demographics, and required work interactions (Joyce, 1977; Joyce & Slocum, 1984; Jackofsky & Slocum, 1988). Collective climates formed on the basis of perceptual consensus represent an intermediate or mid-range concept that may be useful for bridging the strategic organizational and individual levels of analysis.

Variations in collective climate can be systematically described using three dimensions. These are the degree of *consensus* in multidimensional climate perceptions (which determines whether or not multiple collective climates will be found within the broader organization climate), the *consistency* of specific climate dimensions with one another within collective climates, and the degree of *congruency* of collective climate profiles with variables that have previously been shown to affect climate, such as technology or organization structure (Herman, Dunham, & Hulin, 1975). Variations in the patterns of collective climates along these three dimensions provide the basis for describing organizational climate.

Collective climates are perceptions of particular organizational practices that are diffused through relational networks to affect individuals' behavior. Organizations influence climate perceptions in a myriad of ways, but particularly through structure, technology, and control systems. We believe that variations in structure, technology, and control systems are significantly influenced by decisions made by the dominant elite of an organization in response to their perceptions of the strategic context of the firm. The following section presents a typology of strategic contexts. These different contexts are then shown to be related to identifiable characteristics of climate.

Strategic Context and Organizational Adaptation

The emphasis of much research in the domain of organization theory has been on explicating those factors that affect the design and adaptation processes found in organizations. Astley and Van de Ven (1983) synthesize four perspectives that qualitatively represent different views of organization structure, behavior, and managerial roles. The *system-structure* view proposes that behavior of individuals is shaped (Weber, 1947; Fayol, 1949). The basic structure of an organization is composed of roles that predefine behavioral expectations, duties, and responsibilities for all employees. Shared organizational goals impose a need for uniformity, coherence, and integration. The manager's function in the adaptation process is to perceive, process, and respond to changes in the environment by rearranging roles in the organization to ensure survival and effectiveness. Identifying subsystems within the organization that need to respond to changes in the environment, selecting transformation processes, and assigning internal resources efficiently to achieve the goals of the organization are major roles in the adaptation processes.

The *strategic choice* perspective argues that organizations are constructed, sustained, and changed by the manager's enactment of an environment (Child, 1972; Weick, 1979). According to this perspective, choice of organization design, transformation processes, and outputs is more in accordance with political considerations than with technical considerations. The environment is not viewed as an imperturbable constraint. It is achieved through elites choosing strategies and deploying resources to capitalize on the firm's distinctive competencies.

The *natural selection* perspective is based on the population ecology model of organization theory (Hannan & Freeman, 1977). Drawing on Darwin's theory of evolution, its proponents argue that organizations, like organisms in nature, depend for survival on their ability to gain an adequate supply of resources necessary to sustain their existence. Organizations are seen as being severely constrained in their ability to adapt their structure to different niches of their setting for survival. As a result, in the long run, it really does not matter what managers and decision makers do. The strategic choices they make about the deployment of key resources are influenced by their niche. If the niche that an organization occupies no longer continues to attract enough resources to sustain the organization's viability, that form becomes "selected out."

The *collective-action* perspective on adaptation proposes that survival is best achieved through collaboration between organizations. This collaboration could occur, for example, in a regulated and controlled social environment (Emery & Trist, 1973). The Tobacco Trust established by leading U.S. tobacco companies to help shape research linking cancer and smoking illustrates such collaboration. These interorganizational networks negotiate exchanges between members of different organizations as they jointly shape their environment. Interdependent organizations take on specified roles within a normative framework. This framework defines each organization's duties and rights in relation to the collectivity. These norms permit each organization to act independently, but within the collective interests of all organizations sharing the common concern.

Hrebiniak and Joyce (1985) capture the richness of the Astley and Van de Ven review by indicating that these perspectives posit two distinct themes of adaptation. The first theme is determinism-voluntarism, and the second is strategic choice. Determinism-voluntarism refers to the impact of the environment and external stakeholders on the functioning of the firm. In the natural selection perspective, top managers have relatively little influence over the countervailing powers in the firm's environment. In the strategic choice perspective, these environmental powers are low. If top managers have high choice, the power of external stakeholders is low. Hrebiniak and Joyce (1985) state that it is the interaction between these themes that can further facilitate our understanding of organizational behavior. Our earlier logic avers that strategic contexts afford structure, technology, and control systems that form the basis of climate perceptions. It follows then that different strategic contexts would lead to the formation of different organizational climates.

The Hrebiniak and Joyce themes of adaptation are shown in a matrix in Figure 4.1. Quadrant 1 basically illustrates the conditions or assumptions underlying the natural selection perspective — that is, low strategic choice and high environmental determinism. For organizations to survive, the organization must have power over its environment to extract salient resources. Large-scale organizations are favored, while small organizations often fall victim to the forces of their environment. Economic rationality governs decision makers. There is an emphasis on efficiency through tight controls and monitoring systems.

At the opposite extreme in Figure 4.1 are organizations existing under munificent environmental conditions (quadrant 3). Confronted with high strategic choice and low environmental determinism, top managers can pursue various strategic choices. Because of the abundance of resources, the organization is free to design itself in modes that would be difficult under more constrained conditions.

In quadrant 2, both strategic choice and environmental determinism are high. Under these conditions, managers are constrained by external factors that affect their organizations. They may operate in other conditions where such constraints are absent or inconsequential. For example, Miles and Cameron (1982) described how firms in the cigarette industry, despite governmental regulations, controls, and mandatory warnings to consumers about the detrimental effects of their products on consumers' health, were able to enter other markets—such as breweries—where they were less constrained.

In quadrant 4, both strategic choice and environmental determinism are low. Adaptation takes place by chance since managers in this quadrant apparently exhibit no coherent strategy to take advantage of managing their environment. Managers "muddle through" their decision-making process. Although they may have an array of strengths, they cannot capitalize on any one of them. Organizations in this quadrant therefore exhibit few distinctive competencies, and other organizations severely impact their effectiveness. To ensure survival, organizations in this quadrant must move to another strategic context. It is the relative mix and fit among inappropriate internal capabilities that renders these organizations powerless and their survival questionable.

Table 4.1 summarizes the impact of the strategic context

**Figure 4.1. Relation of Strategic Choices and Environmental Determinism
in Organizational Adaptation.**

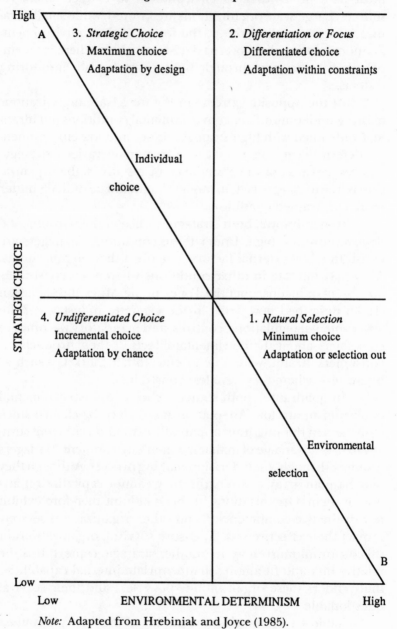

Note: Adapted from Hrebiniak and Joyce (1985).

themes on selected organizational attributes. The formation of organizational climates and their properties (consistency, consensus, and congruency) can be enhanced when it is understood how the organizational attributes that are the stimuli for climate perceptions vary as a function of strategic context. Since much of the information about how organizational attributes vary by strategic context can be traced to prior research, we will review that literature and the resulting consequences for climate consistency, consensus, and congruency.

Quadrant 1 — Low Strategic Choice, High Determinism

In quadrant 1, top management's choice of strategy may be constrained. Cost leaders or defenders (Miles & Snow, 1978) tend to dominate this quadrant. To achieve economies of scale and become an efficient producer of goods and/or services, the manufacturing, engineering, and finance subsystems dominate strategic choice decision-making processes. Rules regulate the flow of information between organizational members to be sure of a high level of formal integration. Members' roles are tightly prescribed by formal job descriptions and sequential technological interdependencies. Reward systems are formal. Salaries and perquisites are based on a manager's location in the hierarchy, tenure in the system, and contributions to efficiency (Kerr & Slocum, 1987).

In these strategic contexts, large organizations typically display a fundamentally bureaucratic form of structure. As a result of the high emphasis on rationality and consistency in such organizations, we would expect a high degree of consensus in climate perceptions. The extensive use of rules and standard operating procedures ensures that individuals from different functional areas are exposed to similar work practices and procedures. Extensive socialization practices establish a highly effective internalized set of controls. Aspects of climate dealing with such issues as performance-reward contingencies, hierarchical leadership, and autonomy show considerable similarity across individuals within the organization. This would yield a high level of consensus among individual psychological cli-

Table 4.1. Effects of Four Adaptation Processes on Selected Organizational Variables.

Organizational Variables	Quadrant 1	Quadrant 2	Quadrant 3	Quadrant 4
Strategic Choice	Low	Differentiated	High	Incremental
Generic Strategy	Defender	Analyzer	Prospector	Reactor
Power Bases	Manufacturing Finance Engineering	Manufacturing Marketing Planning	Marketing R&D	Diffuse
Reward System				
• Performance Based	Weak	Moderate	Strong	Low
• Hierarchy Based	Strong	Moderate	Weak	High
Structure				
• Formalization	High	Moderate	Low	Hybrid
• Administrative Intensity	High	Moderate	Low	
• Technological Interdependence	Sequential	Pooled	Reciprocal	
Organizational Metaphor	Lean and mean; Efficiency	Efficiency and effectiveness	Let a thousand flowers bloom; Effectiveness	None

mates. When aggregated to the collective climates level, we would therefore expect one, or at most only a few, collective climates to be found within the organization due to the presence of this consensus. The climates would therefore reflect the low strategic choice and high determinism characterizing their context.

The collective climates, which together comprise the broader organizational climate, should be highly internally consistent. The organization's emphasis on rationality and the use of extensive control procedures ensure adherence to this rationality. Climates characterized as high in centralization would be rated as high on the use of hierarchical, as opposed to more informal, influence processes. Formality rather than informality should characterize much of the decision making and relationships among co-workers.

Under these strategic conditions, organizations do what they do "because they must, or else!" (Thompson, 1967, p. 3). As a consequence, only those organizations subscribing to environmentally determined allowable variations will survive. Climates should be highly congruent with their technology and environment. Unacceptable performance consequences for organizations failing to meet their contingencies is expected. The machinelike pursuit of logic and rationality in response to a constraining environment should be mirrored in aggregate climate perceptions of that situation at the organizational level of analysis. This results in high levels of consistency, consensus, and congruency. Under more munificent conditions, deviations from such tight coupling of strategic context, organizational practices and procedures, and climate perceptions might be allowable.

Quadrant 3—High Strategic Choice, Low Determinism

In quadrant 3, top management has a great deal of discretion to choose among alternative strategies to achieve the firm's competitive advantages. Risk taking, creativity, and a munificent environment offer top management a choice of enacting various business strategies by which the firm may compete. Under these conditions, decision making is not tightly coupled to organizational goals. Decision makers engage in "slack search" (Hrebiniak & Joyce, 1985). The munificence afforded by the environment allows them to undertake activities with no clear or immediate benefit. This search may yield considerable benefit to the firm in the long run. Under these conditions, top managers may choose a prospector business strategy (Miles & Snow, 1978). Following this strategy, decision makers are freed to pursue new market or product opportunities, as opposed to solving technical problems within a constraining environment. Top management exercises little formal control over member behaviors. Very few administrators are assigned to planning and integrating various functions and/or departments in the organization.

Under these conditions, consensus of climate perceptions would be lower than under the low-choice, high-determinism situation. The organization's structure and processes are not linked to a single superordinate goal. Control systems monitor outputs and not behaviors (Ouchi & Maguire, 1975). Multiple reward and promotion systems, management practices, and personnel selection procedures would characterize these organizations. Individuals would experience different "realities," in part because the organization embodies them in its differing systems, and in part because it fails to enforce adherence to any one of them. The organizational climate would likely contain many collective climates reflecting the different experiences of individuals in such firms.

Climates in this context would probably be less congruent with elements of technology and environment due to the degree of "forgiveness" afforded by the highly munificent strategic situation. Some climates may even represent highly consistent attempts at doing things that are not congruent with environmental contingencies. In more hostile situations, this would result in severe, and perhaps even fatal, consequences for the firm. Under the conditions of this quadrant, incongruent multiple climates are allowed to propagate until the looser controls and performance requirements characterizing this situation are encountered.

Quadrant 2—High Strategic Choice, High Determinism

In quadrant 2, choice is high, but it is differentiated because of the countervailing power and resources in the environment. In some areas, the organization can gain a distinctive competence by pursuing new products in existing business areas. These current domains therefore offer the firm some strategic choice. Alternatively, faced with constraints in its primary markets, organizations may diversify into more munificent markets. In these they encounter less competition, lower regulation, or fewer threats from potential substitute products. In these businesses, high choice exists despite the determinism encountered in the core business. This results in the coexistence of both choice and determinism in the context of a single corporate (as opposed to business-level) strategy.

In this strategically interesting situation, organization climates would display characteristics found under both of the preceding strategic contexts. First, there would be a fair degree of consensus, but not to the same extent as that encountered under quadrant 1 conditions. Multiple climates would be found, but they would not be as numerous as those found in quadrant 3. In segments of the business that are tightly constrained, few climates would be expected. Where the business segment is less constrained, more climates are expected. The final number of collective climates would be a consequence of the number of business segments being served by the organization, as well as of the particular strategic situations faced by each.

These climates should be internally consistent. Congruency with environmental contingencies would be similar to the preceding arguments concerning consistency. For business segments that are highly constrained, high congruency would be expected. For those segments that are less constrained, congruency would be less critical. Thus, looking across all collective climates composing a given organizational climate, we would expect a higher rate of congruency (percent climates congruent with context on basis of prior research) than for the high-choice situation. We expect a lower rate of congruency for the high-determinism, low-choice condition.

Quadrant 4 — Low Strategic Choice, Low Determinism

In quadrant 4, the organization is in transition. There are few environmental constraints imposed on the organization by key stakeholders. Top managers, however, are unable to mobilize the resources of their firm. As a result, the organization's strategic choice process can be described as disjointed and its strategic posture reactionary. It is the lack of a coherent internal structure that delimits the choices available to these organizations. Rewards systems tend to be predicated on the status quo, with little focus on obtaining results. A lack of coherent internal structure prevents the organization from making key adaptation decisions. Top managers exercise little choice over key structural contingencies (formalization, administrative intensity, or technological interdependence) that affect the firm's organizational design.

Organizational climates under this condition should be characterized by low degrees of consensus, high inconsistency, and a lack of congruity with environmentally imposed conditions. The strategy formation process can be viewed as a process for rendering very difficult decision situations manageable (Hrebiniak & Joyce, 1985). This formation process is characterized in terms of agreement concerning both means and ends. When there is disagreement about both what is to be accomplished (ends) and how it is to be accomplished (means), the decision situation is problematic. This requires a so-called "inspirational" decision-making strategy (Thompson, 1967). These conditions are frequently encountered in strategy formation and formulation (Joyce & Hrebiniak, 1988). The process of strategy formulation is intended to produce options that are both technically feasible and politically acceptable. This renders these problematic situations more manageable and allows rational decision-making processes to proceed.

The organization's inaction in the face of strategic opportunities suggests that successful strategy formulation has not taken place. Considerable dissension remains concerning the firm's direction and the means of maximizing the strategic opportunities. Consequently, we would expect to find a lack of climate consensus at the individual level. A large number of multiple, but competing, collective climates at the group and/or division level should emerge. In the extreme, no agreement in perceptions could exist. In this case, no aggregate climates would exist at all (James, 1982; Joyce & Slocum, 1984; James, Joyce & Slocum, 1988). An organization would be essentially "climateless." This would represent an extreme condition, similar in some respects to Durkheim's (1951) concept of anomie.

Because agreement has not been obtained about means, fractionation of the organization's control systems and basic regulating mechanisms would be present. Climates emerging in response to individuals' interpretations of these systems would be likely to be highly inconsistent. Since the firm has not addressed how it would posture itself in relation to its environment, many incongruities within multiple climates would exist. A lack of consensus, high inconsistency, and high incongruity would characterize the climates of firms in this situation. These contribute to managers' apparent helplessness in the face of what other firms would regard as high levels of strategic opportunity.

Conclusions

This chapter has suggested that the characteristics of organizational climates — described in terms of the properties of a set of collective climates comprising them — can be influenced by the strategic context of the firm. This strategic context imposes a variety of choices and constraints on structure, processes, and control systems within the organization. The resulting structural differences across organizations operating in different strategic contexts are hypothesized to yield collective climates with differing attributes in terms of consistency, consensus, and congruity. These characteristics of collective climates were traced to the strategic context and adaptation process of specific organizations. It is our conjecture that deviations from these patterns of relationship will be associated with each organization's viability.

An important question based on these arguments is the

extent to which concepts from organization theory can be used to extend the theory of climates. The basic unit of theory for climate research is the individual. So what contribution can variables at relatively "distant" units of analysis provide to such a theory? We believe that including concepts from multiple levels of analysis is appropriate in organizational psychology and behavior. The inclusion of these concepts has both practical and theoretical implications.

Theoretically, we must understand where climate perceptions come from. Certainly, they are constructed by individuals through processes of meaning creation and attachment. These meanings are not created in a vacuum, but emerge in response to various properties of the stimulus situation. Organization climate is concerned with the patterns of meaning attached to features of organizational settings. These settings have consistently been shown to be related to characteristics of the firm's strategic context. Recent theoretical developments in organization theory suggest the relevance of classifying these contexts by the degree of choice and determinism that they afford management in the creation of structures, processes, and control systems. Strategic context circumscribes and delimits the allowable variations in organization climates that can be created through these processes.

If this is true, then all climates are not equally likely, given the properties of the organization's strategic context. Practically speaking, climates that are inconsistent with strategically prescribed patterns could be taken as evidence of maladaptation. The performance implications of such maladaptation remain to be explored and are of both theoretical and practical interest.

The inclusion of strategic context in theories of organizational climate also raises another interesting theoretical issue. The concept of organizational climate can be traced to attempts to operationalize the environmental component of Lewin's famous equation $B = f(P, E)$ (Lewin, 1947). Fundamentally, climate research has been concerned with attempting to represent the environment in psychological terms and to explore the antecedents and consequences of these representations in organizations.

Paradoxically, *aggregate* concepts of the climate have unintentionally accomplished just the opposite. Psychological climates have been based on the individual's descriptions of organizational practices and procedures. They have therefore been consistent with the intentions of climate research based on the individual's descriptions. When these individual scores have been aggregated to represent the climates of groups, divisions, or organizations, the effect has been to produce descriptions that have less and less to do with the environment, and more and more to do with the unit of analysis that the aggregation is based on. Thus, when we ask an individual to describe his or her work setting, it is clear that we are asking for a perception of the environment. When these scores are aggregated to the work group level, however, it is no longer clear that the average score attributed to the group reflects *its* environment. Some variance in the individual-level scores represents responses to stimuli now contained within the boundary of the group (other members of the work group, for example). So, to some degree the work group is describing itself as well as its environment. As the level of aggregation increases, more and more of what is being described is contained within the boundary of the unit of analysis being described. When we have constructed scores for organizational climate in this fashion, we have produced measures of the organization's perception of itself, rather than of the environment appropriate to the level of analysis being studied.

Organization climates, then, have rarely been the climates of organizations, but rather aggregate perceptions of the *characteristics* of organizations. An analogy would be self-assessments of personality at the individual level of analysis. While these are interesting and potentially quite important, they are not consistent with the notion of climate as environment. Organizational and psychological climate have thus differed substantially in terms of their reliance on environment as a fundamental defining property of the respective constructs. Perceptions of strategic context may represent a true organization climate.

References

Astley, W. G., & Van de Ven, A. (1983). Central perspective and debates in organizational theory. *Administrative Science Quarterly, 28*, 245–273.

Child, J. (1972). Organization structure, environment, and performance: The role of strategic choice. *Sociology, 6,* 1–22.

Drexler, J. A. (1977). Organizational climate: Its homogeneity within organizations. *Journal of Applied Psychology, 62,* 38–42.

Durkheim, E. (1951). *Suicide: A study in sociology.* New York: Free Press.

Emery, R. E., & Trist, E. L. (1973). *Towards a social ecology: Contextual appreciations of the future in the present.* New York: Plenum.

Fayol, H. (1949). *General and industrial management.* London: Pitman.

Glick, W. H. (1985). Conceptualizing and measuring organizational and psychological climate: Pitfalls in multilevel research. *Academy of Management Review, 10*(3), 601–616.

Guion, R. M. (1973). A note on organizational climate. *Organizational Behavior and Human Performance, 9,* 120–125.

Hannan, M., & Freeman, J. (1977). The population ecology model of organizations. *American Journal of Sociology, 82,* 929–964.

Hellriegel, D., & Slocum, J. W., Jr. (1974). Organizational climate: Measures, research, and contingencies. *Academy of Management Journal, 17,* 255–280.

Herman, J. B., Dunham, R. B., & Hulin, C. L. (1975). Organizational structure, demographic characteristics, and employee responses. *Organizational Behavior and Human Performance, 13,* 206–232.

Hrebiniak, L. G., & Joyce, W. F. (1985). Organizational adaptation: Strategic choice and environmental determinism. *Administrative Science Quarterly, 30,* 336–349.

Jackofsky, E. F., & Slocum, J. W., Jr. (1988). A longitudinal study of climates. *Journal of Organizational Behavior, 9,* 319–334.

James, L. A. (1982). Aggregation bias in estimates of perceptual measures. *Journal of Applied Psychology, 67,* 219–229.

James, L. A., & Jones, A. P. (1974). Organizational climate: A review of theory and research. *Psychological Bulletin, 81,* 1096–1112.

James, L. A., Joyce, W. F., & Slocum, J. W., Jr. (1988). Comment: Organizations do not cognize. *Academy of Management Review, 13*(1), 129–132.

Joyce, W. F. (1977). *Antecedents and Consequents of Collective Climates in Organizations.* Unpublished doctoral dissertation, Pennsylvania State University.

Joyce, W. F., & Hrebiniak, L. G. (1988). Power, politics, and organization design. In M. Bazerman, R. Lewicki, & B. Shepard (Eds.), *Research in negotiation* (Vol. 2, pp. 151–173). Greenwich, CT: JAI Press.

Joyce, W. F., & Slocum, J. W., Jr. (1979). Climates in organizations. In S. Kerr (Ed.), *Organizational behavior* (pp. 317–333). Columbus, OH: Grid.

Joyce, W. F., & Slocum, J. W., Jr. (1982). Correlates of climate discrepancy. *Human Relations, 35,* 951–972.

Joyce, W. F., & Slocum, J. W., Jr. (1984). Collective climate: Agreement as a basis for defining aggregate climates in organizations. *Academy of Management Journal, 27,* 721–742.

Kerr, J., & Slocum, J. W., Jr. (1987). Managing corporate culture through reward systems. *Academy of Management Executive, 1,* 99–108.

Lewin, K. (1947). Frontiers of group dynamics. *Human Relations, 1,* 5–41.

Miles, R., & Cameron, K. (1982). *Coffin nails and corporate strategy.* Englewood Cliffs, NJ: Prentice-Hall.

Miles, R., & Snow, C. P. (1978). *Organizational strategy, structure, and process.* New York: McGraw-Hill.

Ouchi, W., & Maguire, M. (1975). Organizational control: Two functions. *Administrative Science Quarterly, 20,* 559–569.

Poole, M. S. (1985). Communication and organizational climate: Review, critique, and a new perspective. In R. D. McPhee & K. Tompkins (Eds.), *Organizational communication: Traditional themes and directions* (pp. 79–108). Newbury Park, CA: Sage.

Schneider, B. (1975). Organizational climates: An essay. *Personnel Psychology, 28,* 447–479.

Schneider, B., & Reichers, A. E. (1983). On the etiology of climates. *Personnel Psychology, 36,* 19–39.

Schneider, B., & Snyder, R. A. (1975). Some relationships between job satisfaction and organizational climate. *Journal of Applied Psychology, 60,* 318–328.

Tagiuri, R., & Litwin, G. H. (Eds.). (1968). *Organizational climate:*

Explorations of a concept. Cambridge, MA: Department of Research, Graduate School of Business Administration, Harvard University.

Thompson, J. D. (1967). *Organizations in action.* New York: McGraw-Hill.

Weber, M. (1947). *The theory of social and economic organization* (A. M. Henderson & T. Parsons, Trans.). New York: Free Press.

Weick, K. (1979). *The social psychology of organizing* (2nd ed.). Reading, MA: Addison-Wesley.

PART TWO

METHODOLOGICAL ISSUES

The chapters in Part Two address two different methodological issues, one concerning the *collection* of data, the other the *analysis* of data that have been collected. Organizational climate researchers, in particular, have been very concerned with quantitative issues in data collection and data analysis. Scholars in the organizational culture tradition have also been concerned with data collection, but their approach has traditionally been more qualitative.

In Chapter Five, Rousseau presents a multilayered model of the attributes of culture and argues for the utility and appropriateness of different methods for collecting data on those different layers. Thus, she presents information on both qualitative and quantitative approaches to the study of culture, describing the layers of culture (and climate) for which different methods may prove most enlightening. In addition, the chapter contains reference to, and some examples of, the numerous survey measures that have been developed for the assessment of culture in organizations.

Dansereau and Alutto, in Chapter Six, present an elegant treatment of the data analysis issues involved when researchers desire to use individuals' perceptions for the description of units of analysis beyond the individual (for example, teams, departments, organizations). Dansereau and Alutto provide a real service to climate and culture researchers by explicating the issues involved in such aggregation. In addition, they present each issue with examples and carry several examples through the entire chapter. Perhaps of most interest to researchers will be their application of their language and methods to issues involved in the aggregation of qualitative data. As an outcome of their presentation regarding levels issues in quantitative data, Dansereau and Alutto are able to identify analogous issues requiring attention by qualitative researchers to ensure the reliability and validity of data interpretation.

These two chapters reveal that in climate and culture research, as in other research, there is no "best" methodology or "best" unit of analysis. They offer numerous examples of the choices researchers can make about how they collect data and how they can validly support the generalizations they make to particular units of analysis. In combination, these chapters also present appropriate cautions about the collection and analysis of climate and culture data. More important, they show that the reliable collection of data and the valid analysis of data are both possible by following a set of clear guidelines for making these methodological decisions.

Chapter 5

Denise M. Rousseau

Assessing Organizational Culture: The Case for Multiple Methods

Quantitative assessment of culture is controversial. Organizational culture research using structured interviews, Q-sorts, and standardized questionnaires melds a well-established construct in the social sciences with a highly sophisticated measurement technology. But what might appear on the surface to be a reasonable combination of concept and operationalization is in fact a disputed one, interjecting issues of epistemology, ethics, and values into research methodology. This chapter examines the nature of the culture construct, its theoretical roots, the epistemological models underlying it, and the strengths and weaknesses of both the qualitative and quantitative methods for studying it. It also clarifies the meaning of quantitative methodology, considers the distinction between assessment and interpretation, and explores ethical issues in assessments of culture. Finally, current techniques for quantitative assessment of culture are reviewed and critiqued, and suggestions are made for future culture research.

Note: My thanks to Benjamin Schneider, Jennifer Chatman, Cathy Enz, and Marshall Sashkin for their insightful comments. I am indebted to Lou Pondy for ideas regarding public versus private research methods. Sam Pokbaz originally created the graphics.

153

The Culture Construct

Culture typically has been treated by anthropologists (Geertz, 1973; Wallace, 1970) and organizational researchers (Smircich, 1983) as a set of cognitions shared by members of a social unit. These cognitions are acquired through social learning and socialization processes that expose individuals to a variety of culture-bearing elements. These elements include the observable activities and interactions, communicated information, and material artifacts that form the social experience. Despite different substantive interests, organizational theorists who write about culture repeatedly employ terms that, as Barley (1983) indicates, bear a family resemblance (Table 5.1).

Notions of shared values, common understandings, and patterns of beliefs and expectations underlie our views on the nature of culture. Organizational researchers, though conceptualizing culture similarly, have assessed widely different elements. These elements vary in their subjectivity or objectivity, as well as in their observability and availability to both researchers and organization members. Examples include:

- organizational heroes (such as calling enlisted men who assist the launch of F-14s "the fighter pilots of the deck"; Roberts, Rousseau & LaPorte, 1990)
- tales of how the boss reacts to incidents of failure or success (such as a manager handing an ingenious employee a banana from his lunch to provide immediate positive reinforcement, hence the Golden Banana Award; Peters & Waterman, 1982)
- rites and rituals (such as the funeral parlor operator opening the window in the death room to signify freshness and life; Barley, 1983)
- behavioral norms (such as laying low when a mistake occurs or being patient with newcomers; Cooke & Rousseau, 1988).

In effect, we seek widely different types of information and probe varied types of knowledge in the study of culture.

Despite a family resemblance in conceptualization and

Table 5.1. Culture Definitions.

Source	Definition
Becker & Geer (1970)	Set of common understandings, expressed in language.
Kroeber & Kluckhohn (1952)	Transmitted patterns of values, ideas, and other symbolic systems that shape behavior.
Louis (1983)	Three aspects: (1) some content (meaning and interpretation) (2) peculiar to (3) a group.
Martin & Siehl (1983)	Glue that holds together an organization through shared patterns of meaning. Three component systems: context or core values, forms (process of communication—for instance, jargon), strategies to reinforce content (such as rewards, training programs).
Ouchi (1981)	Set of symbols, ceremonies, and myths that communicate the underlying values and beliefs of the organization to its employees.
Swartz & Jordon (1980)	Pattern of beliefs and expectations shared by members that produce norms shaping behavior.
Uttal (1983)	Shared values (what is important) and beliefs (how things work) that interact with an organization's structures and control systems to produce behavioral norms (the way we do things around here).
Van Maanen & Schein (1979)	Values, beliefs, and expectations that members come to share.

definition, inconsistency and confusion plague much of the writing on culture in organizations. Schein (1984) treats culture as unconscious assumptions and regards conscious expectations as artifacts. Cooke and Rousseau (1988), in contrast, treat culture as normative beliefs shared by members of a social unit, defining physical manifestations (for example, green army fatigues and insignia of rank) as artifacts. Scholars focus essentially on a *preferred* set of culture elements (for instance, unconscious assumptions [Schein, 1984]; stories [Martin & Siehl, 1983]; behavioral norms [Cooke & Rousseau, 1988; Rousseau, 1989, in press]), defining residual elements not included in that set as "artifacts." This usage can sometimes signal the role of artifacts as elements with lower status on the conceptual totem pole. For example, Schein (1986b, p. 31) argues, "If we do not recognize that overt behavior, opinions, and feelings are *merely* artifacts [emphasis added], not the underlying culture, we are in danger of rushing in with superficial culture audits and measuring instruments that give us only surface indicators." *Superficial* is a highly value-laden term when it refers not to the thoroughness of the assessment or analysis, but rather to the appropriateness of the focus of study. Moreover, writers often use the term *culture* simultaneously to mean different things, employing it both to define a particular social unit (such as Eskimos and IBMers) and to describe specific social processes (for instance, values and norms reflected in a service orientation or a marketing emphasis)—see Barley (1983), for example.

The Elements of Culture. In many respects, it is not the definitions of culture that vary so widely across organizational researchers, but the types of data researchers collect. Schein (1984) focuses on unconscious assumptions implied in the action and speech of organization members. Martin and Siehl (1983) examine the values ("corporate ideologies") observable in patterned sequences of events, rituals (such as meeting top executives at the airport), and artifacts (for example, standardized office furniture conveying conformity and individual invisibility). Cooke and Rousseau (1988) address the behaviors it takes to fit in and get ahead—that is, evidence of behavioral norms attached to a social unit (for instance, "don't make waves" or "appearing to work very hard"). Various organizational assessments based on member perceptions tap the structures giving pattern to organizational activities and integrating members, while a myriad of descriptive writings have talked about the material artifacts of organizational life from blue suits, crew cuts, and officer insignia to United Way and Golden Banana pins (see Peters & Waterman, 1982; Weick, 1987). These investigations all tap things cultural, that is, elements in some manner consistent with the family of definitions attached to culture in organizational research. But their focus varies widely.

To help focus culture research and operationalizations on relevant factors, we might consider a description of some major elements of culture, organized from readily accessible to difficult to assess (Figure 5.1). At the perimeter, material artifacts reflect the physical manifestations and products of cultural activity, which might even survive after the individuals and their social unit cease to exist (examples include logos, badges). Structures reflect those patterns of activity—decision making, coordination and communication mechanisms, and so on—that are observable to outsiders and whose functions help solve basic organization problems, such as coordination and adaptation (Cooke & Rousseau, 1981). Behavioral norms, that is, member beliefs regarding acceptable and unacceptable behavior, promote mutual predictability, but they may be difficult to note without direct information from members (for instance, consequences associated with substandard performance, competitive or cooperative relations between peers). Values—that is, the priorities assigned to certain states or outcomes, such as innovation versus predictability and risk seeking versus risk avoidance—necessitate informants. Finally, unconscious assumptions, not directly knowable even to members, require researcher-member interaction over time for assessment to be made (such an example might be siblinglike rivalry between a CEO's subordinates). Configuring culture as layers of processes (that is, interpretative-behavioral, conscious-unconscious), varying in depth, accessibility, and malleability, is characteristic of models employing multiple dimensions to describe culture (for example, Kilmann, Saxton, Serpa, & Associates, 1985). Moreover, a framework linking multiple elements, describing transmission of one facet through use of others, is consistent with the notion that culture is something an organization *is* rather than *has* (Sathe, 1985).

Culture has many elements, layered along a continuum of subjectivity and accessibility. More objective elements become vehicles for transmission of less tangible, more subjective facets

Figure 5.1. Layers of culture.

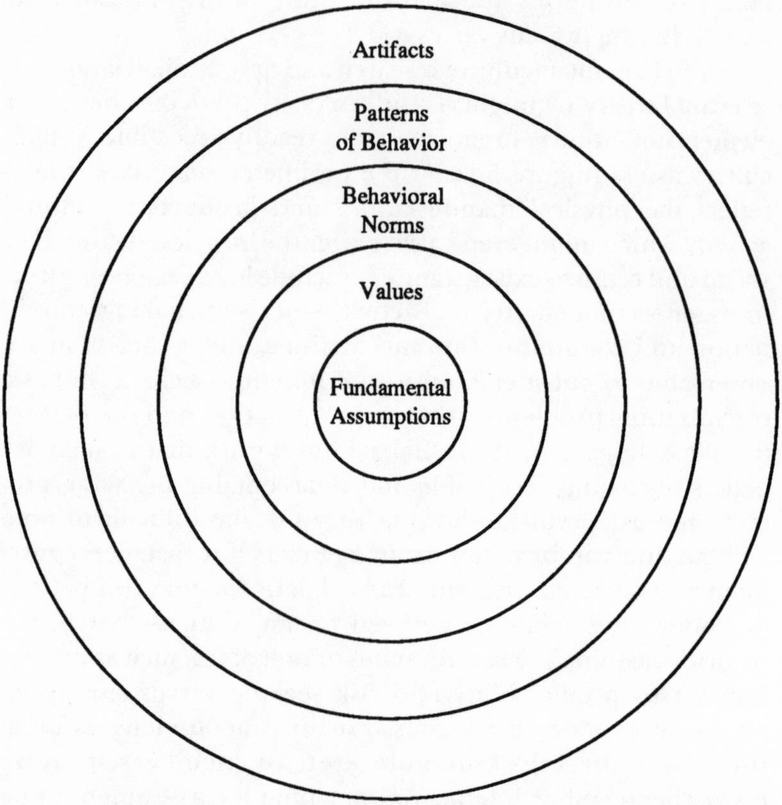

Artifacts

Patterns
of Behavior

Behavioral
Norms

Values

Fundamental
Assumptions

of culture. Material artifacts and other physical manifestations
of social systems and the patterns of activities and interactions
members observe and carry out (such as decision making and
communicating) can constitute major elements of culture when
organizational processes directly related to these — use of formal structures, for example — are under investigation. In contrast, if one chooses to focus on deeper layers of culture, for
instance in studies of socialization and assimilation, the more
tangible culture elements such as the way people respond to
mistakes can be construed as transmitters of the highly internalized and often unconscious aspects of culture (an example
would be member fear of failure).

As noted earlier, the layers of culture associated with values, beliefs, and expectations constitute the primary elements in organizational researchers' conceptualizations of culture. Interest in the values, beliefs, and expectations characterizing a social unit and in the interpretations individuals make of these is consistent with a cognitive-based view of culture as an "enacted environment." Weick (1979) argues that individuals develop an organized view of the world by constructing meanings for events through identification of patterns (for instance, $x \rightarrow y \rightarrow z$). This constructed view of the world reduces equivocality and uncertainty of events and typically involves the efforts of two or more people in the process of interpreting and attaching meanings to such patterns, hence the expression "social construction of reality." Behavioral norms are an example of a social construction experienced by members; these norms require mutuality and sharing as a basis for their existence. Values are preferred states often manifested in observable behaviors ("revealed preferences"). Finally, hidden assumptions — the deepest, most subjective elements of culture — may color all others though they may not be well understood even by members.

In this continuum from unconscious processes to highly observable structures and patterns of activity, the concept of climate in organizations becomes relevant. Elsewhere (Rousseau, 1988) I have argued that climate reflects individual perceptions of the organization and thus focuses on a class of cognitions or *descriptive beliefs* individuals hold regarding organizational properties (managerial trust, supportiveness, participativeness in decision making, and so on). Descriptive beliefs tell us "what *is*" in the eye of the beholder and are influenced by individual characteristics, position in the organization, and organizational factors; they contrast with normative beliefs ("what should be done"), which are more strictly a product of cultural processes. Climate as a product of individual psychological processes (and the individual's potentially idiosyncratic experience of the organization) and culture as a unit-level phenomenon that is derived from social interaction are distinct constructs. Researchers have at times confused climate

with culture because aggregation of individual climate perceptions into unit-level scores has employed measures of consensus
or intraunit agreement to justify this aggregation. The assumption is made that agreement means shared perception (which
implies that members interact to create this shared worldview).
However, few climate studies investigate the role of interaction
or social contact in shaping shared perception (Joyce & Slocum,
1984). An individual can provide information on climate even
when his or her responses do not agree with those of another
unit member. But, by definition, the individual cannot provide
meaningful data on culture unless his or her responses in some
way converge with those of other members. Note that differentiating climate from culture raises questions regarding the
meaning of *shared* climate perceptions (Does agreement make
these perceptions cultural? Are "unshared" perceptions in a
culture measure really climate?) The key distinction between
climate and culture may be in the content of the measure
(descriptive versus normative) and not the sharedness of the
data.

Researchers show a tendency to choose *their* particular
layer of culture, defining what is left as less important, or as a by-
product or vehicle for the transmission of the "deeper" elements
of culture. These varied layers of culture and their differential
availability for study by an outsider suggest that multiple methods are needed to tap the range of cultural elements and
processes.

I argue that based on the literature on culture in organizations and other social systems,

1. Culture is a social process associated with a unit in which
    members share a common set of elements — assumptions
    and worldviews, values, behavioral norms, patterns of ac-
    tivities, and material artifacts.
2. These elements differ in the degree to which they are con-
    sciously experienced by members.
3. Cultural elements vary in their accessibility to outsiders and
    in the degree to which members must actively provide

information and interact in their interpretation before outsiders can understand and represent them.

4. Existence of these layers of elements is common to all units
    with sufficient social stability (for example, common his-
    tory, stable membership) to sustain a culture.

5. As yet, whether the content of each layer is unique to a
    particular social unit and the extent to which cultural ele-
    ments generalize in content and function across units—
    particularly those that researchers characterize as "organi-
    zations"—are empirical questions.

Why Qualitative Methods in Culture Research?

Advocates of qualitative methods have taken several positions
supporting qualitative research and countering the use of quantitative culture measures. Louis (1983) and Smircich (1983) have
argued that culture reflects a social construction of reality
unique to members of a social unit, and that this uniqueness
makes it impossible for standardized measures to tap cultural
processes. Schein (1984, 1986b) argues that quantitative assessment conducted through surveys is unethical in that it reflects
conceptual categories not the respondent's own, presuming unwarranted generalizability. Deal (1986) suggests that traditional
academic methods applied to studying culture "sterilize" the
construct and reflect a relabeling of old approaches to studying
organizations.

Two issues are actually being raised here: (1) whether
cultural processes are in any way amenable to quantitative assessment, and (2) more generally, what the relative strengths and
weaknesses are of quantitative and qualitative assessments in
tapping how individuals experience the organization. This debate stems from the resurgence of qualitative methodology in
organizational research and controversy regarding the assumptions on which it is predicated.

Organizational sociology has long employed ethnography in its study of organizations (for example, see Whyte, 1949).
Its offshoot, the field of organizational behavior—which is

rooted in both sociology *and* industrial and organizational psychology — has come to be characterized by the quantitative methodologies of the latter.[1] A turning point came in the late 1970s when a trend toward "reclaiming" qualitative methods for organizational research emerged (Van Maanen, 1979). This movement emphasizes within-unit interpretations of the meaning of organizational phenomena, eschewing reports of their distribution, pattern, and generalizability across organizations (Morgan & Smircich, 1980). It reflects a view of organizational phenomena as particular and idiosyncratic rather than as replicable and well defined. Appearing in the field of organizational behavior concurrently with the growth of interest in qualitative assessment, the concept of culture has become almost inextricably linked with that methodology.

Role of the Unconscious. The rationale for the use of qualitative methods in culture research is largely predicated on the presumed inaccessibility, depth, or unconscious quality of culture. Some elements of culture are defined as layers of cognition of which members are unconscious or relatively unaware (Schein, 1984). Assumptions can be so deeply embedded that they are difficult to bring to the surface and examine. Schein argues that only a complex interactive process of joint inquiry between insiders and outsiders can uncover fundamental assumptions. Such assumptions, he argues, tend to drop out of awareness and become implicit, because unlike the situation with corporate ideology or slogans, there is no need to remind members of assumptions that are an integral part of their worldview. For example, a competitive, "us versus them" view of the world might characterize high-level government officials heading departments competing for resources and political clout. Rivalry, low trust, and defensiveness may become second nature, part of the psychodynamics of government agencies (Peck, 1988).

Some writers — like Smircich (1983) in discussing "root metaphors" — treat culture as a frame of reference through which one perceives the world, a frame of reference that is difficult for an individual to be cognizant of but accessible when insiders and outsiders interact to explore its meanings and workings. Schein (1985) relates the example of an organization characterized by emotional outbursts and conflict, where both appear to be intrinsically a part of the firm's problem-solving process. In that organization, members could not discover whether an idea had merit without subjecting it to extensive debate and did not question the appropriateness of the emotion and conflict generated by the idea-screening process. Extensive probing revealed a widespread fear of failure that members were reluctant to face. The notion of fundamental assumptions members share as an unconscious core can be expanded not only to include beliefs or worldviews, but also basic emotions (anxieties, fears, attractions) that work and relationships evoke. Sociotechnical theorists in the Tavistock tradition have developed models of workplace psychodynamics in which the individuals' relations with the work group and its task parallel those of child to parent and siblings (Bion, 1959; Hirschhorn, 1988). Fear, anxiety, love, and bonding are engendered in these interactions, which can be understood through processes of transference similar to those employed by psychotherapists in understanding and treating clinical patients (Hirschhorn, 1988).

Fundamental assumptions about organizing that even members cannot access go beyond the detailed descriptions of overt phenomena characteristic of ethnomethodology and involve active participation and probing by researchers. Researchers, in turn, must nonetheless set aside their own conceptions of organizing and meaning to probe those of others. Use of standardized surveys and/or interviews might require respondents to report on more than they are really able to—what Nisbett and Wilson (1977) describe as "telling more than we can know." Some scholars argue that to avoid generating data reflecting demand characteristics associated with structured research methods, a less structured approach allowing probing and feedback from respondents to verify interpretations is necessary.

Organization Uniqueness. Another issue is the possible uniqueness of an organization's values and beliefs such that an outsider cannot form a priori questions or measures. Schein (1984) argues that Likert's (1967) Systems 4 and Ouchi's (1981) Theory

Z reflect only employee ideologies, not basic culture types, in the absence of an extensive cross-organizational database. Stereotypical or overgeneral categories, reducing the wide variety of possible organizational forms and cultures to an idealized or model few, might be construed as a weakness of an a priori structured approach to tapping culture. Moreover, the specific types assessed might reflect ethnocentrism among organizational development practitioners or organizational behavior researchers, something Schein (1984) labels an "American optimism" that anything can be changed or bettered. Types designated as good or bad by researchers also become themselves value-laden.

These arguments are rooted in the notion of culture as a highly subjective unconscious process. This treatment is *not* consistent, however, with the majority of scholarly definitions of culture (Table 5.1), where the emphasis has largely been on behavior patterns and values. Nor is it congruent with actual operationalizations of culture. Siehl and Martin (1983) describe culture in a series of case studies focusing on behavioral patterns and artifacts. Barley (1983) uses descriptions of activities (for example, opening windows in the room where a person has died) and language (for instance, using the word *sleep* as a euphemism for death) to characterize the culture of the funeral industry. In these and other cases, language, overt behaviors and physical evidence are the sources of culture data.

Epistemology. Proponents of qualitative methods have sometimes linked the essential meaning and content of culture to qualitative methods on epistemological grounds. Epistemology, philosophies of knowing and knowledge, offers a variety of different constructions regarding what is knowable and how learning occurs. Morgan and Smircich (1980) employed a subjective-objective continuum to characterize what constitutes knowledge under the different worldviews that social scientists might adopt. Conceiving of reality as a concrete structure, a state to be viewed and measured, the highly objectivist scientist employing a positivist approach uses laboratory experiments and surveys to gain knowledge regarding what are essentially the univocal terms and conditions of the world. In contrast, models in which reality emerges from symbolic relations and the meanings individuals attach to interactions interject subjectivity into concepts of reality and make constantly calibrated measurement devices far less appropriate. When the individual's interpretations are primary causes of behavior, standardized instruments will not produce unequivocal results. Thus reality as social construction requires measurement systems that are more flexible, interactive, and person- and situation-specific.

Morgan and Smircich (1980) link social construction with techniques of ethnomethodology. They argue that an inquiry aimed at understanding the production of commonsense, shared knowledge in different areas of everyday life is achieved by ethnomethodology's identification of a subjective and agreed-on social order. Moreover, they argue that the products of this research will be unable to meet the demands of a more positivist view requiring that measurement and indeed the phenomena studied be univocal. In the study of socially constructed phenomena, they argue that quantitative assessment is unsatisfactory and inappropriate. When culture is viewed as fundamental assumptions invented by a social group to integrate itself and cope with its environment, it may be difficult for members to directly describe it. Epistemologically, a different way of knowing culture may be required.

Ethics. Finally, and perhaps most controversial, is the assertion by Schein (1984) that accessibility of information on culture raises certain ethical concerns. Researchers employing a survey or questionnaire to study organizations behave unethically, Schein argues, by purporting to speak for respondents through aggregated survey data rather than using the informants' own words. He argues that summary categories and aggregations of information misrepresent the respondents' views. Externally derived categories need not conform to the organization members' worldview—which is consistent with Morey and Luthans's (1984) discussion of emic ("insider") and etic ("outsider") perspectives.

In sum, proponents of qualitative methods argue that culture is most appropriately assessed by such processes because:

1. The fundamental content of culture is unconscious and highly subjective.
2. Interactive probing is required to access otherwise inaccessible and unconscious cultural material.
3. Each culture is idiosyncratic and unique and requires nonstandardized assessments.

Opposition to quantitative culture assessment, closely allied with advocacy of qualitative study, maintains that:

1. Culture is not univocal, but as a highly subjective social construction it cannot properly be studied by researcher-constructed categories and scales with unchanging calibrations across field sites.
2. Categorization of constructs on an a priori basis by researchers doing field research misrepresents the experiences of respondents, and thus is invalid.
3. Use of researcher-derived categorizes is a distortion of the respondent's perspective and is thus unethical.

The Case for Multiple Methods

Different layers of culture are amenable to different research methods. Starting at the point of greatest subjectivity in Figure 5.1, assumptions unconsciously held are difficult to assess without interactive probing. Member fears and defenses are elusive psychodynamics difficult to elicit without interaction. In contrast, characteristic patterns of behaviors (norms) regarding how members should (or should not) act are far more accessible. The method appropriate to assessing culture depends on those elements we choose to examine. In the layered model of culture shown in Figure 5.1, observations by outsiders and responses to structured instruments become more appropriate as we move from the center outward. As the elements of culture we are interested in become more conscious (values), behavioral (norms), or observable (artifacts), these are accessible by both standardized and nonstandardized assessments. In both instances, assessments must be subjected to the rules of evidence, which in the case of culture means that members must agree or show consensus in the description or responses they provide. It has not always been evident in descriptive writings on culture how much consensus really exists.

Public and Private Research Methods. Framing the choice of method based on the subjectivity of the research introduces the notion of public and private research methods (Pondy & Rousseau, 1980). Public methods are those that can be specified in advance of implementation (that is, as in the case of recipes and other standardized performance programs), consistently observable by others, and replicable across subjects, sites, and data sets. Private methods are researcher-specific, involving cognitions, judgments, and experiences only indirectly communicable to others. Although both private and public methods can involve interaction and customization, private methods are less constrained, standardized, and specified. Public methods are construed as tapping more "objective" factors, emphasizing the collection of certain types of data or information (such as ratings on a specific continuum) available across subjects and sites, whereas private methods involve collecting data that are idiosyncratic, impressionistic, and not necessarily comparable across members or units. In a debate on the role of quantitative and qualitative methods in organizational research, Pondy and Rousseau (1980) took issue with this objective-subjective construction, suggesting that public and private methods involve not just data collection processes, but data analysis as well (Figure 5.2). Potential combinations of public and private methods for data collection and analysis create opportunities to synthesize the strengths of both quantitative and qualitative methodologies.

Traditional qualitative methods combine impressionistic data collection with interpretive analysis. Classic quantitative methods couple standardized assessment with statistical analysis. Nonetheless, a rich eclecticism can yield statistical analyses

Figure 5.2. Public and Private Methods.

	Data Collection	Data Analysis
Public	Standardized, Prespecified	Statistical, Rules and heuristics
Private	Impressionistic	Interpretive

of impressionistic data (for example, Sutton & Rafaeli, 1988), allowing both exploration of new topics such as emotions and rigorous analysis despite the absence of well-specified a priori constructs. Private assessment coupled with public analysis can open up new areas of study where structured instruments are unavailable or possibly inappropriate. Similarly, standardized data collection combined with interpretive analysis allows researcher experience with a particular type of instrumentation to inform scholars and practitioners about varieties of interpretations, implications, and parallels.

Interpretation of quantitative data essentially mirrors clinical judgment, often reflecting forms of template matching. The example of the Jade Merchant applies here. When a raw jade stone is marketed in Southeast Asia, a "window" is cut on its surface by the merchant to show the varied color and depth within. An experienced buyer of jade matches what he or she sees through the window (color, depth, shading) with the thousands of other pieces (templates) seen in a lifetime in the trade, and from there assesses the jade's value and potential as an elegant statue or piece of jewelry (Green, 1986). Researchers experienced with a particular instrument possess similar templates, patterns from a variety of different administrations that can inform us differently about phenomena under study than could traditional statistical analysis.

In my own experience with an inventory assessing the behavioral norms characterizing organizations (Cooke & Rousseau, 1988; Rousseau, in press), I have repeatedly observed that certain organizations actively promoting norms involving team spirit and goal achievement nonetheless manifest a (contradictory) strong power orientation as well (for example, forcing, building power bases, evoking one's authority). One set of norms is seemingly at odds with the other. Follow-up reveals that this exercise of power is often a transition, reflecting how the organization implemented the change to what might be considered an "excellent" organization (that is, top-down). This pressure for change exerted by top management falls away as the new team-oriented approach is institutionalized. As with most clinical uses of standardized instruments, complex patterns are apparent to the experienced user that would otherwise be lost in a prespecified statistical analysis and summary of the data. Both the jade merchant and the researcher are shaped by experience. Note here that when interpretation is applied at the analysis phase (by feedback from the respondents), organization members are engaged in an interaction that can establish or refute the veridical nature of the data and researcher interpretations and also assist them in realizing meanings and processes not otherwise available to them (Roberts & Rousseau, 1989).

Current Quantitative Approaches to Measuring Culture

Quantitative approaches to collecting data on organizational culture consist of public, replicable, standardized procedures for obtaining and scoring information on the elements within culture's conceptual domain. Such methods include highly structured procedures, techniques, and instrumentation, such as interview schedules, questionnaires, and Q-sorts. The essence of this approach is a priori structuring of stimuli to which organization members are exposed during data collection. The common content participants respond to facilitates the application of uniform categorization and scoring systems useful for data summary, comparison, analysis, and reduction, as well as for replication and cross-validation. Note, however, that structured assessment producing a readily scorable set of information facilitates, but does not necessitate, statistical analysis. Analytical strategies are essentially a separate issue. Assessment is the focus of this chapter.

Common Content. Obtaining information about cultural factors quantitatively involves a priori identification of a feasible set of dimensions, categories, or elements likely to be uncovered. Theory and previous research and experience are sources of this feasible set. Identifying a feasible set of variables requires:

1. *Well-grounded constructs*: Dimensions to be assessed require a basis in previous theory and research, supporting the assumption that certain dimensions are generalizable or generic across situations or organizational settings. The more rigorous the assessment scheme, the more grounded this assumption in theory and research. Rigor is not and should not be treated as synonymous with quantitativeness, but refers to the strength of inference made possible by a given research study (Staw, 1985). Relevant terms here are confidence, specification, generalizability, and replication.

2. *Choice of a unit of measurement*: Organization members require a frame of reference to make use of standardized descriptors (for instance, short/tall, participative/authoritarian). Whether the phenomena studied are organizational, functional, or departmental must be specified. Failure to do this creates problems in obtaining consensus across respondents, as was the case in much of the early research on organizational climate (Rousseau, 1988). In the case of culture, the focal unit—such as firm, department, or work group—must be specified. Failure to do so risks the ambiguity that also plagued much of the early climate research. When the existence of climates is inferred based on statistical agreement at a specific level of aggregation although units go unspecified (for example, "Management is trustworthy," "Decisions are referred upward") rather than

respondents' actual descriptions of a particular unit ("Managers in this department are trustworthy," "Decisions are referred upward to the executive level"), the reality of aggregated climate anywhere other than in the researcher's mind is questionable.

3. *Choice of a focus*: When priorities are set among possible dimensions for study, certain factors are assessed and others omitted. Though all research omits some variables while addressing others, omissions are often quite obvious when measures are specified a priori. No quantitative assessment (or in fact any other) can be all things to all people. Exclusion of certain variables is inevitable.

Subjects, Informants, or Respondents? Organization members participating in studies of their organization's culture play a different role in research depending on the type of assessment conducted. *Informants* interact directly with researchers, using their own terms and concepts to express their point of view, structuring to some extent the direction of the research through their answers to researcher questions. Members who react to stimuli provided by the researcher, such as structured questions, a questionnaire response format, or cards on a Q-sort, serve as *respondents* in the research. A good deal of organizational research employs key informants (that is, individuals construed to have special or more complete information than others in the organization). Qualitative research on culture to some extent focuses upon key informants, who are often drawn from the organization's elite—its executives and middle managers. Informants, identified as those possessing special or more complete knowledge, are often relied upon for veridical information without systematic assessment of their reliability. In contrast, data provided by respondents tends to be subjected to rules of evidence to confirm accuracy or confidence (for example, statistical tests in the research on climate [James, 1982]) and consensual validation (for example, interrater agreement). Research that employs members as respondents tends to be more cross-sectional in nature, involving more members from diverse positions and perspectives in organizations, a pattern which has an impact on the content of the cultures revealed by these distinct approaches as well as on their apparent or observed intensity and distribution (see section on results below). Both approaches contrast with methods treating members as subjects, such as participant observation (Whyte, 1949), field stimulation (Salancik, 1979), and unobtrusive measures research (Webb, Campbell, Schwartz, & Sechrest, 1966) where individual employees are the passive objects of study.

Some Quantitative Measures of Culture. For this chapter, a search was conducted of the existing literature on quantitative assessments of culture. In identifying what researchers are doing with this methodology, it is first necessary to specify what falls into the category of quantitative culture assessment for the purposes of this chapter, and what is excluded. Research employing a standardized a priori specified response set constitutes quantitative assessment. When the context of this response set is any of the elements comprising culture as summarized in Figure 5.1, an aspect of culture is assessed. Thus, studies assessing behavioral norms attached to organizations and their subunits, values espoused regarding organizational actions or preferred outcomes, and other cultural elements with an organizational frame of reference would be included here. Traditional "values" scales such as the Organizational Value Dimensions Questionnaire (Shartle, 1965, 1966) would be excluded because despite the label, they assess the individual respondent's own point of view regarding what is good or poor, acceptable or unacceptable. Practitioner-oriented inventories that lack research supporting their psychometric integrity (as cited by Jones & Pfeiffer, 1975; Ott, 1989) are typically omitted here unless there is evidence of widespread use. Also excluded is what might be tagged as "old wine in new bottles" — that is, climate surveys labeled "culture inventories." These include questionnaires assessing traditional climate concepts such as atmosphere, involvement, communication, and supervision by means of an "organizational culture survey" (see Glaser, Zamanou, & Hacker, 1987, for an example). Note again that climate represents individual perceptions or descriptive beliefs regarding organizational experiences, while culture is essentially shared social cognitions within a unit.

Given the model of culture as layers of elements varying in observability and accessibility, it would be reasonable to expect quantitative assessments of culture to focus on more observable elements. Such is the case. Table 5.2 summarizes the content, structure, psychometric properties, and applications of seven examples of quantitative assessments of culture. Their content varies from values regarding priorities or preferences (for example, Sashkin & Fulmer, 1985; Enz, 1986; O'Reilly, Chatman, & Caldwell, 1988) to behavioral norms, expectations regarding how members should behave and interact with others (for example, Allen & Dyer, 1980; Kilmann & Saxton, 1983; Cooke & Lafferty, 1984, 1989). The focus of these quantitative assessments is on cultural elements that constitute the middle range, between objective and subjective, based on the framework described earlier. These cross-sectional approaches to assessing culture facilitate assessments of many members' perspectives. In no case are key informants, such as executives, relied on to provide culture descriptors, but rather multiple members' perspectives are assessed.

Content. Measures of behavioral norms surveyed here show a fair amount of overlap in the dimensions used to assess this aspect of culture. The task-people distinction underlies the conceptual models used by both Kilmann and Saxton (1983) and Cooke and Lafferty (1984, 1989) consistent with the prominence given this dimension in leadership research (for example, Blake & Mouton, 1964) and in personality theory (for instance, Cooke & Lafferty, 1989). The conceptual framework underlying both instruments has task versus people intersect with another dimension, yielding a two-by-two model in the Kilmann-Saxton Culture-Gap Survey (1983) and a circumplex in the Organizational Culture Inventory (OCI) (Cooke & Lafferty, 1989). The second dimensions in the two models also resemble each other. Kilmann and Saxton characterize the latter dimension as short- versus long-term, operationalizing that in terms of support and relationships versus innovation and freedom, whereas the OCI

Table 5.2. Some Culture Assessment Instruments.

Title:	Norms Diagnostic Index (Allen & Dyer, 1980)	Kilmann-Saxton Culture-Gap Survey (Kilmann & Saxton, 1983)
Aspect:	Behavioral norms.	Behavioral norms.
Focus:	Norms, the building blocks of culture, are the expected, accepted, and supported ways of behaving.	Descriptions of what actually happens and expectations of others. Instrument assesses separately actual operating norms and norms that should be operating if performance, job satisfaction, and morale are to be increased.
Dimensions:	Seven primary scales: Performance Facilitation, Job Involvement, Training, Leader-Subordinate Interaction, Policies and Procedures, Confrontation, and Supportive Climate. Scales were derived from both factor analyses and judgment (Allen & Dyer, 1980)	Four scales reflecting a two-by-two framework (Technical/Human and Short Term/Long Term): Task Support, Task Innovation, Social Relationships, and Personal Freedom.
Levels:	Individual level of measurement.	Individual level of measurement aggregated to work group.
Format:	Likert scales (1 to 5, 6 = Don't know) k = 38.	Paired comparisons (k = 28).
Reliabilities:	Not reported.	KR-20 internal consistency reliabilities were .57, .23, .72, to .26 for the above scales. Test-retest reliabilities (one month) ranged from .83 to .94.
Consensual validity:	Not reported.	Not tested.
Construct validity:	Not reported.	Stable four-factor solution across samples (Saxton, 1987). Scales may be multidimensional.
Criterion-related validity:	Scales have low to moderate correlations with the Job Descriptive Index (Smith, Kendall, & Hulin, 1969), with high correlations between the NDI's Supportive Climate and the JDI's Work and People scales.	Weak relations with group and organizational morale (Saxton, 1987).
Settings:	Manufacturing and retail firms, migrant labor camps.	U.S. for-profit and not-for-profit organizations.
Title:	Organizational Culture Inventory (Human Synergistics, 1986)	Organizational Value Congruence Scale (Enz, 1986)
Aspect:	Behavioral norms.	Similarity of individual values to those of top management.

Focus:	Behaviors that facilitate fitting into the organization and meeting expectations of co-workers.	Organizational values are preferences or priorities held by a group or individual regarding their organizations' actions or outcomes. Perceived congruence between the individual and organization affects both employee and management behavior.
Dimensions:	Twelve scales arranged in a circumplex (based on the intersection of two dimensions: Task/People and Security/Satisfaction): Humanistic/Helpful, Affiliation, Approval, Conventionality, Dependence, Avoidance, Oppositional, Power, Competitive, Perfectionism, Achievement, Self-Actualizing.	Single score summed over twenty-two items (for example, professionalism, profits, adaptability, high morale). Top five rank ordering of values "any company should have" also assessed.
Levels:	Individual-level assessment. Frame of reference can be varied in the instructions. Aggregated to work group and organizational levels.	Individual-level measurement.
Format:	1 to 5 Likert scales (k120).	Likert scales (1 to 4; 5 = Don't know; Enz, 1986; 1 to 7 scale; Enz, 1988). (k = 22)
Reliabilities:	Cronbach's alpha ranging from .70 to .96 (Cooke & Rousseau, 1988; Roberts, Rousseau, & LaPorte, 1990). LISREL analysis indicates half the scales might be multi-dimensional, loading on more than one factor (Aquino & Rousseau, 1990).	Split-half reliabilities of .87 and .95 in different samples (Enz, 1988).
Consensual validity:	Within-unit agreement on OCI responses (Cooke & Rousseau, 1988; Roberts, Rousseau, & LaPorte, 1990).	Not tested.
Construct validity:	Stable factor solution across samples (Cooke & Rousseau, 1988; Roberts, Rousseau, & LaPorte, 1990).	No consensus between top management and department employees on value congruity (Enz, 1988).
Criterion-related validity:	Concurrent correlations between culture styles and satisfaction, propensity to leave, person-job fit (Roberts, Rousseau, & LaPorte, 1990) and organizational performance (Rousseau, in press).	Perceived value–congruity correlates significantly with departmental power. Perceived congruity accounted for departmental power more so than did actual or latent value congruity (Enz, 1988). Top management's perceptions of a department's value congruity correlates most highly with department power.
Settings:	Business firms in United States, Canada, New Zealand, Thailand, and Western Europe; U.S. military units, FAA; nonprofit organizations.	Quick-service restaurant chain and robotics firm.

Table 5.2. Some Culture Assessment Instruments, Cont'd.

	Organizational Culture Profile (O'Reilly, Chatman, & Caldwell, 1988)	*Organizational Beliefs Questionnaire* ("Pillars of excellence"; Sashkin & Fulmer, 1985)
Title:		
Aspect:	Values.	Values shared by organization members.
Focus:	Values regarding what is important, how to behave, or what attitudes are appropriate.	Value functions that must be present to get work done (based on Parsons's [1968] organizational functions framework).
Dimensions:	Fifty-four items sorted via a Q-sort technique into nine categories (from most to least characteristic), generated following review of academic and practitioner literatures on culture (for example, being innovative, an emphasis on quality, fairness, flexibility, decisiveness, being calm, being precise, fitting in). Yields an overall profile of organization across fifty-four items. Items chosen to minimize redundancy and social desirability and to enhance generalizability across organizations and readability	Ten values: enjoying work, being best, innovating or taking risks, attending to details, valuing people, attaining top quality, communicating, growing in production/ profit, managing "hands on," believing in a common "organizational philosophy."
Levels:	Individual descriptions of actual organization. Also used to obtain individual preferences regarding organizational values (Organizational Culture Preference). Person-organization fit computed by comparing Preference scores with aggregated Organizational scores.	Individual.
Format:	Nine categories, forced symmetrical distribution. (k = 54)	Five-point Likert scales (strongly agree to strongly disagree). Items are phrased to avoid social desirability bias: For each scale one item is stated positively and the other negatively and the wording constructed to make it difficult to determine item's desirability. (k = 20)
Reliabilities:	Test-retest reliability (one year) of Organizational Culture Preference Q-sort is .73 for sixteen M.B.A. students (Chatman, 1988).	None reported.
Consensual validity:	Interrater agreement ranged from .80 to .90 for eight accounting firms.	Relatively low within-organization variance in responses (Sashkin & Fulmer, 1985).

Construct validity:	Industry experts identified specific accounting firms by their aggregated profiles (Chatman, 1988).
Criterion-related validity:	Person-organization fit predicts incentive to stay in organization, satisfaction, and commitment.
	Not reported.
Settings:	Accounting firms, business school students.
	Not reported. Norms have been proposed for score needed to achieve particular levels of "excellence" (Sashkin & Fulmer, 1985).
	Business organizations (N = 100), management students.
Title:	*Corporate Culture Survey* (Glaser, 1983)
Aspect:	Strength and type of culture — that is, "shared values and beliefs."
Dimensions:	Types — Based on Deal and Kennedy's (1982) description of culture types: Tough Guy/Gal Macho, Work Hard/Play Hard, Bet Your Company, and The Process cultures. Strength — widely shared values and philosophy of management and other indicators of intensity.
Levels:	Individual descriptions of their present organizations. Is also used to obtain an "ideal" or desired culture profile and to compute "gap" between ideal and actual.
Format:	Likert scales (0 to 4) (k = 50).
Reliabilities:	Not reported.
Consensual validity:	Not reported.
Construct validity:	Not reported.
Settings:	Business organizations.

refers to the second dimension as security- versus satisfaction-oriented (along the lines of Maslow's need hierarchy). In both instruments, this second dimension refers to the degree to which individuals are encouraged to avoid conflict and protect themselves, or to innovate and take risks. Thus, to some extent, these instruments contrast a risk-averse, behavior-inhibiting set of norms with behavior-enhancing growth-oriented expectations. Together, these instruments suggest that norms derived from theories of behavior in organizations share a common focus (tasks or people) and reflect both behavior-inhibiting (for example, risk-averse) and behavior encouraging (for instance, risk-seeking) expectations.

The other instrument focusing on behavioral norms, the Norms Diagnostic Index (NDI; Allen & Dyer, 1980), is reminiscent of a climate survey, containing a collection of different dimensions along which organizations can be described (such as performance facilitation, training, supportive climate, and so on) without an underlying integrative framework. The parallel between the NDI and a climate survey may reflect the fact that the NDI is the oldest of the surveys reviewed here, embodying the transition from climate to culture as a popular concept for organizational assessment.

Values are assessed in the Organizational Beliefs Questionnaire (Sashkin & Fulmer, 1985), Organizational Values Congruence Scale (Enz, 1986, 1988), Corporate Culture Survey (Glaser, 1983), and Organizational Culture Profile (O'Reilly, Chatman, & Caldwell, 1988). Their content is diverse, with Sashkin and Fulmer (1985) and O'Reilly, Chatman, and Caldwell (1988) employing such dimensions as innovation, quality, and common culture. In contrast, Enz (1986) uses somewhat more abstract constructs such as professionalism, control over environment, and social well-being. Glaser's (1983) survey yields atheoretical categories scored along dimensions of the popular book *Corporate Culture: The Rites and Rituals of Organizational Life* by Deal and Kennedy (1982).

In short, the content of inventories assessing values and behavioral norms does vary. Certain dimensions do, however, appear on several questionnaires, expressed either as values or

Table 5.3. Generic Dimensions for Cultural Values and Behavioral Norms.

	Dimensions	
Task	*Interpersonal*	*Individual*
Descriptions		
Innovation	Communication	
Quality	Valuing people	Freedom
Analysis	Fairness	Self-expression
Risk taking	Fitting in	Flexibility
Perfectionism	Team spirit/morale	
	Examples	
Value	Fear of failure	Honesty	Self-actualization
	Prefer status quo	Integrity	
Behavioral	Never make a	Approval seeking	Personal expression
	mistake		
Norm	Challenge new	Open communication	
	idea		

as behaviors. When overlapping dimensions are considered, three general categories are evident (Table 5.3):

1. Task-related values and behaviors, such as risk taking and quality
2. Interpersonal values and behaviors, such as supporting and communicating
3. Individual values and behaviors addressing the enhancement of organization members personally, including freedom and self-expression

Together, these dimensions reflect an etic perspective on cultural elements. Moreover, values and behaviors can be expressed in similar terms, even though values and norms are distinct concepts. For example, expressing a preference for creativity and actually supporting and rewarding it are distinct social phenomena, though a core theme exists. Comparable dimensions of the type listed in Table 5.3 may apply across several distinct types of culture elements, such as hidden assumptions, norms, values, and patterns of activity. Assumptions and values may be configured in terms of task as well as interpersonal and individual foci, as in the case of group psychodynamics involving risk aversion (task), interunit conflict (interpersonal), and limited member autonomy (individual). The same may be true for behavioral norms, which might promote innovation (task), teamwork (interpersonal), and personal discretion and judgment (individual). For example, cultural analyses of high-risk organizations such as nuclear power plants frequently stress the predominance of controlling and restrictive task, interpersonal, and individual values and norms while advocating the need for innovation, teamwork, and operator discretion particularly in crisis situations (Hirschhorn, 1983; Perrow, 1984; Rousseau, 1989).

Consensus. Though consensus is a sine qua non for identification of a norm and also for the attribution that a particular preference or priority is an organizational value, it is noteworthy that consensual validity has not been reported in any published form for several of the instruments surveyed here. The OCI (Cooke & Lafferty, 1984, 1989) demonstrates moderate — that is, squared correlation ratios of approximately 12 percent — within-unit agreement (Cooke & Rousseau, 1988; Roberts, Rousseau, & LaPorte, 1990), with consensus strongest when within-subunit agreement is investigated (for example, by department, level, military operating unit). Sashkin and Fulmer (1985) also examined within-organization covariance for the Organizational Beliefs Questionnaire and found it to be relatively low, while in contrast Enz (1988) found virtually no consensus between top management and employees within specific departments on values the organization purported to espouse. Failure of the other researchers to test for consensus indicates, however, that a major methodological concern has yet to be satisfied in the use of individual-level data to describe something about the organization or unit.

Where consensus is tested, results question the generalizability of the notion that organizations have a strong pervasive dominant culture. Rather, data suggest that organizations may in fact be strongly subcultural, with behavioral norms operating at the level of the subunit. Some theory supports this (Schneider & Reichers, 1983). Cooke and Rousseau (1988) found that the organizations they surveyed were strongly subcultural by functions—marketing, production, and so on—but also by organizational level. Norms supporting achievement, personal initiative, and teamwork characterized higher organization levels in contrast to norms supporting conflict avoidance, competition, and dependence characteristic of lower levels in organizations. That such norms differentiate hierarchical levels suggests a link between organizational structure and cultural elements.

The lack of consensus among members of different units regarding the organizational values demonstrated in Enz's (1988) research also suggests that members of different organization levels can experience divergent priorities and outcome preferences. Enz goes on to argue that congruence when it exists between departmental and top-management values is associated with greater power and influence for congruent departments. Although evidence for the subcultural nature of organizational norms and values is provided by several quantitative assessments, Chatman (1988) found substantial convergence in organizational values reported by respondents from different levels of public accounting firms using her Organizational Culture Profile. In sum, where qualitative research has highlighted uniformity and mutuality in descriptions of culture, evidence from quantitative assessments of culture suggests that the differences can be as striking as the similarities.

Dominant cultures are characteristic of some but not all organizations, necessitating perhaps more attention to varied patterns and distributions of cultural elements in organizations. The various patterns of agreement evident in quantitative assessments suggest two distinct attributes of culture: intensity and integration.

Intensity is the extent to which members of a unit agree on the norms, values, or other culture content associated with the unit. Organizations with strong norms promoting service or entrepreneurship have intensive cultures, whereas new organizations or those in transition (due to culture change or member turnover) have weaker, less intensive cultures. Intensity is evident when intraunit agreement among members regarding culture content is great. Greater consistency in member behavior is expected where intensive cultures are evident.

Integration is the extent to which units within an organization share a common culture. Organizations with a pervasive dominant culture, such as hierarchically controlled power-oriented military units (Rousseau & Cooke, 1988) have highly integrated cultures. In contrast, firms structured functionally — as in the case with many manufacturers — might have strong subcultures (for instance, engineering versus marketing) and a weaker overall corporate culture. Low cultural integration is associated with within-firm differentiation in goals, structures, and personnel practices. Integration is in effect an intensive culture at the organizational level.

Since culture involves a diverse array of values and beliefs, organizations may simultaneously have a strong dominant culture (for example, regarding how business is conducted — quality versus quantity, risk aversion versus innovation) and intensive subcultures as well (for instance, regarding how people are to be treated — teamwork in manufacturing and entrepreneurship in sales). Recent research on nuclear-powered aircraft carriers reveals such a pattern, where the organization's dominant, shared culture emphasizes power and dependence while particular subunits also stress achievement, teamwork, and individual participation in technical decisions (Rousseau & Cooke, 1988). Quantitative assessments facilitate intra- and interunit comparisons — in fact requiring them to establish the instrumentations' psychometric properties — and can reveal a diversity of cultural patterns.

Research Results

Use of quantitative assessments for statistical inferences has resulted in testing of a number of hypotheses and research questions. Some general findings are reviewed here.

1. *Is there intraunit agreement on organizational values and behavioral norms?* As described earlier, diverse patterns are in

evidence, though in general consensus on values and norms exists within departments, functions, and levels of organizations. The degree of consistency between units varies in organizations and cannot be assumed.

2. *What influences do dominant cultures have on organizational process or outcomes?* Little systematic research — quantitative or qualitative — exists on the impact of culture on organizational effectiveness. When different types of organizational strategies are considered, research (Cooke & Rousseau, 1988; Roberts, Rousseau, & LaPorte, 1990; Rousseau & Cooke, 1988; Rousseau, in press) suggests that organizations with reliability-oriented strategies (avoiding error and operating predictably and without catastrophe, as is the case in military operations and air traffic control) have behavior-inhibiting norms (for instance, risk aversion, hierarchical control, conflict avoidance, critical opposition). Organizations with performance-oriented strategies (growth, adaptability, innovation) are characterized by behavior-enhancing norms (creativity, self-expression, teamwork, encouragement). Thus culture and strategy may well be linked. A recent study suggests successful charitable fund-raising campaigns have more achievement-oriented and self-expressive norms than those that raise less money. Less successful campaigns are associated with norms of conflict avoidance and competition (Rousseau, in press).

3. *Is culture related to other organizational characteristics and processes?* Congruity between subunit members' beliefs regarding values and those of top management correlate with departmental power (Enz, 1986), suggesting that the pattern of cultural elements within an organization affects subunit access to and influence over top management. Although behavioral norms are differentiated across levels in organizations, there is a systematic pattern in the *types* of norms characterizing higher and lower levels. High-level executives report that achievement, self-actualization, humanistic, helpful, and affiliative behavior predominate, while lower-level employees report an emphasis on dependence, conventionality, and approval (Cooke & Rousseau, 1988). In

short, executives experience the workplace as more team-oriented and creative, whereas their employees see it as more controlling and inhibiting.

4. *What influences do cultures have on individual outcomes?* Allen and Dyer (1980) found correlations between their measure of culture and job satisfaction. Saxton (1987) found weak relations between cultural dimensions and group and organizational morale. Roberts, Rousseau, and LaPorte (1990) found significant relationships between behavioral norms and member satisfactions, propensity to stay, person-organization fit, and (lack of) role conflict. Organizational norms supporting what they termed a *satisfaction* culture — (emphasizing achievement, self-expression, humanistic/helpful, and affiliative norms) produced positive effects on these outcomes, while *security-oriented* norms such as power, perfectionism, conventionality, and approval were negatively related to these individual outcomes.

5. *How idiosyncratic are cultural elements to specific organizations?* Martin and Siehl (1983) have argued that members believe their own organizations to be unique to such a great extent that this belief is itself highly generalizable. Ideally tests of whether cultural elements are unique to particular organizations or generalizable across them should come from independent assessments of several organizations without a priori categories or cultural dimensions. Such comparative analyses are not currently available. However, quantitative assessments using a priori dimensions of culture have revealed patterns of behavioral norms and values common to several organizations. Effects of level, strategy, and function noted earlier suggest that certain behavioral norms may characterize specific types of organizations or positions. But it must be noted that while quantitative analysis often seeks patterns and generalizability and qualitative research idiosyncrasy and distinctiveness, more comparative qualitative research is necessary to resolve this research question.

Future Research on Culture

The tendency to treat culture as univocal—having one meaning and set of elements—has deprived the field of the rich array of theory and hypotheses such a complex concept can generate. Methodological debates, prejudices, and preferences seem to have stifled much of the constructive work that might have been expected in the decade or so since culture first entered the organizational behavior mainstream. The potential remains to be fulfilled.

Quantitative assessment offers opportunity for inter-organizational comparisons to assess often-assumed relations between culture and organization success, strategy, and goals. Qualitative research can explore the meanings behind the patterns. Some questions remain: If top managers really do have different sets of norms and expectations than their subordinates, what implications do these have for the values and priorities the organization embodies, the service or products it produces, and the integration of members into the organization? How do members of organizations with weak cultures (where mutuality or shared beliefs are lacking) make sense of their environment? If culture changes mean unfreezing of old values and beliefs, how do people interpret and react to times of transition and how do they relearn a culture?

The layers of culture elements different theorists have described are more than just a typology; they also represent a framework that organization members must master to become integrated into the organization. What do they learn first? Behavioral norms? Or priorities and values? Is it easier to socialize members when material and symbolic artifacts are pervasively in evidence? What are more commonly shared: behavior norms, values, or basic assumptions? What is the impact of disagreement among members regarding these?

How members internalize culture from their experiences with the organization is a critical topic of study if we are to better understand the nature of cultural elements, and the impact of norms, values, and basic assumptions on behavior, sense making and membership. Though culture has widely been discussed as a process — that is, what the organization *is* — it has not really been studied as one. Research must go beyond description to explore learning, socialization, and change.

These research questions offer great opportunity. Failure to apply a variety of methods to assessing culture limits our understanding of it. Characterizing cultural elements in terms of generalizable dimensions fosters interunit comparisons and understanding of systematic effects, while qualitative probing can explore how members interpret and internalize these features. Clearly there is a need for both etic and emic perspectives. The structured assessments described here yield a number of etic categories found to be applicable in diverse organizational settings. Dimensions of task performance, interpersonal relations, and individual integrity are relevant descriptors in all organizational settings. How these are affected idiosyncratically by the personality and style of executives or the subjective interpretations made by members requires the combined resources of quantitative and qualitative methods — the logical next step.

Conclusion

Culture research remains an unpaid promissory note in the field of organizational behavior. Driven largely by methodological preferences and a topical subject matter rather than by theory, we are still in the earliest phases of understanding culture's role in organizations.

Notes

1. The author holds degrees in both anthropology and industrial and organizational psychology. She recalls her first industrial and organizational psychology course (about 1972), in which the instructor said, "In this field, only the methods and not the findings generalize."

References

Allen, R. F., & Dyer, F. J. (1980). A tool for tapping the organizational unconscious. *Personnel Journal*, 192–199.

Allen, R. F., Kraft, C., Allen, J., & Certner, B. (1987). *The organizational unconscious: How to create the corporate culture you want and need.* Morristown, NJ: Human Resources Institute.

Aquino, K., & Rousseau, D. M. (1990). Confirmatory factor analysis on comparable measures of personality and organizational culture. Manuscript under review.

Barley, S. R. (1983). Semiotics and the study of occupational and organizational cultures. *Administrative Science Quarterly, 28*, 393–413.

Becker, H. S., & Geer, B. (1970). Participant observation and interviewing: A comparison. In W. Filstead (Ed.), *Qualitative methodology* (pp. 133–142). Chicago: Rand McNally.

Bion, W. (1959). *Experiences in groups.* New York: Basic Books.

Blake, R. R., & Mouton, J. S. (1964). *The managerial grid.* Houston: Gulf.

Chatman, J. A. (1988). *Matching people and organizations: Selection and socialization in public accounting firms.* Unpublished doctoral dissertation, University of California at Berkeley, School of Business Administration.

Cooke R. A., & Lafferty, J. C. (1984). *Level V Organizational Culture Inventory.* Plymouth, MI: Human Synergistics, Inc.

Cooke, R. A., & Lafferty, J. C. (1989). *Organizational Culture Inventory.* Plymouth, MI: Human Synergistics, Inc.

Cooke, R. A., & Rousseau, D. M. (1981). Problem solving in complex systems: A model of system problem-solving applied to schools. *Educational Administration Quarterly, 17*, 15–41.

Cooke, R. A., & Rousseau, D. M. (1988). Behavioral norms and expectations: A quantitative approach to the assessment of organizational culture. *Group and organization studies, 13*, 245–273.

Deal, T. E. (1986). Deeper culture: Mucking, muddling, and metaphors. *Training and Development Journal*, 32–33.

Deal, T. E., & Kennedy, A. A. (1982). *Corporate cultures: The rites and rituals of organizational life.* Reading, MA: Addison-Wesley.

Enz, C. (1986). *Power and shared values in the corporate culture.* Ann Arbor, MI: UMI.

Enz, C. (1988). The role of value congruity in intraorganizational power. *Administrative Science Quarterly, 33,* 284–304.

Geertz, C. (1973). *The interpretation of cultures.* New York: Basic Books.

Glaser, R. (1983). *The corporate culture survey.* Bryn Mawr, PA: Organizational Design and Development.

Glaser, S. R., Zamanou, S., & Hacker, K. (1987). Measuring and interpreting organizational culture. *Management Communication Quarterly, 1,* 173–198.

Glick, W. H. (1985). Conceptualizing and measuring organizational and psychological climate: Pitfalls in multilevel research. *Academy of Management Review, 10*(3), 601–616.

Green, T. (1986, August). The rich and risky trade in jade. *Smithsonian,* pp. 17, 28–40.

Hirschhorn, L. (1983). *Beyond mechanization: Work and technology in a postindustrial age.* Cambridge, MA: MIT Press.

Hirschhorn, L. (1988). *The workplace within: Psychodynamics of organizational life.* Cambridge, MA: MIT Press.

James, L. R. (1982). Aggregation bias in estimates of perceptual agreement. *Journal of Applied Psychology, 67*(2), 219–229.

James, L. R., Hater, J. J., Gent, M. J., & Bruni, J. R. (1978). Psychological climate: Implications from cognitive social learning theory and interactional psychology. *Personnel Psychology, 31,* 783–813.

James, L. R., & Sells, S. B. (1981). Psychological climate: Theoretical perspectives and empirical research. In D. Magnusson (Ed.), *Toward a psychology of situations: An interactional perspective* (pp. 275–295). Hillsdale, NJ: Erlbaum.

Jones, J. E., & Pfeiffer, J. W. (1975). *The 1975 annual handbook for group facilitators.* San Diego, CA: University Associates.

Joyce, W. F., & Slocum, J. W., Jr. (1984). Collective climate: Agreement as a basis for defining aggregate climates in organizations. *Academy of Management Journal, 27,* 721–742.

Kilmann, R. H., & Saxton, M. J. (1983). *The Kilmann-Saxton Culture-Gap Survey.* Pittsburgh, PA: Organizational Design Consultants.

Kilmann, R. H., Saxton, M. J., Serpa, R., & Associates. (1985). *Gaining control of the corporate culture*. San Francisco: Jossey-Bass.

Kroeber, A. I., & Kluckhohn, C. (1952). *Culture: A critical review of concepts and definitions*. New York: Vintage Books.

Likert, R. (1967). *The human organization*. New York: McGraw-Hill.

Louis, M. R. (1983). Organizations as culture-bearing milieux. In L. R. Pondy, P. J. Frost, G. Morgan, & T. C. Dandridge (Eds.), *Organizational symbolism*. Greenwich, CT: JAI Press.

Martin, J., & Siehl, C. (1983). Organizational culture and counterculture: An uneasy symbiosis. *Organizational Dynamics, 12*(2), 52–64.

Morey, N. C., & Luthans, F. (1984). An emic perspective and ethnoscience methods for organizational research. *Academy of Management Review, 9*, 27–36.

Morgan, G., & Smircich, L. (1980). The case for qualitative research. *Academy of Management Review, 5*, 491–500.

Nisbett, R. E., & Wilson, T. D. (1977). Telling more than we can know: Verbal reports on mental processes. *Psychological Review, 84*, 231–259.

O'Reilly, C. A. (1983). *Corporations, cults, and organizational culture: Lessons from Silicon Valley firms*. Paper presented at the August meeting of the Academy of Management, Dallas, TX.

O'Reilly, C. A., Chatman, J. A., & Caldwell, D. (1988). *People, jobs, and organizational culture* (working paper). University of California at Berkeley, School of Business Administration.

Ouchi, W. G. (1981). *Theory Z: How American business can meet the Japanese challenge*. Reading, MA: Addison-Wesley.

Parsons, T. (1968). *The structure of social action* (2 vols.). New York: Free Press.

Peck, M. (1988). *A different drum: Community making and peace*. New York: Simon & Schuster.

Perrow, C. (1984). *Normal accidents: Living with high-risk technologies*. New York: Basic Books.

Peters, T. J., & Waterman, R. H. (1982). *In search of excellence: Lessons from America's best-run companies*. New York: Harper & Row.

Pondy, L. R., & Rousseau, D. M. (1980). *Quantitative versus qualitative methods: An issue of public and private methods.* Paper presented at the August OB/OD/OT Doctoral Consortium, Academy of Management, Detroit.

Roberts, K. H., & Rousseau, D. M. (1989). Research in nearly failure free high reliability organizations: Having the bubble. *IEEE Transactions, 36,* 132–139.

Roberts, K. H., Rousseau, D. M., & LaPorte, T. R. (1990). *The cultures of high reliability military organizations* (working paper). University of California at Berkeley, School of Business Administration.

Rousseau, D. M. (1988). The construction of climate in organizational research. In C. L. Cooper & I. Robertson (Eds.), *International review of industrial and organizational psychology* (Vol. 3). New York: Wiley.

Rousseau, D. M. (1989). The price of success? Security oriented cultures in high reliability organization. *Industrial Crisis Quarterly, 3,* 285–302.

Rousseau, D. M. (in press). Normative beliefs in fund-raising organizations: Linking culture to organizational performance and individual responses. *Group and Organization Studies.*

Rousseau, D. M., & Cooke, R. A. (1988). Cultures of reliability and performance: A field study of the USS Carl Vinson. Paper presented at the August meeting of the Academy of Management, Anaheim, CA.

Salancik, G. R. (1979). Field stimulations for organizational behavior research. *Administrative Science Quarterly, 24,* 638–649.

Sashkin, M. (1983). *Pillars of excellence — The organizational beliefs questionnaire.* Bryn Mawr, PA: Organization Design and Development.

Sashkin, M., & Fulmer, R. (1985). *Measuring organizational excellence culture with a validated questionnaire.* Paper presented at the August meeting of the Academy of Management, San Diego, CA.

Sathe, V. (1985). *Culture and related corporate realities.* Homewood, IL: Irwin.

Saxton, M. J. (1987). *The validation of the Kilman-Saxton culture-gap*

*survey to test a theory of work group cultural norms and an explora-
tion of a nomological network of culture.* Unpublished doctoral
dissertation, University of Pittsburgh.

Schein, E. H. (1984). Suppose we took culture seriously. *Academy
of Management OD Newsletter*, Summer 1984, 2ff.

Schein, E. H. (1985). *Organizational culture and leadership: A dynamic view.* San Francisco: Jossey-Bass.

Schein, E. H. (1986a). A rejoinder to Sashkin and further clarification. *Academy of Management OD Newsletter*, Winter, 6–7.

Schein, E. H. (1986b). What you need to know about organizational culture. *Training and Development Journal, 40*, 30–35.

Schneider, B. (1972). Organizational climate: Individual preference and organizational realities. *Journal of Applied Psychology,
56*, 211–217.

Schneider, B., Parkington, J. J., & Buton, V. M. (1980). Employee
and customer perceptions of service in banks. *Administrative
Science Quarterly, 25*, 252–267.

Schneider, B., & Reichers, A. E. (1983). On the etiology of climates. *Personnel Psychology, 36*, 19–39.

Shartle, C. L. (1965). *Organizational value dimensions questionnaire:
Business firm.* Columbus: Ohio State University, Bureau of
Business Research.

Shartle, C. L., & Stogdill, R. (1966). *Manual for value scale: The
Business Firm (Form BBR-65)* Columbus: Ohio State University,
Program for Research in Leadership and Organization.

Siehl, C., & Martin, J. (1983). *Measuring organizational culture*
(working paper). Stanford University, School of Business.

Smircich, L. (1983). Concepts of culture and organizational
analysis. *Administrative Science Quarterly, 28*, 339–358.

Smith, P. C., Kendall, L. M., & Hulin, C. L. (1969). *The measurement
of satisfaction in work and retirement.* Chicago: Rand McNally.

Staw, B. M. (1985). Repairs on the road to relevance and vigor:
Some unexplored issues in publishing organizational research. In L. L. Cummings & P. J. Frost (Eds.), *Publishing in the
organizational sciences* (pp. 96–107). Homewood, IL: Irwin.

Sutton, R. I., & Rafaeli, A. (1988). Untangling the relationship
between displayed emotions and organizational sales: The

case of convenience stores. *Academy of Management Journal, 31,* 461–487.

Swartz, M., & Jordon, D. (1980). *Culture: an anthropological perspective.* New York: Wiley.

Uttal, B. (1983, Oct. 17). The corporate culture vultures. *Fortune.*

Van Maanen, J. (1979). Reclaiming qualitative methods for organizational research. *Administrative Science Quarterly, 24,* 520–526.

Van Maanen, J., & Schein, E. H. (1979). Toward a theory of organization socialization. In B. Staw (Ed.), *Research in organizational behavior: Vol. 1* (pp. 209–264). Greenwich, CT: JAI Press.

Wallace, A.F.C. (1970). *Culture and personality.* New York: Random House.

Webb, E. J., Campbell, D. T., Schwartz, R. D., & Sechrest, L. (1966). *Unobtrusive measures: Nonreactive research in the social sciences.* Chicago: Rand McNally.

Weick, K. (1979). Cognitive processes in organizations. In B. Staw (Ed.), *Research in organizational behavior: Vol. 1.* Greenwich, CT: JAI Press.

Weick, K. E. (1987). Organizational culture as a source of high reliability. *California Management Review, 29,* 112–127.

Whyte, W. F. (1949). The social structure of the restaurant. *American Journal of Sociology, 54,* 302–310.

Chapter 6

Fred Dansereau, Jr.
Joseph A. Alutto

Level-of-Analysis Issues in Climate and Culture Research

As other chapters of this book show, interest in climate and culture has found expression in a full range of publication outlets, including popular books and articles as well as scholarly journals. Popular publications exhort readers to change the culture or climate of organizations by hiring a "Lee Iacocca type" of leader, by emulating the societal values of the Japanese, or by creating institutional values supportive of "thriving on chaos" through the hiring and training of employees. These approaches seem to assume that the achievement of organizational success in reforming climate or culture occurs through interventions at the person, group, organizational, and societal levels of analysis—although it is rarely clear which type of intervention might prove most effective under a given set of conditions. Interestingly, in more scholarly presentations, there is often a similar concern with, and confusion about, the implications of levels of analysis for understanding the dynamics of forming culture or climate.

This chapter attempts to place the level-of-analysis issues that arise in discussions of climate and culture into a perspective that will allow consistent treatment and development. Although

Note: We gratefully acknowledge the comments of Benjamin Schneider and Irwin Goldstein on an earlier version of this chapter.

193

the approach discussed in this chapter relies heavily on a specific body of statistical reasoning, the reader should not feel overwhelmed by the methodological presentation. Instead, the reader should keep in mind the overriding purpose of this chapter—to emphasize the importance of overtly considering levels of analysis in theory construction and data analysis.

To organize the presentation of one approach to integrating the theoretical positions and research procedures used in the study of climate and culture at a variety of levels of analysis, this chapter uses four types of theoretical and empirical analyses, described and computerized by Dansereau, Alutto, and Yammarino (1984) and Dansereau and others (1986) single-level analysis, multiple-level analysis, multiple-variable analysis, and multiple-relationship analysis. An initial overview, which describes various issues in culture and climate research in terms of the four analyses, illustrates the purpose of each analytical approach. As each stage of analysis is described in a subsequent section of the chapter, alternative theoretical positions and research procedures are derived from previous studies of climate and culture.

Overview

Single-Level Analysis. To illustrate and show a need for single-level analysis, it is helpful to review a distinction made by Dansereau, Alutto, and Yammarino (1984) from the perspective of culture and climate research. To do so, let us consider the "value added" by each of four levels of analysis (persons, dyads, groups, and collectives) when we view one set of individuals. The *person* (or the lowest) level of analysis treats individuals as independent of each other. This allows for the issue raised by Louis (1985, p. 93) in her discussion of culture. She states, "Individual differences in the level of cultural participation . . . should not be overlooked as a contributor to variance. . . ." Groups add a particular type of dependency among individuals. This dependency stems from the direct interaction of individuals with each other. With this view, at least two particular forms of linkage become important: dyads and groups. In the *dyad* case individuals interact on a one-to-one basis, independent of other individuals with whom they may interact. This allows for the approach used by Falcione, Sussman, and Herden (1987), in which they focus on climate in terms of two-person dyads. In a *group*, defined as composed of three or more individuals, the interactions between two focal individuals may depend on their direct interactions with one or more other persons. This perspective can be seen in Schein's (1985) focus on the role of the leader in the formation of cultures in groups. Finally, the *collective* (or highest) level of analysis adds the notion that the dependencies among individuals are based on linkages that go beyond direct interpersonal interactions. Here, the notions of structure, hierarchical status, chain of command, and echelons (Miller, 1978) come into play. This approach can be seen in Glick's (1985) discussion of climate and of organizational-level processes.

Single-level analysis focuses on one level of analysis (for example, groups) with the objective of determining whether that level is or is not a locus of a particular aspect of culture or climate. The term *locus of culture* or *climate* is from Louis (1985), and is meant to suggest the possibility that a particular aspect of culture or climate may or may not be indigenous to a particular level of analysis. A decision to accept a level of analysis (for example, the group level) as appropriate, as we will see, requires an additional decision about how to view the units of analysis (all the groups) at that level. In contrast, a decision to reject a level of analysis as a locus means that we do not select the units of analysis at that level. Essentially, single-level analysis allows for decisions about these matters.

Multiple-Level Analysis. Research on culture and climate, however, has moved considerably beyond a consideration of only one level of analysis, which leads to a need for multiple-level analysis. For example, Van Maanen and Barley (1985) focus on (1) ecological (collective-level), (2) differential interaction (group- and dyad-level), and (3) individual (person-level) aspects of culture. The view of individuals (the person level) taken by Van Maanen and Barley (1985) differs from traditional individual-difference views where individuals are viewed as independent of each other. Likewise, different authors take different approaches to the appropriate levels of analysis for climate. For example, according to James, Joyce, and Slocum (1988), climate associates with the person *and* organizational levels of analysis. According to Glick (1988), climate emerges at the organizational level of analysis. Thus, Glick (1988) rejects a level of analysis of interest to James, Joyce, and Slocum (1988) – the person level. The antithetical nature of the two positions becomes apparent when we recognize that one cannot simultaneously reject and accept a particular level of analysis.

Multiple-level analysis allows for consideration of a variety of combinations of cultural or climate foci. Some combinations may include one or a few levels of analysis (persons only, persons and groups), whereas other combinations may include many levels of analysis (persons, dyads, groups, and collectivities). These combinations serve to identify, in multiple-level terms, the locus of a particular aspect of culture or climate. Such analyses also seem to clarify the antithetical nature of different combinations of levels of analysis.

Multiple-Variable and Multiple-Relationship Analyses. To allow for approaches that combine levels of analysis in very different (antithetical) ways, multiple-variable analysis focuses on how different variables or aspects of culture and climate may associate with different (antithetical) combinations of levels of analysis. For example, when the debate about climate between Glick (1988) and James, Joyce, and Slocum (1988) is viewed from this perspective, the authors' positions, although antithetical, both become plausible because the positions may refer to different aspects of climate (variables). Likewise, although the view of Van Maanen and Barley (1985) of individuals differs from traditional individual-difference views, both views become plausible because one can view each perspective as associated with different variables or concepts.

Finally, multiple-relationship analysis allows culture and climate to serve as moderators of various relationships among variables. In addition, it adds a consideration of time as a factor in the emergence of culture and climate at various levels of analysis.

Summary. We can focus first on single-level analysis provided that we recognize the interdependence among the four analyses, or that: (1) an interpretation at one level of analysis (single-level analysis) changes depending on interpretations at other levels of analysis (multiple-level analysis), (2) antithetical alternatives at one or many levels of analysis can become complementary because different variables may associate with different combinations of levels of analysis (multiple-variable analysis), and (3) many previous approaches contain assertions about the situations that are conducive to the development of climate or culture (multiple-relationship analysis).

Single-Level Analysis

Theoretical Issues

Single-level analysis focuses on one level of analysis (for example, the group level) and allows for four views of that level. Two alternative views allow for the possibility that a particular level does not serve as the locus of a particular aspect of culture or climate (the equivocal and inexplicable alternatives), whereas two other views allow for the possibility that a particular level of analysis serves as the locus of a particular aspect of culture and climate (parts and wholes).

Wholes. Although most previous researchers of climate and culture focus on at least one of the four key levels of analysis (persons, dyads, groups, or collectives), they view the selected level as containing "whole" units of analysis (that is, they focus on differences *between* the units of analysis at a level of analysis). The following four sets of examples illustrate this point for the person, dyad, group, and collective levels of analysis, respectively. First, Schneider (1987) focuses on person-level variables such as personality. Presumably, personality reflects the individual differences among (or *between*) individuals—and individuals with similar personalities may form a climate or culture. Second, Falcione, Sussman, and Herden (1987) focus on the identification of dyadic climate. According to their definition of climate, both members of a dyad experience a similar or shared climate. As such, this approach focuses on the commonness of individuals within dyads and on differences among (or *between*) dyads. Third, at the group level, Schein (1985) focuses on the common experiences of individuals within groups. Accordingly, he concentrates on similarities within groups (common experiences) and differences among (or *between*) groups. Fourth, at the collective level a number of researchers have focused on between-collective differences. Joyce and Slocum (1984) attempt to identify clusters that contain individuals who are similar on climate variables. Climate then varies and covaries among (or *between*) clusters or collectives. James (1982) and Riley (1983) focus on differences among (or *between*) organizations with the assertion that individuals within an organization share a similar set of experiences. Finally, Smircich (1983) describes a set of approaches that focus on differences among (or *between*) societies, sometimes with the assertion that organizations within one society are similar.

As should be apparent for each level of analysis (person, dyad, group, department, organization, society), previous research on climate and culture tends to focus on differences mainly between entities at that level of analysis. In each approach, the objects contained within an entity (for example, persons in a group) tend to be viewed as interdependent and homogeneous. The notions of homogeneity and interdependence reflect the idea of "commonness" or "shared meanings" often used in definitions of climate and culture. As a result of this commonness or homogeneity *within* one unit of analysis (for example, a group), climate and culture are predicted to vary mainly between persons, dyads, groups, or collectivities. Dansereau, Alutto, and Yammarino (1984) call this plausible view of one level of analysis a *wholes* perspective because the scores within an entity (a group) at a level of analysis (the group level) homogenize; therefore, differences among (or *between*) entities (groups) should be considered. In these approaches, climate or culture varies among (between) rather than within persons, dyads, groups, or collectives. The wholes perspective allows for the comparative analysis described by Louis (1985) that focuses on what is unique to a particular setting, or on how settings (groups) are different.

Parts. A second view of commonness among individuals, which has received less attention in climate and culture research, Dansereau, Alutto, and Yammarino (1984) call a *parts* view. In this view, each unit (for example, a group) shows the same (common) differences within itself as do other units (for example, all groups). Approaches of this type typically contain some notion of universalism. As pointed out by Rousseau (1985), organizational behavior theories often do not focus on similarities within all entities. Nevertheless, a parts view has been used for the four key levels of analysis (persons, dyads, groups, and collectivities). As Smircich (1983) points out, the work on culture and climate by Lévi-Strauss, among others, focuses on the identification of universalistic *within*-person bits that are common to all persons. In this type of work, individuals are of interest, but the focus is on the identification of the principles that apply within *all* individuals. At the dyad level of analysis, there are few theories of climate and culture, but the work of Hollander (1958) illustrates one way to view dyad parts. To the extent that superiors in a dyad always have more authority or power relative to subordinates, one can seek to identify variables that always reflect this power differential *within* dyads. At the group level, Graen and Scandura (1987) propose that superiors differentiate the subordinates in their work groups into "in" and "out" groups. Specifically, they assert that dyadic organizing occurs *within* a superior's work group. At the collective (departmental) level, Miller (1978) suggests that organizations are defined in terms of a set of interdependencies among the components (groups) *within* collectives (organizations). In a similar way, Katz and Kahn (1978) focus on five functional subsystems (production and so on) that characterize the various interdependent parts *within* organizations.

As should be apparent, the key message is that whenever

variability is hypothesized and/or assumed to be operating within a level, and the same variability is assumed to be operating for all instances of that level (that is, universalistically), it will be referred to as a parts view. This perspective allows for the point made by Louis (1985) that efforts should be made to understand culture in terms of what is common across all settings (for example, within all groups).

Wholes and Parts. Table 6.1 summarizes the point that we can view a level of analysis (for example, groups) in two ways. From a wholes perspective, a group is viewed as an undifferentiated (homogeneous) unit of analysis (containing shared perceptions) — see Schneider and Reichers (1983), Falcione, Sussman, and Herden (1987), Schein (1985), Joyce and Slocum (1984), Jones (1983), Riley (1983), and Smircich (1983). In contrast, from a parts perspective, a group is viewed as a differentiated (heterogeneous) unit of analysis where each group shows a similar (common) differentiation — see Smircich (1983), Hollander (1958), Graen and Scandura (1987), Miller (1978), and Katz and Kahn (1978).

The Equivocal View. In addition to holding these two views, researchers sometimes attempt to specifically reject a level of analysis. For example, James and Jones's (1974) definition of psychological climate, as associated with only the person level of analysis, requires an ability to reject higher, or more inclusive, levels of analysis (for instance, dyads, groups, and collectives). Likewise, Glick's (1988) definition of organizational climate, as associated with only the organizational level of analysis, requires an ability to reject lower levels of analysis (for example, persons, dyads, and groups). One way to conceptualize this alternative is to suggest, as did Dansereau, Alutto, and Yammarino (1984), that we reject a level of analysis when valid variation and covariation occur both within and between the entities at a level of analysis. For instance, a variable such as job satisfaction may vary between and within groups. In such a case we would have what seems to be simultaneous wholes and parts conditions, which is analytically correct but theoretically misleading. In fact, we may

Table 6.1. Illustration of Wholes and Parts Approaches
in Culture, Climate, and Other Research.

Level of Analysis	Units of Analysis	
	Wholes	*Parts*
Person	ASA framework (Schneider & Reichers, 1983; Schneider, 1987)	Universalistic within-person bits (for example, Lévi-Strauss)
Dyad	Interpersonal climate (Falcione, Sussman, Herden, 1987)	Differentiation in dyads (Hollander, 1958)
Group	Leadership and group culture (Schein, 1985)	In-groups and out-groups (Graen & Scandura, 1987)
Collective (department)	Collective climate (Joyce & Slocum, 1984)	Interdependent groups (Miller, 1978)
Collective (organization)	Structural approach (Jones, 1983; Riley, 1983)	Functional view (Katz & Kahn, 1978)
Collective (above organizations)	Cultural and corporate management (see Smircich, 1983)	Studies of interdependencies within societies

have some homogeneous groups and some heterogeneous groups. In addition, however, we may have individuals so heterogeneous in attitudes, beliefs, perceptions, and so on that they vary freely between wholes and parts at a level of analysis of interest. Such situations occur because a lower level of analysis (for example, the person level) is free to vary within and between the level of analysis of interest (for example, groups). As a result, no consistent "commonness" occurs at the level of analysis of interest. This situation is called an *equivocal condition* because we do not have a basis for selecting either a wholes or parts perspective and cannot infer "commonness" at the level of analysis of interest (see Nachman, Dansereau, & Naughton, 1983, 1985, for illustrations). This alternative allows for situations where only a lower level of analysis serves as the locus of culture or climate. For instance, Louis (1985) suggests that a department rather than an organization may serve as the basis for culture.

Table 6.2. Definition of Alternative Conditions for Single-Level Analysis.

Unit of Analysis	Variation and Covariation		Difference
	Between Entities	Within Entities	Between Versus Within
Wholes	Systematic	Error	Yes
Parts	Error	Systematic	Yes
Equivocal (reject level)	Systematic	Systematic	No
Inexplicable (reject level)	Error	Error	No

Inexplicable View. To complete the list of alternatives requires an *inexplicable* condition where error (no variation or near zero covariation) occurs between and within units at a level of analysis, which also indicates a rejection of a level of analysis. When viewed in terms of variation, this condition is particularly interesting because we can say that all of the entities at a particular level of analysis have the same score. Thus, in a sense, the objects at a level are all the same (do not vary) in terms of a particular variable or concept of interest. Therefore, there is insufficient variation to discern differences among the objects. For example, we can say that a variable may reflect industry characteristics, and if all organizations of interest are embedded in the same industry, the variables will not vary between organizations. In this example the inexplicable condition rejects the organizational level of analysis.

Summary. Table 6.2 lists the four alternative views of one level of analysis in terms of their predictions about variation and covariation within and between entities at one level of analysis.

Qualitative Research Issues

From a qualitative perspective, as Louis (1985, p. 76) states, "When knowledge of culture is the object or end purpose it is important to compare a number of settings, sifting until what is common across settings vis-à-vis some aspect of culture emerges with clarity." To illustrate in a simplified way how we might use single-level analysis in a qualitative way, let us focus on only two settings (two groups). As a researcher examines the groups, he or she may find any of the four alternatives.

First, individuals may differ to such an extent that a researcher cannot identify sufficient similarity to say there is a group climate or culture (an equivocal view). Second, individuals in each group may homogenize such that one group shows more and the other shows less of a particular culture or climate characteristic. In this way a researcher detects, as Louis (1985) suggests, what is unique to each setting (group) by focusing on differences among settings (whole groups). Third, a researcher may find that the two groups are similar in the way individuals organize themselves within each group (a parts view). In this way, as Louis (1985, p. 76) suggests, a researcher detects "what is common across settings [groups]." Fourth, a researcher may find that all individuals in all groups are similar (an inexplicable view). This would mean that a researcher detects communality across all settings (groups) to such an extent that there is no valid variation that a researcher can explain at the group level.

Figure 6.1 illustrates the four alternative views in schematic form. The circles represent persons. The shading represents the degree that a particular aspect of climate or culture (variable) applies to each individual—more shading indicates more of the variable. The rectangles indicate that a group effect is induced due to the shading of the circles. In the wholes alternative we observe that the individuals in group A are sufficiently similar, as are the individuals in group B; we can consider these individuals as homogenized into groups. In addition, the groups differ (heterogeneity between groups). In the parts case, the individuals show similar differences within each group, so that we observe that these individuals form similar groups. In the equivocal case the individuals are sufficiently different so that we observe only individuals, not groups. For the inexplicable conditions, we observe communality among the individuals across all the groups. In this inexplicable case, we may need to observe further whether the groups are contained in the same collectivity. Although the inexplicable condition suggests a need to consider multiple levels of analysis, let us first consider how these four conditions might be identified at one level of analysis through quantitative methods.

Quantitative Research Issues

Previous quantitative approaches to the study of culture and climate allow for the following three scores for variables that empirically distinguish at one level of analysis among the four conditions listed in Table 6.2 and illustrated in Figure 6.1: Total scores, between-cell scores, and within-cell scores. Obviously, if we use the average $(\bar{X})$ of the scores on a variable (X) for individuals in a group and distribute it back to individuals, we have a score that varies only between groups (let us call this a *between-cell score*, $\bar{X}$). But we know from the analysis of variance that the *total score* (X) for each individual equals the group average $(\bar{X})$ plus the deviation of that score (X) from that average $(\bar{X})$ (let us call this a *within-cell deviation score*, $X - \bar{X}$), and state

$$X = (X - \bar{X}) + \bar{X}$$

Figure 6.1. Schematic Illustration of Four Alternatives at the Group Level of Analysis.

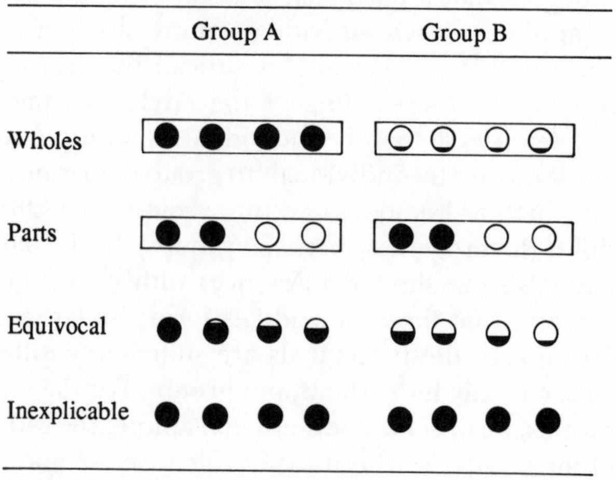

Table 6.3. Illustration of Calculation of Total, Between-Cell, and Within-Cell Scores.

Individual	Cells Group	Variable X*			Variable Y*		
		X	$\bar{X}$	$X - \bar{X}$	Y	$\bar{Y}$	$Y - \bar{Y}$
Mary	A	1	1	0	1	1	0
Jane	A	1	1	0	1	1	0
Curly	A	1	1	0	1	1	0
Moe	B	3	3	0	3	3	0
Harry	B	3	3	0	3	3	0
Edith	B	3	3	0	3	3	0
Archie	C	5	5	0	5	5	0
Larry	C	5	5	0	5	5	0
Meathead	C	5	5	0	5	5	0
Column Number		1	2	3	4	5	6
Units of Analysis		$N=9$	$J=3$	$N-J=6$	$N=9$	$J=3$	$N-J=6$

* X and Y are total scores, $\bar{X}$ and $\bar{Y}$ are cell averages (between-cell scores), and $(X - \bar{Y})$ and $(Y - \bar{Y})$ are within-cell scores.

Notes: Between-eta correlations are: column 1 correlated with column 2 for variable X, and column 4 correlated with column 5 for variable Y. The within-eta correlations are: column 1 correlated with column 3 for variable X, and column 4 correlated with column 6 for variable Y. The between-cell correlation is the correlation of column 2 with column 5. The within-cell correlation is column 3 correlated with column 6. (See Dansereau, Alutto, & Yammarino, 1984, and Markham, 1988, for a description of all possible correlations among these scores.)

Table 6.3 illustrates the calculations of these scores. The use of these three scores also results in a clear definition of the degrees of freedom for the four alternatives. For example, suppose we consider 276 (N) individuals embedded in 83 (J) work groups. The degrees of freedom for the scores for each alternative are as follows:

$$\begin{array}{lll} \text{Wholes} & J - 1 = & 82 \\ \text{Parts} & N - J = & 193 \\ \text{Reject Level} & N - 1 = & 275 \end{array}$$

The degrees of freedom of course add as follows:

$$(N-1) = (N-J) + (J-1)$$
$$275 = 193 + 82$$

Therefore, the issue becomes whether there are 275 persons, 82 independent groups, or 193 interdependent but different individuals within groups.

One-Variable Case. Guion (1973) perhaps first suggested the need to consider empirically the degree to which a climate variable is homogeneous within groups and reflects differences among groups. In fact, Guion (1973) suggested that to induce a wholes case, perhaps all scores should be the same within each group.

Within- and between-eta correlations provide an indication of the degree to which scores agree or do not agree within groups (cells). A *between-eta correlation* (η_B) is the correlation of the total score (X) with the between-cell score $(\overline{X})$. It is called an eta correlation because this value squared equals eta squared in a one-way analysis of variance. If all of the scores in a group agree, this correlation equals 1. A *within-eta correlation* (η_W) is the correlation of the total score X with the within-cell score $(X - \overline{X})$. If all the scores in a group are the same value, this correlation is indeterminate (or zero) because $\eta_B^2 + \eta_W^2 = 1$.

Dansereau, Alutto, and Yammarino (1984) provide two sets of intervals for use in deciding whether a variable varies mainly between cells $(\eta_B = 1)$, within cells $(\eta_W = 1)$, or within cells and between cells. This procedure responds to Guion's (1973) warning about variance, but is somewhat more liberal. For example, to induce a whole-group condition, scores within groups should be very similar (that is, at least 75 percent (30°) to 63 percent (15°) of the variance $[\eta_B^2]$ should occur between groups and less than 25 to 37 percent should occur within groups). They use the ratio (called an E ratio) of the between- to within-eta correlations (η_{BX}/η_{WX}) to decide among the four conditions. Although the procedures provided by Dansereau, Alutto, and Yammarino (1984) allow for a distinction among the four conditions shown in Table 6.2, as suggested by James (1982) and Kenny and LaVoie (1985), the F ratio from the one-way analysis of variance provides a test of the significance of the eta correlations. The intervals for E and the F ratios are as follows:

> Significant E and F ratios > 1 indicate wholes
> Significant E and F ratios < 1 indicate parts
> Nonsignificant E and F ratios indicate equivocal
> Indeterminate E and F ratios indicate inexplicable

Therefore, by focusing on the eta correlations and F ratios, this approach offers a response to the issues raised by Guion (1973) and James (1982).

To illustrate the use of this approach in climate research, consider the results presented by Drexler (1977). He created cells based on organizations and reported a between-eta squared of .42, which indicates a between- (organization) eta correlation of .65 and a within- (organization) eta correlation of .76. Using the procedures described earlier, we conclude that the climate measure varies about equally between and within groups (an equivocal condition). The statistically significant F ratio, reported by Drexler (1977), does not indicate a wholes condition because we cannot assert that the between-eta correlation is larger than the within-eta correlation.[1]

Because of the equivocal nature of these results, the debate between James, Joyce, and Slocum (1988) and Glick (1988) about Drexler's (1977) results seemed inevitable. Moreover, the need to go beyond the one-variable case becomes clear. Glick (1988) argues that even though the variation between organizations is less than the variation within organizations, the between-organization variation is valid. In contrast, James, Joyce, and Slocum (1988) argue that the lack of strong between-organization variation precludes an induction of whole organizations. The assertion by Glick (1988) seems to require a demonstration that between-organization variation is valid. Such an assertion can be considered by demonstration of construct (or predictor criterion) validity for the between-organization variation and a lack of validity for the within-organization variation.[2] To do so requires a consideration of more than one variable.

Two-Variable Case. Sirotnik (1980) focuses on the two-variable case in organizational climate research and uses total, between-cell, and (pooled) within-cell correlations. A *total correlation* (r_{TXY}) equals the correlation of total scores (X and Y). A *between-cell correlation* (r_{BXY}) equals the correlation based on cell averages ($\bar{X}$ and $\bar{Y}$) for two variables. A *within-cell correlation* (r_{WXY}) is the correlation based on the within-cell scores ($X - \bar{X}$ and $Y - \bar{Y}$) for two variables. Because of the independence of these two correlations, a standard Z test and an "A" test (Dansereau, Alutto, & Yammarino, 1984) indicate whether a between-cell correlation (r_{BXY}) is larger than a within-cell correlation (a wholes condition), or vice versa (a parts condition). In addition, these tests allow a determination of whether the two correlations do not differ but both are systematic and greater than zero (an equivocal condition) or equal to zero (an inexplicable condition). Thus, data indicate which of the alternatives shown in Table 6.2 seem more likely. The criteria used to decide among the alternatives based on within- (r_{WXY}) and between-cell correlations (r_{BXY}) are as follows:

$|r_{BXY}| - |r_{WXY}|$ = Significant positive Z and A indicate wholes
$|r_{BXY}| - |r_{WXY}|$ = Significant negative Z and A indicate parts
$|r_{BXY}| - |r_{WXY}|$ = Nonsignificant Z and A indicate equivocal
$\qquad (r_{BXY} = r_{WXY} \neq 0)$ or inexplicable
$\qquad (r_{BXY} = r_{WXY} = 0)$

In Drexler's (1977) data, if he had demonstrated that a measure of performance correlated .90 with climate based on between-organization scores and .00 based on within-organization scores, we would have reason to believe the between-organization scores showed validity. In contrast, if performance correlated .90 based on both the within- and between-organization scores, we would have had no reason to believe the between-organization scores showed more validity than the within-organization scores. In the former case, we could view Glick's (1988) position as more likely. In the latter case, we could view the position of James, Joyce, and Slocum (1988) as more likely.

Combining the One- and Two-Variable Cases. The so-called *WABA equation* — described by Dansereau, Alutto, and Yammarino (1984) and derived from Robinson's (1950) work, as pointed out by Markham (1988) — is the covariance theorem rewritten so as to combine the one- and two-variable cases. Using the notation just defined, the WABA equation is

$$r_{TXY} = \eta_{BX} \eta_{BY} r_{BXY} + \eta_{WX} \eta_{WY} r_{WXY} \tag{1}$$

In other words, the total correlation (r_{TXY}) equals the multiplication of the between-eta correlations for X and Y (η_{BX}, η_{BY}) and the between-cell correlation (r_{BYY}) plus the multiplication of within-eta correlations for X and Y (η_{WX}, η_{WY}) and the within-cell correlation (r_{WXY}). Therefore, a total correlation equals a between component ($\eta_{BX} \eta_{BY} r_{BXY}$) plus a within component ($\eta_{WX} \eta_{WY} r_{WXY}$). In a wholes condition, a total correlation equals the between-cell component. In a parts condition, the total correlation equals the within-cell component. In an equivocal condition a significant total correlation is formed by both the within- and between-cell components. In an inexplicable condition, a nonsignificant total correlation equals both the near-zero between- and within-cell components. By performing the tests for the one- (η_B, η_W) and the two- (r_{BXY} versus r_{WXY}) variable cases, we can determine whether a wholes, parts, equivocal, or inexplicable condition seems more likely at one level of analysis.

To summarize, this empirical approach, which allows for a selection based on culture and climate data among the four alternatives shown in Table 6.2, has the following characteristics. It is sensitive to the magnitude of effects as suggested by Guion (1973), the tests of statistical significance described by James (1982), and the correlations described by Sirotnik (1980). At the same time, it takes into account Robinson's (1950) work on the ecological fallacy with the WABA equation. Moreover, unlike contextual analysis, this approach does not require that a dependent variable be assumed to be at a lower level of analysis. (See Dansereau, Alutto, & Yammarino, 1984, and Markham,

1988, for a comparison of this approach with contextual analysis.)

This approach provides an integrated set of empirical indicators that reinforce an issue raised by Schneider (1975) about focusing on differences among (between) groups (cells) — if one expects homogeneous groups (similar scores in each unit) to obtain variation in scores, one needs to sample variables that vary among groups. Moreover, if a variable varies about equally between and within cells (an equivocal condition), the between-cell variation may show greater construct (or predictor crite-rion) validity than the within-cell variation. Finally, when most of the variation in a variable occurs within groups (a parts condition), the between-cell component will reduce in magni-tude and will not result in an induction of wholes.

Multiple-Level Analysis

Unlike single-level analysis, which focuses on *one* level of analy-sis, multiple-level analysis provides one way to combine levels of analysis and to select, on a theoretical and empirical basis, among four (antithetical) alternative views of *two* or more levels of analysis at a time.

Theoretical Issues. To derive a simplified set of theoretical alter-natives for multiple levels of analysis, let us consider the four alternatives that result if we allow only two alternatives at each level of analysis — accept (wholes or parts) or reject (equivocal or inexplicable). For the two-level case, we can say that a *cross-level* formulation means we accept both levels of analysis. A *level-specific* formulation means we accept a lower level of analysis and reject a higher level of analysis. An *emergent* formulation means we reject a lower level of analysis and accept a higher level of analysis. A *null* formulation means we reject both levels of analy-sis. Table 6.4 illustrates the four alternatives in two ways. First, the summary for each level indicates whether a level of analysis is accepted or rejected. Second, the listing of yes or no indicates one way in which a level of analysis is accepted or rejected.

Table 6.4 uses the person level as an example of a lower

**Table 6.4. Illustration of Linkage Between Single- and
Multiple-Level Analyses.**

Single-Level Analysis	Multiple-Level Analysis			
	Emergent	Level-Specific	Cross-Level	Null
Higher Level (Organization Level)				
Wholes	Yes	No	Yes	No
Parts	No	No	No	No
Equivocal	No	Yes	No	No
Inexplicable	No	No	No	Yes
Summary	Accept	Reject	Accept	Reject
Lower Level (Person Level)				
Wholes	No	Yes	Yes	No
Parts	No	No	No	No
Equivocal	No	No	No	No
Inexplicable	Yes	No	No	Yes
Summary	Reject	Accept	Accept	Reject
Example	Glick's (1988) view of organizational climate.	James, Joyce, & Slocum's (1988) view of psychological climate.	James, Joyce, & Slocum's (1988) view of organizational climate.	Reject both levels of analysis.

level of analysis and the organization level as a higher level of
analysis to illustrate the implications of this approach for climate research. Specifically, James, Joyce, and Slocum (1988)
make a distinction between organizational and psychological
climate. Psychological climate involves acceptance of the person
(lower) level of analysis and rejection of higher levels of analysis
(a level-specific formulation). Thus, psychological climate reflects differences within or among (independent) individuals.
Organizational climate defined by James and Jones (1974) involves an acceptance of the person (lower) level of analysis *and* of
the organizational (higher) level of analysis (a cross-level formulation). In contrast, Glick (1988) seems to reject the person
level of analysis and accepts the organizational level of analysis

(an emergent formulation). The lower panel illustrates how the positions of Glick (1988) and James, Joyce, and Slocum (1988) fall under one of the four alternatives. Because of the antithetical (mutually exclusive) nature of these alternatives (level-specific, cross-level, and emergent), the debate between Glick (1988) and James, Joyce, and Slocum (1988) was inevitable.

Unlike the relatively recent debate about these alternatives, contemporary theories tend to specify less clearly the implications of a theory for multiple levels rather than one level of analysis. The ASA (attraction, selection, attrition) framework (Schneider, 1987) asserts that person-level effects may apply to higher levels of analysis (a cross-level view) or may not apply to higher levels of analysis (a level-specific view). If this framework states that person-level variables always create climate at higher levels of analysis, it asserts a cross-level formulation. If the model states that person-level variables do not always create climate at a higher level of analysis, the model asserts a level-specific formulation. If the model states that person-level variables sometimes do and sometimes do not apply to higher levels of analysis, the model asserts a cross-level formulation under some conditions and a level-specific formulation under other conditions. A need to define the nature of such conditions is obvious. (For example, we might hypothesize that the amount of time that individuals have worked together may influence whether a cross-level specification seems appropriate. This issue is considered in more detail in the section on multiple-relationship analysis.)

Significantly, more ambiguity arises with the interpersonal (dyadic) approach to climate of Falcione, Sussman, and Herden (1987). The model suggests that dyadic processes may be: (1) level-specific at the person level of analysis (the perceptual measurement-individual attribute approach), (2) cross-level and apply to higher and lower levels of analysis (multiple measurement–organizational attribute approach), or (3) level-specific and emergent (that is, it applies to only the dyad level). The last interpretation is possible because Falcione, Sussman, and Herden (1987) suggest that perceptual individual measures are not included, thereby eliminating the applicability of the lower (person) level of analysis.

Schein's (1985) approach describes group processes in terms of personal as well as group characteristics (a cross-level formulation that includes levels of analysis below the group). The model applies to higher levels of analysis only if a collective functions as a group. In other words, collective-level differences only occur when collectives are viewed as groups. Thus, the model is level-specific and rejects levels of analysis above the group.

Joyce and Slocum's (1984) view uses perceptual measures to aggregate to the department level (the model is cross-level and includes levels below the department). The clustering of departments apparently does not apply to differences among organizations. Thus, the approach is specific to the department level (level-specific) and rejects levels of analysis above the department. The models of culture at higher (organization and societal) levels of analysis seem to be cross-level and apply to lower levels of analysis (groups, dyads, and persons). They also seem to be level-specific and do not apply to levels above the organizational or societal level. Finally, Riley's (1983) approach also focuses on collective variables that apply to the organization and lower levels of analysis (cross-level), but not to higher (societal) levels of analysis (level-specific). In addition, however, Riley (1983) views person-level processes as contingent on higher-level processes. Table 6.5 summarizes the theories from the perspective of multiple levels of analysis. The focus on multiple levels of analysis by these theorists seems to stem in part from the nature of organizational contexts, which create opportunities and problems.

Qualitative Research Issues. In terms of qualitative research, Louis (1985) has raised questions about the assumption that the locus of culture is always the organization (or collective) level of analysis. Using multiple-level analysis we can allow for this possibility, as well as for two "problematic" cases described by Louis (1985).

Figure 6.2 illustrates a case where the locus of culture is the collective (organizational) level of analysis, as well the group, dyad, and person levels of analysis. Figure 6.2 uses the same notation and procedures as were used for Figure 6.1, except that ovals represent dyads and pentagons represent collectives. As shown in the figure, there are (1) differences among persons, represented by the shading of circles that represent persons; (2) differences among dyads, represented by the shading of circles

Table 6.5. Illustation of Multiple Levels of Analysis.

Approach	Key level	Multiple-Level Hypotheses
ASA framework (Schneider & Reichers, 1983; Schneider, 1987)	Person	Person-level effects may or may not aggregate to levels above person level. Level-specific indicates "psychological climate." Cross-level indicates organizational climate.
Interpersonal climate (Falcione, Sussman, & Herden, 1987)	Dyad	May be level-specific, cross-level, or emergent as well as contingent or multiplexed.
Group culture (Schein, 1985)	Group	Is cross-level in that it applies to the person as well as group level. This approach probably does not apply above group level; therefore it is also level-specific.
Collective climate (Joyce & Slocum, 1984)	Collective (department)	Does not apply above collective level (level-specific). Also applies to levels below collective (cross-level).
Collective culture (Jones, 1983)	Collective (organizations)	Cross-level. Applies from collective to at least the dyad level. Probably does not apply above collective level (level-specific).
Collective culture (contingency) (Riley, 1983)	Collective	Interaction between collective and lower levels (a contingency formulation). Structure emerges from lower level (cross-level). Other processes seem level-specific.
Collective above organization level (see Smircich, 1983)	Collective	Often applies to levels below collective level (cross-level) and not to levels above the collective (level-specific).

Figure 6.2. Illustration of Cross-Level Wholes (Two Collective Cultures).

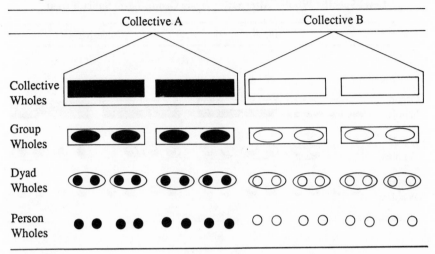

within the ovals (dyads); (3) differences among groups repre-sented by the shading of the ovals (dyads) within the rectangles (groups); and (4) differences among collectives represented by the shading of rectangles (groups) within the pentagons (collec-tives). In such a situation, as is apparent from the figure, it does not matter which level of analysis a researcher examines because the same differences occur at all levels.

The problem that this cross-level collective (organiza-tional) perspective poses is that it is only one of several ways to view an organizational context. As an example of one alter-native, consider the point made by Louis (1985) that organiza-tions may form subcultures. These subcultures may reflect lower-level collective differences such as differences between top management and other members of the organization, and dif-ferences among vertical slices of an organization (divisions) or horizontal slices of an organization (hierarchical levels, depart-ments). In addition, groups within an organization may form subcultures. Thus, when we assume that culture can only be associated with the organizational level, we may make an error. This error occurs because when we observe individuals as per-sons, they may differ due to differences among entities at lower

**Figure 6.3. Schematic Illustration of a Cross-Level and
Level-Specific Wholes Alternative (Four Group-Level Subcultures).**

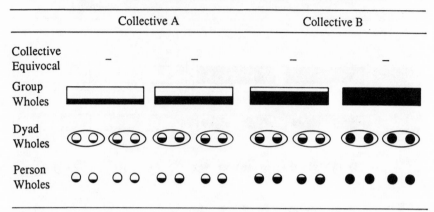

levels of analysis (for example, differences among groups) within an organization rather than due to differences among collectives. Figure 6.3 illustrates this alternative view of the same setting that was considered in Figure 6.2.

This situation—where valid differences occur between groups, dyads, and persons but not between collectives—is a level-specific condition. In this condition, as shown in Figure 6.3, groups vary to such an extent that the groups do not fit into the collective level, which is unlike the cross-level case shown in Figure 6.2. The difference between the situations, represented by Figures 6.2 and 6.3, is analogous to the distinction between psychological climate and group climate, described previously for climate research, with a key difference. In the culture example the lower level of analysis is groups, not persons.

The problem posed by always assuming that the collective (organizational) level is *the* locus of culture should be apparent. If we observe differences among groups, in the cross-level case (Figure 6.2) such differences do reflect differences among collectivities, whereas in the level-specific case (Figure 6.3) such differences reflect only differences among groups, not among collectives. In the latter case we cannot say that differences among persons reflect organizational-level cultures. In the former case

we can say that differences among persons reflect organizational-level cultures. As should be apparent, to understand one
level of analysis (for example, the collective level) we at least need
to consider the level of analysis (for example, the group level)
immediately below the level of analysis of interest.

A second problem, described by Louis (1985), illustrates a
need to also consider the level of analysis immediately above the
level of analysis of interest. As Louis (1985, p. 77) points out,
"Another error associated with the 'organizational' culture assumption is that of attributing to the organization whatever
cultural context is detected within the setting. This occurs, for
example, when a researcher discovers that employees at, say,
AVCO Bank of Anytown are cautious and thus concludes that a
fundamental characteristic of AVCO's culture is caution. What
the researcher in such a situation has failed to consider is the
possibility that he or she has in fact picked up on a characteristic
of Anytown's culture rather than one belonging to the banking
industry." Thus, even if we observe an organizational (collective-
level) configuration we need to consider whether a higher level
of analysis (in this example, the city) may account for the collective effect.

This suggests that although traditional anthropological
approaches often focus on the observation of individuals as
"natives" in a particular culture (Gregory, 1983), levels-of-
analysis issues still occur. When one observes the behavior of
"natives," the question becomes whether an observation reflects
characteristics of persons, dyads, groups, or collectives. For
example, suppose one observes differences among individuals
in commitment to goals and objectives. The question that arises
is whether these observations reflect (1) differences among the
personalities of individuals (person wholes), (2) exchanges that
might occur among individuals on a one-on-one dyadic or
group basis (dyad and group wholes), or (3) differences among
collectives (wholes or parts), or some combination of levels of
analysis. This suggests the necessity of tracing and identifying
the various potential linkages among individuals that may occur
and deciding which observations associate with what levels of
analysis. Obviously, such efforts may produce a variety of defini-

tions of appropriate levels of analysis for different aspects of climate and culture (psychological and organizational climate; cultures and subcultures).

Quantitative Research Issues. The following brief description of a setting studied by Dansereau, Alutto, and Yammarino (1984) illustrates the multiple-level-of-analysis structure of data that often occurs in organizations. The managers studied by Dansereau, Alutto, and Yammarino (1984) were viewed in terms of three levels of analysis. First, because data were collected at only one time period, one score was assigned to each manager. Thus, the study began with 276 mangers (wholes). Second, because each individual reported to one of 83 superiors, these 276 managers were viewed as potential members of their superior's work group. Thus, these managers can be viewed as J (or 83) whole work groups, or as $N - J$ (or 193) interdependent persons embedded in work groups (that is, as work group parts). Third, in this setting, each individual was classified, based on organizational records, as a member of one of eight collectives (defined by higher and lower level in the management hierarchy, and crossed by membership in the production, support, maintenance, and adaptive collectives). Depending on the level of analysis of interest, the degrees of freedom for the analysis of scores could vary as follows:

Person (Subordinate)

Wholes (J)	276

Group Level

Total (N)	276
Parts $(N - J)$	193
Wholes (J)	83

Collectivity Level

Total (N)	83
Parts $(N - J)$	75
Wholes (J)	8

In addition to defining levels in this way, Dansereau, Alutto, and Yammarino (1984) report a cross-level effect. One set of variables that referred to freedom from various constraints associated with the person, group, and collective wholes.

This structure of organizational contexts illustrates the simple point that whole (between-group [cell]) scores at a lower level of analysis serve as the total scores at the next higher level of analysis. In their study, Dansereau, Alutto, and Yammarino (1984) focused first on the group level of analysis and performed single-level analysis. When wholes were obtained at the group level of analysis, the between-group scores (group averages) were analyzed at the collective level. This procedure allows a response to the criticism of Drexler's (1977) work made by James (1982). Drexler (1977) aggregated individual scores on climate to between-group scores without any consideration of the within- and between-group variation and covariation. Therefore, as James (1982) points out, Drexler (1977) provided no empirical justification for aggregating individual scores to the group level. Obviously, analysis of within- and between-group variation and covariation could have provided an empirical justification for group-level aggregation.

Dansereau, Alutto, and Yammarino (1984) and Dansereau and others (1986) describe and illustrate in detail one method that is based on data to decide how variables associate with the four conditions listed in Table 6.4. Essentially, single-level analysis is performed at each of several levels of analysis and for *each* level of analysis one selects one of the four alternatives (wholes, parts, equivocal, and inexplicable). A consideration of the results from single-level analysis at several levels, two at a time, allows a selection among the multiple-level alternatives (cross-level, level-specific, emergent, and null) for any number of levels of analysis.

This approach responds to the requirement from traditional statistical procedures of independence among objects or entities. This requirement can be stated in multiple-level-of-analysis terms as follows: The effects at a higher level of analysis should be equivocal or inexplicable (a level-specific formulation). We can meet this requirement in two ways. First, every time we analyze results at any one level, we can assume or assure that the entities that serve as the basis for the analysis do not aggregate to the next higher level of analysis. Second, we can test, as described here, whether entities at a lower level of analysis do not aggregate to a higher level of analysis.

In this way, we can see that the comment by Glick (1985) that culture and climate researchers assert interdependence but assume independence applies not to just the person level of analysis, but to any level of analysis. The empirical demonstration of a level-specific effect provides data that support an assumption of independence. Therefore, it is not sufficient to say that data should be collected and analyzed only at the level of analysis of interest. It is necessary to add that when individuals embed in multiple levels of analysis, as in organizations, we should consider not only the level of analysis of interest (for example, groups) but also the level of analysis immediately above (for example, collectives). A general rule is to analyze the levels of analysis immediately above the levels of analysis of interest until one finds an equivocal condition (a level-specific result). It also seems appropriate to consider at least the level of analysis immediately below the levels of analysis of interest. As we will see, if this approach is not followed, the unit of measurement will not align with the theoretically based unit of analysis — a serious problem in climate research described by Glick (1985).

From this general rule, we can see the error in some criticisms of previous research on climate and culture. Glick (1988) criticizes James, Joyce, and Slocum (1988) because they sample person-level perceptions of groups (organizations). Because the theory of James, Joyce, and Slocum (1988) is cross-level, it includes persons. Therefore, the theory clearly requires a researcher to sample at the person level of analysis. The problem is *not* that the sampling frame is wrong, but rather the frame is incomplete relative to the cross-level nature of the theory. In other words, it is also necessary to sample levels of analysis above the person level. The assertion by Glick (1988) that if he specifies that climate emerges at the organizational level, he need sample only differences among organizations, is also incomplete. If

Table 6.6. Illustration of Multiple-Variable and Multiple-Relationship Analyses for Culture and Climate.

Approach	Key Level	Multiple Variables		
ASA framework	Person	Person-level variables	→Climate →	Behavior outcomes
Interpersonal climate	Dyad	Factors peculiar to dyad	→Climate →	Behavior outcomes
Group culture	Group	Group shared experiences	→Culture →	Behavior outcomes
Collective climate	Collective (department)	?	→Collective climate →	Behavior outcomes
Collective culture organization	Collective (organizations)	Structure variables	→Collective culture →	Behavior outcomes
Collective culture (Contingency)	Collective (organizations)	Structure variables	→Multiple cultures →	Multiple* outcomes
Collective above organization level	Collective (above organizations)	Cultural societal variables	→Collective cultures →	Behavior* outcomes

* Contingencies hypothesized.
Note: Refer to Table 6.5 for references for each approach.

climate does not hold at levels of analysis below the organizational level, lower levels need to be analyzed empirically. Therefore, previous research tends to be incomplete, not wrong, when viewed from the perspective of multiple-level analysis.

Multiple-Variable Analysis

Theoretical Issues. Table 6.6 illustrates, for the theories described previously, that researchers who study culture and climate often have interest in more than one or two variables. For example, the ASA framework views person-level variables (for instance, personality variables) as a source of climate, which in turn relates to behaviors or various outcomes (for example, performance).

To extend the level-of-analysis procedures to any number of variables, Dansereau, Alutto, and Yammarino (1984) suggest the use of a continuum (multiple-variable analysis). At one end of the continuum, all variables relate (a *related-variables case*); at the other end of the continuum, all variables are independent (an *unrelated-variables case*). Two cases form the middle of the continuum. The *generally related case*, much like a regression equation, means that more variables relate than are independent. The *generally unrelated case* means that more variables are independent than relate. A midpoint occurs where as many variables relate as are independent. Dansereau, Alutto, and Yammarino (1984), Dansereau and others (1986), and Dansereau and Markham (1987a, 1987b) describe these alternatives in more detail.

The unrelated case is of interest when a researcher wants to establish the difference between climate and some other variable (for example, satisfaction). The related case is of interest when a researcher wants to focus, for example, on the three sets of variables shown in Table 6.6 (see, for instance, Jones & James, 1979). The generally unrelated case is of interest when a researcher wants to develop dimensions of climate that are independent of (unrelated to) each other, where each dimension contains items that relate (see, for example, Springer & Gable, 1980; Wallace, Ivancevich, & Lyon, 1975). Finally, the generally related case is often of interest when a researcher wants to focus on the relationship of multiple independent measures of climate that relate to one or several dependent, outcome, or behavioral variables (see, for example, Angle & Perry, 1986; Kelly & Worthley, 1981; Hollmann, 1976; LaFollette & Sims, 1975; Lincoln, Handa, & Olson 1981; Payne, Fineman, & Wall, 1976; Whitely & England, 1977).

For any set of variables, we can assert any one of the four cases because these alternatives are antithetical (mutually exclusive). Of particular interest from a level-of-analysis perspective is an ability to assert different alternatives for within-cell and between-cell correlations. For example, we can assert an unrelated (null) formulation for within-cell correlations and a generally related (multiple-regression-type) formulation for between-cell correlations, which results in the assertion of a wholes condition. Therefore, one can test assertions about levels of analysis for any number of variables.

In a similar way, we can ask whether different aspects of culture and climate imply different combinations of levels of analysis. For example, if cultural variables refer to values that are widely held, perhaps it should be viewed at the collective level of analysis. If climate refers to more specific procedures used to implement values, perhaps climate variables reflect group-level effects. Obviously, both of these examples raise theoretical issues whose resolution seems to lie in analyses that tell us how different variables associate with different levels of analysis.

Qualitative Research Issues. Perhaps the most straightforward illustration of the potential usefulness of multiple-variable analysis comes from Louis (1985, p. 78) in her discussion of the differences between organizational and intraorganizational levels of analysis: "For example, consider the case of the proverbial tensions between sales and production groups. We would expect to find that each group's culture reinforces a somewhat negative orientation toward the other group. If we wished to reduce the tensions, mandating 'harmony' and imposing integrating structures would be unlikely to succeed without giving some attention to the subcultural reinforcers of historic tensions." However, the subcultural tensions themselves may include different (group-level) variables and processes rather than organization-level processes.

To illustrate further how this approach might be helpful in qualitative research, let us use another example from Louis (1985). At the collective level of analysis, after the fashion of the cross-level perspective illustrated in Figure 6.2, we can say that the motto "we try harder" may have a special meaning that applies to Avis as opposed to other collectives. We might ask, in line with the level-specific formulation illustrated in Figure 6.3, whether the maintenance and personnel groups vary in the way they interpret this motto and act on it. Thus, we can specify different variables, concepts, or issues for the two antithetical views illustrated in Figures 6.2 and 6.3, and in the process allow for multiple loci for culture and climate.

In a more general sense, qualitative research sometimes focuses on expressions (outcomes) of culture—for example, rites, symbols, language, gestures, physical setting, artifacts, networks, myths, sagas, legends, and folktales (see Trice & Beyer, 1985, p. 394, for illustrative definitions). Level-of-analysis issues arise when a researcher attempts to identify the relationship between culture and expressions (outcomes) of culture. Let us consider language. Some aspects of language undoubtedly reflect shared meanings at a level of analysis above the organizational level. Other aspects of language, however, may be peculiar to organizations or industries. For example, the term *BOF* takes on meaning in a steel company (BOF means basic oxygen furnace), but little meaning outside such a setting. Contrast this with the more generalized meanings that have become associated with CPU, bit, bytes, and the like due to processes in the computer industry. At the interpersonal (dyad or group level) special language may emerge. For example, in 1988, Democratic party presidential candidate Michael Dukakis was observed speaking a form of Greek only understandable by his immediate family. Finally, Martin, Feldman, Hatch, and Sitkin (1983) describe stories that do not vary significantly between organizations. What is not known is whether these stories vary between societies or are common across all societies. Clearly, qualitative research offers great potential to elaborate on the variables that might associate with one or many of several levels of analysis that are plausible in organizations.

Quantitative Research Issues. Dansereau, Alutto, and Yammarino (1984), Dansereau and others (1986), and Dansereau and Markham (1987a, 1987b) describe the empirical procedures for multiple-variable analysis in detail. Essentially, relationships among variables are assessed based on within-cell *and* between-cell correlations.

A key feature of multiple-variable analysis comes from its ability to allow for different variables to associate with different level(s) of analysis. For example, some variables may reflect individual perceptions or personalities (psychological climate). Other variables may reflect organizational climate as well as person-level differences (for instance, organizational climate as defined by James & Jones, 1974). Still other variables may reflect organizational-level processes that do not hold at lower levels of analysis (for example, the view of organizational climate reflected in Glick, 1985). The use of within- and between-cell correlations allows us to identify the climate and culture variables that hold for different levels of analysis. In this way, antithetical alternatives may hold in one setting but different variables may associate with these alternatives.

This approach suggests that factor analysis and cluster analysis (Joyce & Slocum, 1984), often used in studies of culture and climate, can be performed on within- and between-cell scores. To use factor and cluster analyses, it is necessary to decide beforehand the appropriate (within and between) scores to input to cluster analysis. We may find very different clusters depending on whether we assume wholes or parts. For example, to perform their analysis, Joyce and Slocum (1984) had to assume whole persons. Thus, their results indicate very little about collectives and provide information only about the way individuals clustered based on differences among whole persons for the specific set of variables of interest. Instead, cluster analysis can be used to identify "groups" that have high versus low values on a particular set of climate *variables* for a particular level of analysis.

Multiple-Relationship Analysis

Theoretical Issues. Multiple-relationship analysis amounts to performing, under different conditions, the three analyses described thus far: single-level analysis, multiple-level analysis, and multiple-variable analysis (which in combination provide a method for associating multiple variables and multiple levels of analysis). Multiple-relationship analysis simply focuses on whether relationships among variables are the same (a *multiplexed* formulation) or vary (a *contingent* formulation) under different conditions. The work of Miner (1975) illustrates this approach in general terms. He defines four conditions (hier-archical, professional, task, and group orientation), and associ-ates these variables with the group or organizational levels of analysis. Depending on the condition, different person-level motivation variables relate to person-level performance.

The work of Schneider (1975) and Schneider and Bowen (1985) illustrate this type of analysis in organizational climate research. Specifically, they seem to assume that organizations may have more or less of a climate for service. Within a condi-tion of a strong organizational climate for service, groups in an organization with a high degree of this climate are hypothesized to be more successful and more likely to remain intact than groups in the same organization with less of a climate for service. Presumably, for organizations where the climate is not for service (but perhaps for some other outcome), the rela-tionship between group climate for service and various out-comes may hold (a multiplexed formulation) or may not hold (a contingent formulation).

The fact that researchers often associate climate and culture with higher levels of analysis (groups and collectives) increases the importance of multiple-relationship analysis. These approaches to climate and culture do not suggest that all individuals accept a climate or culture. Instead, they seem to suggest that all individuals may face the same climate or culture. Obviously, a measurement problem results when a researcher uses the reports of new individuals who may not accept a culture or climate. Consequently, it seems necessary to identify vari-ables and measures that capture culture or climate regardless of individual acceptance. Although the phrasing of questions so that they refer not to the individual but to the situation may help, it must be empirically determined whether a variable reflects differences among groups or organizations.

The requirement that a measure of climate or culture be shown empirically to associate with a particular level of analysis is important. As pointed out by Gregory (1983), a finding that a variable does not aggregate to the organizational level does not mean a lack of a culture or climate effect, or a weak climate or culture. It simply means that the level of analysis of interest does not serve as the basis for cultural or climate differences. From this perspective, a "weak" culture means, for example, that individuals tend to face less of a particular dimension of culture (for example, less autonomy) as compared to others (where autonomy is high). A weak culture or climate refers to a low level of a particular variable as perceived by all individuals. In contrast, when variables do not aggregate to a theoretically specified level of analysis, we cannot say that the level of analysis *serves* as the basis for climate or culture in a particular situation.

Qualitative Research Issues. Multiple-relationship analysis seems particularly useful as a way to consider the conditions under which culture may emerge or be observed. For example, Louis (1985) suggests that culture may be easier to observe under conditions that disrupt routines (for example, mergers, new CEO, new individuals, and start-ups). Here again the question becomes, to what level of analysis do these disruptions apply? Do they apply to only some persons, some groups, some portions of a collectivity, and so on? Similarly, in terms of the stages that may need to be passed for a culture to develop, we can view each stage as a condition.

With the identification of conditions we can study what happens in each case. For example, we might study the difference between new groups and old groups and observe equivocal (person-level) effects for the new groups and group wholes for the older groups. Likewise, we might study one set of new groups over time and find equivocal (person-level) results at time 1, and group wholes at time 2. Alternatively, we might find (1) group wholes at each time period, and (2) that all of the groups increase or decrease over time. (For a more detailed description of time as it relates to levels of analysis, see Dansereau, Alutto, & Yammarino, 1984.) Regardless of what we observe, the need to define clearly the conditions under which the observations are made should be apparent.

Quantitative Research Issues. From a quantitative perspective, interest can be in the ability of a climate or culture variable to moderate the relationship between two other variables. In this case, once a climate or culture variable associates with a higher level of analysis, one can use bimodal and other splits or cluster analysis to identify conditions for performing multiple-relationship analysis. For each condition, within and between scores at the person, dyad, and group levels can be examined. For the case of two conditions, the following correlations (in addition to the eta correlations for each condition) are calculated:

> Between-cell correlation in condition $1 = B1$
> Between-cell correlation in condition $2 = B2$
> Within-cell correlation in condition $1 \; = W1$
> Within-cell correlation in condition $2 \; = W2$

Using single-level analysis, we can test the difference of the between- and within-cell correlations. Within conditions, a significant positive difference of $B1 - W1$ indicates wholes and a significant negative difference of $B1 - W1$ indicates parts. A nonsignificant difference indicates an equivocal or inexplicable condition. Therefore, for *each* condition four alternatives are plausible (wholes, parts, equivocal, and inexplicable), which results in the sixteen alternatives described, in detail, in Dansereau, Alutto, and Yammarino (1984), Dansereau and others (1986), and Dansereau and Markham (1987a, 1987b). In a real sense, multiple-relationship analysis allows single-level, multiple-level, and multiple-variable analyses to be performed for each of several conditions and adds a consideration of whether these analyses yield different (contingent) or similar (multiplexed) results for different conditions.

One particularly interesting possibility offered by multiple-relationship analysis comes from the debate between Glick (1988) and James, Joyce, and Slocum (1988). Suppose, as suggested by Glick, a climate for competition depends on emergent organizational-level processes. Thus, we can examine group-level effects within organizations that face high competitiveness (condition 1) and those that experience less competition (condition 2). We may theorize that the relationship of group climate for competitiveness with various criterion variables may be high for competitive organizations and low for noncompetitive organizations (a contingent formulation), or that the relationship of group competition and outcomes does not depend on the organization's competitiveness (a multiplexed formulation). The point, of course, is that the definitions of climate and culture from Glick (1988) and James, Joyce, and Slocum (1988), although antithetical in terms of levels of analysis, may interact and produce outcomes.

Because Dansereau, Alutto, and Yammarino (1984), Dansereau and others (1986), and Dansereau and Markham (1987a, 1987b) have described the empirical procedures for distinguishing between multiplexed and contingency formulations, we will only briefly consider the implications of this approach for other methods. Obviously, the main difference between multiple-relationship analysis versus moderated multiple regression (and the interaction term in an analysis of variance) is that it provides information about the appropriate level of analysis for data. Once the appropriate level of analysis is identified in each condition, moderated multiple regression or an analysis of variance may become appropriate. Until the levels of analysis are clearly identified, however, the use of the more traditional approaches is problematic because they assume known levels and units of analysis. Moreover, the same issues arise when one attempts to assess stability and changes over time (see Dansereau, Alutto, & Yammarino, 1984).

A Final Issue

Although consideration of levels of analysis may appear appropriate primarily for abstract intellectual and research purposes, such issues have very applied implications (see, for example, Dansereau & Markham, 1987a, 1987b). The success of attempts to change climate or culture (for example, whether to instill a "service" orientation, or concern for quality production) may depend on focused change efforts at an appropriate level of analysis. For example, Schneider's (1987) ASA approach suggests that climate arises from individuals. If this is correct, changing climate requires attention to the retention, selection, and attraction of individuals (a person-level approach to the organization). In contrast, Schein's (1985) view seems to suggest that culture arises from group or interpersonal processes. Therefore, based on this approach, the most effective approach to modifying culture would be to focus on controlling changes in group processes. Finally, Glick (1988) suggests that climate may result from emergent, organizational-level, processes. Thus, if one accepts this position, attempts at controlled change of climate should involve concentration on issues such as structure, competition among organizations, technology, and so on. Obviously, different climate- or culture-related variables may associate with different levels of analysis, and applied attempts to change climate and culture may require coordinated attention to multiple levels of analysis. Moreover, if different aspects of culture operate at different levels, it is conceivable that, whether or not it is helpful, a change in group-level culture (subculture) may have no impact on organizational culture.

Summary and Conclusion

The four analytical approaches described in this paper as a set provide a framework for attempting to identify the loci of culture and climate at multiple levels of analysis. Single-level analysis allows for the acceptance or rejection of one level of analysis as a locus of culture, whereas multiple-level analysis allows for viewing culture and climate as associated with multiple levels of analysis. Multiple-variable analysis allows for different combinations of levels of analysis to associate with different variables. Finally, multiple-relationship analysis allows for all analyses under different conditions.

These analyses have allowed us, on a theoretical and empirical basis, to distinguish among the views of James, Joyce, and Slocum (1988) about organizational climate (a cross-level formulation) or psychological climate (a level-specific formulation), and Glick (1988) about organizational climate (an emergent formulation). As a result, debates such as those involving Glick and James, Joyce, and Slocum may eventually be resolved by properly constructed databases. In a similar way, debates about cultures and subcultures may find their resolution in observations from a multiple-level-of-analysis perspective.

Thus, unlike research in other areas, it seems that previous theories and research methods used for examining culture and climate have led us to a very desirable state in which there are in existence clearly contradictory theoretical positions and a sophisticated set of qualitative and quantitative methods. Now it is possible to develop and test with data the antithetical alternatives as a means of confirming our existing theories and deciding whether new theories are necessary, including formulations involving new combinations of variables and levels of analysis. The choice seems simple. We either continue to partially test our theories about culture and climate or subject them to the full array of alternatives that have been described in the literature and arise from the specification of variables and appropriate levels of analysis.

Finally, it seems clear that many researchers concerned with culture or climate have particular preferences for either qualitative or quantitative approaches and, within these perspectives, preferences for methods of dealing with level-of-analysis problems. This chapter does not argue for reliance on one method for addressing the level issue. Instead, we are suggesting that whatever perspective a researcher uses, it should explicitly focus on the level issue during both the formulation of theory and the analysis of data. In the absence of such activity, it will be impossible to build a consistent body of knowledge about the antecedents and consequences of particular dimensions of culture or climate. Thus, if a reader finds the specific analytical approach presented in this chapter to be too limited, other approaches can be used. The critical issue is that future research and theory building must consider appropriate and competing multiple levels of analysis.

Notes

1. If we prefer, we can argue that degrees of freedom influence the degree to which variables should vary within or between organizations. Thus, we might say that there is a statistically

significant between-group effect. To do so, however, requires that the strength of the effect (practical significance) be considered as well. In this example, the strength is weak, but the effect is statistically significant.

2. To make this argument we must recognize that error can be defined in two ways. First, error may mean a lack of variation. In this case, we can require that a variable must vary more between organizations than within organizations. Second, we can say that low variation does not mean error. Instead, we can say that error is capricious and that a large amount of variation may represent error and that even though small in magnitude, variation may be valid. To demonstrate this second alternative requires a demonstration of the validity of the small amount of variation — thus the need for predictor-criterion validity.

References

Angle, H., & Perry, J. (1986). Dual commitment and labor-management relationship climate. *Academy of Management Journal, 29*, 31–50.

Dansereau, F., Alutto, J. A., & Yammarino, F. (1984). *Theory testing in organizational behavior: The variant approach.* Englewood Cliffs, NJ: Prentice-Hall.

Dansereau, F., Chandrasekaran, G., Dumas, M., Coleman, D., Ehrlich, S., & Bagchi, D. (1986). *Data enquiry that tests entity and correlational/causal theories: Application and users guide.* Williamsville, NY: Institute for Theory Testing.

Dansereau, F., & Markham, S. (1987a). Levels of analysis in personnel and human resources management. In K. Rowland & J. Ferris (Eds.), *Research in personnel and human resources management.* Greenwich, CT: JAI Press.

Dansereau, F., & Markham, S. (1987b). Superior-subordinate communication: Multiple levels of analysis. In F. Jablin, L. Putnam, K. Roberts, & L. Porter (Eds.), *Handbook of organizational communication: An interdisciplinary perspective.* Newbury Park, CA: Sage.

Drexler, J. A. (1977). Organizational climate: Its homogeneity within organizations. *Journal of Applied Psychology, 62*, 38–42.

Falcione, R., Sussman, L., & Herden, R. (1987). Communication climate in organizations. In F. Jablin, L. Putnam, K. Roberts, & L. Porter (Eds.), *Handbook of organizational communication: An interdisciplinary perspective*. Newbury Park, CA: Sage.

Glick, W. (1985). Conceptualizing and measuring organizational and psychological climate: Pitfalls in multilevel research. *Academy of Management Review, 10*(3), 601–616.

Glick, W. (1988). Response: Organizations are not central tendencies: Shadowboxing in the dark, round 2. *Academy of Management Review, 13*(1), 133–137.

Graen, G., & Scandura, S. (1987). Dyadic organizing. In L. Cummings & B. Staw (Eds.), *Research in organizational behavior*. Greenwich, CT: JAI Press.

Gregory, K. (1983). Native-view paradigms: Multiple cultures and culture conflicts in organizations. *Administrative Science Quarterly, 28*, 359–376.

Guion, R. M. (1973). A note on organizational climate. *Organizational Behavior and Human Performance, 9*, 120–125.

Hollander, E. P. (1958). Conformity, status, and idiosyncrasy credit. *Psychological Review, 65*, 117–127.

Hollmann, R. (1976). Supportive organizational climate and managerial assessment of MBO effectiveness. *Academy of Management Journal, 19*, 560–577.

James, L. R. (1982). Aggregation bias in estimates of perceptual agreement. *Journal of Applied Psychology, 67*(2), 219–229.

James, L. R., & Jones, A. P. (1974). Organizational climate: A review of theory and research. *Psychological Bulletin, 81*, 1096–1112.

James, L. R., Joyce, W. F., & Slocum, J. W. (1988). Comment: Organizations do not cognize. *Academy of Management Review, 13*, 129–132.

Jones, A. P., & James, L. R. (1979). Psychological climate: Dimensions and relationships of individual and aggregated work environment perceptions. *Organizational Behavior and Human Performance, 23*, 201–250.

Jones, G. R. (1983). Transaction costs, property rights, and organizational culture: An exchange perspective. *Administrative Science Quarterly, 28,* 454–467.

Joyce, W., & Slocum, J. (1984). Collective climate: Agreement as a basis for defining aggregate climates in organizations. *Academy of Management Journal, 27,* 721–742.

Katz, D., & Kahn, R. (1978). *The social psychology of organizations* (2nd ed.). New York: Wiley.

Kelly, L., & Worthley, R. (1981). The role of culture in comparative management: A cross cultural perspective. *Academy of Management Journal, 24,* 164–173.

Kenny, D., & LaVoie (1985). Separating individual and group effects. *Journal of Personality and Social Psychology, 48,* 339–348.

LaFollette, W. R., & Sims, H. (1975). Is satisfaction redundant with organizational climate? *Organizational Behavior and Human Performance, 13,* 257–278.

Lincoln, J., Handa, M., & Olson, J. (1981). Cultural orientations and individual reactions to organizations: A study of employees of Japanese-owned firms. *Administrative Science Quarterly,* 1981, *26,* 93–115.

Louis, M. R. (1985). An investigator's guide to workplace culture. In P. J. Frost, L. F. Moore, M. R. Louis, C. C. Lundberg, & J. Martin (Eds.), *Organizational culture* (pp. 73–93). Newbury Park, CA: Sage.

Markham, S. (1988). The pay for performance dilemma. *Journal of Applied Psychology, 73,* 172–180.

Martin, J., Feldman, M., Hatch, M., & Sitkin, S. (1983). The uniqueness paradox in organizational stories. *Administrative Science Quarterly, 28,* 438–453.

Miller, J. G. (1978). *Living systems.* New York: McGraw-Hill.

Miner, J. (1975). The uncertain future of the leadership concept: An overview. In J. Hunt & L. Larson (Eds.), *Leadership frontiers.* Kent, OH: Kent State University Press.

Nachman, S., Dansereau, F., & Naughton, T. (1983). Negotiating latitude: A within and between group analysis of a key constraint in the vertical dyad linkage theory of leadership. *Psychological Reports, 53,* 171–177.

Nachman, S., Dansereau, F., & Naughton, T. (1985). Levels of analysis and the vertical dyad linkage approach to leadership. *Psychological Reports, 57,* 661–662.

Payne, R. L., Fineman, S., & Wall, T. D. (1976). Organizational climate and job satisfaction: A conceptual synthesis. *Organizational Behavior and Human Performance, 16,* 45–62.

Riley, P. (1983). A structurationist account of political culture. *Administrative Science Quarterly, 28,* 414–437.

Robinson, W. E. (1950). Ecological correlations and the behavior of individuals. *American Sociological Review, 15,* 351–357.

Rousseau, D. (1985). Issues of level in organizational research: Multilevel and cross-level perspectives. In L. L. Cummings & B. M. Staw (Eds.), *Research in organizational behavior* (pp. 1–38). Greenwich, CT: JAI Press.

Schein, E. (1985). *Organizational culture and leadership: A dynamic view.* San Francisco: Jossey-Bass.

Schneider, B. (1975). Organizational climate: Individual preferences and organizational realities revisited. *Journal of Applied Psychology, 60,* 459–465.

Schneider, B. (1987). The people make the place. *Personnel Psychology, 40,* 437–453.

Schneider, B., & Bowen, D. (1985). Employee and customer perceptions of service in banks: Replication and extension. *Journal of Applied Psychology, 70,* 423–433.

Schneider, B., & Reichers, A. (1983). On the etiology of climates. *Personnel Psychology, 36,* 19–40.

Sirotnik, K. (1980). Psychometric implications of the unit-of-analysis problem (with examples from the measurement of organizational climate). *Journal of Educational Measurement, 17,* 245–282.

Smircich, L. (1983). Concepts of culture and organizational analysis. *Administrative Science Quarterly, 28,* 339–358.

Springer, J., & Gable, R. (1980). Dimensions and sources of administrative climate in development of four Asian nations. *Administrative Science Quarterly, 29,* 671–688.

Trice, H., & Beyer, J. (1985). Using six organizational rites to change culture. In R. H. Kilmann, M. J. Saxton, R. Serpa, &

Associates, *Gaining control of the corporate culture*. San Francisco: Jossey-Bass.

Van Maanen, J., & Barley, S. (1985). Cultural organization: Fragments of a theory. In P. J. Frost, L. F. Moore, M. R. Louis, C. C. Lundberg, & J. Martin (Eds.), *Organizational culture* (pp. 31–53). Newbury Park, CA: Sage.

Wallace, M., Ivancevich, J., & Lyon, H. (1975). Measurement modifications for assessing organizational climate in hospitals. *Academy of Management Journal, 18*, 82–97.

Whitely, W., & England, G. (1977). Managerial values as a reflection of culture and the process of industrialization. *Academy of Management Journal, 20*, 439–453.

PART THREE

APPLYING CLIMATE
AND CULTURE CONSTRUCTS

How useful are the climate and culture constructs? Does usefulness mean that culture or climate correlates with the financial performance of organizations? Does usefulness mean that climate and culture constructs help us understand why organizations look and feel the way they do? Does usefulness mean that climate and culture are related to the ways organizations deal with each other? These are some of the questions addressed in the chapters in this section.

Siehl and Martin, in Chapter Seven, directly confront the issue of the relationship between organizational culture and financial performance. They develop the argument that the usefulness of the culture construct is not to be found in the financial performance of organizations but in the understanding it yields about the organization as a human system. In addition, they logically show that the seemingly straightforward connection between financial performance and culture portrayed in the popular media may be moderated by numerous conditions external to the organization (like turbulence in the environment). In addition, they present the reasonable argument that since no one can agree on how to measure "financial performance," how can culture be related to it? These cautions on expecting a relationship between culture and financial performance are useful because they suggest that achieving the holy grail — that is, a relationship between culture and financial performance — is only one standard for evaluating the usefulness of the culture construct.

In Chapter Eight, Kopelman, Brief, and Guzzo explicate many of the intermediate linkages between culture and productivity, in a way documenting the point made by Siehl and Martin that there are many effects on financial performance. Of course, the implicit idea behind expecting a relationship between culture and financial performance is that culture is somehow reflected in productivity. Kopelman, Brief, and Guzzo show that even the relationship between culture and productivity has numerous potential moderators. In their chapter, the focus is on how the culture of an organization may influence that organization's human resource practices and how those human resource practices, in turn, influence productivity. Thus, in Chapter Eight, we see documentation — through a review of the existing literature — of the contributions human resource practices make to productivity.

In Chapter Nine, Thompson and Luthans present behavior management strategies for creating particular climates and cultures. They show how a behavioral perspective can be applied to create particular kinds of messages through consciously and carefully designed organizational reward strategies. In their chapter, they outline seven properties of organizational culture and the ways behavioral principles may be used to create, change, and maintain culture.

Mirvis and Sales, in Chapter Ten, show through a fascinating history of an acquisition and buyback that (1) cultures may be best understood when one culture confronts another and (2) cultures may persist over long periods of time when confronted with external pressure for change. Perhaps most important, they show that a failure by organizations to consider the operating culture of an organization they acquire will yield negative consequences for both parties to the acquisition The details about these negative consequences presented by Mirvis and Sales will prove instructive to any organization considering an acquisition, either as acquirer or acquiree. A clear message from this chapter is that the culture construct provides a framework for understanding how acquisitions, and by implication other forms of forced change in organizations, may yield negative unintended consequences.

In Chapter Eleven, I argue that the climate construct has considerable usefulness when it is conceptualized in a strategic mode. By a strategic mode I mean that climate is most useful when it is focused on some goal of organization like innovation, safety, or service. The chapter focuses on the climate for service and shows how the service climate construct can be used to not only understand the ways employees understand their own organization but how customers who come in contact with the organization also understand and are affected by the climate for service.

A final chapter in *Organizational Climate and Culture* is by Pettigrew. He first discusses the conceptual, methodological, and applications issues raised in the prior chapters; then, he presents a series of issues and problems for future thinking about these constructs. In his overview of the prior chapters, Pettigrew reflects on the historical antecedents of research and thinking about climate and culture, presenting an insightful and frequently funny commentary on whence cometh the constructs. In his look to the future, Pettigrew forcefully argues for a view of organizations as cultural and political systems. In addition, he presents a contextualist view of organizational competitiveness and change, showing how internal organizational features interlock with various external attributes to produce organizational effectiveness.

These chapters provide rich perspectives on how useful the climate and culture constructs can be. They capture the idea that the ways in which employees experience their workplaces have implications for how organizations can be changed, how we cannot expect climate and culture to explain *everything* about organizations, and how the climate and culture of organizations have implications for the ways organizations relate to each other and to the customers with which they come in contact.

Chapter 7

Caren Siehl
Joanne Martin

Organizational Culture: A Key to Financial Performance?

The quantity of organizational culture research has increased dramatically during the last decade (see, for example, Barley, Meyer, & Gash, 1988), in part because so much of it has held out a tantalizing promise: that culture may be a key to enhancing financial performance. Supposedly, articulating the "right" set of cultural values will: create excitement, high morale, and intense commitment to a company and its objectives; clarify the behaviors expected of employees; galvanize their potential productivity; and, through these activities, ultimately improve the financial performance of the organization (see Baker, 1980; Kilmann, Saxton, Serpa, & Associates, 1985; Martin, Feldman, Hatch, & Sitkin, 1983; Ouchi, 1981; Pascale & Athos, 1981; Schein, 1985; Schwartz & Davis, 1981). These are all functionalist claims, although some — the cognitive clarification and morale claims, for instance — are less immediately utilitarian than others (for example, the link to financial performance).

The objective of this chapter is to argue that this subset of organizational culture research is on the "wrong track," that the promise of a link between organizational culture and financial performance is empirically unsubstantiated — perhaps impossi-

Note: The authors wish to thank Debra Meyerson and Benjamin Schneider for their comments on earlier versions of this chapter.

241

ble to substantiate. In the first part of this chapter, we review published empirical research that claims to have found a link to financial performance. We delineate ways that this work (including our own) is conceptually limited, methodologically flawed, and, therefore, empirically inconclusive. In the second section, we discuss practical reasons for this shortage of solid empirical evidence. The inherent methodological difficulties of exploring the relationship between culture and financial performance are analyzed. In the third and final section, we challenge the theoretical and political assumptions implicit in this or any utilitarian functionalist approach to the study of culture.

We are not questioning claims of a link to financial performance in order to declare the "death" of culture research (see Calas & Smircich, 1987), although we do recognize the risks inherent in questioning a functionalist approach. As Staw (1984) has convincingly argued, "Organizational researchers have had difficulty in sustaining interest in models that do not explain at least some variance in outcomes such as performance." Staw suggests that interest in decision making and attribution declined because of this problem. The risk, of course, is that culture research may succumb to a similar lack of interest if links to financial performance are not found.

We believe that organizational culture is a fruitful topic of study, whether or not support for functionalist arguments is found. Our point in this chapter is that it is unwise and misleading to justify studying culture in terms of its links to financial performance, since such a link has not been—and may well never be—empirically demonstrated. The first step in this argument is to define what is meant by the problematical terms, *culture* and *financial performance*.

Defining Culture

Researchers vary dramatically in how they define culture and what they study, when they claim to be studying culture. Below we use a matrix framework for analyzing the various ways researchers have operationalized the concept of culture. We then use the patterns of relationships among the cells of the matrix to distinguish three different paradigms of culture research, each of which defines culture in a different way. (The material immediately following is adapted from Martin & Meyerson, 1988, where fuller descriptions of these concepts, as well as a justification for the use of the term *paradigm*, can be found. We describe the matrix and paradigms from the perspective of researchers, but similar frameworks are also used by cultural members to describe their own experiences in an organization.)

A Matrix Framework. A matrix, like that in Table 7.1, can be used to summarize a description of a culture. Across the top of the matrix are the aspects of organizational life that researchers study when they say they are studying culture. These include formal practices (such as structure, job descriptions, and formal, written policies), informal practices (for example, behavioral norms), and artifacts such as rituals, stories, special jargon, humor, and physical arrangements (including dress, interior decor, and architecture).

"Generalist" cultural research includes many of these manifestations in a cultural portrait, as illustrated in Table 7.1. In contrast, "specialist" research focuses primarily on a single manifestation of culture, for example, only informal behavioral norms or only stories. While a specialist study can increase understanding of a single cultural manifestation, it cannot offer the breadth and depth of insight that comes with a generalist analysis of the full range of the manifestations of a particular culture.

Cultural researchers use content themes, listed down the left-hand side of the matrix, to unify their descriptions of the cultural manifestations they choose to study. For example, as can be seen in Table 7.1, an egalitarian theme might be used to explain such cultural manifestations as informal superior-subordinate relationships, a cafeteria used by all, and an absence of reserved parking spaces. Researchers vary in the kinds of content themes they use. Most stress relatively superficial, value-laden content themes such as the need for innovation, egalitarianism, a holistic concern for employee well-being, or the importance of "bottom-line" profitability.

Table 7.1. Matrix Analysis of an Integration Paradigm Cultural Description

		Cultural Manifestations					
Content Themes		Practices		Artifacts			
Espoused	Enacted	Formal	Informal	Rituals	Stories	Jargon	Physical Arrangements
Egalitarian sharing	Egalitarian sharing	Answer own telephone "Perk" distribution based on need, not status Consensual decision making	Informal superior-subordinate relations				One cafeteria Nonreserved parking spaces
Confront conflict	Confront conflict	Open-door policy to discuss problems	Many arguments in groups	Hard-fought softball game		"Fighting"; "Kill him"	

Others seek deeper themes—for instance, preconscious fundamental assumptions (see Schein, 1985), hidden symbolic meanings, or other aspects of deep interpretations (see Gahmberg, 1987; Moxnes, 1987). For example, Barley (1983) uses the theme of "life-restoration" to explain, using semiotic analysis, a wide range of funeral directors' activities. The matrix approach can be used to summarize all these various ways of operationalizing culture.

Espoused Versus Enacted Content Themes. One further distinction, included in the matrix, is crucial to understanding the shortcomings of the studies reviewed in this chapter. Content themes may be espoused or they may be enacted (see Argyris & Schön, 1978). *Espoused content themes* are expressed opinions—what cultural members say they think, believe, or do themselves, or what they say others in their milieu think, believe, or do. *Enacted content themes*, in contrast, are abstractions that capture aspects of how people actually behave, rather than how they say they behave. Thus, a person may describe his or her work group as valuing open confrontation of conflict (an espoused content theme), but long-term observation of this group in a wide variety of circumstances may reveal the opposite pattern of actual behavior (enacted content theme).

This espoused versus enacted distinction is important because people often want to portray themselves attractively—in their own eyes as well as in the eyes of others. Furthermore, their attitudes about work, either positive or negative, can affect what they perceive and remember and which opinions they express. These familiar impression management and social desirability biases can affect cognitions, attitudes, and reports of behavior, even when anonymity is protected. For these reasons, espoused content themes must be kept conceptually distinct from enacted content themes. Furthermore, research on the prevalence of attitude-behavior inconsistency (for instance, Salancik, 1977) clearly indicates that, under most conditions, espoused and enacted content themes are unlikely to be highly correlated. Therefore, it is important that researchers study more than espoused content themes.

Because of the difficulties caused by impression management and social desirability biases, as well as attitude-behavior inconsistencies, many cultural researchers have preferred in-depth, qualitative methods to "penetrate the front" of espoused content themes and to develop a richly detailed, context-specific understanding of actual behavior (for example, Gregory, 1983; Smircich, 1981; Van Maanen & Barley, 1984). Those researchers who seek an understanding of preconscious assumptions or deep symbolic meanings are even more strenuous in their insistence on the superiority of in-depth, clinical approaches (for example, Schein, 1987) or the long-term participant-observation methods favored by ethnographers. Although a full discussion of this methodological debate is beyond the scope of this chapter, it is important to note here that researchers who advocate the use of qualitative methods tend to study a wider range of cultural manifestations in order to "penetrate the front" of espoused content themes.

Because espoused and enacted content themes are conceptually distinct and may be empirically independent as well, cell entries in a matrix may be inconsistent with each other. This possibility is important because the pattern of relationships among cell entries in a matrix reveals the essence of the way culture is being defined and studied. Such patterns provide a key to understanding the differences among the three paradigms of culture research described below.

The Integration Paradigm. Those who use the Integration Paradigm focus on those cultural manifestations that are consistent with each other. When Integration Paradigm research is summarized using the matrix format, every cell entry in the matrix is consistent with every other cell. For example, Integration Paradigm research might describe how a content theme (such as the importance of confronting conflict) is espoused in a philosophy of management statement and enacted, consistently, in formal practices, informal behavioral norms, and so on. Because of this intercell consistency in the matrix, an Integration Paradigm cultural portrait is like a hologram, in that when a hologram breaks each part encapsulates the whole.

Only one matrix is needed for an Integration Paradigm cultural portrait, because all cultural members are said to share the same view of the culture. Table 7.1 is an example of an Integration Paradigm cultural portrait. The consistent pattern of relationships among the cells of this matrix, and the fact that only one matrix is needed, implies that this paradigm is defining culture in terms of that which is shared—the "social glue" that holds members together in an organizationwide consensus.

The Integration Paradigm also defines culture as that which is clear, rather than ambiguous: "an area of meaning cut out of a vast mass of meaninglessness, a small clearing of lucidity in a formless, dark, always ominous jungle" (Berger, 1967, p. 23). There are three defining characteristics, then, of the Integration Paradigm: consistency, organizationwide consensus, and the denial of ambiguity.

The Differentiation Paradigm. The cultural portraits characteristic of the Differentiation Paradigm include some cultural manifestations that are inconsistent with each other. For example, a CEO might espouse the importance of participative management and yet make decisions without consultation, in an authoritarian manner.

Differentiation Paradigm researchers also question the existence of organizationwide consensus. Instead, they argue that cultural boundaries coalesce around subcultures—for example, levels of a hierarchy, an occupation, or a friendship group. Thus, any Differentiation Paradigm matrix would have some intercell inconsistencies and a full portrait would include one matrix for each subculture. Whereas the Integration Paradigm assumes unity and harmony, the Differentiation Paradigm permits the analysis of inequalities and conflicts.

Finally, the Differentiation Paradigm portrays each subculture as an island of lucidity; ambiguities are relegated to the intersections among subcultures, in the same way swift currents create channels among islands. The defining characteristics of the Differentiation Paradigm, then, include inconsistency, subcultural consensus, and the channeling of ambiguity.

The Ambiguity Paradigm. The third paradigm—the Ambiguity Paradigm—describes the relationships among cultural manifestations as neither clearly consistent nor clearly inconsistent with each other. Instead, the relationships among manifestations is confused (due to a lack of knowledge or an excess of complexity) or contradictory (in the sense that a paradox implies a contradiction that cannot be resolved).

Cultural portraits constructed from an Ambiguity Paradigm perspective show a lack of organizationwide consensus and a lack of consensus within clear subcultural boundaries. Instead, individuals seem to be like nodes in a web, connected by shared concerns to some but not all the surrounding nodes. When a particular issue becomes salient, one pattern of connections becomes relevant. That pattern would include a unique array of agreements, disagreements, and domains of ignorance, complexity, or contradiction. A different issue would draw attention to a different pattern of connections—and different sources of confusion.

Rather than being a "small clearing of lucidity in a formless, dark, always ominous jungle," the Ambiguity Paradigm portrays culture as the jungle itself. The three defining characteristics of the Ambiguity Paradigm are lack of clarity, lack of consensus, and the acknowledgment of ambiguity.

Table 7.2 juxtaposes the defining characteristics of these three paradigms and cites examples of representative research. We believe that any adequate portrait of an organizational culture should include aspects of all three paradigms—that is, some cultural manifestations that demonstrate organizationwide consistency and consensus, some inconsistencies and subcultural groupings, and some inescapable ambiguities. In contrast, most cultural researchers do not cross these paradigmatic borders.

As we will see in the next section, culture researchers who seek a link to financial performance usually work within only a small subset of the matrix and within only one paradigm. Before reviewing these studies, however, we need to look at how they operationalize and define financial performance.

Table 7.2. Summary of the Three Paradigms of Organizational Culture Research.

Defining Characteristics	Paradigm Name		
	Integration	Differentiation	Ambiguity
Level of consistency	Only consistent elements mentioned	Some inconsistency	Lack of clarity
Degree of consensus	Organization-wide consensus	Consensus within, not between, subcultures	Issue-specific consensus, dissension, and confusion
Orientation to ambiguity	Denial	Channeling	Acknowledgment
Metaphor	Hologram, clearing in jungle	Islands of clarity	Web, jungle
Representative studies	Barley (1983) Clark (1970, 1972) Martin, Feldman, Hatch, & Sitkin (1983) Ouchi (1981) Pascale & Athos (1981) Peters & Waterman (1982) Schein (1981, 1983, 1985) Selznick (1957) Siehl & Martin (1984) Wilkins (1983, 1984)	Gregory (1983) Louis (1983) Lukas (1987) Martin & Siehl (1983) Riley (1983) Van Maanen & Barley (1984)	Brunsson (1985) Calas & Smircich (1987) Feldman (1983/1984) Golding (1987) Grafton-Small & Linstead (1987) March & Olsen (1976) Siehl (1988) Starbuck (1983) Weick (1979)

Defining Financial Performance

Culture researchers have followed the lead of researchers in other domains that specialize in studying financial performance. Although no single, uniformly accepted operationalization of performance has emerged, culture researchers generally operationalize performance with financial ratios. For example, four standard ratios that are frequently utilized include return on assets, return on equity, return on sales, and earnings per share. Each of these ratios taps a different aspect of financial performance and, in a sense, has a different limitation. For example, risk-adjusted earnings per share show a clear bias toward the concerns of shareholders and investors, while return on sales may be of broader interest. Such collections of ratios are highly correlated (for example, Martin, Anterasian, & Siehl, 1988) and are a reasonably well-accepted indicator of how well an organization is meeting the financial interests of various stakeholders, such as customers, investors, and employees.

This does lead, however, to a significant problem that is evident in most of the research linking culture to financial performance. The financial ratios that are used to opera-tionalize performance are generally computed at the level of the firm. These measures of financial performance are congruent with the assumption, characteristic of Integration Paradigm research, that an entire firm contains a single culture. Re-searchers seeking a link between culture and financial perfor-mance have failed to grapple with the financial performance implications of the Differentiation Paradigm's emphasis on sub-cultures and the Ambiguity Paradigm's emphasis on a lack of certainty.

Reviewing the Evidence of a Link to Financial Performance

The empirical studies that have examined the relationship be-tween culture and financial performance began with the as-sumption that a firm has a single, organizationwide culture. These studies then tested, to some extent, three versions of the culture–financial performance relationship: (1) a direct link between the two concepts, so that certain broad types of "strong" cultures are said to cause superior performance; (2) a direct link between particular aspects of culture and perfor-mance with the direction of causality reversed; and (3) con-tingency variants of the direct arguments for example, that superior performance results only when a firm's culture is con-

gruent with its business strategy. Below, we review a representative—but not all-inclusive—sample of the empirical evidence
regarding each of these versions of the argument.

The Direct Culture-Performance Link. The first direct version of
the culture-performance argument posits that the key to profitability is having the appropriate type of "strong" culture. Although definitions of the appropriate type vary, as discussed
below, those researchers who study this issue implicitly share a
definition of a "strong" culture as one where espoused values are
consistent with behavior and where all (or most) employees
share the same view of the firm. This is an Integration Paradigm
portrait of consistency (across cells of the matrix) and organizationwide consensus—a portrait of harmony, in that people at all
levels of the hierarchy share the values espoused by management. Organizational cultures that fail to generate this kind of
consistency and consensus concerning the "appropriate" or
"strong" content themes are, then, considered "weak" cultures.

For example, Ouchi (1981) and Pascale and Athos (1981)
argue that the financial success of some Japanese and American
firms is attributable to their "strong" cultural emphasis on certain humanistic values, such as concern for the personal well-
being of employees, an emphasis on consensual decision-making, and so forth. These ideas echo the themes of the human
relations movement (Leavitt, 1978; McGregor, 1960). The idea
that humanistic reforms will eventually have financial benefits is
not new, but firm empirical support for the idea has remained
elusive.

Ouchi and Johnson (1978) presented an in-depth portrait
of the cultures of two electronic companies, demonstrating
through careful interviews and observation that a particular
theoretically derived set of humanistic values was shared among
executives in one company and not in the other. These humanistic values include a concern for people, collective decision
making, and long-term employment. The financial performance (as measured through profitability and sales) of the
humanistic company was then shown to be superior.

The two companies were selected (using data from a

panel of expert judges) in order to maximize the differences between two "ideal-type" control systems (Type A and Type Z). As the authors indicate, the selection procedure is similar to the common procedure in psychology of administering a test to screen for the trait under study and then choosing to study those who score highest and lowest on the characteristics being investigated. This sampling procedure yields a true comparative sample rather than a representative sample. Although carefully executed, the procedure carries risks of small numbers, as well as the potential instabilities associated with studying statistical "outliers."

Ouchi and Johnson interviewed every person at the level of vice president or above in both companies. In addition, each officer of the company was asked to complete a questionnaire and to take home a spouse questionnaire to his spouse (all officers were male). In total, thirteen company A executives and sixteen company Z executives participated in the study. By interviewing only executives, Ouchi and Johnson are implicitly stating that the perceptions of executives about the culture are the same as the perceptions of other lower-level employees. If this assumption is incorrect (and it is entirely believable that it could be), then the limitations of the individual-level sampling procedure may have led to unwarranted conclusions about cultural consistency and organizationwide consensus, putting the financial performance conclusions of the study into doubt. Table 7.3 summarizes the sampling procedures and the measures of culture and performance used in this study and in the other studies described below.

Using a larger sample of organizations than Ouchi and Johnson, Peters and Waterman (1982) described the cultures of sixty-two financially successful firms, making similar claims of a link between a particular type of "strong" culture and superior performance. The authors of this vivid, powerful, and popular book admit in their introduction that their study lacks the rigor of traditional scientific research. The sixty-two companies were a convenience sample, apparently drawn from a list of McKinsey clients. Samples of cultural members were selected in a nonrandom fashion, often by the firm's management. As in the Ouchi and Johnson study, Peters and Waterman focused primarily on the top managers of these firms. Once again, the subculture of the single most powerful group in the firm was treated as equivalent to a unitary, firmwide culture.

Interviews with these managers were apparently open-ended and unstructured (little detail is given). Illustrating their generalizations with copious, memorable anecdotes, the researchers defined the "strong" cultures of these sixty-two firms as sharing eight characteristics (see Table 7.3). Some of these characteristics were humanistic, such as caring about people, while others were market-related, such as "backing fanatics" about product quality and making heroes of innovators.

The measures of financial performance were relatively sophisticated, as can be seen in Table 7.3. Financial ratios were used to measure the performance of firms in the original convenience sample. Those firms with poor performance levels for their industry were simply excluded from the sample, opening the possibility that the residual "superior performance" group would regress toward the mean over time. No comparison groups of less successful companies or companies with different kinds of cultures were included in the sample.

A subsequent follow-up of the companies in Peters and Waterman's sample ("Who's Excellent Now," 1984) demonstrated some inadequacies of these methodological choices. Focusing on measures of financial performance only, this article concluded that fourteen of the original sixty-two "superior performers" would either not pass the financial tests described in the book or had subsequently suffered significant earnings decline. Although this journalistic follow-up was not a full-blown scientific study, it did make it clear that Peters and Waterman's articulate and vivid book did not establish a solid empirical link between culture and financial performance.

A third study also sought evidence of a direct link between these two concepts, using more sophisticated sampling procedures for both the organizations and the subjects within the organizations. Denison (1984) studied a convenience sample of thirty-four firms representing twenty-five different industries as defined by Standard and Poor's four-digit industry code.

Table 7.3. Summary of Culture-Financial Performance Studies.

Researchers' names:	Ouchi & Johnson (1978)	Peters & Waterman (1982)	Denison (1984)	Gordon (1985)	Martin, Anterasian, & Siehl (1988)
Type of organizations	Electronics firms	Business firms, representing six industry segments	Business firms representing twenty-five different industries	Utility companies, manufacturing firms, and financial institutions	Business firms from the 1980 Fortune 500
Number of organizations	2	62	34	63	100
Sampling procedure for organizations	Comparative sample to maximize differences between two "ideal-type" organizational control systems	Convenience sample of companies considered to be innovative and excellent	Convenience sample (companies are client firms of ISR that voluntarily choose to be part of the survey)	Convenience sample (intentionally included firms in either a dynamic marketplace, a nondynamic marketplace, or one undergoing change; part of a larger study conducted by Hay and Associates)	Random sample
Type of subjects	Employees at the level of vice president or above including officers of the company	Top managers	Employees at all levels in the firm, but not all divisions in the firm, are represented	Upper-level managers	Annual reports
Number of subjects	29	Not reported	43,747	Not reported	100
Sampling procedure for subjects	Hand-picked	Hand-picked	Semirandom (the firm selected the divisions to be surveyed, but within a division, the selection was random)	Hand-picked to focus on "the top of the pyramid"	Random sample

Measure(s) of culture (as reported by the researchers)	Members' reports of firm characteristics regarding: 1. length of employment 2. individual versus collective decision making 3. responsibility 4. frequency of evaluation 5. type of evaluation 6. type of career path 7. concern for people	Researchers' judgment of the degree to which the firm exhibited eight attributes: 1. a bias for action 2. close to the customer 3. autonomy and entrepreneurship 4. productivity through people 5. hands-on value-driven 6. stick to the knitting 7. simple form, lean staff 8. loose-tight properties	Members reports' of organizational practices and conditions were averaged into twenty-two indexes. All scores were then averaged to arrive at a score for the entire organization on each index. The two indices were found to be related to financial performance and organization of work and decision-making practices.	Member reports of "how the company operates," including questions about the clarity of company direction, top-management communication, individual initiative, action orientation, and human resource development. Data were averaged to determine a "cultural profile" for the firm.	Externally espoused content themes, in annual reports, were analyzed to determine an espoused content theme profile for the firm. Eight profiles emerged: people, pride in products, quality, innovation, social responsibility, customer service, finances, and economy.
Measure(s) of financial performance (as reported by the researchers)	• Profitability of the firm • Dollar sales • Level of debt financing	• Measures of growth 1. Compound asset growth from 1961 to 1980 2. Compound equity growth from 1961 to 1980 3. Average ratio of market value to book value • Measures of return on capital and sales 1. Average return on capital for 1961–1980 2. Average return on equity (1961–1980) 3. Average return on sales (1961–1980)	• Income-investment ratios • Income-sales ratios	• Profitability of the firm • Growth in revenues for the firm	• Return on assets • Return on equity • Return on sales • Earnings per share

These industries were as diverse as metal mining, guided missiles and space vehicles, and electrical services. The companies in the sample were a convenience sample in the sense that they were client organizations of the University of Michigan's Institute for Social Research that voluntarily chose to be involved in the larger-scale "Survey of Organizations" at some point between 1966 and 1981.

"Culture" was measured by administering a standardized questionnaire to a sample of employees. Firms nonrandomly selected divisions to be studied, but within divisions, employees were randomly selected. This was a large sample of 43,747 employees, representing all levels of the hierarchies of thirty-two firms. Each employee's responses to the questionnaire were averaged into twenty-two indices, including such topics as organizational climate, leadership, peer relations, group process, work design, and satisfaction. In addition, a number of measures of financial performance were obtained on the thirty-two firms, including return on investment, return on sales, and performance against competitors.

Given the ambitious scope of this project, it is noteworthy that only two of the indices were reported to be significantly correlated with financial performance (as measured by the income-investment ratio and the income-sales ratio): the organization-of-work index and the decision-making practices index. The organization-of-work index is a composite of four survey items that reflect the degree to which respondents say work is sensibly organized, work methods are adapted to changing conditions, decisions are made at appropriate levels, and the goals of the organization are perceived by the individual as clear and reasonable. The decision-making practices index is a two-item measure indicating the degree of involvement that individuals say they have in decisions that affect them and the extent to which they say information is shared across the levels of the organization. These two indices, measuring reported decision making and work organization procedures, were labeled, by the researcher, as indicative of a "widely-shared participative culture."

This study defines and measures culture in a manner that

is quite different from that adopted by most culture researchers, perhaps because this questionnaire was designed for use in numerous other, "noncultural" research projects. The questionnaire items measure employees' reports about behavior. In the terms used here, these are espoused content themes, not measures of actual behavior. Therefore, they are open to the biases associated with impression management, social desirability, and attitude-behavior inconsistency discussed earlier. Even when anonymity is guaranteed, subjects' responses can be influenced by desires to control the ways they present themselves and the organizations where they work. In addition, the topics of the questions (particularly organizational climate, work design, and job satisfaction) seem to bear more relation to these well-established research traditions than to the ways culture is usually defined.[1]

Furthermore, the language in these questions is generated by the researcher, not the organizational member. Therefore we cannot know whether employees would spontaneously come up with these categories of experience. We also cannot know whether categories such as "participative management," "teamwork," or "cooperation" have similar meanings across organizational contexts. Thus, the comparative statistics that can be used on such measures may well mask incommensurabilities.

These criticisms are not unique to Denison's study. Similar criticisms have been made of all the cultural studies that have used standardized, researcher-generated questionnaire items or phrases as stimuli to gather cultural members' descriptions of what they or others think, value, or do. Such "cultural" measures appear to have two important advantages. They can be quantified and, arguably, they can in some cases be compared—comparisons of cultures being essential for theory building. However, most culture researchers are particularly sensitive to the necessity of "penetrating the front" of social desirability inherent in espoused content themes and opinions. From this perspective, these kinds of measures of culture are seriously inadequate.

These difficulties in the measurement of culture, however, must be balanced against the methodological strengths of this study. The sample of individuals, if not firms, is relatively large and randomly selected. Performance is carefully measured at multiple points in time. Keeping both strengths and caveats in mind, it is noteworthy that Denison found that companies in a "widely-shared participative culture" had superior returns on investment and sales. Similar results were found when performance against competitors was used in place of the direct performance measures. Denison argues that contingency theory would predict that in stable environments, participation should have had an adverse effect on performance. Thus, by comparing companies from a diverse set of industries and from differing environments, the performance impact of participation should have lessened. Because the effect continued to be significant, these results suggest that this type of "strong" culture was effective, independent of contingency variables such as firm strategy and environmental uncertainty.[2]

A fourth study—by Gordon (1985)—also purports to examine the direct version of the culture-performance argument. The organizations in Gordon's convenience sample consisted of fourteen utility companies (electric, gas, and local telephone companies), eighteen manufacturing firms (all in highly competitive marketplaces and all with products that employed some element of high technology), and thirty-one financial institutions (banks and insurance companies). Cultural data were collected through a survey of a nonrandom sample of the top mangers of the firm (sample size is not mentioned). Top managers included the four or five levels of management from the CEO down. Culture was measured by obtaining the perceptions of these top managers concerning eleven "values," such as clarity of company direction, innovation, top-management communication, individual initiative, action orientation, and human resource development. These data were averaged for each company to determine a "cultural" profile.

For all of the companies in the sample, performance was measured by the amount of profitability for the year the survey was conducted and for two subsequent years. In addition, for the dynamic-marketplace companies (the manufacturers), the performance measure was augmented to include growth in revenues for the same time period. A comparison was made between a company's performance data and the industry's average performance (profitability and growth) for the same years. High-performing companies were then isolated and contrasted with low-performing companies, those operating below the industry average, or mixed performers. Companies that had average performance were not included in the analysis. Among the fourteen utility companies, six were labeled as high performers and four as low performers. Five of the eighteen manufacturing firms were labeled high performers and thirteen were labeled mixed performers. Of the thirty-one financial institutions, eight were labeled high performers and twelve were low performers.

The results of this study showed virtually no significant differences between the low and high performers of the three industries for any of the eleven "values." Only one difference was found to be significant at the .01 level. The high-performing utility companies were perceived to be more open in dealing with conflicts than the low-performing companies.

This study has many of the same failings as the studies described earlier. As in Peters and Waterman's work as well as Ouchi and Johnson's, the reports of a nonrandom selection of top managers is presented as representative of the firm as a whole, implying organizationwide consensus without sufficient data. In addition, this is a "specialist" study of only one cultural manifestation — the relatively superficial espoused content themes that may well be uncorrelated with the behaviors of most cultural members. Finally, the use of researcher-generated categories in the standardized questions leaves open the issue of whether similar categories would be spontaneously used by cultural members when describing their experiences in the firm.

In summary, the first, direct version of the culture-performance argument has received very limited empirical support. These studies are plagued by methodological shortcomings in the sampling procedures, sample size, and the measurement of culture and/or performance. Similar difficulties are evident in studies examining the second version of the culture-performance argument.

The Direct Performance-Culture Link. The second version also posits a direct link between particular aspects of culture and superior financial performance. In the second version the order of causality is reversed so that a firm's performance level is now what influences the content of the culture. Empirical support for this second version, like the first, is scarce.

Martin, Anterasian, and Siehl (1988) randomly selected 100 organizations from the 1980 *Fortune* directories of the 500 largest U.S. industrial corporations. A systematic content analysis of the photographs and texts of these firms' annual reports produced measures of the extent to which the top management of the firms externally espoused ten types of content themes. These theme profiles were used as input into a cluster analysis, which yielded eight distinct clusters of firms. The eight types were labeled in terms of the espoused theme receiving greatest emphasis, although each type included some emphasis on other themes as well: People (a mix of humanitarian and teamwork concerns), Pride in Products, Quality, Innovation, Social Responsibility, Customer Service, Finances (emphasis on the importance of the firm's "bottom line"), and Economy (emphasis on the state of the national economy).

This study has some of the same advantages as the Denison study. The sample of firms is relatively large (and in this case random). The measures of culture are quantified and, perhaps, comparable across firms. In this study, the espoused content themes were independently generated by these cultural members, not developed in response to researcher questions.

Unfortunately, these advantages are counterbalanced by important disadvantages. This is a severely limited "specialist" study of espoused content themes drawn from a text designed by top management for public relations purposes. These content themes are obviously not equivalent to enacted behavior and they may well not represent the opinions of lower-level employees in these firms. Thus, as a measure of culture, this study has severe inadequacies.

Martin, Anterasian, and Siehl (1988) used an index incorporating four measures of financial performance (return on assets, return on equity, return on sales, and earnings per share) at only one point in time. Control variables often associated with performance (firm size, market competitiveness, industry) were also included. In this study, as in the Denison study, relatively sophisticated measures of performance variables were coupled with relatively superficial, quantitative indicators of culture.

Results of this study showed relatively little support for this second, more limited, version of the culture-performance argument. The performance levels of the seven theme types of the firms did not differ significantly with one exception: the Social Responsibility firms had significantly higher performance levels than the firms emphasizing the state of the economy. Firms in the People cluster were not unusually profitable or unprofitable.

These results for the Economy cluster are congruent with the findings of previous attribution studies of annual reports, which found that firms tended to blame poor performance on the state of the economy in an attempt to escape blame and improve their public image (Bettman & Weitz, 1983; Salancik & Meindl, 1984; Staw, McKechnie, & Puffer, 1983). A similar impression management explanation can be made for the high-performing firms in the Social Responsibility cluster. Those firms that espoused the importance of social responsibility had, during the previous year, been criticized for behaving in a socially irresponsible manner, for example, by polluting the sea with oil spills or causing erosion because of deforestation.

The results of this study, then, suggest that any direct association between espoused content themes and financial performance may be relatively weak. Further, these results indicate that the direction of causality, to the extent it exists at all, may be reversed; financial performance levels may cause certain themes to be espoused, in order to improve the firm's image and offer a socially desirable explanation for unusually high or low profit levels.

A broader and less cynical form of this reverse causality explanation is also possible: high levels of performance may make it possible to espouse (and enact) certain types of cultural content themes. According to this version, high levels of performance provide the organizational slack and excess resources that "pay for" the expenses associated with enacting humanitarian values such as job security, caring about people, and giving to the community. Without these excess resources, it would be difficult, if not impossible, for an organization to sustain a humanitarian culture. To date, this proposition has not been subjected to conclusive empirical testing, although the middling performance levels of firms in the People cluster suggest that empirical support may not be forthcoming.

The results of this reverse causality interpretation cannot be assessed without further research because of the strong limitations of the kind of data described earlier. Themes espoused by top management to external constituencies, as in annual reports, may be the aspect of culture that is least likely to be related to a firm's financial performance. If values impact financial performance by galvanizing employees' commitment and productivity, then future research must focus on internally enacted aspects of culture, rather than externally espoused themes. Given this focus, it would be essential to study the perceptions of employees at all levels of the organization, not just top management. And, longitudinal studies of both culture and performance (with *adequate measures of each*) are essential for the assessment of questions of causality.

Another possibility is suggested by Schein's (1981) assertion that the most important aspect of culture is the set of fundamental assumptions that underlie a culture. Perhaps a link to financial performance will be found when deeper levels of cultural phenomena, such as assumptions, are studied. Until such studies are conducted, a question mark must be placed next to claims that levels of financial performance can influence the content of particular aspects of a culture or that certain types of culture lead to superior financial performance.

Contingency Studies of the Direct Culture-Performance Link. The third version of the culture–financial performance proposition consists of variants of a contingency argument. The most common variant is a claim that firms with cultures congruent with their business strategies are better performers than firms that lack this congruency (Bourgeois & Jemison, 1982; Phillips & Kennedy, 1980; Schwartz & Davis, 1981; Tichy, 1982). These authors argue that when a firm's culture clashes with its strategy, confusion and conflicts of interest increase, strategies are resisted, and the firm's financial performance ultimately may be impaired. For example, the cautious, tradition-bound culture of the "bell-shaped man" at AT&T was challenged by the firm's decision to enter the highly competitive, fast-paced field of information processing, at least temporarily impairing the firm's performance. In contrast, when culture and strategy are synchronized, such difficulties are said to be minimized, with a concomitant beneficial effect on financial performance.

Evidence supporting this third, contingency version of the culture-performance relationship has been confined, for the most part, to short, almost anecdotal descriptions of case studies of single organizations. To the best of our knowledge, no detailed, in-depth, ethnographic case studies investigating this point of view have been done. Limited strategy-relevant data from a larger sample of firms is, however, available in the study by Martin, Anterasian, and Siehl (1988) described earlier.

Two strategies were studied: degree of diversification (an index based on measures of the number of four-digit SIC codes, the number of lines of business in the annual report, a specialization ratio, a Herfindahl-based index, and an entropy index) and level of riskiness of a firm's financial policies (an index based on beta, total risk, and the ratio of debt to equity). These strategies were selected for several reasons. Riskiness and diversification have been related to organizational survival (Hannan & Freeman, 1977). Furthermore, there are plausible reasons why these particular strategies may link the value types described earlier to financial performance. When a firm adopts a relatively risky financial strategy, or when it becomes more diversified, employees may be put under additional strain. More risky strategies may present a threat to employees' financial and emotional security, as jobs are threatened or company ownership is transferred. Similarly, employees' shared interests may decrease as diversification increases, since product-driven common concerns may be few. Under these conditions, some types of content themes should be more likely to emerge than others. It was argued that two alternative hypotheses were plausible.

One alternative is that greater diversification and more risky financial strategies may create conditions that make the espousal of humanitarian concerns desirable. For example, espousing people-oriented values might provide a common set of interests and a cohesiveness that might otherwise be absent in a highly diversified company, where different interest groups struggle for economic resources. Emphasis on the value of employees as individuals might also carry a promise of security otherwise missing in a firm prone to taking financial risks. These can be seen as impression management arguments. The problems created by more risky and more diversified strategies, such as employee insecurity and a lack of shared interests, are partially compensated for by top management's espoused values, emphasizing humanitarian rather than financial concerns. Such espoused humanitarian concerns, of course, may be quite inconsistent with the effects of risky financial and diversification strategies that threaten employees' financial and emotional security.

The opposite alternative is also possible. In firms that adopt less risky financial strategies, there should be less rapid turnover and more geographical stability, enabling employees to get to know each other personally. In specialized firms, employees who share task-oriented concerns about similar products may be more likely to develop the personal concerns that must be present if "concern for people" values are to be credible. Thus, more specialization and less riskiness may create the homogeneity of interests and personnel stability that are congruent with humanistic values (for instance, Leavitt, 1978; McGregor, 1960). This latter viewpoint is congruent with the consistency and consensus emphasis of the Integration Paradigm approach to culture, rather than the more cynical impression management position described above.

Finally, if either viewpoint were supported (that is, if an association between these types of content themes and these strategies could be found), then the contingency argument could be tested. The contingency argument can be summarized as: Firms that manifest a culture-strategy congruency should have higher financial performance levels than firms that lack such congruency.

In order to determine if the clustering of firms, according to the content themes emphasized in the annual reports, was related to choice of strategy, a multivariate discriminant analysis (MDA) was performed. In order to avoid the unreliability associated with small cluster size, only the seventy-two organizations from the four largest clusters (People, Products, Social Responsibility, and Finances) were included in this analysis. The riskiness and diversification indices were used as independent variables for classification.

The results of the MDA provided some evidence of a "culture"-strategy fit. The more risky financial strategy was associated with humanitarian content themes, in accord with the impression management argument. Diversification did not have enough explanatory power to enter the model.

In another analysis, the weights associated with placement in the discriminant space were used to classify the seventy-two organizations into one of the four content theme clusters listed above. Those organizations that were correctly classified into the appropriate type, using weights derived from the MDA, would be exhibiting evidence of a "culture"-strategy fit. According to the contingency hypothesis, firms that were correctly classified by this analysis should have higher performance levels than those firms that were not correctly classified.

Within each of the four types, the correctly classified firms — that is, those exhibiting a culture-strategy fit — did not have significantly higher performance levels than the incorrectly classified firms (those not showing evidence of a culture-strategy fit). A similar analysis, contrasting correctly and incorrectly classified firms from all four types simultaneously, also yielded no significant differences in financial performance levels. Contrary to the hypothesis, no evidence supporting the contingency approach to predicting financial performance was found.

In addition to the methodological limitations discussed above, this study focused on only two strategies: financial riskiness and degree of diversification. The results of the study may be due, not to flaws in the contingency argument, but to the choice of strategies studied. Although these two strategies have been shown to be related to organizational survival (Hannan & Freeman, 1977), survival is not the same as superior financial performance, particularly when the latter is measured only at a single point in time. Perhaps marketing strategies, particularly those that bear on a firm's definition of its distinctive competence, will present a more fruitful direction for research on the strategy-contingency argument.

The model proposed by Barney (1986) is in accord with this suggestion. Barney argues that organizational culture will be a source of sustained competitive advantage and thus, by implication, a source of sustained superior financial performance only when three conditions are met. First, the culture must be valuable in the sense of enabling positive economic consequences. Second, the culture must be rare, and third, the culture must be imperfectly imitable. Because not all firms have cultures with these attributes, organizational culture will not be a source of competitive advantage for all firms. This model is a provocative variant of the contingency argument presented earlier, but it has yet to be tested empirically.

A further variant of the contingency argument was proposed by Wilkins and Ouchi (1983). They argued that if an organization is facing conditions of high ambiguity, complexity, and interdependence of transactions, then a "strong" culture will result in greater efficiency and, by implication, improved performance. But under conditions of low complexity and low uncertainty, culture will be less efficient than other forms of control and, by implication, will result in lower performance. Again, this variant of the contingency argument has yet to be systematically tested.

Quinn and McGrath (1985) have also proposed a contingency argument linking culture to performance. They suggested that the type of culture must be congruent with the type of environment in order that certain outcomes, including performance, will occur. Working with a competing-values framework (Quinn, 1984; Quinn & Cameron, 1983; Quinn & Kimberly, 1984), they specifically link a rational culture, whose organizational purpose is the pursuit of clear objectives, with improved performance (efficiency, productivity, and profit) under the environmental condition of high intensity/low uncertainty. These predictions about the contingent nature of the relationship between culture and performance have yet to be tested empirically.

Finally, it is important to point out that some of the culture literature implicitly assumes that an organization's culture may significantly impair an organization's effectiveness and thus negatively impact its financial performance. For example, some kinds of shared cultures may prevent organizational members from perceiving diverse and/or unexpected opportunities and may inhibit them from pursuing activities that are inconsistent with the culture, but may be potentially critical to organizational effectiveness in a turbulent environment (for example, Crozier, 1964; Porter, 1980; Tichy, 1983). Research has failed to address this issue. Finally, there are numerous performance-related questions that emerge from the Differentiation and Ambiguity Paradigm approaches to studying culture. For example, are there conditions under which subcultural differentiation (for instance, Martin & Siehl, 1983; Wilkins & Ouchi, 1983) or open tolerance for ambiguity (for example, March & Olsen, 1976; Weick, 1979) have positive or negative impacts on performance?

Summary. Although this review of studies seeking a link between culture and financial performance is not complete (several unpublished studies, for example, are not included), it is, we believe, representative of the scope of this kind of research. These culture researchers have tended to be "specialists," focusing primarily on content themes rather than the full range of cultural manifestations. Further, they have generally examined relatively superficial content themes, such as policy-specific beliefs, rather than deeper, preconscious assumptions or symbolic interpretations. They tend to focus on espoused, rather than enacted, content themes. Most important, they tend to work exclusively within the Integration Paradigm, creating severe limitations in the ways they are defining culture.

In addition to these limitations in the definition and measurement of culture, these studies have not definitively established an empirical link to financial performance. Three versions of this link were examined and the evidence supporting each was found to be weak. In the next section, we explore the possibility that this lack of support is not the result of the lack of a relationship, but rather is due, in part, to the difficulties of testing these relationships.

Empirical Intractability

It is important to acknowledge the empirical difficulties inherent in examining the relationship between culture and performance. For generalized statements to be made about a link between culture and financial performance, a large sample of organizations is needed. And, in order to acquire a deep and thorough understanding of a variety of cultural manifestations (including relatively deep interpretations and taken-for-granted, perhaps unconscious, assumptions), a large investment of time, money, and patience is required—in even one firm. Special skills, such as ethnographic methods or clinical interviewing techniques, may be necessary, particularly if deeper aspects of culture are being studied (Schein, 1987; Van Maanen, 1979).

Gathering these kinds of cultural data in a large number of organizations is nearly impossible. It simply takes too much time. Yet, many researchers are understandably reluctant to rely on culture measures that are insufficiently rich or close to the phenomenon.

It is virtually impossible to conduct in-depth case studies of the cultures of more than a few sites. The usual methodological caveats—for example, about taking comparable measures across sites and using appropriate comparison groups—are essential and very difficult to execute. Some researchers have developed repeatable quantitative measures that tap a variety of cultural manifestations, not just espoused content themes (for example, Kilmann, Saxton, Serpa, & Associates,

1985; Martin, Sitkin, & Boehm, 1985; Siehl & Martin, 1988). However, these measures lack the breadth, depth, and richness that many cultural researchers find essential.

In addition, most culture researchers are reluctant to become involved in building fully specified models of financial performance, including all the usual control variables (such as size, market competitiveness, industry, and so forth) that researchers in other domains consider essential for a full understanding of financial performance. Indeed, data on a wide range of these control variables is essential for identification purposes, if causal modeling techniques are to be used. For these reasons, studies of the culture-performance relationship that involve adequate aggregated data are a methodological nightmare.

These methodological difficulties are severe in and of themselves. Yet they fail to even allude to a much tougher problem: time. Perhaps a link between culture and financial performance exists, but it does not reliably become evident within a short (one-year) time frame. If this is so, a cross-sectional design would reveal no relationship and an erroneous conclusion would be drawn. If longitudinal data on culture and financial performance were available, important questions about causality could be addressed. For example, are informal behavioral norms generally stable over time independent of changes in formal policy? What is the lag between the adoption of a new cultural direction and its impact, if any, on financial performance? If there is an association between culture and financial performance, what is the direction of causality: do certain content themes influence performance, as is usually implied, or does the level of financial performance determine what themes are expressed, or is the relationship reciprocal? In order to address these important issues, however, all of the methodological difficulties discussed above would have to be addressed at every time period to be studied.

To further complicate matters, it may be inappropriate to address the question of a relationship between culture and financial performance with organization-level data. As Barney (1986) suggests, cultural variables may impact financial performance only under some specialized conditions. For example, the impact may only occur in firms where certain specific cultural assumptions block the implementation of particular change programs. If studies rely exclusively on aggregated data drawn from large random samples of organizations, this limited kind of impact of cultural variables on financial performance will be missed. Such a point of view suggests that some research should focus on longitudinal case studies of organizations facing similar kinds of trouble.

Furthermore, it is possible that performance has been inappropriately conceptualized. Even if a financial focus is perhaps appropriate, in some firms, culture is related to profit stabilization or growth, while in others, it is related to the maximization of profits in the short term. In addition, it may be that financial performance measures should incorporate consideration of "intermediate factors," such as differential tax structures in various industries, scrappage, and technology-based economies of scale. It is possible that culture has a direct impact only on nonfinancial aspects of financial performance, such as morale, commitment, mental and physical health, and job satisfaction. Culture might impact financial performance indirectly, through such variables as productivity, quality control, turnover, or absenteeism.

When these other aspects of performance are considered, different kinds of variables become relevant. Perhaps, rather than looking internally to a firm's strategies, the appropriate focus is external to the organization. To cite only one possibility, organizations that are heavily resource-dependent, or that face an unusually turbulent environment, may try to reduce uncertainty by stabilizing, rather than maximizing, profits. If so, degree of resource dependency or environmental turbulence may impact which values are articulated to organizational constituencies and which financial objectives are sought.

Expansion of the types of variables considered, to include such other contingencies as environmental turbulence or resource dependency, might well increase the chances of finding a link between culture and performance. In addition, such a major change in the focus of culture research would link this domain of inquiry to other streams of financial performance research, and to the mainstream of organizational theory, more broadly defined (see Chapter Four in this volume).

Finally, an emphasis on traditional outcome variables, such as financial performance, may well obscure the importance of organizational processes, such as innovation and creativity. Such processes are significant independent of a direct link with performance-related outcome variables, particularly if we can begin to distance ourselves from existing functionalist paradigms, and consider the perspective of those people, such as lower-level employees, who benefit less fully and directly, if at all, from an improvement in profitability. We agree with the argument that such processes may ultimately be more important and fundamental than traditional outcomes (Staw, 1984). Clearly this is a critically important avenue for future research.

Is the Focus on a Link Between Culture and Performance Problematic?

The existing research on the relationship between organizational culture and financial performance, and some of the difficulties of conducting such research, have been addressed. Now, we turn to the third focus of this chapter. We believe that it is critical to discuss the potentially negative ramifications of focusing on the link between culture and performance. All of the functionalist suggestions for improving culture-performance research, detailed in the previous section, may be on the "wrong track." We believe there are several significant reasons why a focus on performance may be hampering the development of our understanding of culture specifically and, more generally, of how culture relates to other aspects of organizational theory.

First, a continued functionalist focus on financial performance reinforces applied, managerial thinking rather than theory development. Searching for a link between culture and performance confines researchers to the existing functionalist paradigm of what organizations are, and what they should be doing. If we continue, either explicitly or implicitly, to use culture as yet another determinant of performance-related outcomes, we will fail to realize the full potential of studying culture. Many cultural researchers (we are relatively recent converts to this point of view) do not conceive of culture as yet another variable to add to the domain of organizational theory.

Rather than conceptualizing culture as "caused" by some variables and as "causing" other outcome variables to increase or decrease, these cultural researchers argue that, instead of being a variable, culture is a metaphor for organizational life (Smircich, 1983). A full presentation of these ideas requires exploration of the epistemological roots and methodological implications of this approach to theory building. Although such an exploration is beyond the scope of this paper, introductions to some of these ideas, with specific reference to culture research, can be found elsewhere (for instance, Schein, 1987; Van Maanen, 1979; Van Maanen & Barley, 1984).

When researchers look at organizations "as if" they were cultures, they can enrich our understanding of organizational life in new and unexpected ways. Already, interest in culture has opened and reopened neglected areas of inquiry—for example, by exploring the organizational relevance of symbolism, structuration, semiotics, deconstruction, and ideology (see Barley, 1983; Gahmberg, 1987; Jermier 1985; Moxnes, 1987; Pondy, 1977; Riley, 1983). These cultural studies bring us far beyond the traditional variables of organizational theory, such as structure, firm size, technology, job satisfaction, motivation, and leadership.

By drawing attention to the multiple interpretations that people generate to understand, legitimate, or question their activities at work, these studies offer a deeper understanding of what goes on inside organizations. Examination of the patterns of relationship among cultural manifestations gives us a fuller comprehension of the consistencies, inconsistencies, and ambiguities that constitute the texture of organizational life. These approaches to the study of cultures lead us to insights unavailable within current paradigms of organizational theory.

Furthermore, for some researchers in the field of organizational behavior, exposure to qualitative cultural studies has led to a new appreciation for the depth of understanding that can emerge from the sophisticated use of ethnographic methods. In addition, if culture research supplements its traditional focus on internal organizational workings with a greater consideration of environmental concerns, then culture studies may suggest more complex and subtle ways to contribute to theories of institutionalization, resource dependence, and organizational learning. None of these contributions — potential or already achieved — is predicated on finding a link between culture and performance.

Indeed, seeking a culture-performance link may not only deflect energy from potentially innovative avenues of inquiry; it may even have pernicious social effects. Organizational behavior research has been criticized as biased to serve managerial, rather than individual or societal, interests (for example, Braverman, 1974; Clawson, 1980; Nord, 1974). Such criticism has been directed specifically at culture research (for instance, Calas & Smircich, 1987; Jermier, 1985; Stablein & Nord, 1985), particularly that research which has sought links between culture and performance. The potential of such links raises ethical questions as to "in whose best interests is this research being conducted?" (Deetz, 1985). Even cultural studies of ESOPs, worker cooperatives or labor unions (as yet undone) are not necessarily immune to this problem.

Some specific examples should make this negative potential evident. To the extent that culture researchers focus on the ideologies espoused by top management, they may be studying efforts to indoctrinate employees in a value system that exploits their potential for enthusiasm, commitment, and productivity, facilitating the direction of resulting profits to the disproportionate benefit of higher-level employees and stockholders. Thus, the arguments of those who admiringly describe culture as a managerial control mechanism can be restated as attempts to maintain ideological hegemony and exploit the productivity of those who do not control or own the means of production.

A more moderate version of this argument (and one that pertains to all studies of culture, not just those that seek a link to performance) begins with the premise that culture is cognitive and emotional, as well as behavioral. While many would concede some aspects of the control of behavior to organizations, we are particularly uneasy about facilitating control of employees' thoughts and emotions. This can present particularly severe problems for women and minorities, especially in organizations where management's espoused values are clearly articulated and conformity is expected. Such "strong cultures" are almost always initiated and controlled by white males. In such contexts, cultural conformity may be particularly difficult—and undesirable—for those who are demographically (or otherwise) dissimilar (for example, Ouchi, 1981). Even if clearly articulated, widely shared cultures were shown to be a key to improved financial performance, these cultural environments might be precisely the contexts where women and minorities would encounter the most discrimination.

These are only a few of the reasons a focus on the relationship between culture and performance may have negative effects. An implicit managerial bias leads many researchers to continue to advocate and pursue this relationship in spite of a glaring lack of empirical support and potentially insurmountable difficulties in gathering reliable data. We would conclude by asserting that, rather than continuing in this quest, as culture researchers we should instead seriously consider the issues raised above. The concept of culture holds too much promise to be sold short as just another intervening variable in existing models of the determinants of organizational performance.

Notes

1. Space limitations make it impossible for us to address, except obliquely, the question of how culture differs from other familiar concepts, such as climate, commitment, job satisfaction, and so on. This is a far more difficult request than it first appears because many—but by no means all—culture researchers do not have functionalist objectives. Also, many cultural researchers prefer idiographic and qualitative methods. Most important, many culture researchers would argue that, rather than being a variable, culture is a metaphor for organizational life (Smircich,

1983). When culture is conceived of as a metaphor in this manner, a request to define the difference between culture and other more familiar variables misses the point. Given the focus of this volume, it may be helpful to note that the culture researchers who seek a link to financial performance are generally more similar to climate researchers than they are to the qualitative, idiographic culture researchers described in this footnote.

2. We understand that Denison, in an as-yet unpublished manuscript, has extended his study of financial performance longitudinally, with perhaps an additional five years of data. This will be an important improvement in the measurement of financial performance, a variable that Denison has already measured as well as any cultural researcher. The question, of course, is whether the measures of culture have also been significantly improved.

References

Argyris, C., & Schön, D. A. (1978). *Organizational learning: A theory of action perspective.* Reading, MA: Addison-Wesley.

Baker, E. L. (1980). Managing organizational culture. *Management Review, 69,* 8–13.

Barley, S. R. (1983). Semiotics and the study of occupational and organizational cultures. *Administrative Science Quarterly, 28,* 393–414.

Barley, S., Meyer, G. W., & Gash, D. (1988). Cultures of culture: Academics, practitioners, and the pragmatics of normative control. *Administrative Science Quarterly, 33*(1), 24–61.

Barney, J. B. (1986). Organizational culture: Can it be a source of sustained competitive advantage? *Academy of Management Review, 11,* 656–665.

Berger, P. (1967). *The sacred canopy.* Garden City, NY: Doubleday.

Bettman, J. R., & Weitz, B. (1983). Attributions in the boardroom: Causal reasoning in corporate annual reports. *Administrative Science Quarterly, 28,* 165–183.

Bourgeois, L., & Jemison, D. (1982). Analyzing corporate culture in its strategic context. *Exchange: The Organizational Behavior Teaching Journal, 7*(3), 37–41.

Braverman, H. (1974). *Labor and monopoly capital: The degradation of work in the twentieth century.* New York: Monthly Review Press.

Brunsson, W. (1985). *The irrational organization.* New York: Wiley.

Calas, M., & Smircich, L. (1987). *Post-culture: Is the organizational culture literature dominant but dead?* Paper presented at the International Conference on Organizational Symbolism and Corporate Culture, Milan, Italy.

Clark, B. R. (1970). *The distinctive college: Antioch, Reed, and Swarthmore.* Chicago: Aldine.

Clark, B. R. (1972). The organizational saga in higher education. *Administrative Science Quarterly, 17,* 178–184.

Clawson, D. (1980). *Bureaucracy and the labor process.* New York: Monthly Review Press, pp. 11–35.

Crozier, M. (1964). *The bureaucratic phenomenon.* Chicago: University of Chicago Press.

Deetz, S. (1985). Ethical considerations in cultural research. In P. J. Frost, L. Moore, M. R. Louis, C. C. Lundberg, & J. Martin (Eds.), *Organizational culture: The meaning of life in the workplace.* Newbury Park, CA: Sage.

Denison, D. R. (1984). Bringing corporate culture to the bottom line. *Organizational Dynamics, 12,* 4–22.

Feldman, M. (1984). Policy expertise in a public bureaucracy (doctoral dissertation, Stanford University, 1983). *Dissertation Abstracts International, 44,* 2281A.

Gahmberg, H. (1987). *Semiotic tools for the study of organizational cultures.* Paper presented at the International Conference on Organizational Symbolism and Corporate Culture, Milan, Italy.

Golding, D. (1987). *Certainty as a symbolic artifact of management.* Paper presented at the International Conference on Organizational Symbolism and Corporate Culture, Milan, Italy.

Gordon, G. C. (1985). The relationship of corporate culture to industry sector and corporate performance. In R. H. Kilmann, M. J. Saxton, R. Serpa, & Associates, *Gaining control of the corporate culture.* San Francisco: Jossey-Bass.

Grafton-Small, R., & Linstead, S. (1987). *Artefact as theory: all roses lead to Milano.* Paper presented at the International Conference on Organizational Symbolism and Corporate Culture, Milan, Italy.

Gregory, K. L. (1983). Native-view paradigms: Multiple cultures and culture conflicts in organizations. *Administrative Science Quarterly, 28,* 359–376.

Hannan, M., & Freeman, J. H. (1977). The population ecology of organizations. *American Journal of Sociology, 82,* 929–964.

Jermier, J. (1985). When the sleeper wakes: A short story extending themes in radical organization theory. *Journal of Management, 11,* 67–80.

Kilmann, R. H., Saxton, M. J., Serpa, R., & Associates (1985). *Gaining control of the corporate culture.* San Francisco: Jossey-Bass.

Leavitt, H. J. (1978). *Managerial psychology.* Chicago: University of Chicago Press.

Louis, M. R. (1983). Organizations as culture-bearing milieux. In L. R. Pondy, P. J. Frost, G. Morgan, & T. C. Dandridge (Eds.), *Organizational symbolism.* Greenwich, CT: JAI Press.

Lukas, R. (1987). Political-cultural analysis of organizations. *Academy of Management Review, 12,* 144–156.

McGregor, D. (1960). *The human side of enterprise.* New York: McGraw-Hill.

March, J., & Olsen, J. (1976). *Ambiguity and choice in organizations.* Bergen, Norway: Universitets Forlaget.

Martin, J. (1981). Stories and scripts in organizational settings. In A. Hastorf & A. Isen (Eds.), *Cognitive social psychology.* New York: Elsevier–North Holland.

Martin, J., Anterasian, C., & Siehl, C. (1988). *Externally espoused values and the legitimation of financial performance* (working paper). Palo Alto, CA: Stanford University, Graduate School of Business.

Martin, J., Feldman, M. S., Hatch, M. J., & Sitkin, S. B. (1983). The uniqueness paradox in organizational stories. *Administrative Science Quarterly, 28,* 438–453.

Martin, J., & Meyerson, D. (1988). Organizational cultures and the denial, masking, and amplification of ambiguity. In M.

Moch, L. Pondy, & H. Thomas (Eds.), *Managing ambiguity and change*. New York: Wiley.

Martin, J., & Siehl, C. (1983). Organizational culture and counterculture: An uneasy symbiosis. *Organizational Dynamics, 12*(2), 52–64.

Martin, J., Sitkin, S., & Boehm, M. (1985). Founders and the elusiveness of a cultural legacy. In P. J. Frost, L. Moore, M. R. Louis, C. C. Lundberg, & J. Martin (Eds.), *Organizational culture*. Newbury Park, CA: Sage.

Moxnes, P. (1987). *Deep roles: An archetypal model of organizational roles*. Paper presented at the International Conference on Organizational Symbolism and Corporate Culture, Milan, Italy.

Nord, W. (1974). The failure of current applied behavioral science: A Marxian perspective. *Journal of Applied Behavioral Science, 10*, 557–578.

Ouchi, W. G. (1981). *Theory Z*. Reading, MA: Addison-Wesley.

Ouchi, W. G., & Johnson, J. B. (1978). Types of organizational control and their relationship to emotional well-being. *Administrative Science Quarterly, 23*, 293–317.

Pascale, R., & Athos, A. (1981). *The art of Japanese management*. New York: Simon & Schuster.

Peters, T., & Waterman, R. H., Jr. (1982). *In search of excellence: Lessons from America's best-run companies*. New York: Harper & Row.

Phillips, R., & Kennedy, A. A. (1980, December). Shaping and managing shared values. *McKinsey Staff Paper*.

Pondy, R. (1977). Language is a leadership game. In M. McCall & M. Lombardo (Eds.), *Leadership: Where else can we go?* Durham, NC: Duke University Press.

Porter, M. (1980). *Competitive strategy*. New York: Free Press.

Quinn, R. E. (1984). Applying the competing values approach to leadership: Toward an integrative framework. In J. G. Hunt, D. Hosking, C. Shriesheim, & R. Stewart (Eds.), *Managerial work and leadership: International perspectives*. Elmsford, NY: Pergamon.

Quinn, R. E., & Cameron, K. (1983). Organizational life cycles and shifting criteria of effectiveness: Some preliminary evidence. *Management Science, 29*, 33–51.

Quinn, R. E., & Kimberly, J. R. (1984). The management of transitions. In J. R. Kimberly & R. E. Quinn (Eds.), *New futures: The challenge of transition management.* Homewood, IL: Dow Jones–Irwin.

Quinn, R. E., & McGrath, M. (1985). The transformation of organizational cultures: A competing values perspective. In P. J. Frost, L. Moore, M. R. Louis, C. C. Lundberg, & J. Martin (Eds.), *Organizational culture: The meaning of life in the workplace.* Newbury Park, CA: Sage.

Riley, P. A. (1983). A structurationist account of political culture. *Administrative Science Quarterly, 28*, 414–437.

Salancik, G. R. (1977). Commitment and the control of organizational behavior and belief. In B. M. Staw & G. R. Salancik (Eds.), *New directions in organizational behavior.* Chicago: St. Clair Press.

Salancik, G. R., & Meindl, J. R. (1984). Corporate attributions as strategic illusions of management control. *Administrative Science Quarterly, 29*, 238–254.

Schein, E. H. (1981). Does Japanese management style have a message for American managers? *Sloan Management Review, 21*, 63–67.

Schein, E. H. (1983). The role of the founder in creating organizational culture. *Organizational Dynamics, 12*(1), 13–28.

Schein, E. H. (1985). *Organizational culture and leadership: A dynamic view.* San Francisco: Jossey-Bass.

Schein, E. H. (1987). *The clinical perspective in fieldwork.* Newbury Park, CA: Sage.

Schwartz, H., & Davis, S. M. (1981). Matching corporate culture and business strategy. *Organizational Dynamics, 9*, 30–48.

Selznick, P. (1957). *Leadership and administration.* New York: Harper & Row.

Siehl, C. (1988). *The role of ambiguous stories in creating an illusion of consistency* (working paper). Los Angeles: University of Southern California, School of Business.

Siehl, C., & Martin, J. (1984). The role of symbolic management:

How can managers effectively transmit organizational culture? In J. G. Hunt, D. Hosking, & R. Stewart (Eds.), *Managerial
work and leadership: International perspectives.* Elmsford, NY:
Pergamon.

Siehl, C., & Martin, J. (1988). Measuring organizational culture:
Mixing qualitative and quantitative methods. In M. O. Jones,
M. Moore, & R. Schneider (Eds.), *Organizational ethnography:
Field studies of culture and symbolism.* Newbury Park, CA: Sage.

Smircich, L. (1981). Studying organizations as cultures. In G.
Morgan (Ed.), *Research strategies: Links between theory and
method.* Philadelphia: Pennsylvania State University Press.

Smircich, L. (1983). Concepts of culture and organizational
analysis. *Administrative Science Quarterly, 28,* 339–358.

Stablein, R., & Nord, W. (1985). Practical and emancipatory
interests in organizational symbolism: A review and evaluation. *Journal of Management, 11,* 13–28.

Starbuck, W. (1983). Organizations as action generators. *American Sociological Review, 48,* 91–102.

Staw, B. M. (1984). Organizational behavior: A review and refor-
mulation of the field's outcome variables. In M. Rosenzweig &
L. Porter (Eds.), *Annual review of psychology, 35,* 627–666.

Staw, B. M., McKechnie, P. I., & Puffer, S. M. (1983). The justification of organizational performance. *Administrative Science
Quarterly, 28,* 582–600.

Tichy, N. M. (1982). Managing change strategically: The technical, political, and cultural keys. *Organizational Dynamics,
11*(2), 59–80.

Tichy, N. M. (1983). *Managing strategic change: Technical, political,
and cultural dynamics.* New York: Wiley.

Van Maanen, J. (1979). The self, the situation, and the rules of
interpersonal relations. In W. G. Bennis, D. E. Berlew, E. H.
Schein, & F. I. Steele (Eds.), *Interpersonal dynamics: Essays and
readings on human interaction.* Homewood, IL: Dorsey.

Van Maanen, J., & Barley, S. (1984). Occupational communities:
Culture and control in organizations. In B. Staw & L. Cummings (Eds.), *Research in organizational behavior* (Vol. 6). Greenwich, CT: JAI Press.

Weick, K. (1979). *The social psychology of organizing.* Reading, MA: Addison-Wesley.

Who's excellent now: Some of the best-seller's picks haven't been doing so well lately. (1984, November 5). *Business Week,* pp. 76–94.

Wilkins, A. (1983). Organizational stories: Symbols which control the organization. In L. R. Pondy, P. J. Frost, G. Morgan, & T. C. Dandridge (Eds.), *Organizational symbolism.* Greenwich, CT: JAI Press.

Wilkins, A. (1984). The creation of company cultures: The role of stories and human resource systems. *Human Resource Management, 23,* 41–60.

Wilkins, A., & Ouchi, W. G. (1983). Efficient cultures: Exploring the relationship between culture and organizational performance. *Administrative Science Quarterly, 28,* 468–481.

Wuthnow, R., Hunter, J., Bergesen, A., & Kurzweil, E. (1984). *Cultural analysis.* Boston: Routledge & Kegan Paul.

Chapter 8

Richard E. Kopelman
Arthur P. Brief
Richard A. Guzzo

The Role of
Climate and Culture
in Productivity

The primary concern of this chapter is with how the environment of work contributes to work effectiveness. The environment is characterized in terms of organizational *culture* and *climate*; effectiveness is depicted in terms of *productivity*. Based largely on data about the determinants of productivity, causal connections between culture, climate, and productivity are explored.

The chapter begins by examining the meaning of culture and its indicators. It reviews varied perspectives on culture and offers a brief assessment of the status of the culture construct. The climate construct is then similarly examined. Discussed next is the relation between organizational climate and productivity, with particular attention given to psychological processes mediating this relation. An orienting model provides the framework for the chapter. Throughout, the chapter emphasizes culture, climate, and productivity as they relate to the human resource management practices of organizations.

Organizational Culture: Meaning, Indicators, and Applications

Two Meanings of Organizational Culture

In anthropology, the concept of *societal* culture has generated a considerable degree of controversy. Indeed, an early comprehensive review of the concept produced more than 100 definitions (Kroeber & Kluckhohn, 1952). At present, several prominent definitions, and their associated schools of anthropology, exist. There is, however, general agreement that the various perspectives can be meaningfully classified into two categories (Chilcott, 1987; Goodenough, 1964; Swartz & Jordan, 1980): (1) the phenomenal perspective, focusing on observable behaviors and artifacts; (2) the ideational perspective, focusing on shared meanings, symbols, and values.

A similar bifurcation of approaches has emerged in connection with the concept of *organizational* culture. Some writers and researchers attend to observable phenomena such as rites, rituals, stories, and creeds (for example, Beyer & Trice, 1987; Deal & Kennedy, 1982; Hickman & Silva, 1987; Martin & Siehl, 1983). Others emphasize the shared—and often taken-for-granted or preconscious—values, beliefs, and assumptions held by members (for instance, Sathe, 1983; Schein, 1985; Smircich, 1983). Values, beliefs, and assumptions are not as clearly discernible as overt behaviors or codified creeds. In fairness, however, it should be noted that virtually all writers have recognized that the concept of organizational culture pertains to both observable and ideational aspects of organizational behavior.

Thus, while most conceptual definitions of organizational culture recognize the existence of two levels of culture (observable manifestations and underlying, interpreted meanings), specific research methods and accompanying operational definitions have limited the scope of most inquiries to one level or the other. It might also be noted that two of Smircich's (1983) widely cited five culture themes (cross-national and corporate culture) focus on observables. The other three themes—cognitions, symbolisms, and unconscious processes—relate to less observable interpretations. Curiously, Smircich and Calas (1987) classified several ideationally oriented organizational culture theorists (such as Schein, 1985) as representative of the phenomenal, observable culture camp. Apparently, the latter three of the Smircich themes have been reserved for those writers who are not "managerially biased," who seek the "reformation of social arrangements" (Smircich, 1983, p. 353), and who promote the "emancipatory interest" (Smircich & Calas,

1987, p. 242). We regard Schein's (1985) work as characteristic of the ideational school.

Some writers have extended the definition of organizational culture to include formal management practices (for example, Akin & Hopelain, 1986; Martin & Siehl, 1983; O'Toole, 1985). In our opinion, though, when organizational culture is defined this broadly it loses conceptual clarity. It no longer refers just to shared meanings and manifestations (the "why" of organizational behavior), but also to specific formal practices (the "what"; see Schneider and Rentsch, 1988).

Indications of Organizational Culture

Organizational researchers attending primarily to observable phenomena have employed a variety of measurement techniques. Some, in preparing case studies, have obtained information from published sources and/or personal interviews (for example, Deal & Kennedy, 1982; Hickman & Silva, 1987; Peters & Waterman, 1982). In-depth ethnographies rely on extensive participant and nonparticipant observations (for instance, Harris & Sutton, 1986; Sapienza, 1987). Examinations of rites and stories have been performed based on content analyses of published accounts of such phenomena (Beyer & Trice, 1987; Martin, Feldman, Hatch, & Sitkin, 1983).

Proponents of the ideational school have largely relied on either of two major approaches in collecting data on organizational culture: in-depth interviews or survey questionnaires. One thoughtful and comprehensive work within the ideational school is Schein's *Organizational Culture and Leadership: A Dynamic View* (1985). According to Schein, there are no reliable, quick ways to identify shared values. Rather, it is necessary to rely on firsthand observations and iterative, clinical interviews. Complicating matters a bit, Schein refers to basic values (that is, ideal modes of conduct and end states; see Rokeach, 1969, 1973) as *assumptions* and uses the term *values* solely to describe espoused values. Yet, Schein's "assumptions" truly are basic value statements. Indeed, the theoretical basis and content of these statements comes from Kluckhohn and Strodtbeck's *Variations in*

Value Orientations (1961), which describes basic values or terminal goals.

Based on the view that it is necessary to uncover preconscious beliefs in order to assess organizational culture, Schein (1985, p. 135) asserts that the search for cultural assumptions may be "elusive even after months of study." Indeed, he adds, "culture does not reveal itself easily. It is clearly there, but to articulate it and describe it requires great patience and effort" (p. 136). Further, he cautions that the "deciphering of a cultural paradigm . . . is difficult and hazardous" (p. 312). Along these lines, Sathe (1983, pp. 6–7) asserts that "reading a culture is an interpretive, subjective activity." For Wilkins (1983, p. 37) the process is "something of an art."

In light of the apparent ambiguity and subjectivity inherent in the ideational approach to "measuring" organizational culture, one might wonder whether the whole enterprise is not somewhat akin to contact lenses — in the eye of the beholder. However, this skepticism is not really warranted, at least insofar as Schein's work is concerned. He has developed guidelines for a ten-step systematic process of assessment that includes an iterative interview program, conceptually grounded in a theory of values. Further, critical incident–based general protocols have been developed for individual and group interviews pertinent to each value orientation (for example, the trustworthiness of people, the ideal distribution of power). Pertinent to the validity of Schein's organization-specific interpretations, it appears that most of these specific interpretations were accepted by members of the client organizations. Some interpretations, though, were resisted. Given the developmental work that has been achieved, we question whether it might not be possible to develop construct-valid, standardized measures (perhaps using projective methods) to tap fundamental value orientations.

As noted earlier, organizational culture, as indicated by value orientations, also has been assessed through various survey instruments (for instance, Harrison, 1972, 1987; Hebden, 1986; Hofstede, 1980; O'Toole, 1985; Tucker & McCoy, 1988; also see Chapter Five in this volume). An evaluation of either the conceptual merits or the construct validity of evidence pertaining to the various questionnaire instruments that purport to measure organizational culture is beyond the scope of this chapter. We accept the *possibility* that value orientations held by members of an organization may be amenable to valid measurement. While we recognize that espoused personal values may be inconsistent with actual behaviors (Argyris & Schön, 1978), this does not meant that it is impossible to measure values with a standardized survey instrument. However, to date little empirical construct-validation research has been published pertinent either to objective or subjective measures of organizational culture. Perhaps this reflects a paucity of advanced widely accepted theorizing about the nature and dimensionality of culture. Yet, if Schneider's (1987) Attraction-Selection-Attrition model is valid, there is reason to believe that, over time, organizational members will come to share a common value orientation. It remains to be seen if current culture measures are up to the task of discerning such differences across organizations.

Applications of the Culture Construct

Numerous claims have been made in the popular and professional literatures regarding the utility of the concept of organizational culture. It has been argued that knowledge of organizational culture can be useful in planning mergers and acquisitions, and also for strategic planning (Wilkins, 1983). Failed mergers have frequently been "explained" post hoc in terms of "culture clash." It has also been suggested that knowledge of organizational culture can be helpful to organizations and individuals in connection with recruitment, selection, and career planning (Deal & Kennedy, 1982; Sathe, 1983). Further, it has been implied that knowledge of organizational culture may be useful in developing a "strong" culture, thereby providing several benefits. These include increased member identification, commitment, and cooperation (Martin, Feldman, Hatch, & Sitkin, 1983; Ouchi, 1981; Pettigrew, 1979); greater behavioral clarity and individual "sense making" (Deal & Kennedy, 1982; Louis, 1983); greater consistency in decision making and performance (Hickman & Silva, 1987; Sathe, 1983); enhanced individual acculturation and socialization (Louis, 1983); and more successful succession planning (Schein, 1983, 1985). Unfortunately, these claims are largely speculations that await systematic investigation.

It has also been suggested, to the contrary, that organizational cultures may be far less diverse than is widely thought (for example, Martin, Feldman, Hatch, & Sitkin, 1983). Certainly there is evidence that organizations tend to adopt similar *practices*, at least among those that manage to survive (DiMaggio & Powell, 1983; Spender, 1983; Woodward, 1965). As Aldrich (1979, p. 265) puts it, "The major factors that organizations must take into account are other organizations." Today, this phenomenon takes the form of "competitive benchmarking"—that is, comparing performance in various activities across organizations (for instance, inventory turnover), and attempting to imitate the best practices in the industry for each function (see Fuld, 1988; Ghemawat, 1986).

Not only do some writers question the diversity of organizational cultures, others argue that "strong" cultures may actually be dysfunctional. As Schneider (1987) has noted, high levels of member homogeneity may lead to what Argyris (1976) characterized as "dry rot." Organizational research by D. R. Denison (1984) supports this contention. Based on responses from more than 40,000 individuals, it was found that high perceptual agreement among individuals as to ideal organizational practices was positively related to current and short-term organizational performance, but negatively related to long-term organizational performance. Along these lines, the inherent tension between the efficiency and the innovativeness arising from homogeneous and heterogeneous organizations has been noted by many researchers (for instance, Drucker, 1973).

Culture as Phlogiston? We would hope that the debate about the concept of culture does not become moot, as have many scholarly controversies in the past. The debate that emerged in scientific circles in the early 1700s concerning the element phlogiston is one such example. At the time the weight of learned opinion was that phlogiston, an invisible gas, was produced upon combustion. Later it was concluded that phlogiston not only was invisible, it did not exist.

What presently is needed, we suggest, is increased attention to the development of theory-based, construct-valid measures of organizational culture. At the same time, evidence regarding the utility of the culture construct needs to be developed.

An Orienting Framework

Although the construct of organizational culture is in need of development, we can locate it in a conceptual framework that drives our subsequent discussion of culture, climate, and productivity. This framework appears in Figure 8.1. Note that organizational culture is viewed as a product of societal culture. Organizational culture, in turn, provides the context in which organizational climate is nested. The relationship of climate to productivity, with various mediating stages, also is depicted in Figure 8.1. The remainder of this chapter elaborates the model shown in the figure.

The Cultural Context. To what extent do organizational practices reflect cultural influences? And what is the connection, in turn, between an organization's practices and its climate and productivity? These questions, embedded in Figure 8.1, now become the focus of our attention. It should be noted that the practices of interest are those concerned with managing human resources. Of special interest are changes made in such practices with the aim of improving employee productivity.

Broadly speaking, all organizations operate within a societal cultural context, whether we define that context in terms of shared meanings and values or observable behaviors and artifacts. While there are some similarities across cultural contexts (employees get paid, young children are not hired), distinct societal cultures produce unique sets of influences.

Consider the United States as a culture. Although regional differences exist, a number of common practices and influences can be identified. As related to human resource

Figure 8.1. A Model of Climate, Culture, and Productivity.

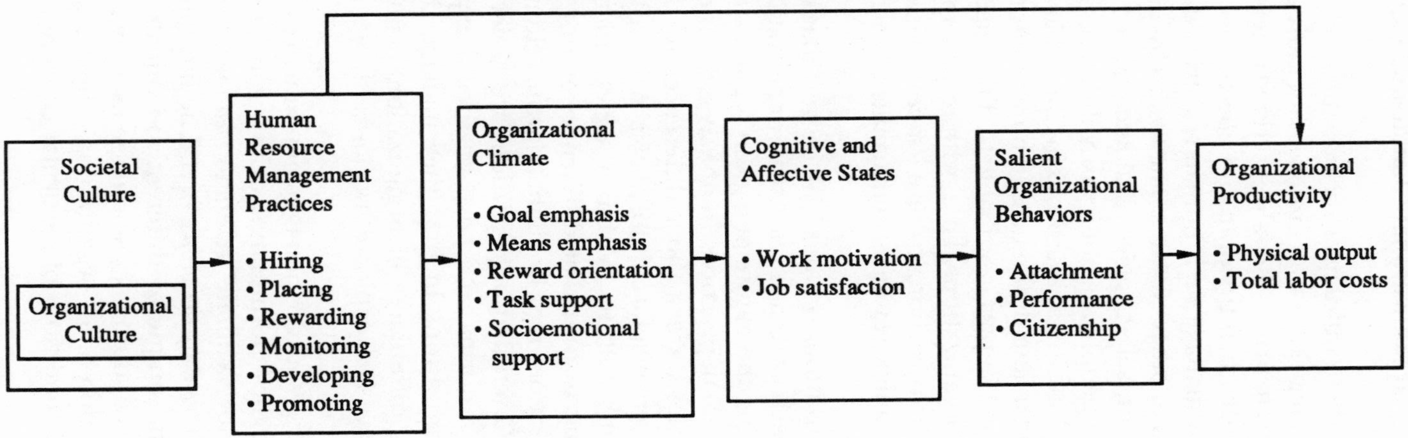

Societal Culture	Human Resource Management Practices	Organizational Climate	Cognitive and Affective States	Salient Organizational Behaviors	Organizational Productivity
Organizational Culture	• Hiring • Placing • Rewarding • Monitoring • Developing • Promoting	• Goal emphasis • Means emphasis • Reward orientation • Task support • Socioemotional support	• Work motivation • Job satisfaction	• Attachment • Performance • Citizenship	• Physical output • Total labor costs

management practices, these influences include the spirit and teeth of EEO and OSHA legislation, an emphasis on individual achievement and entrepreneurism, the value ascribed to leisure, and the reverence for individual freedom and liberty.

U.S. organizations manage their human resources differently than organizations in other cultures. The means by which U.S. organizations recruit, select, place, evaluate, reward, develop, release, and retire people are often vastly different from the way these things are done in organizations in China, Mexico, and many other cultures. These differences in human resource management practices are, in part, ascribable to differences in the cultural contexts of organizations. Thus, with respect to the first question raised in this section, culture — *societal culture* — does indeed influence human resource management practices in organizations.

But what of organizational culture? We suggest that societal differences may have a greater impact than organizational differences in determining the nature of a given organization's human resource management practices. In no way is this meant to imply that organizations are without differences in their cultures. Logically, however, societal culture plays a major role in shaping an organization's culture. Within a society, then, it should not be surprising to find that differences among the cultures of some organizations may be slight (Martin, Feldman, Hatch, & Sitkin, 1983). Given that organizations are subject to the same societal values, norms, and laws, we should expect similarities across organizations in how they manage their human resources. Thus, differences in organizational culture within a society may have less explanatory power than some have claimed.

Certainly, human resource management practices are important ingredients in the determination of an organization's climate. As we argue below, "climate" refers to *meaningful interpretations of a work environment by the people in it*. The interpretations are to some extent unique to different individuals, yet common environmental conditions exist and are used by individuals in their construction of an organization's climate. The common environmental conditions of particular concern here are the practices and conditions maintained by an organization for the purpose of managing its human resources. We turn now to an examination of the relationship of human resource management practices to climate and productivity.

Human Resource Management and Climate. According to the model in Figure 8.1, culture (societal and organizational) influences human resource management practices in organizations. These practices, in turn, should influence organizational climate and, ultimately, organizational productivity. The link between human resource management practices and productivity is addressed next, and then we provide a closer examination of climate and its role as a mediator of the management practices–productivity link.

Various human resource management practices have been implemented in order to raise productivity. Some of the more widespread (and thoroughly researched) practices include the use of financial incentives, feedback, goal setting, systematic selection and placement, training and development, participation in decision making, work redesign, flexible work schedules, organization development, and changes in organizational structure. Reviews of research on these practices have been provided by Guzzo (1988), Guzzo, Jette, and Katzell (1985), and Kopelman (1986), among others.

For the most part, different amounts and forms of these practices have been found to influence productivity, though in varying degrees and circumstances. Goal setting, for example, seems to be a practice that reliably induces productivity gains, at least in the short term. Training is another practice that has been found to have large positive effects on productivity. Redesigning jobs in the direction of increased variety, autonomy, and the like has been shown to yield productivity gains, though such gains are typically smaller than those arising from training or goal-setting inventions. Feedback—especially when it is objective and concrete—can raise productivity. However, when feedback arises from judgments or other relatively nonobjective practices, the productivity gains are often minimal. Financial incentives, too, have been shown to raise productivity, but the effects of financial incentives appear to depend on several boundary conditions. Likewise, systematic approaches to personnel selection have demonstrated positive effects on average performance. The point here is that ample research evidence shows that the appropriate application of human resource management practices can bring about productivity gains.

Why do these gains occur? We theorize that human resource management practices in part influence productivity through their effect on climate—that is, on how people interpret their work environment (see Figure 8.1). For instance, when an organization implements a new financial incentive plan or engages in participative decision making, a change in organizational climate may occur. This change in climate may, in turn, affect employee performance and productivity. Note that we do not assert that all of the effects of human resource management practices on productivity are mediated by changes in climate; productivity improvement practices may affect productivity for reasons other than the changes in climate those practices induce. Nonetheless, we assert that *some* of the consequences of productivity improvement practices reflect changes in climate.

While the above assertion is quite modest, there is surprisingly little evidence that bears directly on it. Few studies exist that have documented changes in climate that result from changes in human resource management practices. Most studies of the relationship of these practices to productivity improvement do not examine change in climate as a mediator of the practices' effects. Nor is climate typically the end variable of interest in research on the impact of human resource management practices.

A recent study by Pfluger (1988) examined changes in climate in response to the implementation of two distinct human resource management practices. Pfluger measured five dimensions of organization climate: autonomy, reward, support, participation, and warmth. (These climate dimensions correspond in part to the dimensions of reward orientation, socioemotional support, task support, and means emphasis as discussed later in this chapter.) Measures on each of these five dimensions were taken prior to the implementation of either of two new human resource management practices. The practices were implemented in nonoverlapping samples and changed such things as leader behavior, feedback, the breadth of job responsibilities, and rewards for performance. Results indicated that predictable changes in specific dimensions of climate resulted from the implementation of the new practices. Thus, organizational climate can change following the implementation of human resource management practices, and change in specific dimensions is determined by the nature of the human resource management practice implemented.

Data from other sources bear on changes in climate in response to variations in human resource management practices. Morse and Reimer (1956) documented changes in perceived autonomy as a result of differing management practices in two experimental conditions. Kopelman (1976) documented how differences in reward system practices were perceived over time in three organizations. Dastmalchian (1986), too, showed that distinct organizational environments (defined partly in terms of human resource management practices) are differentially related to organizational climate.

It seems likely that more than one climate dimension will change when one of the previously mentioned human resource management practices for improving productivity is implemented. The establishment of a financial incentive plan, for example, is likely to change not just the reward orientation dimension of climate (by heightening the salience of pay) but may also alter the socioemotional aspect of climate (to the extent that the administration of monetary rewards affects perceived equity). The use of systematic goal setting may alter not only *what* gets emphasized in the workplace — that is, which ends are sought — but also *how* (means emphasis) those ends are pursued. Increased participation by employees in planning and decision-making processes could affect several climate dimensions, especially goal emphasis, means emphasis, task support, and socioemotional support. Adopting flexible work schedules is a practice that can be expected to have little effect on what gets done (goal emphasis), but it might well affect how things get done (means emphasis). In this regard, flexible working hours were interpreted as enhancing productivity in a situation calling for common resources to be shared (Ralston, Anthony, & Gustafson, 1985).

Thus, changes in human resource management practices designed to improve employee productivity are likely to bring about changes in one or more dimensions of organizational climate. Of course, the dimensions of climate changed can be expected to depend on the character of the particular productivity improvement practice implemented. Further, changes in climate are likely to contribute to the ultimate effect of such practices on productivity.

This analysis is not unlike that provided by Likert (1961). Likert proposed a schema for understanding causal, intervening, and end-result variables in organizations. In this perspective, causal variables included things such as human resource management practices, while end-result variables included productivity. The connection between causal and end-result variables was viewed by Likert as dependent on intervening variables. Though the concept of organization climate had little currency at the time Likert wrote, climate surely fits into his framework as an intervening variable. Perhaps our major departure from Likert's model is that unlike him, we do not assert that all effects of human resource management practices on productivity are mediated by the "intervening variable" climate.

We now take a closer look at the concept of organizational climate.

Organizational Climate

Work environments cannot generally be described as psychologically neat and orderly. Rather, they typically can be represented as a bundle of stimuli presenting ambiguous and conflicting cues. Likewise, organizational members should be viewed as active perceivers and interpreters of their work environments. These environments so perceived and processed can be thought of as psychologically meaningful descriptions of contingencies and situational influences that individuals use to apprehend order, predict outcomes, and gauge the appropriateness of their organizational behaviors (for example, Campbell, Dunnette, Lawler, & Weick, 1970; James & Jones, 1974; Schneider, 1975). Such a cognitively based description of the work environment has also been referred to as *psychological climate* (James & Jones, 1974; Jones & James, 1979).

As indicated above, climate is functional in nature. That is, it serves as a basis for interpretation and, therefore, as a guide to action (for instance, Gellerman, 1959; Georgopoules, 1965; Gilmer, 1966; Litwin & Stringer, 1968; Pritchard & Karasick, 1973; Tagiuri, 1968). Indeed, as Schneider and Rentsch (1988) see it, climate is a "sense of imperative." This sense derives from incumbent perceptions of those organizational policies, practices, and procedures that indicate — through rewards, support, and expectations — the kinds of goals important in the organization and the means by which they are to be accomplished. More specifically, as Indik (1965) and Campbell, Dunnette, Lawler, and Weick (1970) suggest, climate is the psychological process that mediates the relationships between the work environment (conceived as an objective set of organizational policies, practices, and procedures) and work-related attitudes and behaviors. Thus, climate, as we view it, is neither what the work environment is nor how people respond to it; rather, climate is a perceptual medium through which the effects of the environment on attitudes and behavior pass.

As we have construed it, climate is an individual-level variable. Thus, it is expected to reflect individual characteristics involved in the processes of perception and concept formation as well as characteristics of the work environment (Jones & James, 1979). However, as captured by individual descriptions of organizational policies, practices, and procedures, climate is expected to be widely shared within organizational units subjected to the same policies, practices, and procedures. This is most obviously the case because the stimuli being described by the members of the unit are constant or nearly so across individuals. (The phrase "or nearly so" implies, as is evident for example from the results of Graen and his associates [see Dansereau, Graen, & Haga, 1975], that some attributes of the work environment may vary from one worker to another within the same unit.) Another reason climate is expected to be widely shared is that the range of individual differences reflected in climate is likely to be restricted within a unit. This was articulated by Schneider (1987) who, through his Attraction-Selection-Attrition framework, argued that particular kinds of people are attracted to particular settings and those who do not fit leave.

We concur with others that climate is a multidimensional construct with a central core of dimensions that apply across a variety of work environments. Building on prior conceptual efforts to identify this core (for instance, Campbell, Dunnette, Lawler, & Weick, 1970; Payne & Pugh, 1976), we consider the following five dimensions to be common elements of climate:

1. *Goal emphasis* — the extent to which management makes known the types of outcomes and standards that employees are expected to accomplish
2. *Means emphasis* — the extent to which management makes known the methods and procedures that employees are expected to use in performing their jobs
3. *Reward orientation* — the extent to which various organizational rewards are perceived to be allocated on the basis of job performance
4. *Task support* — the extent to which employees perceive that they are being supplied with the materials, equipment, services, and resources necessary to perform their jobs
5. *Socioemotional support* — the extent to which employees perceive that their personal welfare is protected by a kind, considerate, and generally humane management

The notion that the preceding dimensions are common across varying work settings does not imply that the salience of a given dimension is the same across work environments. Furthermore, two organizations may both have a strong goal emphasis, while in one the emphasis may be on quality and in the other on quantity. This varying focus is consistent, for example, with Schneider's (1980) interest in a "climate for service" and Zohar's (1980) interest in a "safety climate."

In sum, we conceptualize climate in terms of: (1) psychologically meaningful descriptions of the work environment that serve as a basis for interpretation and, therefore, as a guide to behavior; (2) an individual-level construct, which likely can be aggregated at the organizational-unit level; and (3) a central core of dimensions that apply across a variety of work environments (but whose content focus may vary between organizational units). It is climate functioning as a guide to behavior that is the primary concern of this chapter. The particular behaviors of interest are those that can be thought of as contributing to an organization's productivity—that is, job performance and citizenship behaviors.

Climate and Productivity

In this part of the chapter, building on the conceptual base supplied by James and Jones (1976), we outline a model of the relationship between climate and productivity. In so doing, we attempt to show that the model is consistent with much of the available though sparse empirical literature. The model we present, however, represents more than a summary of the evidence. It also reflects our views regarding the importance of climate for understanding productivity. We begin with a brief review of the James and Jones model of organizational functioning and a definition of our model's end-result criterion, organizational productivity.

Productivity

In an elaborate model of organizational functioning, James and Jones (1976) argue that climate is tied causally to what they call *end-result criteria*, including promotion rate, productivity indices, turnover rates, and salary progression. This occurs through two mediating mechanisms: (1) organizationally related attitudes and motivation, such as job satisfaction, expectancy, instrumentality, and reward preference, and (2) job behaviors and performance. The particular end-result criterion of current interest is organizational productivity, which we, like

James and Jones, see as an organizational-level variable that is a direct product of individuals' behaviors.

Organizational productivity can be construed as a facet of overall organizational effectiveness. What constitutes organizational effectiveness varies for differing groups with a stake in the organization, whether they may be owners, managers, employees, customers, or the public at large. Moreover, for any given group of stakeholders, the dimensions of organizational effectiveness attended to may be interrelated such that progress along one dimension entails regression along another dimension. For instance, Hage (1965), in his axiomatic theory of organizations, argued that efficiency (a construct closely aligned with productivity) and adaptiveness (or innovativeness) are inversely related. Drucker (1973) echoes this idea. Hence, it is easy to envision how the management of an organization, in some circumstances, has to trade off an emphasis on efficiency for one on creativity. The point we are trying to make is that while organizational productivity is the end-result criterion of current interest, to some stakeholders under some conditions, it simply may not be a particularly salient facet of organizational effectiveness.

Productivity is a concept that expresses the relationship between output and the inputs required for its production. At the most aggregate level, a productivity measure accounts for all output value and input costs. Mahoney (1988) refers to such a measure of productivity as a *total-factor measure*. Economists concerned with national productivity levels are likely to seek total-factor productivity measures for countries of interest. Productivity measures among organizational researchers, however, differ. These measures are almost certainly partial-factor measures of productivity (E. F. Denison, 1984; Mahoney, 1988). That is, only one or a few of the inputs (labor, energy, materials) or perhaps some indirect estimate of output value — such as customer satisfaction or quality — are likely to be estimated. The full productivity ratio (outputs and inputs) is really never assessed at the organizational level by behavioral scientists. Consequently, most organizational research that links human resource management practices to productivity, or climate to productivity, must be understood as involving partial measures of productivity. Such research assumes (most often implicitly) that changes in a partial measure are a valid indication of changes in the total productivity ratio.

While we propose that organizational productivity is a function of individuals' behaviors, very limited theory and research have addressed relationships between such behaviors and productivity at the organizational level (Thomas & Brief, 1984; also see Chapter Six in this volume). It can be assumed, however, that organizational productivity is not a simple sum of unit productivities (Mahoney, 1984). Because of interactions and dependencies in the work process, organizational productivity is likely to be some complex function of unit productivities. Nevertheless, in the following section, matters of such complexity are ignored. Given our limited knowledge, simple relationships between specific sorts of behaviors and organizational productivity will be proposed. In doing so, largely for purposes of exposition, we will focus on organizational productivity construed as either (1) *physical* labor productivity (the ratio of gross physical output to total labor hours), or (2) *economic* labor productivity (the ratio of total dollar outputs to total labor costs). Of course, total labor costs include those expenditures incurred in conjunction with such human resource management practices as recruitment, selection, and training, as well as the costs of compensation and fringe benefits. (For more on the definition and nature of organizational productivity, see Guzzo, 1988, and Kopelman, 1986).

Organizational Behaviors and Labor Productivity

It can readily be seen that gains in productivity can occur through increases in output value (quality or quantity) or decreases in labor costs. Thus, the question arises: What sorts of organizational behaviors influence dollar outputs and/or labor costs? Building on the work of Katz (1964), we can identify three pertinent sorts of behaviors: attachment, performance, and citizenship-related behaviors. Attachment behaviors encompass both attending and staying in the organization and are more commonly referred to in their converse forms, absenteeism and turnover, respectively. The negative organizational consequences of absenteeism and turnover seem to be well known. In this regard, Cascio (1987) details the kinds of separation, replacement, and training costs associated with turnover. He and others (for example, Dalton & Enz, 1988; Mobley, 1982) note various ways turnover may disrupt production or sales. Thus, increasing the attachment behaviors of an organization's employees (thereby decreasing absenteeism and turnover) would logically result in productivity gains. These gains would probably be attributable both to increased output value and decreased labor costs. It should be noted, however, that the effects of increasing attachment behaviors may not invariably be positive. Some investigators have argued, for instance, that turnover may serve the organizationally positive function of replacing low-output employees with those producing at higher output levels (for instance, Martin, Price, & Mueller, 1981; Mobley, 1982; Staw, 1980) or yield more innovation (Dalton & Todor, 1979).

Performance behaviors refer to those activities specified as comprising an employee's formal or prescribed organizational role. These role-prescribed behaviors are those commonly depicted in such organizational documents as job descriptions and performance appraisal forms. For some jobs, performance may be defined in the same terms as output. In such cases it is apparent that increases in performance would be expected to result in productivity gains. However, the performance-productivity relationship would likely be weaker (or possibly even negative) for those jobs for which performance is not defined in terms of output. One can readily identify in virtually any organization jobs designed to support, indirectly, the output produced or service provided. In a manufacturing organization, for example, the accounting department may serve a support function. It may, though, actually require reports and data collection activities that are counterproductive. Simply put, performance on every job in an organization is not seen as equally critical to output; thus the performance-productivity relationship will vary as a function of how central performance for a given job or family of jobs is to total organizational productivity.

Citizenship behaviors, which include components of so-called prosocial organizational behaviors (Brief & Motowidlo, 1986), refer to constructive or cooperative gestures that are not mandatory—that is, not defined in a job description as perfor-mance—but which contribute to organizational effectiveness (for example, Organ, 1988). Examples of such organizationally functional extrarole behaviors supplied by Katz (1964) include cooperating with others, protecting the organization from un-expected dangers, and suggesting organizational improve-ments. Given the broad scope of what constitutes citizenship behaviors, they can be seen to affect dollar output and/or labor costs. We suspect, however, that these effects are often subtle (for example, a worker lending a co-worker some supplies or mate-rials the other lacks) rather than dramatic (such as a worker offering a creative suggestion for reducing labor costs by some sizable margin). Consistent with our suspicion is Organ's (1988, p. 6) assertion that "any single occurrence of it [citizenship behavior] is modest or trivial." He goes on to liken an act of organizational citizenship to a vote in an election for public office. While a single vote is trivial, voting, in the aggregate, sustains the democratic system. Thus, most organizational cit-izenship behaviors might be thought of as maintaining the contributions of attachment and performance behaviors to pro-ductivity; without them, productivity would slowly deteriorate. Nevertheless, as noted, an act of citizenship on occasion may result in a rather dramatic improvement in productivity.

In sum, we have asserted that three sorts of behaviors (attachment, performance, and citizenship) influence organiza-tional productivity. Moreover, it was suggested that the rela-tionships between each of these behaviors and the components of productivity (outputs and inputs) are not necessarily simple ones that currently are well understood. In the next section, we leave behind these complex and ambiguous relationships to address the affective and cognitive antecedents of the productiv-ity-relevant behaviors we have dealt with.

Affective and Cognitive Antecedents
of Productivity-Relevant Behaviors

Organizational climate gets translated into salient organiza-tional behaviors via cognitive and affective states (see Figure

8.1). Bandura (1986, p. 231) asserts that "people act on their judgments of what they can do, as well as their beliefs about the likely effects of various actions." A number of cognitive models of motivation have been advanced that are at least partially consistent with Bandura's assertion. In particular, there are direct parallels to the valence models proposed by a number of theorists, such as Atkinson (1964), Fishbein (1967), Rotter (1954), and Vroom (1964). Expectancy-valence theories predict that the higher the perceived outcome expectancy and the more valued the outcomes, the greater is the motivation to perform the activity. Considerable empirical evidence supports this prediction (see Mitchell, 1974; Schwab, Olian-Gottlieb, & Heneman, 1979). Recall, however, Bandura's assertion that motivation is more than a function of the likely effects of various actions. It also is attributable to people's judgments of what they can do, what Bandura (1977, 1982, 1986) calls *self-efficacy expectations*. Here, all three cognitive sources of motivation — outcome expectancy, outcome valence, and self-efficacy expectations — are seen primarily as influencing performance behaviors. This posture is congruent with that espoused by other work motivation theorists, including Campbell, Dunnette, Lawler, and Weick (1970), Dachler and Mobley (1973), Graen (1969), Lawler (1971), Porter and Lawler (1968), and Vroom (1964).

Alternatively, withdrawal behaviors are seen as being influenced by the kinds of cognitive variables identified above and by affect in the form of job satisfaction (for example, Mobley, Griffith, Hand, & Meglino, 1979; Steers & Rhodes, 1978). This assertion recognizes that while the satisfaction-performance relationship is modest (see Iaffaldano & Muchinsky, 1985), the relationships between satisfaction and both absenteeism (for example, Muchinsky, 1977) and turnover (for instance, Muchinsky & Tuttle, 1979) are considerably stronger. Moreover, Brief and Motowidlo (1986) and Organ (1988) review a number of studies that show that job satisfaction also is a consistently strong predictor of citizenship behaviors. In total, therefore, productivity-relevant behaviors have been proposed to be influenced differentially by various cognitive sources of motivation as well as by how people feel at work or, more specifically, by their job satisfaction. No claim is made, however, that the cognitive and affective variables we have identified are the only or even the most important factors of influence. Other factors, such as technology or markets, may have substantial effects as well.

The Effects of Climate. The arguments presented thus far are summarized in Figure 8.1. As can be seen, we have reasoned that the components of productivity—that is, outputs and labor inputs—are affected directly by three specific sorts of organizational behaviors: attachment, performance, and citizenship. These behaviors are brought about by various cognitive sources of motivation and by affect at work (for instance, job satisfaction). Now we turn to the effects of climate. As shown in Figure 8.1, climate is posited to affect both work motivation and job satisfaction.

      Considerable evidence indicates that dimensions of climate, in fact, are associated with job satisfaction (for example, Friedlander & Margulies, 1969; Pritchard & Karasick, 1973; Litwin & Stringer, 1968). Indeed, some have even argued, erroneously so, that climate and satisfaction are redundant (for instance, Guion, 1973; Johannesson, 1973). Importantly, however, one cannot precisely identify the particular dimensions of climate that are related consistently to satisfaction. This probably is so because how dimensions are labeled conceptually and operationalized varies considerably across studies. Nevertheless, research and thinking about the causes of job satisfaction (for example, Locke, 1976) suggest that each dimension of climate is a likely correlate of satisfaction. For instance, *goal emphasis* and *means emphasis* both may serve to reduce experienced role conflict and role ambiguity and thereby promote satisfaction (see Van Sell, Brief, & Schuler, 1981; Jackson & Schuler, 1985). *Reward orientation* may generate feelings of equity that in turn lead to satisfaction (for example, Pritchard, 1969; Goodman & Friedman, 1971). *Task support* may signal that one's assigned work is significant; it is known that task significance is correlated with satisfaction (see Aldag, Barr, & Brief, 1981; Hackman & Oldham, 1975). Task support may reduce physical strain, which also is known to be related to satisfaction (Chad-wick-Jones, 1969). Finally, *socioemotional support* may affect satis-faction, most obviously because it directly demonstrates to workers that their personal feelings are a concern of others in the organization. Our speculations about the mechanisms that tie climate dimensions to satisfaction should not be taken to imply that we believe each dimension always will be associated with satisfaction. In some cases means emphasis, for example, may reduce ambiguity, yet in others, it may be seen as infringing on the autonomy workers believe is necessary to do their jobs (for instance, House & Mitchell, 1974).

While a number of studies conducted in educational settings indicate that dimensions of climate directly affect moti-vation (see Anderson, 1982), other limited evidence speaks to such direct effects. Of particular interest is a study by James, Hartman, Stebbins, and Jones (1977). Their results, based on data obtained from managerial employees of a large health care company, indicated that "psychological climate was significantly and meaningfully related to various aspects of instrumentality and valence" (p. 251). This direct evidence is supported by a number of studies that show climate to be associated with per-formance through its effects on motivation (for example, Friedlander & Greenberg, 1971; Lawler, Hall, & Oldham, 1974; Schneider & Hall, 1972). Particularly impressive in the climate-performance research area are the programmatic results of Schneider and his colleagues (see Schneider & Bowen, 1985; Schneider, Parkington, & Buxton, 1980)—results that repeat-edly show climate to be related to performance, defined in terms of customer assessments of service quality.

Given the limited literature available on direct climate-motivation relationships, what follows, once again, are merely our speculations about how specific dimensions of climate might be associated with particular cognitive sources of moti-vation. With respect to the likely effects of goal emphasis, the theorizing of Bandura (for example, 1986) supplies a number of insights. First, according to Bandura, goals affect outcome ex-pectancies in that they specify conditional requirements for positive self-evaluation and, if in fact attained, create self-satis-

faction and a sense of fulfillment. Second, goals figure promi-
nently in the development of self-efficacy expectations. Bandura
(1986, p. 470) states: "Without standards against which to measure their performances, people have little basis for judging how
they are doing, nor do they have much basis for gauging their
capabilities." Drawing in part on the work of Locke and his
associates (for example, Locke, Shaw, Saari, & Latham, 1981),
Bandura goes on to recognize that the motivational effects of
goals are not unconditional. The effects are dependent on the
specificity, challenge, and proximity of the goal, as well as on the
strength of commitment to the goal. (For more on the applicability of Bandura's work to the issues raised, see Brief &
Aldag, 1981, and Hollenbeck & Brief, 1988.)

Means emphasis is seen as positively affecting self-efficacy
expectations through clarifying how a given level of performance might be achieved. As suggested earlier, however, the
effects of means emphasis may not always be positive. For instance, as found by Schneider and his colleagues, an emphasis
on rules and procedures to promote efficiency, rather than
service, often leads to employee frustration and reduced motivation to deliver quality service (Schneider & Rentsch, 1988).
This conclusion holds not only for means emphasis but for goal
emphasis, reward orientation, and task support. That is, one
must question goals, means, rewards, and support to obtain
what? As suggested in our discussion of the "productivity" construct and its relationship to organizational effectiveness, activities aimed at obtaining one end-result criterion may impair
the attainment of another. Thus, in seeking to create a climate
that motivates desired organizational behaviors, managers may
be required to trade off one desired behavior for another. A
given climate is unlikely to achieve all possible ends.

Reward orientation signals to workers the organizational
consequences of their behaviors. Therefore, it is seen as enhancing outcome expectations. This intuitively appealing observation is buttressed by Bandura's (1986) recognition that such
expectations are considered to be largely the products of one's
reinforcement history. In the current case, of course, what is at
issue is the individual's reinforcement history at work and, as

emphasized in the preceding paragraph, the question not to be ignored is, "What is reinforced?"

As noted by Campbell and Pritchard (1976), performance, in part, is a function of facilitating and inhibiting conditions not under the control of the individual. Only in recent years has their assertion received the serious attention it deserves—for example, by Schoorman and Schneider (1988). Frequently, facilitating and inhibiting conditions affect the relationship between effort and performance. Here we consider them, in the form of task support, as affecting the motivation that drives effort. In particular, task support is seen as influencing a person's judgment about his or her capability of accomplishing a certain level of performance—in other words, his or her self-efficacy expectation. We deduce that through being supplied with the materials, equipment, services, and resources necessary to perform their jobs, employees come to view themselves as more capable. Perhaps the converse is simpler to see; without the materials, equipment, services, and so on necessary to perform their jobs, employees view themselves as less capable of performing them. Guzzo and Gannett (1988) further discuss the motivational implications of facilitating and inhibiting conditions.

Finally, socioemotional support also is seen as affecting motivation—in this case, valence of outcomes. Our reasoning is that individuals perceived as protecting the welfare of employees will come to be valued. These valued persons become more potent sources of social reinforcement. That is, the valence of such a reward as praise is greater when delivered by a person whom an employee holds in high regard, and high regard is seen as being attached to those who act to protect the welfare of employees.

We have speculated about how dimensions of climate may be tied to job satisfaction and specific components of work motivation. Thus far, we have not considered other potentially important effects of climate. For instance, recent evidence from the goal-setting literature (such as Earley & Perry, 1987) suggests that goal emphasis may not only affect the amount of effort one expends but may also influence how that effort is expended. In particular, goal emphasis may determine how much planning employees engage in to accomplish a task and the sorts of plans they develop. Moreover, like means emphasis, reward orientation, and task support, goal emphasis probably serves to direct attention and effort to specific tasks. Tasks for which goals are set, rules and procedures formulated, rewards allocated, and support given are ones that signal to employees what is expected of them. Clearly, the message carried by these signals would be more influential in directing effort to the degree the signals are consistent. For example, when goals are set for quality but rewards are given only for quantity, a relatively weak message is being sent. Thus, from a managerial perspective, the dimensions of climate require coordination. Without consistency, managers may release opposing forces that cause the organization to vacillate rather than to move forward with unity of effort. And, if such unity can be achieved, the goals of the organization might be advanced further by the resultant organizational syntality (Cattell, 1948). Take the case, for instance, when goal emphasis is supported by a reward orientation that makes goal attainment more attractive and by task support that makes the expectancy of goal attainment more likely (see Hollenbeck & Klein, 1987). Our posture is that the interaction of these three dimensions of climate contributes to organizational momentum beyond the main effects of each dimension.

Conclusion

It now should be obvious that the model depicted in Figure 8.1 is a gross simplification. Equifinalities, interaction effects, and trade-offs are not shown. Moreover, while James and Jones (1976) chose to incorporate various feedback loops and reciprocal relationships in their model, we do not. Our model's contribution is the detail with which the relationships between sets of variables are characterized. For instance, James and Jones discuss the relationship between psychological climate and attitudes and motivation without addressing any specific dimensions of climate. We believe that conceptual detail is essential to framing empirical research whose results will enhance understanding of the psychological processes linking climate to various end-result criteria such as productivity. In addition, we conceive of our model and the discussion of it as a tentative guide to practice. Thus, in closing, we present a summary list of issues that require attention by those responsible for the management of productivity.

1. Given management's goals and objectives, is productivity a strategically important dimension of organizational effectiveness? If so, how should it be operationally defined? In other words, what is the output of interest and how should it be measured; in addition, what are the components of input and how should they be gauged?

2. Given management's chosen definition of productivity, what specific sorts of attachment, performance, and citizenship behaviors are related to output and input? Are some of these organizational behaviors more or less important? Which groups of employees are expected to engage in those role-related behaviors most central to productivity? For those groups, are attachment, performance, and/or citizenship behaviors particularly problematical?

3. Given that management has targeted specific behaviors of particular groups of employees for improvement, what attitudinal and/or motivational factors need to be changed? More specifically, what dimensions of climate can be altered to affect these motivational and attitudinal factors? What might be the unintended consequences of altering any given dimension of climate?

4. What human resource management practices might be changed, within the range of constraints and opportunities presented by the cultural context, to bring about increased productivity?

The preceding list of issues indicates that productivity management must be based on a thorough understanding of the organization's mission, its members, and its climate. Moreover, these questions, together with the model in Figure 8.1, indicate a long and tenuous link between culture and productivity.

References

Akin, G., & Hopelain, D. (1986). Finding the culture of productivity. *Organizational Dynamics, 14*(3), 19–32.

Aldag, R. J., Barr, S., & Brief, A. P. (1981). Measurement of perceived task characteristics. *Psychological Bulletin, 90*, 415–431.

Aldrich, H. (1979). *Organizations and environments.* Englewood Cliffs, NJ: Prentice-Hall.

Anderson, C. S. (1982). The search for school climate: A review of the research. *Review of Educational Research, 52*, 368–420.

Argyris, C. (1976). Problems and new directions for industrial psychology. In M. D. Dunnette (Ed.), *Handbook of industrial and organizational psychology.* Chicago: Rand McNally.

Argyris, C., & Schön, D. A. (1978). *Organizational learning: A theory of action perspective.* Reading, MA: Addison-Wesley.

Atkinson, J. W. (1964). *An introduction to motivation.* Princeton, NJ: Van Nostrand.

Bandura, A. (1977). Self-efficacy: Towards a unifying theory of behavioral change. *Psychological Review, 84*, 191–215.

Bandura, A. (1982). Self-efficacy mechanisms in human agency. *American Psychologist, 37*, 122–147.

Bandura, A. (1986). *Social foundations of thought and action.* Englewood Cliffs, NJ: Prentice-Hall.

Beyer, J. M., & Trice, H. M. (1987). How an organization's rites reveal its culture. *Organizational Dynamics, 15*(4), 5–24.

Brief, A. P., & Aldag, R. J. (1981). The "self" in work organizations: A conceptual review. *Academy of Management Review, 6*, 75–88.

Brief, A. P., & Motowidlo, S. J. (1986). Prosocial organizational behaviors. *Academy of Management Review, 11*, 710–725.

Campbell, J. P., Dunnette, M. D., Lawler, E. E., III, & Weick, K. E. (1970). *Managerial behavior, performance, and effectiveness.* New York: McGraw-Hill.

Campbell, J. P., & Pritchard, R. D. (1976). Motivation theory in industrial and organizational psychology. In M. D. Dunnette (Ed.), *Handbook of industrial and organizational psychology.* Chicago: Rand McNally.

Cascio, W. F. (1987). *Costing human resources: The financial impact of behavior in organizations* (2nd ed.). Boston: PWS-Kent.

Cattell, R. B. (1948). Concepts and methods in the measurement of group syntality. *Psychological Review, 55,* 48–63.

Chadwick-Jones, J. K. (1969). *Automation and behavior.* New York: Wiley.

Chilcott, J. H. (1987). Where are you coming from and where are you going? The reporting of ethnographic research. *American Educational Research Journal, 23,* 199–217.

Dachler, H. P., & Mobley, W. H. (1973). Construct validation of an instrumentality-expectancy-task goal model of work motivation: Some theoretical boundary conditions. *Journal of Applied Psychology Monograph, 58,* 397–418.

Dalton, D. R., & Enz, C. A. (1988). New directions in the management of employee absenteeism: Attention to policy and culture. In R. S. Schuler, S. A. Youngblood, & V. L. Huber (Eds.), *Readings in Personnel and Human Resource Management* (3rd ed.). St. Paul, MN: West.

Dalton, D. R., & Todor, W. D. (1979). Turnover turned over: An expanded and positive perspective. *Academy of Management Journal, 4,* 225–235.

Dansereau, F., Graen, G., & Haga, W. (1975). A vertical dyad linkage approach to leadership in formal organizations. *Organizational Behavior and Human Performance, 13,* 46–78.

Dastmalchian, A. (1986). Environmental characteristics and organizational climate: An exploratory study. *Journal of Management Studies, 23,* 609–633.

Deal, T. E., & Kennedy, A. A. (1982). *Corporate culture: The rites and rituals of corporate life.* Reading, MA: Addison-Wesley.

Denison, D. R. (1984). Bringing corporate culture to the bottom line. *Organizational Dynamics, 13*(2), 4–22.

Denison, E. F. (1984). Productivity analysis through growth accounting. In A. P. Brief (Ed.), *Productivity research in the behavioral and social sciences.* New York: Praeger.

DiMaggio, P. J., & Powell, W. W. (1983). The iron cage revisited: Institutional isomorphism and collective rationality in organizational fields. *American Sociological Review, 48,* 147–160.

Drucker, P. F. (1973). *Management: Tasks, responsibilities, practices.* New York: Harper & Row.

Earley, P. C., & Perry, B. C. (1987). Work plan availability and performance: An assessment of task strategy priming on subsequent task completion. *Organizational Behavior and Human Decision Processes, 39,* 279–302.

Fishbein, M. (1967). Attitude and the prediction of behavior. In M. Fishbein (Ed.), *Readings in attitude theory and measurement.* New York: Wiley.

Friedlander, F., & Greenberg, S. (1971). Effect of job attitudes, training, and organization climate on performance of the hard-core unemployed. *Journal of Applied Psychology, 55,* 287–295.

Friedlander, F., & Margulies, N. (1969). Multiple impacts of organizational climate and individual value systems upon job satisfaction. *Personnel Psychology, 22,* 171–183.

Fuld, L. M. (1988). *Monitoring the competition.* New York: Wiley.

Gellerman, S. (1959). The company personality. *Management Review, 48,* 69–76.

Georgopoules, B. S. (1965). Normative structure variables and organizational behavior. *Human Relations, 18,* 155–169.

Ghemawat, P. (1986). Sustainable advantage. *Harvard Business Review, 64*(5), 53–58.

Gilmer, B. (1966). *Industrial psychology.* New York: McGraw-Hill.

Glick, W. H. (1985). Conceptualizing and measuring organizational and psychological climate: Pitfalls in multilevel research. *Academy of Management Review, 10,* 601–616.

Goodenough, W. H. (1964). *Explorations in cultural anthropology.* New York: McGraw-Hill.

Goodman, P. S., & Friedman, A. (1971). An examination of Adams' theory of inequity. *Administrative Science Quarterly, 16,* 271–288.

Graen, G. (1969). Instrumentality theory of work motivation: Some experimental results and suggested modifications. *Journal of Applied Psychology Monograph, 53,* 1–25.

Guion, R. M. (1973). A note on organizational climate. *Organizational Behavior and Human Performance, 9,* 120–125.

Guzzo, R. A. (1988). Productivity research: Reviewing psychological and economic perspectives. In J. P. Campbell, R. J. Campbell, & Associates, *Productivity in organizations: New perspectives from industrial and organizational psychology.* San Francisco: Jossey-Bass.

Guzzo, R. A., & Gannett, B. A. (1988). The nature of facilitators and inhibitors of effective task performance. In F. D. Schoorman & B. Schneider (Eds.), *Facilitating work effectiveness.* Lexington, MA: Lexington Books.

Guzzo, R. A., Jette, R. D., & Katzell, R. A. (1985). The effects of psychologically based intervention programs on worker productivity: A meta-analysis. *Personnel Psychology, 38,* 275–291.

Hackman, J. R., & Oldham, G. R. (1975). Development of the job diagnostic survey. *Journal of Applied Psychology, 60,* 159–170.

Hage, J. (1965). An axiomatic theory of organizations. *Administrative Science Quarterly, 10,* 289–320.

Harris, S. G., & Sutton, R. I. (1986). Functions of parting ceremonies in dying organizations. *Academy of Management Journal, 29,* 5–30.

Harrison, R. (1972). Understanding your organization's character. *Harvard Business Review, 50*(3), 119–128.

Harrison, R. (1987). Harnessing personal energy: How companies can inspire employees. *Organizational Dynamics, 14*(4), 5–20.

Hebden, J. E. (1986). Adopting an organization's culture: The socialization of graduate trainees. *Organizational Dynamics, 15*(1), 54–72.

Hickman, C. R., & Silva, M. A. (1987). *The future 500: Creating tomorrow's organizations today.* New York: New American Library.

Hofstede, G. (1980). *Culture's consequences: International differences in work related values.* Newbury Park, CA: Sage.

Hollenbeck, J. R., & Brief, A. P. (1988). Self-regulation in the workplace: Towards a unified approach to understanding worker attitudes and behavior. In R. S. Schuler, S. A. Youngblood, & V. L. Huber (Eds.), *Readings in personnel and human resource management.* St. Paul, MN: West.

Hollenbeck, J. R., & Klein, H. J. (1987). Goal commitment and the goal setting process: Problems, prospects, and proposals for future research. *Journal of Applied Psychology, 72,* 212–220.

House, R. J., & Mitchell, T. R. (1974). Path-goal theory of leadership. *Journal of Contemporary Business, 3,* 81–98.

Iaffaldano, M. T., & Muchinsky, P. M. (1985). Job satisfaction and job performance: A meta-analysis. *Psychological Bulletin, 97,* 251–273.

Indik, B. P. (1965). Organization size and member participation: Some empirical tests of alternative explanations. *Human Relations, 18,* 339–350.

Jackson, S., & Schuler, R. (1985). A meta analysis and conceptual critique of research on role ambiguity and role conflict in work settings. *Organizational Behavior and Human Decision Processes, 36,* 16–78.

James, L. R., Hartman, E. A., Stebbins, M. W., & Jones, A. P. (1977). Relationships between psychological climate and a VIE model for work motivation. *Personnel Psychology, 30,* 229–254.

James, L. R., & Jones, A. P. (1974). Organizational climate: A review of theory and research. *Psychological Bulletin, 81,* 1096–1112.

James, L. R., & Jones, A. P. (1976). Organizational structure: A review of structural dimensions and their conceptual relationships with individual attitudes and behavior. *Organizational Behavior and Human Performance, 16,* 74–113.

Johannesson, R. E. (1973). Some problems in the measurement of organizational climate. *Organizational Behavior and Human Performance, 10,* 118–144.

Jones, A. P., & James, L. R. (1979). Psychological climate: Dimensions and relationships of individual and aggregated work environment perceptions. *Organizational Behavior and Human Performance, 23,* 201–250.

Katz, D. (1964). The motivational basis of organizational behavior. *Behavioral Science, 9,* 131–146.

Kluckhohn, F. R., & Strodtbeck, F. L. (1961). *Variations in value orientations.* New York: Harper & Row.

Kopelman, R. E. (1976). Organizational control system responsiveness, expectancy theory constructs, and work motivation:

Some interrelations and causal connections. *Personnel Psychology, 29,* 205–220.

Kopelman, R. E. (1986). *Managing productivity in organizations.* New York: McGraw-Hill.

Kroeber, A. L., & Kluckhohn, C. (1952). *Culture: A critical review of concepts and definitions.* New York: Vintage Books.

Lawler, E. E. (1971). *Pay and organizational effectiveness: A psychological view.* New York: McGraw-Hill.

Lawler, E. E., Hall, D. T., & Oldham, G. R. (1974). Organizational climate: Relationship to organizational structure, process, and performance. *Organizational Behavior and Human Performance, 11,* 139–155.

Likert, R. (1961). *New patterns of management.* New York: McGraw-Hill.

Litwin, G. H., & Stringer, R. A. (1968). *Motivation and organizational climate.* Cambridge, MA: Harvard University, Graduate School of Business Administration, Division of Research.

Locke, E. A. (1976). The nature and causes of job satisfaction. In M. D. Dunnette (Ed.), *Handbook of industrial and organizational psychology.* Chicago: Rand McNally.

Locke, E. A., Shaw, K. N., Saari, L. M., & Latham, G. P. (1981). Goal setting and task performance: 1969–1980. *Psychological Bulletin, 90,* 125–152.

Louis, M. R. (1983). Organizations as culture-bearing milieux. In L. R. Pondy, P. J. Frost, G. Morgan, & T. C. Dandridge (Eds.), *Organizational symbolism* (pp. 23–44). Greenwich, CT: JAI Press.

Mahoney, T. A. (1984). Growth accounting and productivity: Comments. In A. P. Brief (Ed.), *Productivity research in the behavioral and social sciences.* New York: Praeger.

Mahoney, T. A. (1988). Productivity defined: The relativity of efficiency, effectiveness, and change. In J. P. Campbell, R. J. Campbell, & Associates, *Productivity in organizations: New perspectives from industrial and organizational psychology.* San Francisco: Jossey-Bass.

Martin, J., Feldman, M. S., Hatch, M. J., & Sitkin, S. B. (1983). The uniqueness paradox in organizational stories. *Administrative Science Quarterly, 28,* 438–453.

Martin, J., & Siehl, C. (1983). Organizational culture and counterculture: An uneasy symbiosis. *Organizational Dynamics, 12*(2), 52–64.

Martin, T. N., Price, J. L., & Mueller, C. W. (1981). Job performance and turnover. *Journal of Applied Psychology, 66,* 116–119.

Mitchell, T. R. (1974). Expectancy models of jobs satisfaction, occupational preference, and effort: A theoretical, methodological, and empirical appraisal. *Psychological Bulletin, 81,* 1053–1077.

Mobley, W. H. (1982). *Employee turnover: Causes, consequences, and control.* Reading, MA: Addison-Wesley.

Mobley, W. H., Griffith, R. W., Hand, H. H., & Meglino, B. M. (1979). Review and conceptual analysis of the employee turnover process. *Psychological Bulletin, 86,* 493–522.

Morse, N., & Reimer, E. (1956). The experimental change of a major organizational variable. *Journal of Abnormal and Social Psychology, 52,* 120–129.

Muchinsky, P. M. (1977). Organizational communication: Relationship to organizational climate and job satisfaction. *Academy of Management Journal, 20,* 592–607.

Muchinsky, P. M., & Tuttle, M. L. (1979). Employee turnover: An empirical and methodological assessment. *Journal of Vocational Behavior, 14,* 43–77.

Organ, D. W. (1988). *Organizational citizenship behavior: The good soldier syndrome.* Lexington, MA: Lexington Books.

O'Toole, J. (1985). *Vanguard management: Redesigning the corporate future.* Garden City, NY: Doubleday.

Ouchi, W. G. (1981). *Theory Z.* Reading, MA: Addison-Wesley.

Payne, R. L. & Pugh, D. S. (1976). Organizational structure and climate. In M. D. Dunnette (Ed.), *Handbook of industrial and organizational psychology.* Chicago: Rand McNally.

Peters, T. J., & Waterman, R. H. (1982). *In search of excellence: Lessons from America's best-run companies.* New York: Harper & Row.

Pettigrew, A. M. (1979). On studying organizational cultures. *Administrative Science Quarterly, 24,* 570–581.

Pfluger, R. (1988). *The effect of two interventions on specific dimensions of organizational climate.* (Unpublished doctoral dissertation,

New York University.) *Dissertation Abstracts International,* *50*(028), 775.

Porter, L. W., & Lawler, E. E. (1968). *Managerial attitudes and performance.* Homewood, IL: Irwin.

Pritchard, R. D. (1969). Equity theory: A review and critique. *Organizational Behavior and Human Performance, 4,* 176–211.

Pritchard, R. D., & Karasick, B. W. (1973). The effect of organizational climate on managerial job performance and satisfaction. *Organizational Behavior and Human Performance, 9,* 126–146.

Ralston, D. A., Anthony, W. P., & Gustafson, D. J. (1985). Employees may love flextime, but what does it do to the organization's productivity? *Journal of Applied Psychology, 70,* 272–279.

Rokeach, M. (1969). *Beliefs, attitudes and values: A theory of organization and change.* San Francisco: Jossey-Bass.

Rokeach, M. (1973). *The nature of human values.* New York: Free Press.

Rotter, J. B. (1954). *Social learning and clinical psychology.* Englewood, Cliffs, NJ: Prentice-Hall.

Sapienza, A. M. (1987). Imagery and strategy. *Journal of Management, 13,* 543–555.

Sathe, V. (1983). Implications of corporate culture: A manager's guide to action. *Organizational Dynamics, 12*(2), 5–23.

Schein, E. H. (1983). The role of the founder in creating organizational culture. *Organizational Dynamics, 12*(1), 13–28.

Schein, E. H. (1985). *Organizational culture and leadership: A dynamic view.* San Francisco: Jossey-Bass.

Schneider, B. (1975). Organizational climates: An essay. *Personnel Psychology, 28,* 447–479.

Schneider, B. (1980). The service organization: Climate is crucial. *Organizational Dynamics, 9,* 52–65.

Schneider, B. (1987). The people make the place. *Personnel Psychology, 40,* 437–453.

Schneider, B., & Bowen, D. E. (1985). Employee and customer perceptions of service in banks: Replication and extension. *Journal of Applied Psychology, 70,* 423–433.

Schneider, B., & Hall, D. (1972). Toward specifying the concept of work climate: A study of Roman Catholic diocesan priests. *Journal of Applied Psychology, 56,* 447–455.

Schneider, B., Parkington, J. J., & Buxton, V. M. (1980). Employee and customer perceptions of service in banks. *Administrative Science Quarterly, 25,* 252–267.

Schneider, B., & Reichers, A. E. (1983). On the etiology of climate. *Personnel Psychology, 36,* 19–39.

Schneider, B., & Rentsch, J. (1988). Managing climates and cultures: A futures perspective. In J. Hage (Ed.), *Futures of organizations.* Lexington, MA: Lexington Books.

Schoorman, F. D., & Schneider, B. (Eds.) (1988). *Facilitating work effectiveness.* Lexington, MA: Lexington Books.

Schwab, D. P., Olian-Gottlieb, J. D., & Heneman, H. G. (1979). Between-subjects expectancy theory research: A statistical review of studies predicting effort and performance. *Psychological Bulletin, 86,* 139–147.

Smircich, L. (1983). Concepts of culture and organizational analysis. *Administrative Science Quarterly, 28,* 339–358.

Smircich, L., & Calas, M. B. (1987). Organizational culture: A critical assessment. In F. M. Jablin, L. L. Putnam, K. H. Roberts, & L. W. Porter (Eds.), *Handbook of organizational communication: An interdisciplinary perspective* (pp. 228–263). Newbury Park, CA: Sage.

Spender, J-C. (1983). The business policy problem and industry recipes. In R. Lamb (Ed.), *Advances in strategic management* (Vol. 2). Greenwich, CT: JAI Press.

Staw, B. (1980). The consequences of turnover. *Journal of Occupational Behavior, 1,* 253–273.

Steers, R. M., & Rhodes, S. R. (1978). Major influences on employee attendance: A process model. *Journal of Applied Psychology, 63,* 391–407.

Swartz, M., & Jordan, D. (1980). *Culture: An anthropological perspective.* New York: Wiley.

Tagiuri, R. (1968). The concept of organizational climate. In R. Tagiuri & G. H. Litwin (Eds.), *Organizational climate: Explorations of a concept.* Boston: Harvard University Press.

Thomas, A., & Brief, A. P. (1984). Unexplored issues in productivity research. In A. P. Brief (Ed.), *Productivity research in the behavioral and social sciences*. New York: Praeger.

Tucker, R. W., & McCoy, W. J. (1988). Can questionnaires measure culture: Eight extended field studies. Paper presented at the 96th convention of American Psychological Association, Atlanta, GA.

Van Sell, M., Brief, A. P., & Schuler, R. (1981). Role conflict and ambiguity: Integration of the literature and directions for future research. *Human Relations, 34*, 43–71.

Vroom, V. H. (1964). *Work and motivation*. New York: Wiley.

Wilkins, A. L. (1983). The culture audit: A tool for understanding organizations. *Organizational Dynamics, 12*(2), 24–38.

Woodward, J. (1965). *Industrial organization: Theory and practice*. London: Oxford University Press.

Zohar, D. (1980). Safety climate in industrial organizations: Theoretical and applied implications. *Journal of Applied Psychology, 65*, 96–102.

Chapter 9

Kenneth R. Thompson
Fred Luthans

Organizational Culture: A Behavioral Perspective

Organizational culture is a complex and pervasive part of any working environment. While there does not seem to be agreement as to what culture is and how pervasive it is in an organization, there is a general consensus that it is a major component affecting performance and behavior. However, given its importance, organizational culture still remains an elusive concept that seems to defy concrete treatment in research and application. The consequence is that an apparently important part of organizational life is somewhat ignored and misused by both managers and those who study organizations.

We propose to look at organizational culture in a way that will help facilitate an understanding of culture formation, maintenance, and change. We propose to view culture from a behavioral perspective. This article links behaviorism, learning, and organizational culture in a framework that aids an understanding of organizational culture. First, the concept of culture will be defined in cognitive and then behavioral terms. Some implications of viewing culture in behavioral terms will then be considered. Seven properties of culture emerge from the behavioral framework that facilitate an understanding of organizational culture. Using these seven properties of culture, the formation,

Note: The authors wish to thank Benjamin Schneider for his comments on an earlier draft of this manuscript.

319

maintenance, and change of culture in organizations will be discussed.

Organizational Culture: Cognitive Perspectives

There is considerable disagreement about the definition of organizational culture. Some authors have even gone so far as to develop a typology to describe the various definitions and schools of thought about culture (Allaire & Firsirotu, 1984). Lucas (1987, p. 152) notes that "organizational cultures are, in their effect, solutions to contradictions which exist 'naturally' from the perspective of organizational members." Johannisson (1987, p. 5) views culture as "intrinsic organizing. As it represents an environment that people have jointly created, it leads them to join in coordinated effort without any explicit sanction by a power center." Meyerson and Martin (1987) expand on the definition provided by Berger and Luckmann (1966, p. 623) by defining cultures as "socially constructed realities and, as such, the definition of what culture is and how cultures change depends on how one perceives and enacts culture." Gregory (1983, p. 364) views culture as "learned ways of coping with experience."

Smircich (1983) attempts to clear up the confusion surrounding the definition of culture by categorizing three approaches to culture. Culture can be viewed as an independent variable (or external variable) brought into the organization, as an internal variable within an organization, or as a root metaphor for conceptualizing organizations.

The External Perspective. The external perspective views culture as an independent variable. Smircich (1983) notes that in this view culture is considered to be a background factor (almost synonymous with country), an explanatory variable, or a broad framework influencing the development and reinforcement of beliefs. She feels the literature can be segmented into a macro focus (examining the relationship between culture and organization structure) and a micro focus (investigating the similarities and differences in attitudes in different cultures).

The external perspective of culture focuses attention on the values, beliefs, and predispositions about organizations, work, and authority of individuals in a culture. These values, beliefs, and predispositions would be developed external to the organization through the social interactions that individuals have with referent groups, families, friends, and other work and nonwork experiences and groups. These values, beliefs, and predispositions would vary over nationalities and, one might infer, there would be less variability within national cultures. Using this perspective, any organization is only a context in which these cultural variables become manifest. An organization is, from this standpoint, passively shaped by the predispositions of its employees.

The Internal Perspective. The internal perspective is a second way that culture and organizations are linked. Smircich (1983) notes that researchers such as Louis (1980), Siehl and Martin (1981), Deal and Kennedy (1982), Tichy (1982), and Martin and Powers (1983) recognize that organizations are themselves culture-producing. The internal approach to culture focuses on the unique "rituals, legends, and ceremonies" (Smircich, 1983, p. 344) that evolve by placing people in an environment that the top management and/or founders of organizations create through rules, structure, norms, and goals. "Typical variables considered in this stream of research are structure, size, technology, and leadership patterns" (Smircich, 1983, p. 344). At a macro level, these internal structural dimensions seem to be important in the development and maintenance of an organization's culture, especially when one organization is compared to another.

However, these internal variables do not seem to be the only factors influencing culture, since culture is not a monolithic construct that exists for all members of an organization. Within an organization, there can be different views of the organization's culture depending on the individual and the groups to which the individual belongs. Pennings and Gresov (1986) make this distinction by describing culture as a relationship between six subsystems at two levels: the industry or societal (external) level and the organizational (internal) level.

They recognize the importance of linking predispositions from outside the organization with attributes within the organization as major determinants of organization culture. Under these conditions, it is quite possible that a highly differentiated culture could evolve where there would be strong links horizontally in the organization but weak links with the external culture and vice versa. In the latter case, the organization would be similar to a Type J organization as described by Ouchi and Jaeger (1978).

It is thus possible that organization members might have differences in their own set of perceptions regarding the organization's culture. Pennings and Gresov (1986) allow for this possibility, because they link their own model to Louis's (1983) work. Pennings and Gresov (1986, p. 329) define organizations as "culture-bearing milieux" that can be understood "within the framework as elaborations of the concept of subsystem fragmentation, with strong horizontal linkages (a nested culture), strong vertical linkages (overlapping), or both. . . ." In essence, then, organizations are really sets of different perceptions of the organization's culture held by individuals and groups in the organization and manifested through various subcultural predispositions. In addition, an individual may be a member of several of the various groups that form through informal and formal actions via this natural process. There may be different defined cultures for each group and even individual differences within each group.

The notion of various cultures or subcultures within a single organization raises some very interesting questions. Is there a dominant culture? How does this dominant culture evolve? Are there conflicting subcultures in organizations? How are these conflicts resolved? Lucas (1987, p. 144) applies the idea of *negotiated order*. Various subcultures influence other subcultures in such a manner that the views of the subculture may become the dominant culture in the organization. The dominant culture has the most influence on the organization.

But why would being a member of a dominant culture be important to organizational members? Often it would not be, since individuals would have formed their own causal map of reality, and as long as that map is not infringed on by others, the individual would be satisfied. However, to reduce ambiguity (Meyerson & Martin, 1987) and to aid in personal goal con-gruence (Wilkins & Ouchi, 1983), there is some propensity by members of groups to influence the dominant organizational culture themes (Morey & Luthans, 1985).

Other variables that can have an effect on culture forma-tion include the physical surroundings (Peponis, 1985) and conditions of the work environment: physical proximity, noise, heat, light, and so forth. While these elements have not been a central stream of research in culture formation, the work of Peponis (1985) would support the conclusion that one cannot ignore them when considering the whole range of possible cultural dynamics.

The Root Metaphor Perspective. The third traditional perspective treats organizational culture as a root metaphor. As stated by Smircich (1983, p. 347), "Some theorists advance the view that organizations should be understood *as* cultures. They leave behind the view that a culture is something an organization *has*, in favor of the view that a culture is something an organization *is*." Hence, culture cannot be separated as a distinct variable in an organization, because it encompasses all parts of the organi-zation. It is simply too encompassing to be treated as a unique element.

Linking the Perspectives. To link the perspectives discussed so far, three dimensions of culture emerge. First, culture comes from people who are influenced by the organization and events out-side the organization. One cannot just look at culture as some-thing that is a product of the organization. An individual's predispositions and thought processes will influence how he or she will react to different situations. The culture that is formed in an organization will be influenced by these individual varia-tions, and therefore will be unique to the individuals that are part of the organization. Second, culture needs to be thought of as something that is not absolute, but constantly evolving as events and people change in the organization. Third, culture cannot be viewed as a monolithic construct. Each individual in the organization has his or her own definition of culture. This definition is similar to but not the same as the various groups of which he or she is a part. There are many subcultures in the organization that conflict, combine, and coexist. Each influences the other and tries to influence the direction of the organization.

What, then, is the cognitive perspective of culture? Comparing the definitions and the external, internal, and root metaphor perspectives leads us to define culture as "socially constructed realities that provide learned ways of coping with experiences." This is close to the definitions of Gregory (1983) and Berger and Luckmann (1966) and includes learning the notion of multiple realities. Significantly, this definition implies that a learning process is at the heart of culture. The "socially constructed realities" part of the definition implies that social interaction is important. Using the plural of *reality* implies that culture is an evolving process based on a changing definition of reality.

Are behaviors relevant to the definition of organizational culture? O'Reilly and Caldwell (1985) suggest this possibility. Citing research from social learning theory, they note that individuals in social settings may learn which behaviors and opinions are rewarded and punished merely by observing others. Such social or vicarious learning may shape behaviors and attitudes in organizations. In addition, others—such as Opp (1981)—focus on recurrent behavior as the major force behind culture value formation.

Hence, there seems to be an acknowledged connection between behaviors and the development of culture. These aspects of culture are important to a behavioral perspective. Armed with a definition of culture and a sense of the various perspectives on culture, we now suggest a behavioral perspective on culture that, we believe, will help to clarify how culture is formed, maintained, and changed within a dynamic organizational setting.

A Behavioral View of Organizational Culture

An operant approach to understanding behavior can be presented very simply: As Skinner (1938) maintains, behavior is a function of its consequences. Environmental consequences tend to influence behaviors when a connection is made between the behavior and its consequences. One learns once the association is made between behavior and these consequences. The behavioral approach, then, is strongly associated with learning.

Relating behaviorism and learning to culture is complicated by the various cognitive perspectives on culture that have been reflected in the literature. As noted earlier, culture may be defined in a very limited fashion, or it can be defined as synonymous with the organization. These different meanings of culture suggest part of the reason why it is very difficult to get an operational definition of culture and to understand the various dynamics that are part of culture formation and maintenance.

To try to demystify culture, we present a simple example of how a new employee learns the level of performance that is expected by management. Various interactions between the employee and management or the employee and other employees convey expectations of levels of performance. For now, we will only look at interactions between the employee and management. As soon as the employee enters the organization, management may articulate some expectations about performance. As the employee completes a task, management may or may not reinforce the employee's performance. For example, when the employee does an outstanding job and management does not respond, there is no reinforcement of that level of effort. When management does not respond to lower levels of performance, again there is little conveyed to the employee regarding what is an acceptable level of performance. Only when management responds to particular levels of performance is there a connection made between performance behaviors and management desires. This connection may reinforce or not reinforce future performance, depending on the consequences.

Now let us look at the same example using behavioral

terminology. The employee has learned to associate a level of performance with a consequence, feedback by management. When providing positive feedback, management has reinforced the behavior of the employee. When neutral feedback is provided, it neither reinforces nor undercuts the behavior. Negative feedback would reduce the frequency of future behavior. But, does this behavior interaction represent culture? Based on our definition above, it is what *leads to* culture, because the employee has learned how to cope with experiences by defining a range of appropriate behaviors. The feedback *transmits* culture. We argue, then, that culture is transmitted through the behavior-consequence transaction. Once the association is learned, then a part of culture is learned. As an increasing number of behavior-consequence transactions occur, a sense of the full spectrum of an organization's culture is acquired and becomes part of the cognitive interpretation of the culture for that individual.

But how can a behaviorist consider cognitive connections made by an individual? While a strict Skinnerian would not allow for that possibility, the introduction of Social Learning Theory (SLT) by Bandura (1976, 1977) does. SLT provides for cognitive processes both in learning connections between the environment and appropriate behaviors and in learning through vicarious processes. This SLT extension expands the ability of behaviorism to explain a host of acquired behavior-consequence associations that may not have been learned through direct experience. For through vicarious processes, a person learns about behavioral-consequence connections by observing what occurs to others. In the previous example, not only is the employee who directly experienced management's reaction to the level of performance influenced, but so are the employees that see management's actions or hear about what happened through the informal communication channels (the grapevine).

This process helps to explain how a cognitive interpretation of reality develops within an individual. The matching of behaviors with consequences is facilitated by these direct and indirect experiences. In addition, SLT allows for cognitive interpretation of these events that tend to help define culture for the individual.

SLT's notion of behavioral self-control also provides a greater understanding of behavioral choice than was ever possible under a strict Skinnerian interpretation. SLT allows for a cognitive connection to be made by the individual to manage his or her own behavioral strategies so as to maximize the potential for a desirable outcome. In the preceding example, the employee may work harder while a supervisor that recognizes good performance is present, but not respond when a supervisor is present that does not seem to care about performance. The employee actively tries to influence outcomes and controls his or her own behavior to influence those outcomes. Because of these dimensions, SLT has been considered to be an important theoretical framework for behavioral management that can make substantial contributions toward increasing the effectiveness of the behavioral approach (for an expanded discussion, see Luthans & Martinko, 1987). SLT thus becomes very important in shedding light on the dynamics of culture formation and maintenance.

In addition to learning through behavior-consequence experiences and through vicarious learning, people also learn through antecedent-behavior-consequence links. Learning of antecedent conditions is another important part of behavioral conditioning and is an important part of understanding culture. The use of antecedents implies that employees learn what particular behaviors are appropriate at specific times. For example, one does not swear when customers or bosses are around; however, swearing is acceptable when only the work group is present. Again, culture is learned through the consequences of behaviors, but antecedent conditions (such as when the boss or customers are present) may increase the probability that one type of behavior will lead to the desired consequences. The connection or links of interest are established through direct reinforcement or by vicarious learning.

Defining culture in behavioral terms involves adding a statement to the original cognitive definition that was made earlier. Culture was defined as "socially constructed realities that

provide learned ways of coping with experiences." To this definition we would now add an additional statement that reflects a
behavioral viewpoint. "The socially constructed realities come
about through patterns of direct and vicarious interactions involving the cognitive matching of antecedents-behaviors-consequences that reinforce accepted norms of behavior." This behav-
iorally expanded definition implies that the learned ways of
coping come about through the cognitive matching of behavioral consequences. This cognitive matching is done on the
individual level. However, through the sharing of common experiences, a similar shared vision about the organization's culture
can emerge. Yet, it would be rare to have individuals share
exactly the same vision.

The preceding discussion demonstrates how a behavioral
approach can be applied to an understanding of culture. The
implications of viewing organizational culture from a behavioral perspective can be distilled into seven distinct properties.

Implications of a Behavioral View:
Seven Properties of Organizational Culture

Seven properties emerge when relating behavioral and learning
principles to organizational culture. Each of these properties
contributes to an understanding of organizational culture.

Property 1: **Culture** *Is a Generic Term.* *Culture* is a generic term for
a host of behaviors that connote general operating norms of
conduct for an environment. These behaviors are viewed collectively and are developed into a cognitive construct by the individual. While culture may be articulated in cognitive expressions, its development and maintenance come from
behavioral interactions that tend to confirm or create disso-
nance with the articulated cognition.

Defining organizational culture based on behavioral factors frees us to include a host of behaviors as parts of the puzzle
that create the cognitive construct called organizational culture.
Instead of looking for a monolithic construct, hundreds of

separate behavioral interactions create culture. Hence, organizational culture forms as a natural process of specific human interactions of a particular kind. There is no one event that creates culture. It is not mandated by management, nor by labor. It evolves over time in the minds of organizational participants as the result of antecedent conditions, behaviors, and consequences of behaviors that in turn lead to a pattern of behaviors.

Treating culture this way helps in understanding culture maintenance and change. Instead of viewing culture as an independent variable separate from the organization (see Smircich, 1983), culture becomes part of the organization, a root metaphor as described by Smircich (1983). Under property 1, to change culture or to understand why it is as it is, the environment and behavioral interactions in the organization become the foci of analysis. In addition, the whole life experience of the individual is considered as organization culture evolves from the culture that the organization members have when they enter the organization. This more encompassing view is much more consistent with a behavioral definition of culture and the view, discussed earlier, that culture evolves from the predispositions of members entering the organization. Hence, a broad spectrum of experiences within and outside the organization need to be considered in order to explain how the image of the organization's culture forms within the cognitive framework of the individual.

Property 2: Culture Is Learned. Individuals are moved to behave in ways that lead to desired consequences (Skinner, 1938). Individuals will modify their own behaviors to conform to a cultural norm if it is perceived that compliance will lead to desirable outcomes for the individual (Likert, 1967).

Culture is learned through a connection that is made between behaviors and consequences. If an employee goes out of his or her way to help a customer and management does not respond, that behavior may not be exhibited in the future. Since behaviors are a function of their consequences, culture formation can be thought of as a series of behaviors and consequences. The more that management or a work group reinforces a particular behavior, the more likely it is that it will be exhibited in the future.

Learning those connections between behaviors and consequences aids in building the individual's generic construct that we call organizational culture. If cleanliness in the work environment is not reinforced, then that must not be a value of management. Hence the culture of the organization can be defined as not caring about cleanliness. If a work group defies management by taking long breaks or coming in late, with little response by management, then it may encourage others to exhibit similar behaviors. Through these sorts of behavior-consequence interactions, done one at a time, the culture of the organization is shaped or maintained.

Property 3: Culture Is Transmitted Through a Pattern of Behavioral Interactions. Through a pattern of behavior-consequence interactions, an individual's cognitive map of reality is shaped. Note that this implies that while culture may be shared, it is a personal construct subject to highly individualized interpretation.

Viewing culture as a pattern of behaviors and consequences provides insight into culture development and maintenance. For example, two employees discuss an action by management. Though management wants fast service for customers checking out in a retail outlet, check and charge approval policies slow the process. The employees may discuss the policy and agree that management really does not care about customers because management is reinforcing behaviors that slow customer processing.

Through this one example of management's actions and the interpretations of those actions, there is a subtle defining of one part of the organization's culture. As other events occur, they would tend to reinforce this perception or create another impression of how management wants the customers treated.

The same is true of how an employee learns directly or vicariously of other management values. Questions such as the following are answered through direct and vicarious experiences of the employee:

- How does management treat its employees?
- How does management want outsiders to view the organization?
- What employee behaviors are allowed by management?
- Does hard work pay off?
- How does management respond when you treat customers well?
- Does management care if you are late?
- What is the employee's reaction if another employee is mistreated by management?

Through direct and various behavioral events, an employee learns how management and other individuals in the organization respond to incidents. Their behavioral response provides a consequence that becomes the basis for determining various parts of the organization's culture. This concept is similar to the notion of moments of truth that Albrecht and Zemke (1985) describe when talking about customer service. Each behavior-consequence event is one of those moments of truth that tend to help shape the employee's image of the organization's culture.

Changing culture in light of this behavior-consequence concept involves comprehensive planning and execution. Consistent messages must be conveyed through behavioral interactions and through changes in the employee's environment. If, for example, the desire is to improve customer responsiveness, the manager needs to be consistent in his or her own behaviors to convey that message. Employee behaviors that support service need to be consistently reinforced. Formal company compensation and evaluation systems, other company symbols, and information sources must be structured so that they emphasize the service goals of the organization.

The consistency between various reinforcing agents in the organization is important to the learning process. Learning will be enhanced if there are consistent as opposed to conflicting reinforcements. Conflicting contingencies will only create unclear signals in the employee's mind and lengthen the cultural change process.

Hence, organizational culture is transmitted by means of behavioral interactions through a series of antecedents, behaviors, and consequences as expressed in behavioral terms (see Luthans & Kreitner, 1985, or Scott & Podsakoff, 1985, for a review of the behavioral approach). In cultural formation, it is behaviors that are focused on as the major means of establishing culture. Through behavioral actions people communicate ideas and values. Even if the culture is being transmitted through stories (see Martin, Feldman, Hatch, & Sitkin, 1983, for examples), a behavior—speaking—is involved. Through seeing what happens to others, vicarious learning takes place. Watching another event, while not directly involved, can still result in learning.

Translating culture formation into behavioral terms helps people understand how the process works. People learn more from behaviors than from printed statements and company policies. There is an old adage that "I can't hear what you are saying because your actions are speaking too loud." In essence, organizational participants will interpret actions more than words when forming a cultural definition of the organization. This definition of the culture of the organization will be reinforced by subsequent behaviors and consequences that are exhibited by organizational members that will support or not support the conclusions already made by the individual.

Combining direct experiences with the actions and words of co-workers, an individual quickly forms perceptions of the organization's culture. These perceptions will be maintained unless additional experiences tend not to support the original perception.

Property 4: In an Organization Setting There Are Multiple Reinforcements and Reinforcing Agents. The individual has a variety of wants and needs that can be fulfilled in a host of ways by various individuals and groups in the organization. The individual will become more strongly aligned with the reinforcing agent or agents that meet his or her wants and needs (Lewin, 1947).

Organizational culture formation, maintenance, and change occur in an environment where there are multiple reinforcements and reinforcing agents. In a newly emerging culture, less stable relationships are developed. Much of the initial stage in the formation of an organization centers around the development of a work flow that is effective for the organization. Part of the definition of that work flow is the development of intra- and intergroup relationships that support the organization's goals. As Lucas (1987) indicates, a "negotiated order" occurs between the groups that define many appropriate behaviors that facilitate the functioning of work groups at an acceptable level. While each group may not have a shared vision of the culture, they accommodate each other's vision.

In a new organization, work groups form based on many different factors, as discussed elsewhere (for the classic work in this area see Cartwright & Zander, 1968). Group formation also leads to group norm development — what might be referred to as the various subcultures, as articulated by Johannisson (1987). These various groups become separate reinforcing agents in addition to management and other individuals. Each is a potential reinforcing agent that can either work to support or not support the culture that management desires.

Once a culture is formed, these reinforcing agents work to support or hinder the dominant culture in the organization. Changing the organization involves the identification of the various reinforcing agents, so that an understanding of their effects on the change process might be determined. Integrating those agents that can be supportive while reducing the effect of those agents that are less supportive often becomes an important part of the change process.

In the same way, there are multiple reinforcements in the organization. The individual has many wants and needs that can be fulfilled by the various people and groups in the organization. These reinforcements can also be supportive or nonsupportive of management. For example, the desire to have social contacts may negate an incentive salary plan, although the individual desires both money and social support. Social support may be more important than the loss of income (see Luthans & Kreitner, 1985; and Premack, 1965, for a full discussion).

There are two important aspects of property 4. First, an organization's culture is not controlled solely by management. There are multiple reinforcing agents. Second, there are many things that can be used to reinforce behaviors in an organization. Some of these reinforcements can be more effectively carried out through work groups than by formal management. As such, culture formation, maintenance, and change are all affected by various groups, individuals, and reinforcements. These various agents and reinforcers can support, harm, or be neutral toward management's desires.

Property 5: Each Individual Carries Predispositions That Shape His or Her Interpretation of the Organization's Culture. Previous work and nonwork experiences would affect the individual's perception of the organization. In addition, these previous experiences affect how events would be interpreted and transformed into the employee's "reality of the organization's culture" in the new job experience. Hence the patterns of antecedents-behaviors-consequences may be interpreted differently. These differences will vary as work and life experience vary across the members of the organization.

Predispositions will affect the organization during culture formation, because more people will be new to the organization and each will have a unique predisposition about the organization and values that are brought in from the outside. Pennings and Gresov (1986) would define the new organization as having weak internal links but strong external ones.

Predisposition will affect a mature culture in that change will be made more difficult. Existing perceptions about the organization will be hard to change. This is one of the reasons why management training approaches where a manager goes off to a training program for a week have low success rates. While the manager may have new ideas, the organization has the same perceptions of the manager. New techniques are hard to adopt since they are not reinforced by the work group. It takes much perseverance by the manager to keep with the new techniques until they become accepted by the work group. Group change approaches are considered more effective in this respect because the members are involved in the change process from its inception, hence are more apt to modify their predispositions.

Property 6: A Symbiotic Relationship Exists Between Reinforcing Agent and Target. The influence target depends on the influence agent to fulfill some of his or her needs. And conversely, the influence agent depends on the influence target to meet some of his or her needs. The stronger the needs and the importance that is attached to fulfilling these needs, the greater the accommodation that will be made to influence either the target or the agent to comply with the desires of the other.

There are limits to the degree of accommodation that either party is willing to make, however. This accommodation boundary might be called a *zone of tolerance*, similar to Barnard's (1938/1962) *zone of acceptance* in his acceptance theory of authority. Compliance outside the zone of tolerance would be considered unacceptable, since it would violate basic norms and values that are dear to the influence target.

The symbiotic relationship between agent and target is even more pronounced during culture formation. The power of the influence agent is reduced because there are fewer stable social relationships. This tends to equalize the symbiotic nature of the influence attempt—that is, the agent needs the target just as much as the target may need the agent. This is true of management's relationship with the target as well as with other groups.

Management, for example, may not have a stable core of employees in the new organization. Since management is under pressure to get to a level of performance comparable to more established units, there will be greater pressure on management to accommodate the demands of its employees, at least until a solid core of dependable employees is established.

Similarly, work groups are not yet strongly established in a new organization. Social and safety needs would dictate that individuals will form into some sort of groups. The need to find potential members that "fit with the other group members" will keep groups more pliable. Again, this will be true at least until a central core is established within the group.

Having instability at all levels creates the potential for relatively wide shifts in the perception of the organization's culture until some stability is established. This occurs in a process similar to what Lucas (1987) called a negotiated order. Norms are formed through various interactions that people have as part of the antecedent-behavior-consequence pattern and through vicarious learning patterns. Hence culture is stabilized.

Change, in more mature cultures, will come in incremental stages unless a concerted change effort is applied. This is the premise that drives comprehensive organization development approaches (see Burke, 1982). However, the symbiotic relationships will still govern the negotiated order that prevails and the resulting culture that evolves.

Property 7: Changing an Established Culture Is Difficult. Changing an established organizational culture involves the learning of new sets of appropriate behaviors. Learning these new sets of behaviors involves the changing of organizational consequences so that the new behaviors are reinforced while undesired behaviors have less positive consequences.

It is more difficult to change an existing culture than it is to create a new culture. First, an existing culture already possesses nests of learned antecedents-behaviors-consequences. To change these learned expectancies, a concerted effort is needed to undercut existing perceptions while supporting the new culture through reinforcing desired behaviors by managing the environment to support the new culture. This change process is so difficult that some organizations decide to open new plants with new employees rather than trying to change the culture in existing plants. Some of the moves from the industrial North in the United States to the South have had less to do with unionization than with the ability to create a culture that is more supportive of the organization's goals. This explains part of the difficulty in applying some of the organizational change approaches in different organizational environments (see French, Bell, &

Zawacki, 1989, for a discussion of some of these problems, especially pp. 641–680). Hence, while the property that "culture is learned" may seem simple enough, it has profound implications for a consideration of cultural change.

Linking the Seven Properties

All seven properties can be integrated into a cohesive whole by means of some specific linking conclusions. First, attitudes and behaviors are closely associated in organizational culture. While organizational culture is a cognitive construct, behavioral interactions between people make the culture manifest. Culture can only be changed through changes in behaviors. However, since culture is a cognitive construct, attitudes need to be changed, too. How can attitudes be changed? Through changes in behaviors by those who wish to change the culture. In this manner, the desired changes can be communicated. In addition, the new attitudes need to be reinforced. How can this be done? Through the reinforcement of behaviors that demonstrate the new attitudes. But how does a change in reinforcement of behaviors lead to a change in attitudes?

This becomes somewhat more problematical. Remember that, as stated earlier, the basic tenet of the behavioral approach is that behavior is a function of its consequences. A person will change behaviors if the new behavior leads to a higher probability of receiving a desired consequence (Vroom, 1964, addresses this cognitive process in his classic work on motivation). The main point is that changed reinforcements make it obvious to the individual that there has been a change in what the organization values, and the change is incorporated into his or her perception of the culture of the organization. The individual then has the choice of accepting, accommodating, or rejecting the change. Note that the issue is *not* whether he or she agrees or disagrees with the change in the organization. The issue is whether the individual revises his or her perception of the culture of the organization with the change.

Second, it is clear that while organizational culture is a cognitive construct, it is still built and demonstrated by antece-

dents, behaviors, and consequences. Hence, these three elements ought to be the main focus in understanding what culture
is and how it is to be changed. Behaviors are the primary unit,
the driving force that propagates a vision of culture within an
individual. To influence the perception of the individual, one
must try to influence the antecedents and consequences that
relate to behaviors that are exhibited in the organization. These
are what behaviorists call *environmental factors* (see Luthans &
Kreitner, 1985).

The antecedent conditions consist of environmental factors that would influence the behavior of the individual. If
management is trying to influence the culture of the organization, it would insure that the environment presents a consistent
message that establishes behavioral expectations. This can be
done through the articulation of both goals for the organization
and individual behavioral goals that would assist in reaching
organizational goals. For example, if the goal is friendly service,
management should make it clear that it wants the employee to
act in a courteous manner. Positive outcomes will occur to the
individuals who demonstrate the appropriate behaviors, which
will reinforce behaviors directly or vicariously.

In order for management's desires to remain believable,
and thus have a higher chance of becoming part of the culture,
management has to be consistent in its actions. As we saw above
in the example about concern for customers, other policies and
reinforcement systems ought to be consistent with reaching the
goals that management has articulated. Any mismatch would
bring into question the seriousness of management's desire to
reach the goals and cloud the culture that management is attempting to create.

Management is not the only influence agent in the organization. It is clear from the seven properties that there are a host
of reinforcing agents that influence culture in an organization.
Any of these other agents, such as informal and formal groups,
may be sending congruent or incongruent antecedent images or
reinforcements for behaviors that might support or undermine
the image that the individual has about the organization. For
example, management may be trying to demonstrate that there

is a fair merit system that rewards performance. Negative comments by a work group might give the image that performance is based on politics. These statements would tend to undermine the effectiveness of management's efforts. That is why clear communications and demonstrations of how a policy or practice works helps to increase the probability that individuals will have a better understanding of the process. If the process is not clearly communicated or is difficult to understand, avenues are opened for distortions and confusion.

Third, while direct behavioral interactions are central to an understanding of culture, the environment plays an important role in culture development. It is not enough to articulate what culture is desired. The organization, through its policies and practices, physical surroundings, work flow, and other elements—as described in the previous sections of this article—all tend to support or undermine the culture that is being articulated. Hence, while behaviors may be the elementary unit in conveying an understanding of organizational culture, the environment is an important agent that will tend to reinforce or subvert the behaviors that are being exhibited and will set forth the antecedent conditions that influence the behaviors and perceptions of the individuals in that environment. For example, a clean store with well-stocked and attractive displays reinforces a caring culture about the customer. Employees sense this, as do the customers. In essence, the environment reinforces the desired culture.

Fourth, consistency by the influence agent is central in reinforcing particular cultural norms. Inconsistency will only lead to confusion in the mind of the influence target as to what is desired. Hence, learning will take longer, with the possibility that the wrong associations between behavior and reinforcement will be made. This latter case is called *superstitious behavior* (see Bolles, 1975). The importance of consistency in behavioral responses is discussed in Luthans and Kreitner (1985) and Davis and Luthans (1980).

These four conclusions are central to understanding how culture is formed, maintained, and changed in an organization. They flow from the seven properties and are a natural conclusion of applying a behavioral approach to an understanding of organizational culture.

Summary

Understanding how culture is formed, maintained, and changed in organizations is an important element in understanding individual and group behavior in organizations. To shed light on the dynamics of culture, we have employed a behavioral perspective in this chapter.

A behavioral approach views organizational culture as the result of a pattern of antecedents-behaviors-consequences that tend to support the development of behavioral norms for individuals in the organization. Behaviors that are acceptable to organization participants are reinforced; those that are not are not reinforced. Reinforcements include a host of behavioral consequences that can be social in nature (inclusion, praise, acceptance in activities) or that can be formally reinforced through the organization reward system (pay increases, promotions, status symbols).

Social Learning Theory (SLT) has extended more traditional behavioral approaches to include the notion of cognitive processes and vicarious learning. Making cognitive connections between patterns of reinforcement and in the interpretation of vicarious learning helps to build a cognitive definition of culture within the individual that is then validated through additional work and nonwork experiences.

This chapter has expressed the view that there are many cultures in an organization. The development of a dominant culture is a function of the accommodation of various subcultures to a dominant culture that may or may not reflect the values of any of the individual subcultures. It is through the influence process that a dominant culture evolves.

Seven properties emerge when we consider organizational culture from a behavioral perspective. Each has been reviewed from the perspective of its contribution to an understanding of culture from a behavioral viewpoint and in terms of its implications for culture formation, maintenance, and change.

Management has an obvious stake in the development of a culture that will be compatible with its goals. This chapter has outlined the various aspects of the employees' environment that can affect culture formation and has provided examples of how the environment can be managed. While total control is not possible or desirable, we have argued that culture can be influenced over time, to a significant degree, with consistent application of behavioral principles.

References

Albrecht, K., & Zemke, R. (1985). *Service America: Doing business in the new economy*. Homewood, IL: Dow Jones–Irwin.

Allaire, Y., & Firsirotu, M. E. (1984). Theories of organizational culture. *Organization Studies, 5*, 193–226.

Bandura, A. (1976). Social learning theory. In J. T. Spence, R. C. Carson, & J. W. Thibaut (Eds.), *Behavioral approaches to therapy* (pp. 1–46). Morristown, NJ: General Learning Press.

Bandura, A. (1977). *Social learning theory*. Englewood Cliffs, NJ: Prentice-Hall.

Barnard, C. I. (1962). *The functions of the executive*. Cambridge, MA: Harvard University Press. (Original work published 1938.)

Barnea, A., Haugen, R. A., & Senbet, L. W. (1985). *Agency problems in financial contracting*. Englewood Cliffs, NJ: Prentice-Hall.

Berger, P., & Luckmann, T. (1966). *The social construction of reality*. Garden City, NY: Doubleday.

Bolles, R. C. (1975). *Learning theory*. New York: Holt, Rinehart & Winston.

Burke, W. W. (1982). *Organization development*. Boston: Little, Brown.

Carlzon, J. (1987). *Moments of truth*. Cambridge, MA: Ballinger.

Cartwright, D., & Zander, A. (Eds.) (1968). *Group dynamics: Research and theory* (3rd ed.). New York: Harper & Row.

Davis, T.R.V., & Luthans, F. (1980). A social learning approach to organizational behavior. *Academy of Management Review, 5,* 281–290.

Deal, T. E., & Kennedy, A. A. (1982). *Corporate culture: The rites and symbols of corporate life.* Reading, MA: Addison-Wesley.

French, W. L., Bell, C. H., & Zawacki, R. A. (1989). *Organization development: Theory and practice* (3rd ed.). Homewood, IL: BPI/ Irwin.

Gregory, K. L. (1983). Native-view paradigms: Multiple cultures and culture conflicts in organizations. *Administrative Science Quarterly, 28,* 359–376.

Gupta, N., Jenkins, G. D., & Curington, W. P. (1985, August). *Pay for knowledge: The state of practice.* Paper presented at the annual national meeting of the Academy of Management, San Diego, CA.

Guthrie, E. R. (1935). *The psychology of learning* (2nd ed.). New York: Harper & Row.

Hackman, J. R., & Oldham, G. R. (1976). Motivation through the design of work: Test of a theory. *Organizational Behavior and Human Performance, 16,* 250–279.

Hall, E. T. (1969). *The hidden dimension.* Garden City, NY: Doubleday.

Johannisson, B. (1987). Beyond process and structure: Social exchange networks. *International Studies of Management and Organization, 17,* 3–23.

Kerr, S., & Jermier, J. M. (1978). Substitutes for leadership: Their meaning and measurement. *Organizational Behavior and Human Performance, 20,* 375–403.

Lewin, K. (1947). Group decision and social change. In T. M. Newcomb & E. L. Hartley (Eds.), *Readings in social psychology* (pp. 330–344). New York: Holt, Rinehart & Winston.

Likert, R. (1967). *The human organization.* New York: McGraw-Hill.

Louis, M. R. (1980, August). *A cultural perspective on organizations: The need for and consequences of viewing organizations as culture-bearing milieux.* Paper presented at the annual national meeting of the Academy of Management, Detroit.

Louis, M. R. (1983). Organizations as culture-bearing milieux. In L. R. Pondy, P. J. Frost, G. Morgan, & T. C. Dandridge (Eds.),

Organizational symbolism (pp. 23–44). Greenwich, CT: JAI Press.

Lucas, R. (1987). Political-cultural analysis of organizations. *Academy of Management Review, 12*(1), 144–156.

Luthans, F., & Kreitner, R. (1985). *Organizational behavior modification and beyond: An operant and social learning approach.* Glenview, IL: Scott, Foresman.

Luthans, F., & Martinko, M. (1987). Behavioral approaches to organizations. In C. L. Cooper & I. T. Robertson (Eds.), *International review of industrial and organizational psychology 1987* (pp. 35–60). New York: Wiley.

Martin, J., Feldman, M. S., Hatch, M. J., & Sitkin, S. B. (1983). The uniqueness paradox in organizational stories. *Administrative Science Quarterly, 28*, 438–453.

Martin, J., & Powers, M. E. (1983). Truth of corporate propaganda: The value of a good war story. In L. R. Pondy, P. J. Frost, G. Morgan, & T. C. Dandridge (Eds.), *Organizational symbolism* (pp. 55–77). Greenwich, CT: JAI Press.

Meyerson, D., and Martin, J. (1987). Cultural change: An integration of three different views. *Journal of Management Studies, 24*, 623–647.

Morey, N. C., & Luthans, F. (1985). Refining the displacement of culture and the use of scenes and themes in organizational studies. *Academy of Management Review, 10*, 219–229.

O'Reilly, C. A., III, & Caldwell, D. F. (1985). The impact of normative social influence and cohesiveness on task perceptions and attitudes: A social information processing approach. *Journal of Occupational Psychology, 58*, 193–206.

Opp, K. D. (1981). The explanation of values, problems, and approaches. In G. Dlugos & K. Weiermair (Eds.), *Management under differing value systems.* Berlin: de Gruyter.

Ouchi, W. G., & Jaeger, A. M. (1978). Type Z organization: Stability in the midst of mobility. *Academy of Management Review, 3*, 305–314.

Pennings, J., & Gresov, C. (1986). Technoeconomic and structural correlates of organizational culture: An integrative framework. *Organization Studies, 7*, 317–334.

Peponis, J. (1985). The spatial culture of factories. *Human Relations, 38,* 357–390.

Peters, T. J., & Waterman, R. H. (1982). *In search of excellence: Lessons from America's best-run companies.* New York: Harper & Row.

Premack, D. (1965). Reinforcement theory. In D. Levine (Ed.), *Nebraska symposium on motivation* (pp. 123–180). Lincoln: University of Nebraska Press.

Riley, P. (1983). A structurationist account of political cultures. *Administrative Science Quarterly, 28,* 414–437.

Schneider, B. (1987). The people make the place. *Personnel Psychology, 40,* 437–453.

Schuler, R. S., Ritzman, L. P., & Davis, V. (1981). Merging prescriptive and behavioral approaches for office layout. *Journal of Operations Management, 1*(3), 131–142.

Scott, W. E., & Podsakoff, P. M. (1985). *Behavioral principles in the practice of management.* New York: Wiley.

Siehl, C., & Martin, J. (1981). *Learning organizational culture* (working paper). Stanford, CA: Stanford University, Graduate School of Business.

Skinner, B. F. (1938). *The behavior of organisms.* East Norwalk, CT: Appleton & Lange.

Smircich, L. (1983). Concepts of culture and organizational analysis. *Administrative Science Quarterly, 28,* 339–358.

Smith, P. C., & Kendall, L. M. (1963). The retranslation of expectations: An approach to the construction of unambiguous anchors for rating scales. *Journal of Applied Psychology, 47,* 149–155.

Thompson, K. R., & Luthans, F. (1983). A behavioral interpretation of power. In R. W. Allen & L. W. Porter (Eds.), *Organizational influence processes* (pp. 72–86). Glenview, IL: Scott, Foresman.

Tichy, N. M. (1982). Managing change strategically: The technical, political, and cultural keys. *Organizational Dynamics, 11*(4), 59–80.

Vroom, V. (1964). *Work and motivation.* New York: Wiley.

Wilkins, A. L., & Ouchi, W. G. (1983). Efficient cultures: Exploring the relationship between culture and organizational performance. *Administrative Science Quarterly, 28,* 468–481.

Chapter 10

Philip H. Mirvis
Amy L. Sales

Feeling the Elephant: Culture Consequences of a Corporate Acquisition and Buy-Back

> It was six men of Indostan
> To learning much inclined,
> Who went to see the Elephant,
> (Though all of them were blind),
> That each by observation,
> Might satisfy his mind.
> —John Godfrey Saxe,
> *The Blind Men and the Elephant*

DC, a Midwestern manufacturing firm, developed its first state-ment of company values in the late 1960s. This early statement, reflecting then-CEO Lester Richardson's abiding faith in peo-ple, drew from the behavioral sciences and emphasized per-sonal openness and teamwork as keys to the company culture. These original values were internalized by management in team-building exercises and infused into the organization through participative management.

In 1982 a new CEO and management team took charge at DC. Through a series of position papers, the new leaders devel-oped an updated value statement. This new statement con-cerned itself with employees, but it also dealt with customers, innovation, products, strategy, the profit objectives of the com-pany, and the security of its workforce. It was published in 1984 in a glossy brochure titled "Sharing a Vision." The brochure, distributed to the workforce at large, was meant to herald the new leadership of the firm and to signal some changes in what the company would stand for to its people.

Clearly, Douglas Davis, the new CEO, had a different outlook than his predecessor on managing people and the business. At management meetings and in video presentations to employees, he criticized the time wasted by excessive amounts of participation and argued that a heavy reliance on task forces blurred individual responsibility. In his speeches he stated that the company had to become "lean and mean" in the face of business challenges.

DC people not only heard the words, they saw the changes: Selective staff reductions were undertaken in line with new strategic directions. Top-management meetings became crisper and more businesslike. Division heads were left to develop their own management structures and to manage their people in the way they saw fit. There were few discussions of company philosophy, and group process analysis—a speciality of the old leadership—ceased.

"All of Them Were Blind"

In 1983, one year after the new management team took charge and just prior to the publication of their vision statement, we conducted the biennial Quality of Work Life Survey (QWL) at DC, collecting data from the nearly 1,000 employees of the company. We found that over two-thirds of DC's employees believed top management was placing too much emphasis on profits and not enough on people. Compared with results obtained in the previous QWL survey in 1981, there was an increase in ratings of stress and workload in the company. Some 40 percent reported that DC's new leaders were putting pressure on people to enhance the "bottom line." In turn, over one-quarter said that DC's new top-management team was less committed to participative management than the previous leadership; and there were declines, versus 1981, in ratings of people's say-so in everyday decisions.

In the comments section of the questionnaire, respondents were asked for recommendations that would help make DC a more effective organization. In response, many complained about the amount of "deadwood" in the company and recommended that management "crack down" on poor performers. Finally, people rated the new management team as less innovative than the old one and reported more conflict in the relationships between divisions.

Taken together, these data, in our opinion, signaled *disintegration* in the DC culture. We saw them as evidence that once shared values were in flux and that traditional norms were no longer guiding everyday behavior. When we offered this interpretation in our feedback meeting with top management, we met with sharp disagreement about the meaning and the import of the data.

Davis, the new CEO, was untroubled by the data and attributed them to the continuing "shakeout" in the company. Emphasis on profits and the attendant pressures felt by people were all part of "tough love." In his view, the U.S. business climate required a stronger emphasis on performance and individual accountability. He believed that managers still "cared" about people but were holding them to "higher standards."

Robert Bates, head of DC's largest division, had a different interpretation of the data. "Nobody talks about community anymore or seems to care about it," he said, adding that top managers did not talk about "process" much any more either. In his view, managers were getting the message that bottom-line "results" were what mattered and that how you achieved them was "unimportant."

The new head of Human Resources contended that we (the researchers) were not seeing all of the good things happening in the company. He pointed out that ratings of job satisfaction and commitment to the company remained very high for most DCers and that efforts to form self-managing teams had contributed to even better ratings of job autonomy and peer communication among hourly personnel. Greater autonomy, he further reasoned, might account in part for the increased workload and sense of pressure. In his view, a new kind of culture was taking hold—one in which everybody would work harder but could partake more fully of the "good things" through work enrichment and a gainsharing system.

Round and round the discussion went, some praising what was happening in the company and others challenging it, until Bates—sensing the confusion prompted by the data and the consternation felt by his peers—said that this was like "feeling the elephant." Some were handling the trunk and others grabbing the tail. All were seeing parts of the "truth" but all were blind to the totality of the beast.

The Elephant and Organization Culture: Theory

The elephant, we recognized at once, is an apt metaphor for organization culture. Although we use the image playfully, it is play with a purpose, since the elephant helps us understand the integrity *and* the diversity of culture.

The literature offers up an array of definitions of organizational culture, but all agree on its basic social nature. Some definitions focus on culture's role in unifying the organization. Culture has been labeled the "social glue that holds the organization together" (Baker, 1980, p. 52) or the "more expressive social tissue around us that gives everyday tasks and objectives meaning" (Pettigrew, 1979, p. 574). Other definitions, conversely, focus on the commonly held views within the social organization from which the culture originates and is maintained. Culture is thus defined as a shared system of beliefs, expectations, and meanings (Pettigrew, 1979; Pfeffer, 1981; Schwartz & Davis, 1981) or as an environment distinctive because of common assumptions about "how things are done around here" (Martin, 1982). Key to us in these definitions is that culture is *shared* by the members of the organization and serves to *integrate* the social system.

For our analysis, we consider three realms of culture. Human action, or *behavior* (including language, socialization of new members, and the performance of rituals, traditions, customs), represents the surface realm. Such action is organized through norms, roles, and role relationships. Underlying this realm is one of *values*, through which assumptions about human nature, society, and the self give purpose and significance to actions and legitimacy to organization. The third realm is *philosophy*. As the overarching paradigm that provides a map for action and a means for interpreting and evaluating its consequences, philosophy links behavior and values (Condon & Yousef, 1975; Padilla, 1980).

Three points arise from this conceptualization of culture. First, during normal times, cultures are unified and internally consistent, integrated within and across the three realms. Thus, philosophy expresses values; values are manifest in normative behaviors; and behaviors give meaning to the overarching philosophy. In this sense, culture reflects and maintains the integration of the social organization—it is the elephant in its entirety.

Second, even during normal times, there is some variation within a culture as exhibited and understood by different members of the organization. Given the particular experiences of subpopulations and the individual differences among members of an organization, we can assume that not everyone accepts the stated philosophy of an organization, adheres fully to company norms, or bows equally to the pantheon of organization values. Culture is "shared" to the extent that individual members identify with the larger unit, and, necessarily for the survival of the organization, feel a degree of commitment to it or a preference for this organization over others. Even during normal times, however, we expect to find a *range* of perceptions and experiences among members of an organization—all having a different feeling toward and some blindness to the elephant.

Finally, an organization in flux—as a result of crisis or planful transition—will exhibit crosscurrents in the usually free-flowing culture. Cultural change occurs in bits and pieces in segments of the population, so that during times of transition there are inconsistencies and variation within and across the three realms. Rather than seen as a unity, culture at this time is characterized by disintegration—different parts of the elephant tell a different story of the nature of the beast. The challenge in our work has been to interpret the variation we find in the reports of the "blind men," determining what represents range within a shared paradigm and what is a sign of disintegration in the culture.

Studying Corporate Culture: Method

There is general agreement that studies of corporate culture are best conducted through "inside" inquiry (Evered & Louis, 1981) where researchers are intimately associated with a company and develop "thick descriptions" (Geertz, 1973) of company life. This assumes that knowledge of a culture is tacit and experiential (Louis, 1983) and emerges in situ through critical observation and clinical interviewing (Schein, 1985), checked against the biases and interests of informants and the preconceptions of the researchers themselves.

We agree, in general, with this perspective and have based our study on several years of on-site assessment, at times in an action research role, as well as on periodic interviews with principals in DC and reviews of pertinent documents and memos. In addition, we have measured the pervasiveness of viewpoints on company culture by designing and incorporating into DC's biennial QWL surveys questions about norms and values in the company. On each survey we have also asked specifically about views of major events in the life of DC and the implications these have for work life in the company. We have periodically reported the findings from this research and our interpretations to DC's leaders for critical analysis and comment. Through this feedback and review process the validity of our study has been further strengthened.

An Overview of the Study. Our work with DC began with the company's first Quality of Work Life Survey in 1975 and has extended to the present time. During these years, the company experienced an acquisition by a major U.S. conglomerate (1978), the ascension of new leaders to top management (1982), and most recently, a leveraged buyout by the new management team (1986). By means of surveys, interviews, and review of archival data, we have assessed reactions to each event and its consequences throughout the years.

Table 10.1 provides a timetable of our research activities and their link to events related to cultural change in DC. We have elsewhere reported on the cultural crisis induced by DC's acquisition (Sales & Mirvis, 1984). Here we take a longer-range perspective on the evolution, disintegration, and reintegration of the organization's culture. Our report begins with 1983, the peak of "cultural disintegration" in the company. We move next to the early years (1900–1977) to trace the roots of the "old" DC culture. In the following three sections we review the clash of cultures that resulted from DC's acquisition (1978–1979) and the subsequent changes in the DC culture (1980–1981 and 1982–1983). In the last sections, we discuss the later years (1984–1985 and 1986–1988) and the dynamics by which the organization's culture moved from its height of disintegration toward "reintegration."

Cultural Disintegration: The Elephant — 1983

Once the image of "feeling the elephant" had been proposed to capture the confusion among top management in reviewing the 1983 survey results, we joined the discussion by drawing an elephant to graphically depict how the DC culture was, at that moment in time, marked by competing values and emphases (see Figure 10.1). Our commentary on the "elephant" highlighted competing forces in DC.

- *Profits Versus People.* To get through the tall grass requires the company to earn higher profits, but it also needs people to be "on board." The survey shows that management has been emphasizing profits but risks losing its people orientation and the commitment of its employees.
- *Pressure Versus Vision.* The elephant needs to work harder and smarter in today's environment. Some in top management think this requires a "kick in the butt," while others favor a new vision and direction. Compared with prior years, fewer people in DC now find the company's goals clear and fewer have confidence that DC will achieve them five years hence.
- *Top-Down Leadership Versus Participation.* Some DCers say that

Table 10.1. Ten Years of Culture Change: Timetable and Method.

	DC Organization and Culture	*Research and Intervention*
ROOTS OF THE OLD DC CULTURE		
1900–1970	**Culture of Family Firm** DC Becomes Paternalistic	
1970–1977	**Culture of Participative Management** Lester Richardson as CEO Top-Management Teamwork	Compensation Survey (1975) Work Life Survey (1977)
DISINTEGRATION OF THE OLD CULTURE		
1978–1979	**Clash of Cultures** White Knight Acquisition by GrandCo/Conflicts/Business Systems Imposed	Work Life Survey (1979) Qualitative Study of Impact of Acquisition on DC—I
1980–1981	**Acculturation** Accommodation to GrandCo—"Behavioral Shifts" Preservation of DC Culture "Ethnic Minority"	Work Life Survey (1981) Qualitative Study of Impact of Acquisition on DC—II
1982–1983	**Cultural Disintegration, Split in Top Management** "Acculturative Stress" Appointment of New CEO	Work Life Survey (1983) Qualitative Study of Changing Culture: Feeling the Elephant—I
1984–1985	**Continued Cultural Disintegration** Company Values and Beliefs "Sharing a Vision" Development of New Norms	Work Life Survey (1985) Qualitative Study of Changing Culture: Feeling the Elephant—II
REINTEGRATION IN NEW CULTURE		
1986–1988	**Leveraged Buyout of DC: "Family Again"**	Work Life Survey (1988)

the new leadership stands on its hind legs and threatens people. Others say that management continues to lead by listening to people and letting them participate in decisions. DC's leadership has sent "mixed messages" to people about participative management and is divided over how to lead the company.

• *Innovation Versus Conservatism.* DC does not appear to people

Figure 10.1. Feeling the Elephant: Signs of Deculturation in DC, 1983.

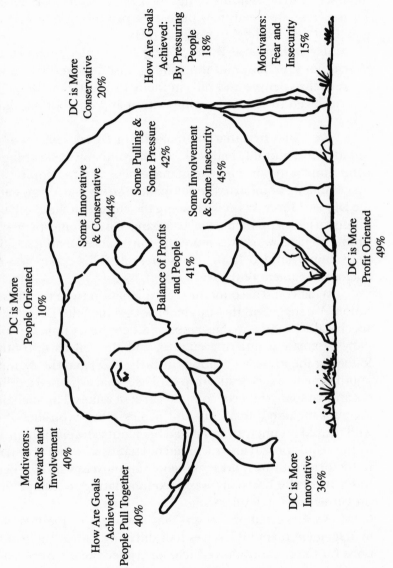

DC is More
People Oriented
10%

Motivators:
Rewards and
Involvement
40%

How Are Goals
Achieved:
People Pull Together
40%

DC is More
Innovative
36%

Some Innovative
& Conservative
44%

Balance of Profits
and People
41%

Some Pulling &
Some Pressure
42%

Some Involvement
& Some Insecurity
45%

DC is More
Conservative
20%

How Are Goals
Achieved:
By Pressuring
People
18%

Motivators:
Fear and
Insecurity
15%

DC is More
Profit Oriented
49%

as being at the "leading edge" of organizational development anymore—not high stepping into the future. Instead, management seems to be "holding things in" (the elephant's rear). People say the company needs new processes, products, and technologies. Can new leadership pull this off?

- *Sitting on Deadwood Versus Blowing the Trumpet.* Some DCers call for sanctions and reprisals against deadwood. Can you revitalize people and retrain them, or must "deadwood" be sacrificed in service to competition and the "bottom line"?

We noted first that the majority of DCers remained "on board" and a plurality believed that the company was keeping its commitment to participative management and to people.

Still, we pointed to the elephant to stress that a segment of the DC workforce was experiencing the culture in the elephant's hindquarters. For them, the company has become primarily profit-oriented, work was more pressure-packed, and decisions were being handed down from on-high. This group was an alienated segment of the workforce.

What could account for their alienation from the organization? We suggested that this had roots in the "old" DC culture, specifically in the way the values had been sewn into the company to create a unifying culture, and then in its uprooting following the firm's acquisition (in early 1978) and the eventual appointment of new leadership (in 1982) that espoused a different and, in some respects, competing set of values. The alienated segment included managers and professionals who identified with the old regimen and who had been unfavorably influenced by the acquisition. It also included old hands who had grown up in the prior culture, and some newer employees who had been hired in as the company was accommodating to competitive pressures and top-level change.

We suggested, moreover, that members of the new top-management team themselves had differing values and aspirations for the organization which, we argued, were contributing as well to the overall lack of integration in the culture. We then asked what was holding them and the company together: "Does the elephant have a heart?" Top management was convinced, at least, that DC's culture was undergoing a change. They resolved to codify its values, locate its "heart," and communicate these to the workforce.

Roots of the "Old" DC Culture (1900–1977)

The "old" DC culture evolved from its early history as a family firm and its later embracing in the 1970s, of participative management.

Culture of Family Firm. DC dates back to the turn of the century, when the founder moved to a port city in the Midwest and established a small plant to design and manufacture printing equipment and materials. From 1920 through 1950 it was known as a fine and decent employer, nonunionized, whose culture was marked by high-minded paternalism. Employees were regarded as "family" and frequently joined the founder at his home for summer picnics and seasonal outings.

In the 1950s control of the company was passed to the founder's oldest son, who began to institute many progressive management practices. Employees, for example, were given and sold shares of stock and met yearly, in the cafeteria, for a boisterous shareholders' meeting. Benefits were expanded to cover health care and longer paid vacations—well ahead of the trend in larger corporations.

Culture of Participative Management. In the mid 1960s the company went public and shortly thereafter experienced a significant business downturn. In the eyes of the newly constituted board of directors, the oldest son had neither the managerial know-how nor the business acumen to turn things around. In hopes of renewing the organization, they appointed in 1970 a new CEO, a younger son of the founder who had been serving as head of the company's main operating division.

The younger son, Lester Richardson, had been characterized by co-workers as extremely tough, intellectually aggressive, and personally insensitive. When he assumed the top leadership post, however, he resolved to change his management style. Through participation in outside T-Groups (which he described as "hellish") and work with behavioral scientists he invited in to consult to DC, he revolutionized his personal style and, along with DC's other top managers, became educated about new managerial models, philosophies, and processes.

Richardson employed an external consultant, a clinical psychologist well versed in organizational development (OD), to facilitate meetings between his direct reports and him. A series of meetings served to build open relationships among them. They developed and shared personal "dreams" about their future and that of the corporation. They defined a common philosophy and management approach based on OD's values and practices. Subsequently, the top managers formed into a corporate management team, committed to examining their working processes and oriented toward consensus-style decision making. Everyone was encouraged to critique and comment on everyone else's function.

This management style was spread into middle management through team building in the divisions in the early 1970s. Divisional management group structures developed and members were trained in group process skills. The company's management-by-objectives system was revised to measure OD activities and reward accomplishments. In keeping with OD principles, a variety of task forces were formed to study organizationwide opportunities for change and improvement. As a result, by the mid 1970s, the firm began to direct its energies toward improving the quality of work life for the hourly workforce in the company and, to this end, instituted the biennial QWL surveys to measure a broad range of people's attitudes and satisfactions. Other innovations ranged from quality circles in one plant to an education and consciousness-raising program to promote better relationships between men and women.

Richardson and his team prided themselves on staying at the "leading edge" of human systems theory and practice. Their rationale was straightforward. It helped them achieve "extraordinary results from ordinary people." They believed that innovation in the human organization would help reduce the "gap between current performance and potential," and thus they

emphasized "people development" in company communications and programs.

In the late 1970s, with participative management as the
centerpiece of the company's life, DC saw business booming, its
workforce up to 1,000 people, and quality of work life flourish-
ing. Through conscious and consistent effort, the wisdom of its
leaders, and the use of consultants as resources, an integrated
culture had evolved at DC. Its philosophy drew from the firm's
familial roots and later emphasis on participative management;
its values stressed the worth of the individual and the authority
of knowledge; and its behaviors were process-oriented and supportive of individual development.

Clash of Cultures (1978–1979)

Disintegration of this family-born and participatively bred
culture began when DC became the target of an unfriendly
takeover bid. The unfriendly bid was averted when DC was
acquired, in 1978, by a "white knight" — a West Coast conglomerate many times its size. The acquirer, to be called GrandCo, was
relatively more traditional in its management style and put a
stronger emphasis on short-term return on investment. This set
up a "clash of cultures" between the firms and threatened the
integrity of the DC culture built up over a decade of concerted
effort.

From the start, it was apparent that DC and GrandCo had
different expectations about this seeming "business deal" and
different models of how it should transpire. DCers, for example,
expected that they would be an active party to all integration
decisions, which would be made by "studying" each company's
ways of doing business and evaluating the advantages and disadvantages. GrandCo, by contrast, had long-established methods
for integrating subsidiaries and expected that its recommendations would be implemented as a matter of course. Underlying
DC's expectations was a cultural commitment to making decisions based on the "authority of knowledge" and through a
participative process. This belief system was "Greek" to
GrandCo executives, who believed in the "power of aristocrats,"

at least in DCers' eyes, and who had "never heard of" participative management.

People's culture is so much a part of them and their lives that they are unaware of it, unable even to describe or define their culture, until it comes into contact with another one. In this instance, despite talking a great deal about their managerial philosophy and values, DC managers had not been so consciously aware of how these were represented in their institutions, mores, and everyday behaviors. Thus DC's management approach—its commitment to process and open disclosure of information—were taken for granted by people within the company simply as part of everyday life. However, when GrandCo officials exhibited a different style, and, by implication, held to different values, DCers became more conscious of what they believed in, how different their company culture was from GrandCo's, and how much they wanted to preserve it.

The terms with which DC characterized these differences are summarized in Table 10.2 in terms of the three realms of culture: behaviors, values, and philosophy.

Business-Related Behavior. Business-related differences between the companies that were a matter of policy, practice, or custom became the focus of early "postacquisition" negotiations between the two parties. GrandCo expected detailed monthly reports from all of its subsidiaries and hosted two in-depth planning meetings per year to review results and develop business projections. GrandCo's systems put a premium on setting realistic financial targets and reaching them. The reviews were normally conducted in the boardroom, where presentations were to be precise and polished.

By contrast, DC executives had used a different approach to running their company. Managers were given liberal capital expenditure budgets and would meet quarterly to review targets and results in a freewheeling atmosphere. Annual planning meetings focused on products and markets, much more so than finance, and projections were revised regularly in line with changing business conditions. Periodic meetings were held with

**Table 10.2. Cultural Differences Between GrandCo and DC
as Discerned in 1980 by DCers.**

	GrandCo	DC
Business-Related Behavior	Monthly reports Two planning meetings Realistic targets "Broadway" presentations	Quarterly reports One planning meeting per year "Stretch" targets Theater-in-the-round
Interpersonal Behavior	Product-oriented Command "Chop-chop" Problem solving fast when routine, slow when complex No confrontations "Close to the chest"	Process-oriented Request Courteous Problem solving slow but implementation fast "Everything on the table" Open disclosure
Values	Financial, numbers people Power of the aristocrats Third-party communication Low levels of responsibility "Protect your ass"	Operations people Authority of knowledge Face-to-face communication High levels of responsibility "Fail forward"
Philosophy	Political Benevolent, authoritarian Control and performance	Familial Participative management "Extraordinary results from ordinary people"

supervisors to review progress and revise targets in a "theater-in-the-round" type of meeting.

Interpersonal Behavior. Relations between the two companies were complicated by differences in norms and behavior. DCers described GrandCo as very "businesslike, crisp, decisive. . . chop-chop," particularly when demanding information and proposing changes in DC. Still, its executives were seen as keeping things "close to the chest" when DCers asked questions and as being unable or unwilling to respond quickly to DC initiatives and recommendations. By contrast, DC spent more time in the process of decision making, openly putting "everything on the table" and looking at alternatives. Its problem-solving processes were "slow as molasses" but implementation was swift because everybody would "buy in."

Values. Differences in the business-related and interpersonal behaviors between the companies led to deeper inferences about the values of GrandCo. DCers came to believe that GrandCo was primarily "profit-oriented" and populated by "numbers" people who did not care about DC's operations or people orientation. "Herds of accountants" came into DC to "find faults" in their bookkeeping systems. Staff executives were followed by "lackeys" who were not empowered to make decisions or were unwilling to "make waves" in the parent company. All of this meant that GrandCo executives operated with low levels of responsibility and a high "protect your ass orientation."

Furthermore, GrandCo people would call to say "I'll be there next Wednesday at 9:00 A.M." without indicating the intent of the meeting, its objectives, or "checking whether it was a convenient time." Such interpersonal norms were "foreign" to DCers and led to the perception that GrandCo operated through command power. They expect a "Yes, sir" attitude, DCers inferred, where decisions are announced through the hierarchy and people are expected to "knuckle under." In turn, DCers' commitment to making decisions on "authority of knowledge" was seen as "Swahili" to financial types at GrandCo.

Philosophy. These differences in behavior and values were encapsulated by DCers in shorthand depictions of the philosophies of each company. GrandCo was a "benevolent-authoritarian" kind of organization in contrast to the "family-oriented" DC. Interestingly, DCers acknowledged that because of its size, structure, and traditions, it was understandable that GrandCo had such a managerial philosophy and was so rife with politics. But they then denigrated it because that was characteristic of "technocracies." What they also reasoned, however, was that "the benevolent-authoritarian value system at GrandCo will find its way into DC unless we work very hard to prevent it."

We have elsewhere ascribed DCers' view of GrandCo to ethnocentrism—the tendency of one group of people to view another through the lens of its own culture and to denigrate it (Sales & Mirvis, 1984). Certainly this attitude was exacerbated by the threatened imposition of GrandCo business systems, which DC executives viewed through their own cultural frames of references. Months of conflict led DCers to see GrandCo executives as of a kind — "bastards," who worked through "henchmen," who did not know a "damn thing about modern management." No doubt the tone of their stereotyping was also a function of "in-group" and "out-group" dynamics and of the many "win-lose" conflicts experienced, with consequent levels of scorekeeping and scapegoating.

Acculturation (1980–1981)

Anthropologists subsume these psychosocial dynamics under the rubric of *acculturation* (Berry, 1980). Interestingly, they point out that the conflicts and crises induced by developmental changes within a culture, or as a result of voluntary migrations, are far less pronounced than those that follow forced occupations and the imposition of the dominant culture's imperatives. Certainly an acquisition can be depicted as a special case of cross-cultural contact in which the processes of cultural change are a function of imposed changes and people's accommodation to new "realities."

We were not privy to any of the strategy meetings held at GrandCo and do not know of their particular designs on DC. On the surface, their executives seemed to be well meaning. GrandCo did not — at least in the first three years — replace any DC executives or institute any policies or controls that an objective observer might find unusual or especially onerous in a conglomerate acquisition. Still, GrandCo's influence on its new subsidiary did effect changes in the "old" DC culture.

Antecedents of Acculturation:
The Influence of the Dominant Culture

Acculturation begins as the influence of the parent company, the dominant culture in an acquisition, is exerted on the traditional

Table 10.3. External Influences and Behavioral Change — 1979–1982.

GrandCo Influence	Traditional Culture	Behavioral Change	Cultural Consequences
New Ownership			
"Slavering Wolf"	People-oriented	Results mandatory	Cash machine
"Big Brother"	Freedom of action	Look over shoulder	Nervous and jerky
New Structure and Controls			
"Amoeba"	Product-oriented	Finance-oriented	Know your numbers
"Octopus"	Home grown— commitment to decisions	Laid on—com- pliance with decisions	GrandCo busi- ness systems
New Reporting Relationships			
"Technocrat"	Human relations	Grin and bear it	No confrontations
"Yes, Sir"	Problem solving: authority of knowledge	Problem solving: reality of power	One down— dependence

culture of the acquired firm. We classify this influence into three types: the influence of new ownership, of new structure and controls, and of new reporting relationships (see Table 10.3).

The Influence of New Ownership. The language used to describe a merger or acquisition conveys the underlying emotional con- tent of a "business deal" (Hirsch & Andrews, 1983). A takeover attempt (a "raid") conveys a far more threatening message than a friendly merger (a "marriage"). Similarly, the relative size and the financial circumstances of both parties (whether, for exam- ple, the larger party is a "savior" or the smaller one a "cash cow") further condition the frame of reference people use in judging the culture of the other organization.

In this instance, DCers characterized the company that first attempted to take them over as a "rapist." This initial set

shaded their perceptions of GrandCo which, though a chival-
rous "white knight" in merger fairy tales, was depicted as a wolf,
"slavering over DC's profits," in top executives' nightmares.
GrandCo's size, twenty times larger than DC, could have been
equated with security and proved reassuring. Instead, GrandCo
was characterized as "Big Brother" always "looking over the
shoulder" of DCers.

To contend with this ominous threat to the organization,
DC's top management concluded that they would have to increase profitability. Good results were "mandatory." Many companies "drift" after an acquisition and, as results decline, the
buyer applies even closer financial scrutiny and sometimes
moves in its own executives (Kitching, 1967). In this case, DC
sought to preempt any such imposition by increasing emphasis
on short-run profitability.

The Influence of New Structure and Controls. Structural changes
and changes in rules and regulations are, to varying degrees,
commonplace in any corporate acquisition. But wanting to
preserve its identity and resistant to any change imposed by
GrandCo, DC was alert to the imposition of new structures and
controls. DCers saw GrandCo as an "amoeba" that would absorb
the company, and staff people termed it an "octopus" trying to
ensnare them. Descriptions of conflict between the two companies were, in turn, filled with boxing, wrestling, and war
imagery.

Mergers and acquisitions also shake up the power structure in a company and create new interdependencies (Kotter,
1985). In the case of DC, the financial departments gained new
clout because of their high-priority dealings with the parent
company. GrandCo was a conglomerate composed of many
different kinds of businesses. Its executives were neither versed
in DC's product line or market, nor did they seem, in the eyes of
DCers, to be very much interested in them. Instead, they managed by the "numbers," and DC's financial community — previously a "second-class citizen" — gained prestige and power.
They could "talk" to GrandCo and GrandCo found that they
could talk dollars and "sense."

The Influence of New Reporting Relationships. After the acquisition, the president of DC, who had previously reported directly to DC's board of directors, was to report to a GrandCo executive. The imposition of a new leader not only changes reporting relationships, it begins to dictate how a company sets its strategy, organizes its operations, and answers to the parent company. This, in turn, establishes cultural superiority and puts the subsidiary in a "one-down" dependency position. In this instance, Richardson had hoped to report directly to the CEO of GrandCo, but instead was assigned to a group vice president. The new parent company, through this assignment, symbolically and in actuality further "put [Richardson] in his place" and established dominance over DC. Taken together, new ownership, new structure and controls, and new reporting relationships made it appear to DC's management that their culture was under siege. "If we don't fight their technocratic steering," said one seasoned DC executive, "we will wither up and become businessmen. . . ."

Consequences of Acculturation: Behavioral Shifts

Each type of influence contributed to changes in the acquired company in the early postacquisition years. DC learned to accommodate to new ownership and adjusted behaviors accordingly (Sales & Mirvis, 1984). There were, for example, predictable pressures from the parent company to achieve higher levels of profitability: GrandCo put "DCers through the wringer" to feed its "profit-hungry" machinery. In turn, DC employees began to discern a difference in the company. In the 1981 QWL survey, some 40 percent said that management had become less interested in the welfare and well-being of DCers and as many said that they personally had less trust in others in the company. Over 50 percent said that they had to work harder on their jobs, and the same percentage said that the acquisition was having a big impact on the organization.

Given necessary new structure and controls, DC began to prepare monthly financial reports. They learned to make polished presentations at the biannual planning meetings and began to impress their superiors at GrandCo with their detailed knowledge of the business and their responsiveness to sharp queries. After some internal debate, top managers adopted GrandCo's conservative budgeting systems and bonus plan even though this meant sacrificing "stretch" targets and no longer "going for the biggies."

Under the influence of new reporting relationships, DCers learned to follow "protocol" when dealing with GrandCo executives and tried to "shield" their managers from "interference" by withholding information and "playing down" the impact of the acquisition. Employees felt the consequences in day-to-day operations. In 1981, nearly 50 percent of the workforce reported an increase in rumors following the acquisition and 30 percent found that their supervisors were blaming top management for integration problems. Interviewees said management was obsessed with GrandCo and was failing to oversee regular operations and stay in touch with people. All of this, in turn, made DC's top management appear "nervous and jerky" in their relationship with GrandCo and "foolish" in their dealings with direct reports.

Despite these influences and behavioral shifts, unwelcome change and incursions into an organization's culture may be resisted. DC's top managers fought GrandCo at every turn and, interestingly, even described themselves as an "ungrateful little brother." One manager analogized DC's early reactions to Kubler-Ross's (1969) model of death and dying, noting that executives were in a state of anger and bargaining with GrandCo over their very existence. DC's executives were thus able, until 1982, to maintain pieces of their culture as an "ethnic minority" in GrandCo. They maintained, for example, key aspects of their compensation plan, preserved their rights to fully disclose financial data to supervisors, and retained their freedom to handle contracts with outside parties without GrandCo oversight. More important, perhaps, the top-management group remained unified in its commitment to preserve DC's "independent identification" and to represent DC's interest openly and authentically to GrandCo officials.

The top-management group at DC continued to meet

regularly to "examine their relationship with GrandCo" and worked with us to develop a more reasonable strategy for dealing with conflicts by "respecting" GrandCo's culture and no longer "fighting for the sake of fighting." Eventually they concluded that they had been their "own worst enemy" and decided to seek out some accommodations with individual GrandCo leaders. These steps—required change in given areas of the business, efforts by some to maintain cultural identity, and finally moves toward more effective accommodation—set the stage for both further acculturation to GrandCo and further disintegration of DC's once unified and unifying culture.

Split in Top Management (1982–1983)

In a 1981 report to top management, we suggested that efforts to counter GrandCo and preserve DC's independence had divided management and exacerbated the clash of cultures. Some, including CEO Richardson, seemed to favor a "strong stand" vis-à-vis value differences with GrandCo. Davis, then head of DC's main division, and others argued that DC should accommodate to "new realities." Some top managers thought Richardson, the standard bearer in participative management, was in a "pissy dilemma"—trying to remain true to his philosophy and values while struggling to deal with superiors who explicitly devalued them. Others saw Richardson as a "hindrance" to effective integration. A few executives believed that he had been too "self-righteous" in dealing with GrandCo. Davis, for instance, opined that top people in both companies "put their pants on the same way" and that the rest of top management was "overreacting." In his view, his peers had better learn to become "big boys" in order to get the business "back on track."

In 1982, there were controversial and, to some, troubling events in the company that would alter its culture in the years ahead. First, a decision had to be made about the firm's structure: whether to retain product divisions or move to a market-oriented model. Davis and the financial people at DC had long been in favor of restructuring DC to form profit centers. This would mean merging several of the product divisions into market-oriented lines of business. Richardson believed such a move would concentrate power into too few hands and deprive managers of desired autonomy and freedom of action. He feared it would give fewer people opportunities to grow and develop and limit their participation in decisions. Davis made the point that economies of scale and market focus should be the prime consideration in making a business decision of this magnitude. He also made his views known to superiors at GrandCo.

Second, there was the matter of executive succession. Richardson was told that he would not find any career opportunities in GrandCo — he was "too much of a maverick." Accordingly, he decided to select an executive vice president to oversee operations while he contemplated his career plans. Two candidates emerged from the participative selection process traditionally used by DC: Davis, clearly an operations man, and Bates, then head of human resources.

Davis was by then well known to GrandCo and was strongly aligned with the financial leadership in DC. Bates, in their eyes, was closely aligned with Richardson and had been the point man in several conflicts with GrandCo. Top managers in DC were divided as to who was better equipped to lead the company. The "participative" process, with GrandCo input, resulted in Davis's appointment. Several weeks later, the company announced it would be adopting a market-oriented structure.

People in DC were divided over the executive vice president and organization structure decisions. The QWL survey in 1983 found that only about half of the workforce (52 percent) understood why these decisions had been made and fewer (48 percent) supported the top-level makeover. One interpretation was that new leadership was essential to "getting along" with GrandCo and that the market-oriented structure would give DC more operational focus. Others feared that DC was "kowtowing" to GrandCo and feared that the management in the new divisions would "lose touch" with the average employee.

Soon DCers were to have an opportunity to judge the impact of these events more fully. Richardson left the company in 1982 — and, for the first time, a non-family member came to head DC. Davis became the CEO and began to speak out against participation and other time-wasting practices. He also changed the sign in front of DC to read: DC — A GrandCo Company.

Continued Cultural Disintegration (1984–1985)

Lester Richardson had these views on the impact of new leadership on the company's culture: "On the one hand, I've always believed and acted like the 'tone is set at the top.' A CEO, by what he says and does, creates and keeps a company's culture alive. I just don't think that Davis [the new CEO] truly believes in participative management. He wants so much to be 'the boss.' Sure he cares about people and will do a super job of running the business side of DC. But the company will change under his leadership. . . . On the other hand, I remind myself that the culture has spread throughout the company and is in the hands of a great many people. They'll practice participative management and they'll really want to develop people. . . . What do you think?"

In our estimation, Davis's leadership and intent to run a "lean and mean" organization divided DCers and was an additional precipitant in the disintegration of the original DC culture. With Davis's ascension to the top post, top management became far less process-oriented. Many more issues were worked out one on one with the principals involved and less group time was devoted to collective problem solving and decision making. Some of the old guard said that the top-management group was not really a group anymore. All were simply subordinates to "the boss."

In 1983, one year after Davis's ascension, 42 percent of the workforce thought the company was putting profits ahead of people. Three years later, in 1985, 51 percent were of this opinion. There were further changes in traditional norms and values. Top management discontinued its team-building work and internal focus on group process. Davis equated these with "navel gazing" and preferred to work in a more consultative, one-on-one fashion with his executives. Pressure for production was increased and people reported that GrandCo was putting DC through the "meat grinder." It became acceptable, even fashionable, to talk about "deadwood" in the company. How do you get results from deadwood? "Light a fire under it!" This is why, in our view, employees began to experience more pressure and more fear on their jobs.

The "elephant" we had drawn in 1983 — with its image of divergent perspectives and conclusions about the state of the organization and its culture — served to focus new top management on the need to articulate its own beliefs and values for the company and, as we suggested earlier, to locate the elephant's "heart." Each member of the management group developed a position paper specifying his or her central values for running the company. Over the course of several months, these positions were refined to complete a roster of beliefs and values that top management regarded as central to the future success of the business and the welfare of its members. The resulting statement of values was distributed to all employees under the title of "Sharing a Vision."

What did the business-directed, results-oriented kicking and the search for the heart bring about? The 1985 QWL survey found a significant decline in middle managers' and supervisors' understandings of the goals of the company and in their confidence in senior management. Compared with 1983 results, confidence in the company's future had declined another 7 percent in the workforce overall. And confidence in top management dropped 15 percent overall. Furthermore, fewer than half of the managers and salespeople were confident the company could compete in its markets.

The survey also revealed continuing signs of cultural disintegration: The data showed that some managers and supervisors were putting pressure on people, were less responsive to their inputs, and were motivating them by fear, while many others continued, in the eyes of their employees, to use involvement, participation, and rewards to run their operations. Relationships among divisions, now organized by market orientation, deteriorated further.

The point we stressed was that the new initiatives coming from top management were countercultural. Attacks on participative management and changes in top-management behaviors signaled that DC no longer valued cherished traditions which, in the eyes of employees, were integral to the company's success. Moreover, emphasis on a "lean and mean" organization was contrary to the ethos of "family feeling," and efforts to crack down on deadwood counterfeited the time-honored tradition of obtaining "extraordinary results from ordinary people." Table 10.4 summarizes our contention that the changes in DC since the new top management's ascension were resulting in cultural cleavages and disintegration.

When we presented these data on inconsistencies in management style and on rivalries between division heads to Davis, he once more discounted our thesis that DC's culture was disintegrating. On the contrary, he believed the results accurately reflected the diversity of managerial styles in the company and suggested that we were "hung up" on the old company culture and that some DC employees were not yet attuned to new business realities.

The HR head pointed out that most DCers gave the company "high marks" on products, customer services, and other elements of the new vision. He also noted that the majority believed that the company treated people with dignity and respect and operated in a fair and ethical manner. "The survey validates what we're doing!" he concluded. We countered that over one-quarter also said that the company was not "practicing what it preached." Another third was simply not "sharing" the vision. We then resurrected the elephant and looked it over again. . . .

Disintegration of Culture and the Decline in Confidence

What fascinated us is that the reported decline in DCers' confidence in management and in the future of the company was by no means matched by DC's business results or prospects. On the contrary, DC had continued to earn record profits, even through recession years, and had expanded its market share. The company also registered record sales rates and paid out record commissions. Certainly managers had become better educated about threats in the general business environment during this

**Table 10.4. Internal Acculturation and Cultural Disintegration —
1983–1985.**

Acculturative Stress	Traditional Culture	Emerging Culture	Cultural Cleavage
Richardson, Old CEO, Retires			
"A Maverick"	Authenticity	Conformity	CEO as culture keeper versus hindrance to integration
"Family Head"	Group management	Lean and mean	Company operates as family versus business
Davis, New CEO, Selected			
"Tough Love"	Human development	Performance	Getting extraordinary from ordinary people versus clearing out deadwood
"Accountability"	Collective	One-on-one	Management via process versus results
New Structure			
"Market-Oriented"	Product groups	Profit centers	Loyalty to company versus to division
"A GrandCo Company"	Autonomy	Pragmatism	Independent identity versus subsidiary
New Philosophy			
"Sharing a Vision"	Take care of people and the rest follows	Take care of business and people follow	Orientation toward people versus toward profits
"A New Culture"	Unified	Diversified	Gap in practice versus preaching

era and still retained their perception of GrandCo as a "profit machine." By 1985, however, nearly all in management felt the relationship with GrandCo was solid and the great majority of the workforce opined that GrandCo and DC had developed a good working relationship under Davis's leadership.

What then accounts for DCers' decline in confidence? To test our own hypothesis that a split in the DC culture was contributing to people's unease and alienation, we analyzed responses to questions on the 1985 survey that directly measured the competing tensions found in the "elephant."

Leadership Versus Participation. Two questions addressed a central division in the company: whether or not people were getting the "right amount" of leadership and direction from top management and whether or not they were seeing the company practice the "right amount" of participative management. These questions fold into a neat two-by-two table showing various combinations of leadership and participation (see Table 10.5). The cell registering too much leadership and too little participation represents a "sweatshop," whereas too little leadership and too much participation would imply that the company is being run like a "bridge club." Too little or too much of both would mean that the company is being under- or overmanaged. Finally, the "right amount" of each was conceptualized as "nirvana."

Table 10.5 illustrates these conditions and Table 10.6 shows how DCers rated the organization in 1985. What is notable is how divided people were as to their views of leadership and participation. Some 20 percent thought the company was

Table 10.5. The Impact of New Top Management: How Much Leadership and Participation.

	Too Little Leadership	Right Amount	Too Much Leadership
Too Little Participation	Undermanaged		Sweatshop
Right Amount		NIRVANA	
Too Much Participation	Bridge club		Overmanaged

Table 10.6. The Impact of New Top Management: DCer's Ratings in 1985.

	Too Little Leadership (%)	Right Amount (%)	Too Much Leadership (%)
Too Little Participation	20	7	8
Right Amount	4	30	6
Too Much Participation	6	6	13

being undermanaged and 13 percent thought it was being overmanaged. A plurality (30 percent) was in nirvana, but the remainder saw various forms of imbalance between leadership and participation.

Fear and Pressure Versus Goals and Rewards. There was also a division of opinion, though less marked, in perceptions of how people are motivated and how goals are accomplished. Some 40 percent of the DC workforce saw people motivated mostly by involvement and rewards and saw goals being accomplished because people pulled together to meet them. By contrast, nearly one in five believed that motivation came from fear and insecurity and that goals were accomplished via management pressure.

Innovation and the Problem of Deadwood. People were also divided as to whether the company was innovative (36 percent) or conservative (20 percent) or a little of each (44 percent). Many reported that "deadwood" was a problem but, again, there was disagreement as to whether management was "too easy" on people (50 percent) or handling the problem effectively (39 percent). Putting the results of these questions together with ratings of the company's relative emphasis on profits versus people, the fragmented feel of the "elephant" could be represented statistically as shown in Figure 10.2.

By 1985, the elephant was carrying an even heavier load in its hindquarters than two years before. About 20 percent of the work force were alienated from the lean and mean DC culture (as they saw it) and many more saw the company down-

Figure 10.2. Feeling the Elephant: Data on Deculturation in DC, 1985.

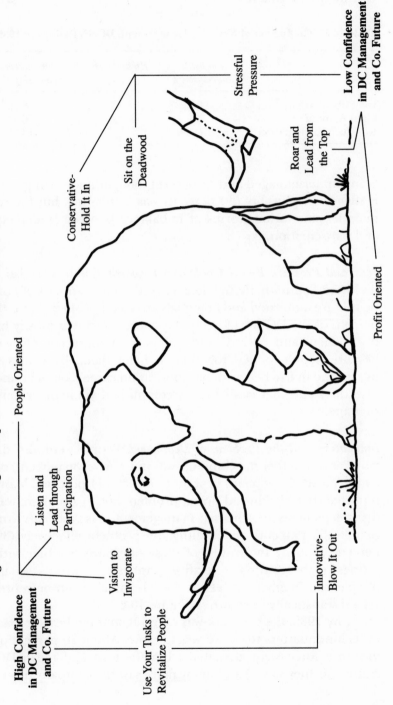

People Oriented

Conservative-
Hold It In

Sit on the Deadwood

Stressful Pressure

Low Confidence in DC Management and Co. Future

Roar and Lead from the Top

Profit Oriented

High Confidence in DC Management and Co. Future

Listen and Lead through Participation

Vision to Invigorate

Use Your Tusks to Revitalize People

Innovative-
Blow It Out

**Table 10.7. Practicing What Is Preached Versus
Confidence in Management.**

Confidence in Top Management	DC Practices What It Preaches		
	Not at all (%)	Somewhat (%)	To a great extent (%)
Low Confidence	62	21	17
High Confidence	8	13	79

grading participation and emphasizing profits over people. By contrast, about 40 percent saw the "new" DC culture embodying the same values as the old one. Finally, 40 percent or so believed DC to be marked by a mix of cultural characteristics, to some degree favorable and to some degree unfavorable. The question we raised with top management was whether or not DC could reach their hearts and regain their full commitment—once deemed necessary in order to obtain extraordinary results from these ordinary employees. Otherwise, we projected the DC culture would continue to fragment and many would see themselves in an increasingly ordinary company culture.

Who's Sharing a Vision? Plainly the new "vision" statement was not reaching them. Most DCers believed that the company manufactured high-quality products, delivered high-quality services, and ran the business with integrity. The majority also said that the company encouraged teamwork, held people responsible for doing their jobs well, and treated individuals with dignity and respect. However, only 56 percent agreed that the company practiced what it preached, and some one in four—nearly all in the elephant's hindquarters—said the company's vision was bogus.

We arrayed the data to compare people's views on whether or not the company practiced what it preached with their confidence in management. As Table 10.7 shows, those who saw practices in line with preachings had far more confidence in the management than those who saw practices as out of line.

Changes in the way DC did business were wrought directly by the influence of GrandCo after the acquisition and changes in management style came indirectly through GrandCo's preference for Davis as new CEO. These changes in behaviors go beyond superficial accommodation to new realities. Culture serves a normative function. The normative message in DC was that "results matter" and that these are achieved through hard work and individual accountability. Participation was no longer to be viewed as essential to the company's success. Instead, it was to be considered in certain instances but not favored or overused lest it impede initiative or blur responsibility.

Culture also serves a symbolic function. The new symbol was that DC was "a GrandCo company." "The acquisition is 'old news,'" said one interviewee; "why do you keep asking questions about it?" In our eyes, at least, the old news had implications for new realities—a stronger profit orientation, less emphasis on people, more pressure and insecurity—what some had feared from the acquisition by GrandCo and now were experiencing at the hands of their own leadership.

To be fair, many embraced the new values and beliefs. "Richardson could have never kept up with this pace," one executive opined; "we've got to move quickly in the marketplace today." Another said, "the new culture matches new business conditions." To be fairer still, many traditional DC practices and values were retained—those as tangible as disclosing and reviewing financial information with supervisors, and others as subtle as asking, not commanding, people to do something. There were signs of politics and flank protection in DC in 1985, but nothing akin to what was ascribed to GrandCo.

What was apparent, in our view, was that top DC executives were now behaving and thinking like "businessmen" and many believed that to be essential to the company's success. What was equally apparent, however, was that a substantial segment of the workforce was either turned off by or indifferent to their leadership and the culture of the organization.

Frankly, DC's top management was distressed at declines in ratings of people's confidence in them and troubled that so many did not see their "vision" in practice. Our thesis—that management was, as a group, sending mixed messages to people about what the company stood for—was discussed openly among the top-management team. We talked over the division in the workforce as to the ideal DC culture and its present state. Members of top management disagreed sharply on whether the company had "lost its bearings." They were divided, too, as to whether Davis was "too much of boss" versus "the kind of leader we need in this day and age." There was also a sharp division as to whether or not GrandCo had "hamstrung" management with its demands on profitability and whether or not the relationship was being managed effectively.

Top management did agree, however, that none of them had that "gleam in the eye" they had shared eight years ago, and they resolved to "do something" to get that back again.

Leveraged Buyout of DC: Family Again (1986–1988)

Early in 1986, in a presentation on the future strategy of the conglomerate, GrandCo raised the specter of a possible DC divestiture. Among themselves DC's top-management group mused over this possibility. They gave Davis the mandate to let GrandCo's president know that if the conglomerate had any plans to divest, "this group wants to be in the running." "There is nothing we can share with you at this time," the top man at GrandCo responded, "but I guarantee you can be in the running with whoever else is interested." In the summer the imminence of divestiture was a rumor; in October it was official; and in December DC's top-management group purchased their company through a leveraged buyout, "for a substantial price but not out of line."

The decision to undertake the buyout apparently came easily to DC's leaders, and the consequences have been exciting and energizing for them. "A great adventure!" the head of HR calls it.

In the first year of the buyout (1987), top managers worked sixty-hour weeks on average and climbed a steep learning curve comparable, in the words of one, to "baptism by fire."

Now constituted as the "officers group," DC's top management has become "a closer-knit group, mutually supportive of each other," even though they meet together less frequently. They not only share an enormous financial obligation, but they are expe-riencing a high degree of respect and trust for each other and deep personal feelings among themselves and their families.

Today there is more of an "urgency" in the officers group. At meetings the agenda is covered expeditiously and decisions made on the spot. When an issue cannot be readily resolved, members of the group most likely defer to Davis, still CEO but less a "boss." There is likewise less tolerance for "deadwood" now. DC feels vulnerable financially, having assumed a large debt and no longer being able to dip into GrandCo's "deep pockets." It is feared that those who are not doing their fair share "may be jeopardizing the whole organization."

Along with responsibility, there is enjoyment of auton-omy regained. Davis says he has more time to devote to running the business since he no longer puts in hours managing the relationship with GrandCo. A return to a single review meeting in the fall has greatly simplified the "burden" of planning and budgeting. Since the buyout, there is also less scrutiny of capital expenditures and more maneuverability through plans for large-scale changes in the company's operations.

Reintegration of the DC Culture. The 1988 survey showed signs of "reintegration" in DC. Quality of work life ratings, down in 1983 and 1985, increased in key areas having to do with trust in management and perceptions that management was interested in the welfare and well being of DCers. The majority of DC people saw the company putting an equal emphasis on people and profits. Longer-term employees — those who worked for DC prior to the acquisition — reported the sharpest increase in their approbation of management and its commitment to people. It is interesting to note, as well, that employees sponsored a party for management, following the buyout, at a local pub and dubbed the gathering "A New Beginning — Family Again."

Certainly DC's culture in 1988 is different from the one we first studied in 1977. DC's managerial philosophy and style is less participative—at the top of the company. However, there is a marked increase in the number of people who participate in decisions through work teams, task forces, and cross-divisional committees compared with years past, and people's ratings of the effectiveness of these groups are extremely favorable. The leadership style of the division heads is viewed as quite participative, and their division management groups have gained the confidence of a greater proportion of DCers.

Richardson was right. The tone is set at the top. Davis has been characterized as a "workaholic," and people in DC say that they have a heavier workload and more pressure on their jobs than ever before. Not all of his direct employees are satisfied with the chances they have to participate in decisions, and some have, in a fashion, become "conformists." However, Richardson was also right that it would be the managers, and supervisors, and everyday working people in DC who would keep the "old" culture alive. The reintegration of the DC culture—now generally accepted as one oriented equally toward people and profits—is most clearly seen in the renewed confidence of the workforce (see Figure 10.3).

Culture Change and the Elephant

There are many ways that a parent company interjects its culture into a subsidiary. Changes come from reporting relationships, control over resources and the imposition of financial controls, and certainly from the replacement of personnel or new reporting relationships, particularly for executive leadership. Furthermore, change comes from the gradual resocialization of existing organization members according to new norms in the process of accommodation to the dominant company's culture. We have seen how GrandCo's culture clashed with DC's during the early stages of this acquisition and how through the process of acculturation, DC came to be aligned with and to some extent assimilated into GrandCo. *Its culture was, however, at risk of disintegration when "old" values and "new" ones divided top management and others within the firm.*

A GrandCo-type culture was not functional for DC, at

Figure 10.3. DCers' Increase in Confidence, 1985–1988.

--- 1985   —— 1988

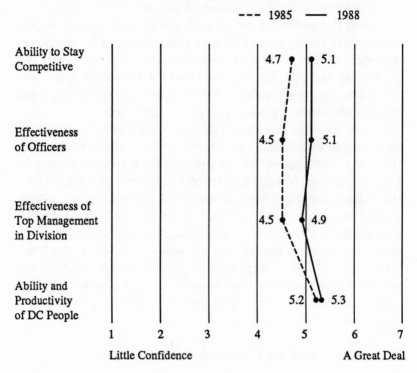

least in the eyes of its people. Moreover, top management's new vision provided neither the normative framework nor the symbolic significance to unify people or capture their hearts. Metaphors of becoming lean and mean and sitting on deadwood did not, in this context, win confidence or gain approbation. On the contrary, they further divided people and threatened DC's familylike atmosphere.

    Certainly the structure and style of the business has changed. It is no longer run by the Richardson family, and the two divisions pretty much go their own way. A more results-oriented ethic has taken hold, although this is now deemed imperative to pay off debt and to avoid another unfriendly takeover attempt. Furthermore, there is less talk about the "good old days" and more about the "trials and challenges" that lie ahead. No one talks any more about the symbols and images of disintegration — the elephant, GrandCo, or even the acquisition.

It is uncertain whether the old mores in DC could have been retained in the face of a more competitive and demanding business environment, with or without the company's acquisition. Richardson thinks so; Davis does not. In any case, Davis's message that the company must face up to new competitive realities has been understood and accepted by most people in DC. It perhaps helps that they recognize that the company again "steers its own course" and has become "family again." They also note that management is more available again, is more celebratory at retirement parties and new employee introductions, and is more apt to join in on company social events. They see that following the buyout the officers distributed stock throughout management and instituted a profit-sharing system that paid out handsomely. These actions make everyone a little more "profit-oriented" but not necessarily at the expense of people, a balance confirmed by the 1988 survey.

The relative weight given to people versus profits was cast in a divisive frame during times of crisis (the acquisition) and change (the new leadership). The presumed tension between the two contributed to our analysis that DC's culture was disintegrating, failing to hold people together. We saw people telling a different story about the organization depending on the part of the elephant they had grabbed. During "normal" times, as we would characterize the postbuyout years, the relationship between people and profits is seen as a balance between the two, with neither one precluding the other. While there is a range of views on this balance, we believe that DCers would agree that all are now feeling the same elephant — the shared culture of their organization.

References

Baker, E. L. (1980). Managing organizational culture. *McKinsey Quarterly*, (Autumn), 51–61.

Berry, J. W. (1980). Acculturation as varieties of adaptation. In A. M. Padilla (Ed.), *Acculturation*. Boulder, CO: Westview Press.

Condon, J. C., & Yousef, F. S. (1975). *An introduction to intercultural communication*. Indianapolis, IN: Bobbs-Merrill.

Evered, R., & Louis, M. R. (1981). Alternative perspectives in the organizational sciences: "Inquiry from the inside" and "inquiry from the outside." *Academy of Management Review, 6*, 385–389.

Geertz, C. (1973). *The interpretation of cultures*. New York: Basic Books.

Hirsch, P., & Andrews, J. (1983). Ambushes, shootouts, and knights of the round table: The language of corporate takeovers. In L. R. Pondy, P. J. Frost, G. Morgan, & T. C. Dandridge (Eds.), *Organizational symbolism*. Greenwich, CT: JAI Press.

Kitching, J. (1967). Why do mergers miscarry? *Harvard Business Review, 45*, 84–101.

Kotter, J. P. (1985). *Power and influence: Beyond formal authority*. New York: Macmillan.

Kubler-Ross, E. (1969). *On death and dying*. New York: Macmillan.

Louis, M. R. (1983). Organizations as culture-bearing milieux. In L. R. Pondy, P. J. Frost, G. Morgan, & T. C. Dandridge (Eds.), *Organizational symbolism*. Greenwich, CT: JAI Press.

Martin, J. (1982). Stories and scripts in organizational settings. In A. Hastorf & A. Isen (Eds.), *Cognitive social psychology*. New York: Elsevier–North Holland.

Padilla, A. M. (1980). *Acculturation*. Boulder, CO: Westview Press.

Pettigrew, A. (1979). On studying organizational culture. *Administrative Science Quarterly, 22*, 570–581.

Pfeffer, J. (1981). *Power in organizations*. Marshfield, MA: Pitman.

Sales, A., & Mirvis, P. (1984). When cultures collide: Issues in acquisition. In J. R. Kimberly & R. Quinn (Eds.), *Managing organizational transitions*. Homewood, IL: Irwin.

Schein, E. (1985). *Organizational culture and leadership: A dynamic view*. San Francisco: Jossey-Bass.

Schwartz, H., & Davis, S. M. (1981). Matching corporate culture and business strategy. *Organizational Dynamics, 9*, 30–48.

Chapter 11

Benjamin Schneider

The Climate for Service: An Application of the Climate Construct

My goal in this chapter is to summarize conclusions I have reached about what organizational climate is, how it can be assessed, and how the construct can be applied. The particular application I discuss concerns the climate for service. More specifically, I first explore the general climate literature with respect to issues concerning the strategic nature of climate, whether organizations contain one or many climates, and what we know about the role of perceptions in climate research.

Second, I discuss the service construct, showing how services differ from goods and the implications those differences have for the design of effective service organizations. I follow this discussion with a review of research my colleagues and I have conducted on the assessment of service climate and on attempts to change organizations to a service climate. I show in this section what I have learned about the application of the climate construct.

It needs to be made clear at the outset that I am interested

Note: I received extraordinarily valuable feedback on earlier versions of this chapter from my colleagues Eric Braverman, Irwin Goldstein, Sarah Gunnarson, and Katherine Klein. For the past fifteen years Daniel Q. Kelly has been financially and psychologically instrumental in pushing forward the thinking and research summarized here.

in service, so that service is my choice for demonstrating the applicability of the climate construct. Were I interested in safety, innovation, or other topics (see Schneider & Gunnarson, 1990), I could have chosen them as the foci for application. In what follows, readers may choose their own focus of interest, be it service, safety, innovation, quality of work life, or whatever. I believe that by following the climate logic and methods I will describe with respect to service, readers can have an enhanced understanding of their own focus of interest.

Climate: Definition and Overview of Some Issues

I define climate as incumbents' perceptions of the events, practices, and procedures and the kinds of behaviors that get rewarded, supported, and expected in a setting. Events, practices, and procedures of organizations have been referred to by me and my colleagues (Schneider & Rentsch, 1988) as the *routines* of a setting; we have called the behaviors that get rewarded, supported, and expected the *rewards* of the setting. In what follows I also adopt this convention as a shorthand to characterize the elements of perception that constitute climate.

I assume that the many routines and rewards of a setting are not only perceived by incumbents but that incumbents attach meaning to these routines and rewards (Schneider, 1975). The meanings attached to routines and rewards communicate a message to employees about what it is that is valued in the setting. Thus, routines and rewards serve a signaling and focusing function, signaling the outcomes that are valued in the setting and focusing energies and competencies on the attainment of those outcomes.

My definition of climate, and the accompanying assumption, require some further development since they subsume several issues that have been discussed in the climate literature. These issues concern the global versus focused nature of climate, and the role of perceptions in climate research, including the issue of aggregating individuals' perceptions to derive climate data for a setting. I present each of these issues in turn, since they constitute a ground against which the figure of service climate will be presented.

Global Versus Strategic Climate

A review of the early climate literature reveals that researchers invariably had some implicit focus for their climate construct in that they emphasized a particular *kind* of climate in their studies. For example, Hall and Schneider (1973) emphasized the climate for psychological success because their framework focused on the kinds of work settings in which people can experience psychological success (Hall, 1971). In Litwin and Stringer's (1968) creative early climate research, the climate emphasized was the climate for the expression of needs for power, achievement, and affiliation. Thus, their research was in large part an attempt to show how "environmental press" promotes or inhibits the behavioral manifestation of particular need states (see Stern, 1970, for similar research on college climate).

There are additional examples of this focus on a particular *kind* of climate. Argyris's (1958) early work emphasized the "right type" climate; Lewin, Lippitt, and White (1939) focused on leadership style and the kinds of "social climate" different leadership styles can create; Fleishman (1953) reported on the way in which a climate for human relations–oriented leadership was reflected in display of that kind of leadership style (thus a "climate for leadership"); and McGregor (1960) explored the climate for participation and control created by managers— what he referred to as "managerial climate."

These early climate studies have led me (Schneider, 1975, 1985) to conclude that some dependent variable or strategic focus of interest has, mostly implicitly, driven research on the climate construct. If safety was the criterion of interest, the facets of the workplace related to a climate for safety were explored (for example, Zohar, 1980); similarly for motivation (Litwin & Stringer, 1968), or quality (Banas, 1988), or innovation (Delbecq & Mills, 1985), or—service. I have argued that this is appropriate since the climate construct in the abstract may subsume almost anything—and frequently it includes almost everything (Schneider, 1975). Thus, implicitly researchers have been cognizant of the importance of a focus for climate, the importance being the necessity to bound the construct in a way that facilitates assessment.

The explicit specification of a criterion of interest moves the study of climate into a strategic mode (see Pennings & Associates, 1985; Pettigrew, 1987). In the strategic mode, climate research presents the challenge of identifying the routines and rewards related to the criterion of interest. Once the routines and rewards that are conceptually likely to facilitate the accomplishment of the specific goal of interest are identified, their status in organizations can be assessed and attempts to change the way they function can be made. The utility of the climate construct is that it explicitly assumes there will be numerous routines and rewards requiring assessment, because it is the perception of multiple routines and rewards that is assumed to communicate the meaning of what is important in a setting.

In summary, climate as an abstract construct seems to include *everything* that occurs in organizations and lacks a strategic focus. One alternative for researchers is to discover what an organization seems to focus on or what strategic goals it pursues. Another alternative, and the one I prefer, is for researchers to choose a focus of interest (say, service or safety or innovation) and discover the extent to which people in the organization perceive the organization to be enacting (Weick, 1979) this focus. In this latter alternative, perceptions of the routines and rewards enacting, say, safety (Zohar, 1980) or innovation (Delbecq & Mills, 1985), should be the focus of the perceptions collected from organizational members.

As is obvious from the above consideration of my definition of climate, and my assumption about how climate functions for people in a setting, perceptions play an important role in climate research. The role of perceptions in climate research takes two forms. First is a consideration of the importance of perceptions in understanding and applying the climate construct. Second, there is the issue of the aggregation of incumbents' perceptions in a setting to produce a climate score for the setting. I discuss each of these in turn.

The Importance of Perceptions in Climate Research. Much of the climate literature since the mid to late 1960s has used individuals' perceptions of the many routines and rewards that characterize a setting as the basic data for climate research. Prior to the mid 1960s, researchers (for example, Lewin, Lippitt, & White, 1939) and diagnosticians (such as Argyris, 1958) assigned a climate label to their own perceptions of the routines and rewards they observed.

Assuming that incumbents' perceptions influenced incumbents' behavior, researchers such as Likert (1967), Schneider and Bartlett (1968, 1970), and Litwin and Stringer (1968) explicitly incorporated incumbents' perceptions of the settings' routines and rewards into their climate measures. The assumption of a connection between incumbents' perceptions and incumbents' behavior still dominates climate research (for example, Jones & James, 1979; Joyce & Slocum, 1982; Schneider & Bowen, 1985; Zohar, 1980). Thus, incumbents' perceptions are the basic diagnostic data of climate research.

Doubts about the reliability and validity of these perceptions have periodically emerged (Guion, 1973; Powell & Butterfield, 1978; Woodman & King, 1978), but recent evidence suggests that these perceptions show interrater reliability within settings (Moeller, Schneider, Schoorman, & Berney, 1988) as well as validity against external judgments across settings (Schneider & Bowen, 1985).

The Data Aggregation Concern. While it is obvious that individuals are the source of perceptions, it is not obvious under what conditions individuals' perceptions may be aggregated to other units of analysis. Thus, individuals' perceptions have been aggregated to yield data for studies contrasting climates for different positions in an organization (Hall & Schneider, 1973), levels in an organization (Schneider & Snyder, 1975), branches of banks (Schneider, Parkington, & Buxton, 1980; Schneider &

Bowen, 1985), Navy ships (Jones & James, 1979), and aggregates of persons with similar perceptions in the organization (Joyce & Slocum, 1982).

The distinction that needs to be drawn here is the difference between the unit of data and the unit of analysis (James, Joyce, & Slocum, 1988). I conclude that perceptions will always come from individuals, but the analysis of individuals' perceptions may occur at any *meaningful* level. That is, perceptions collected from individuals must be such that the level to which they are aggregated makes conceptual sense. This is accomplished by providing respondents with the frame of reference appropriate for the level of analysis for which the data will be used.

For example, statements on a survey about the challenge individuals experience in their job may not be meaningfully aggregated across many respondents in many different jobs to produce an *organization* score on job challenge. This is true because the data collected—individuals' experiences of their own job—do not make conceptual sense when aggregated to a level of analysis beyond one job. Alternatively, a statement on a survey regarding the behavior of a branch manager in a bank branch may permit the aggregation of many respondents' data to provide a bank branch score with respect to the branch manager's behavior.

In summary, perceptions are the basic data for contemporary studies of climate. These perceptions may be aggregated to other levels of analysis when the frame of reference for the perceptions is at the level to which the data will be aggregated (Roberts, Hulin, & Rousseau, 1978; Rousseau, 1985).

Summary. Incumbents' perceptions of the routines and rewards that characterize a setting constitute the climate of organizations. Perceptions of the routines and rewards associated with particular strategic foci of interest (for example, safety or service) constitute the climate of the setting with respect to those foci. In the present chapter, the concern is with service climate. I turn to this topic next, beginning with a brief overview of the small but growing literature on service. This overview is followed by a summary of some research my colleagues and I have carried out on service climate.

Prior to moving to the topic of service, however, I want to repeat my earlier point that service is being used as a convenient foil to reveal the utility of the climate construct. I am particularly interested in service, and so I explicate issues related to service.

Service: Introduction and Overview

Many service organizations are beginning to view service quality or service excellence as a strategic imperative or, at a minimum, a strategic opportunity. Numerous popular books have appeared that emphasize how critical service can be for organizational effectiveness (for example, Peters, 1987; Peters & Waterman, 1982). Indeed, books have appeared on the 100 best service companies (Zemke & Schaff, 1989). These publications have made some companies legends for their service quality. For example, FritoLay is reputed to call on each of the outlets that sells its products at least once per week, Disney management of theme parks are fanatical about cleanliness and friendliness, and Nordstrom never lets a customer leave the department store dissatisfied even if satisfying the customer requires purchasing a product from a competitor to sell to the customer to make him or her happy.

This emphasis on service is more than just hyperbole. IBM achieves about one-third of its revenues on service, about two-thirds of all employed people in the U.S. work in service jobs, and the service sector has produced more than three-quarters of all new jobs in the past decade (Albrecht & Zemke, 1985). Finally, there is increasing concern that poor service quality in the United States may yield an outcome for service industries similar to that experienced in the steel and auto industries—that is, domination by other countries. These concerns have resulted in numerous efforts to identify the service issues that require attention to regain potentially lost strategic advantages. These efforts have taken two tacks, one emphasizing conceptual differences between goods and services, the other attempting to define what service quality means to consumers.

Service Conceptualized. In most reviews of the service literature, Shostack (1977a, 1977b) is given credit for explicating the idea that a service is something different from a good. Building on a small European (for example, Bateson, 1977; Eiglier & Langeard, 1977) and American literature (for instance, Levitt, 1972), Shostack made the argument that services are characterized by intangibility. She proposed that this fact suggests that services yield experiences rather than possessions. Because of this difference, she argued, new ways of thinking about services and the way they should be marketed are required.

A number of papers on this topic—such as Berry (1980) and Lovelock (1981)—quickly appeared. From these efforts, several definitions of service emerged, each of which focused on a unique aspect of service. Three facets (actually continua) kept recurring in these definitions of service (Bowen & Schneider, 1988).

1. The *tangibility-intangibility continuum*—refers to the possession-experience continuum. The relative intangibility of services makes evaluation of service quality more difficult for the producer and the consumer because the outcome of a service is frequently more of an experience than a possession.

2. The *simultaneity continuum*—refers to the time lapse between the production and consumption of services compared to the production and consumption of goods. By implication, many services are produced and consumed simultaneously. For example, a seat on an airplane flight is produced and consumed at the same time. If a seat on a flight on a particular day is not consumed, it cannot ever exist again. In addition, the person who occupies a seat on a flight receives the service as it is being delivered.

   Seats on airplanes reveal two of the major problems services create for the management of service organizations. First, services can be difficult to inventory for future use; a seat on a flight can only exist once. Second, services can be difficult so far as quality control is concerned. This is true because once the service to the consumer is underway it is difficult to jump in to stop the delivery and do a check for quality; the flight cannot easily be called back to replace a nasty cabin attendant.

3. The *customer participation continuum*—refers to the fact that customers participate actively in the production of many of their services. For example, a customer may use an automatic teller machine or provide all of the information a physician needs when seeking services from him or her.

Customers can create problems for organizations because they penetrate the production core (Thompson, 1967) of the organization and cause disruptions (Aldrich, 1979). How to deal with the customer as part of the service production process has been a focus of some service literature. This has been especially evident in writings on operations management by Chase (for instance, Chase, 1978, 1981; Chase & Tansik, 1983) in which differences among services related to the degree of contact the customer has with the organization is a central issue. The point is that service is not *a* thing but a multifaceted construct, with each facet falling on a continuum.

These three continua characterize all services, creating a situation in which the traditional marketing focus on only the external consumer may be shortsighted. Thus, scholars such as Chase (1981) from operations management, Mills (1985) from organizational behavior, Normann (1984) (a human resource management consultant), and Albrecht and Zemke (1985)—who put services marketing on the *New York Times* best-seller list—have documented the ways that management of the internal organization has implications for the services delivered to the consumer. Thus, what began as services *marketing* has become the more broadly conceptualized services *management*. This naturally occurred when it was realized that the internal organization must be managed with service as a strategic focus if the organization is to deliver excellent service to the external consumer. In fact, recent texts on service are called services *management* texts, and they include sections on services marketing, services human resource management, and services operations management (for example, Grönroos, 1990; Lovelock, 1988).

Unlike the traditional marketing literature's focus on goods, services marketers have begun writing about the various "internal markets" (Grönroos, 1990) that require coordination if the consumer is to have a positive service experience (Bowen & Schneider, 1988). This concern for a total organization focus on service is substantiated by research on consumer definitions of what constitutes service quality.

Services Measurement: Implications for Management. The efforts devoted to the conceptualization of services yielded some important insights into the ways service organizations needed to be designed and managed. These insights have benefited from operationalization of the service construct from the customers' perspective. While Schneider (1973) and Schneider, Parkington, and Buxton (1980) had designed measures of service quality in banks, research on the generic attributes of service awaited the efforts of Parasuraman, Zeithaml, and Berry (1985, 1988).

Parasuraman, Zeithaml, and Berry interviewed service customers from different industries and, on the basis of those interviews, designed a measure to assess service along ten dimensions of customer service experiences. The ten dimensions are shown in Table 11.1.

The table shows the diverse standards by which customers judge the quality of the service they receive. These standards, in turn, must be the foci of management if the organization is to be considered a service leader. Obviously, "responsiveness" or "reliability" requires the internal organization to function in coordinated ways with each subsystem (Katz & Kahn, 1978) smoothly integrated to meet customer expectations. Customers, in fact, are most likely unaware of the internal workings of service delivery facilities and they probably do not care about them. Consumers want service delivered reliably and responsively on demand, and service organizations must create routines and rewards to ensure such practices if consumers are to have a positive service experience.

Table 11.1. Dimensions and Examples of Service Quality: Customers' Views.

Reliability:
Consistency of performance and dependability

- Accuracy of billing
- Keeping records
- Performing the service at the designated time

Responsiveness:
The willingness or readiness of employees to provide service

- Calling the customer back quickly
- Giving prompt service

Competence:
Possession of the required skills and knowledge to perform the service

- Knowledge and skill of the contact personnel
- Knowledge and skill of operational support personnel

Accessibility:
Approachability and ease of contact

- Waiting time to receive service is not extensive
- Convenient hours of operation

Courtesy:
Politeness, respect, consideration, and friendliness of contact personnel

- Consideration for the customer's property
- Clean and neat appearance of the contact personnel

Communication:
Keeping customers informed in language they can understand, and listening to them

- Explaining the service itself
- Assuring the customer that a problem will be handled

Credibility:
Trustworthiness, believability, honesty

Credibility is achieved by:
- Company reputation
- Personal characteristics of the contact personnel

Security:
The freedom from danger, risk, or doubt

- Physical safety
- Financial security

Understanding/ Knowing the Customer:
Making the effort to understand

- Learning the customer's specific requirements
- Providing individualized attention

Tangibles:
The physical evidence

- Physical facilities
- Appearance of personnel
- Tools or equipment used to provide the service
- Physical representations of the service

Source: Adapted from Parasuraman, Zeithaml, and Berry (1985).

Bowen and Schneider (1988) have noted that due to the attributes of service (intangibility, simultaneity, and customer participation in production) — described earlier — the management of service organizations has the problem of ensuring high service quality without the ability to control and/or check what is actually delivered to consumers. That is, because of intangibility, simultaneity, and customer participation in the production of their own services, once a service encounter (Czepiel, Solomon, & Suprenant, 1985) is begun, the service is produced, delivered, consumed, and experienced in an uninterrupted sequence. It is then the sequence of production, delivery, and consumption that yields consumer experiences.

Lacking the ability to control the sequence once it has begun, service organization management must resort to less immediate forms of environmental control. That is, management in service organizations must create conditions such that the routines and rewards of the organization focus incumbents' energies and competencies on service excellence. In the terminology of the present chapter, the routines and rewards must create a service climate, a climate that emphasizes the importance of a positive experience for consumers throughout the production, delivery, and consumption sequence. This climate, Bowen and Schneider (1988) argue, serves as a guide to employee behavior such that management intervention into the service sequence is unnecessary; the climate for service serves as a substitute for management control (Kerr & Jermier, 1978). In the next section of the chapter I present some research on the identification of the routines and rewards that create a service climate. I also show the validity of incumbents' perceptions of the climate for service against customer reports of their service experiences.

Elements of a Service Climate

In this section I present results from a series of studies on service climate. The first studies jointly explored relationships existing between employee reports of the service climate in their workplace and customers' experiences of the service they received from the same places (bank branches). The second study delved more deeply into the issue of climate, exploring relationships between the conditions underlying a climate for service and customers' experiences. In this study, we explored the hypothesis that when employees' own welfare is facilitated (through career planning, work facilitation, supervision, and so on), customers of those employees will report superior service experiences.

Climate for Service: Customer and Employee Views. In a series of articles (Parkington & Schneider, 1979; Schneider, 1980; Schneider, Parkington, & Buxton, 1980) I demonstrated support for the hypothesis that employee perceptions of the routines and rewards for service are correlated with customer perceptions of service quality. This support was obtained based on analysis of data collected from surveys designed and administered to both customers and employees of bank branches. The surveys were designed based on interviews with customers and employees, respectively. These interviews focused, for customers, on encounters with particularly excellent or particularly poor service. For employees, the interviews focused on the routines and rewards they believed facilitated or inhibited the delivery of excellent service. Based on these interviews with employees, ten a priori dimensions of routines and rewards defining a service climate were identified. Examples of the issues tapped in each of the ten dimensions are shown in Table 11.2.

In Schneider, Parkington, and Buxton (1980) the survey data were collected from branch customers and employees and then aggregated to the branch level ($N = 23$ branches). Analyses revealed significant correlations between employee reports of the routines and rewards for service in their branch and customer reports of their experiences when they went to the branch for service. Indeed, customer and employee perceptions of service quality received and delivered correlated .67.

These are important results for several reasons. First, the strong relationship validated the collection of climate data from employees in organizations; climate data collected from employees were significantly correlated with external observers'

Table 11.2. Dimensions and Examples of Service Climate Dimensions: Employees' Views.

Bureaucratic Orientation to Service	• Following all rules and procedures • Doing job in routine fashion
Enthusiast Orientation to Service	• Keeping a sense of "family" in the branch • Designing new ways to serve customers
Managerial Behavior	• Planning and goal setting for service delivery
Service Rewards	• Incentives and other rewards for service excellence
Customer Retention	• Active attempts to retain customers • *Not* giving special treatment to big accounts
Personnel Support	• Staffing levels and training permit good service
Operations Support	• Easy access to customer records • Error-free records
Marketing Support	• Understanding of customers • Care in introducing new products/ services
Equipment/Supply Support	• Equipment is available and up and running • Necessary supplies are available

Source: Adapted from Schneider, Parkington, and Buxton (1980).

(customers') perceptions of the same setting. Second, the results were important because they showed that the climate of a service organization extends beyond the formal boundaries of the organization. These results supported suggestions by such diverse writers as Barnard (1948) and Aldrich (1979) that customers may be as much a part of the organization as the employees. Indeed, in services marketing, some writers have referred to customers as "partial employees" (Lovelock & Young, 1979), because they participate in the production of their own services. The significant relationship between employee and customer perceptions lends additional support to the "partial employee" construct.

These results also had implications for data aggregation issues in climate research. Because each customer in a branch may be served on different occasions by different employees and each employee may serve many different customers, the only method by which customer and employee perceptions could be correlated across branches was at the branch level of analysis. In addition, it is clear that, from a strategic perspective, it is what happens in the *branch* to and for customers—not what happens to any *one* customer by any *one* employee—that is crucial for overall service quality in the branch. The branch must thus be organized and managed to deliver service quality to anyone who enters the branch by whomever is available.* These considerations dictated the logic for the branch as the unit of analysis.

Finally, the results were important since later replications have yielded similar results (Brown & Mitchell, 1988; Forum Corporation, 1988; Gunnarson, 1989; Schneider & Bowen, 1985). The replication conducted by the Forum Corporation (1988) is particularly interesting because the data analyses for that project were carried out across fourteen *corporations* based on interviews with 2,374 customers and 3,239 employees. Results from the Forum Corporation study indicate that companies in which employee turnover rates are high are the same companies in which employees reported that they offered poor service quality to customers.

These findings suggest a number of conclusions, all of which indicate that in service organizations the boundary between the internal workings of the organization and the delivery of customer service is not as clear as it may be in goods-producing organizations.

This conclusion resulted in two new streams of work on service climate. One examined employees' perceptions of the human resource practices under which they worked as a correlate of customers' service experiences. The second examined

---

* This is technically only true in branches where all customers—regardless of their account balances—are seen by all tellers. In branches that segment accounts and have different services available to different segments of the market, some tellers see only a very select group of customers and vice versa.

efforts of a more immediate strategic nature, changing an organization to create a climate for service.

Human Resource Practices and Customers' Experiences

In this research, we (Schneider & Bowen, 1985) hypothesized that employees' experiences of routines that went "deeper" than service delivery routines per se might also be related to customer perceptions of service. By "deeper" we meant the organization's general human resource routines (for example, supervision, career programs, socialization of newcomers), not just those related immediately to service delivery. We proposed that human resource practices that exist in a setting create the foundation for employees to deliver service to consumers. In other words, we proposed that behind service climate must be a climate that promotes the conditions in which a service climate may exist. More specifically, we proposed that when employees encounter human resource practices that facilitate a more positive experience for them, they will create a more positive experience for customers.

This hypothesis was based on a number of considerations. First, we (Parkington & Schneider, 1979) had shown that a positive service climate created for employees by management was negatively related to employees' role ambiguity, role conflict, frustration at work, and turnover intentions. Second, we (Schneider, Parkington, & Buxton, 1980) conceptualized our findings of a strong relationship between customer and employee service perceptions in terms of empathy. By this we meant that employees empathize with what customers experience because, in their daily lives, they are customers, too. Expanding on these ideas, we (Schneider & Bowen, 1985) hypothesized that when management provides for employees, employees will provide for customers.

In testing this hypothesis, we also carried out a replication of the earlier Schneider, Parkington, and Buxton (1980) results. These results were essentially fully replicated. For example, the correlation between customer perceptions of service quality received and employee perceptions of service quality delivered was .63 for the 28 replication branches studied (compared to .67 in the original study). Indeed, a correlation of the correlations obtained in the first study and the replication study across all employee and customer perceptions yielded an $r = .69$ (see Table 3 in Schneider & Bowen, 1985).

We carried out some additional analyses regarding customer and employee perceptions of service quality, this time involving turnover intentions of customers and employees (for customers the intention was to switch their accounts elsewhere, as in Schneider, 1973). Data analyses revealed that employee reports of the service quality they offer customers were modestly related to customer turnover intentions. However, customer reports of the service quality they receive were strongly correlated with employee turnover intentions. These results, along with those reported by the Forum Corporation (1988), lend additional credence to the idea that employees are sensitive to customer perceptions and that customer reports of service quality have implications for employee behavior. Bowen (1983) has even shown that employees may put more credence in feedback from the customers they serve than they do in feedback from their supervisors!

The examination of the relationships between human resource practices and customer service perceptions also yielded some significant findings. However, these results were not as strong as those obtained when the two sets of perceptions being correlated both focused on service. For example, correlations between employee and customer perceptions of service were as high as .70 in both the original and the replication studies; the strongest correlation between employee perceptions of human resource practices and customer perceptions of service was .56. However, each of the five dimensions of human resource practices assessed was correlated significantly with customer perceptions of overall service quality.

Summary. Figure 11.1 summarizes the results of the two studies just described, the one on the climate for service and the other on human resource management. The figure shows that an organization's human resource practices are correlated with

Figure 11.1. A Conceptualization of System Effects on Service Quality.

Deeper Organizational Attributes ↓	Managerial competencies and rewards (for example, pay)	Human resource routines (for example, career programs)	Operations routines (for example, information systems)
Service Climate ↓	Managerial competencies and rewards (for example, setting service goals)	Human resource routines (for example, service training)	Operations routines (for example, supplies and equipment necessary to deliver)
Customer Experience ↓	Branch is run smoothly	Staff competence and courtesy	Modern and up-to-date equipment

OVERALL SERVICE QUALITY

customer perceptions of a service climate but that these practices are only one of the keys to a service climate. Also important for a service climate are other issues, such as management's emphasis on service, the adequacy of equipment and supplies, operational support, and so forth (see Figure 11.1). The conclusion—to be detailed in a study to be described next (Schneider, 1990b)—is that a service climate is dependent on many facets of the optimal functioning of the organization, not just on the human resource practices.

Change to a Service Orientation

In the past few years, I have worked with several organizations as they attempt to change to a more service-oriented climate (Schneider, 1990b; Schneider & Schechter, 1990). In one organization, the CEO has attempted to totally transform her financial services company. This decision followed an extensive qualitative diagnosis I accomplished at her request (Schneider, 1990b).

The change process she has adopted is one in which she simultaneously has attempted to make change across functions and levels, always focusing on service excellence. The change process is described in detail in Schneider (1990b), but a sense of the variety of ways she has proceeded to create this service climate may be gleaned from a listing of some of her activities:

- The feedback report I wrote for the CEO was almost 100 pages in length, containing many quotations from the focus-group interviews we conducted with thirty diverse groups of employees. The report contained many comments about the effects the management of the organization has on service. These effects included issues related to staffing, training, supervision, facilities and equipment, and operations and systems, as well as descriptions of the pressures and tensions of work. Nevertheless, the CEO made a copy of the entire report available to any employee in the organization who desired to read it.
- Two meetings of the top-management team (twelve people) were held, in which each member was charged with taking personal responsibility for issues in his or her own domain (for example, systems, human resources) that the report revealed required attention.
- A weekend retreat was then held to share responsibilities across boundaries regarding issues for which everyone had responsibilities (for example, communication, cooperation, coordination, and support on task-related matters).
- In these meetings, the CEO made it clear that service excellence was the goal of all changes and the primary goal of the organization. She emphasized this in all of the changes that followed, arguing that everyone in the organization has a customer—be it internal or external.

These measures, together with the hiring of a person with direct responsibilities for service quality, have produced a new service-focused climate in the company. This focus has culminated in a service plan with status equivalent to the financial plan for the organization. The service plan has the same kinds of targets and tracking mechanisms as the financial plan, but the issues it addresses are unusual. For example, the following kinds of data are being tracked:

- Client/customer service survey data
- Adherence to internal delivery standards (between functions)
- Client/customer mail and phone turnaround time
- Training per employee per month

In addition, the following activities have been made routine in the organization:

- Service accomplishments by different departments are accompanied by celebrations that everyone attends.
- A new employment interview has been designed around service themes in an attempt to ensure the hiring of people with a positive service orientation (Hogan, Hogan, & Busch, 1984).
- A new performance appraisal system has been put in place, built around the same ten dimensions shown in Table 11.1. Thus, employees are now being evaluated on how well they serve others on the same criteria used by customers to evaluate the service provided by the organization.

The goal in this organization was the creation of a total system, strategically focused and service imperative, in which each employee had service (both internal and external) as his or her top priority. Toward this end, the CEO addressed as many of the major subsystems of the organization as she was able to. To do this she used the Katz and Kahn (1978) typology—production, support, maintenance, adaptive, and managerial subsystems—and promoted their coordination and direction on service.

Summary

Service climate is a complex, multidimensional, multilevel construct. However, both at the service climate level and the human resource level, incumbents' perceptions of the way the organization functions are reflected in the quality of service customers say they receive. Further, to change an organization to be more service-oriented may require an open-systems framework for thinking about change, since so many subsystems (Katz & Kahn, 1978) apparently affect the service quality ultimately experienced by the consumer. To change an organization to become one that is perceived to be a service climate requires attention to these multiple dimensions and multiple levels.

Concluding Thoughts

What Is Climate? The work summarized here has proceeded less systematically than I have presented it; retrospect has served an organizing function. However, there has been a constant movement in climate research from a quite general perspective on what organizational climate is to a more strategic focus for climate specification, operationalization, and change. This progress has, in interesting ways, yielded a *general* conceptualization of a *strategic* focus. That is, the strategic focus indicates that *all* subsystems of an organization must be targeted effectively on the strategic goal to create the strategic climate of interest. This strategic focus needs to be the target of climate assessment and management's attempts at climate change.

This conclusion follows from the idea that management in organizations makes choices, implicitly or explicitly, to adopt certain practices and procedures and to reward and support certain behaviors such that even implicit goals become clear to the organization's employees. These practices and procedures and the activities and behaviors that get rewarded and supported play a critical function in organizations—they are the criteria on which employees base their work decisions, and they send a message about what is important to prospective employees as well (Schneider, 1987).

Although the strategic focus of this chapter was the climate for service, it is clear that it could also have been safety, or quality, or innovation (Schneider & Gunnarson, 1990). However, the *strategic focus* of rewards and the *strategic focus* of policies and practices would differ. These differences in foci would produce different climates, because it is the strategic focus of routines and rewards that determines a setting's climate.

What Is the Best Way to Measure Climate? The assessment strategies I have described here have included both surveys and interviews. Neither of these methods is necessarily preferable; they are useful for different purposes. For an organization to change, it must have particular information about itself. This requires in-depth qualitative diagnosis for two reasons. First, management responds much more readily to extensive quotations from employees than they do to numbers. Second, determination of the ways in which specific issues manifest themselves varies greatly from organization to organization. Qualitative data provides managers with evidence about, for example, the precise practices and procedures that inhibit service delivery rather than merely identifying the fact that there are some inhibitory practices and procedures.

For instance, suppose a survey is conducted in an organization and employees report low levels of supervisory support, high levels of intradepartmental conflict, and low participation in decision making. The change agent cannot know the ways by which these are manifest in the organization, and so he or she cannot know precisely what needs to be changed. Conversely, for generic studies across organizations (units, functions, branches) against some strategic goal of interest, surveys may be the preferred procedure for achieving answers to more generic conceptual or research issues in which multiple sites are required for exploring hypothesized relationships.

The two extremes for data collection are presented here for purposes of explication, but there are intermediate possibilities. For example, one alternative would be to have a survey that contained items assessing generic themes that could be used across settings but for each setting the generic items could be supplemented by tailor-made items. The latter items would require some in-depth exploration of issues in a specific organization to identify the ways in which generic concepts become manifest there. Such a methodology would build on early research by Alderfer and Brown (1972) that showed the utility of "empathic questionnaires" for the generation of valid data.

There is still much to do on the development of measures, both quantitative and qualitative, for the assessment of climate.

However, the *purpose* of the assessment — that is, change in a *particular* organization versus research across a number of organizations — may dictate how useful a procedure will be.

What Is the Appropriate Unit of Analysis for Climate? I have not concentrated on this issue in the chapter except where I described the logic for the use of the branch as the unit of analysis in the service climate studies of employee and customer perceptions. However, the issue is a sticky one and must be grappled with by researchers prior to each study, or the ecological validity of the study may be threatened (Roberts, Hulin, & Rousseau, 1978; Rousseau, 1985). Obviously no unit of analysis for research is more appropriate than any other. As with the issue of the assessment of climate, the answer to the question depends on the particular unit of interest — banks, bank branches, or individual employees in branches.

I have recently begun thinking more systematically about the level-of-analysis problem and have reached the conclusion that the key issue is one of variability. By this I mean that each climate researcher or diagnostician must answer the question, At what unit of analysis do I want relatively low within-group variability and relatively high between-group variability?

Consider the following scenario. Suppose you wanted to show that the emphasis a bank branch manager gives to service in the eyes of his or her employees is related to the quality of service customers say they receive from those employees. You ask yourself the following question: Given that this is my question of interest, where do I want relatively low variability? The answer is within each branch. Given this answer, you know you should not ask employees or customers questions on which there is likely to be high variability across respondents within a branch; you want to maximize within-branch homogeneity while, of course, maintaining between-branch heterogeneity. You need to do the latter because, without branch heterogeneity, it is impossible to show a correlation across branches. Thus, just as variability needs to be low within branches, it also cannot be low between branches; the latter would only be useful if you were interested in how branches, collectively, do things.

Some might claim that choosing the level of analysis at which one wants (and does not want) variability is somehow cheating. For example, it might be argued that nature has put variability at some levels of analysis but not at others. However, this argument makes no sense, because all measurement—and thus all variability—is made by humans. The lessons of the scientific enterprise are that regardless of the chosen level of analysis for a study, variability can be shown to exist at levels above and below the target level (Nunnally, 1978). The conclusion is that every climate study must choose its level of analysis prior to the design of questions (either for surveys or for interviews) so that a delicate balance is achieved between obtaining within-unit and between-unit homogeneity and heterogeneity. A secondary conclusion is that, of course, there is no best unit of analysis for climate (or any other) studies. A caution here is that if organizational-level diagnoses are to be accomplished and used as a basis for truly organizational-level change, the focus of the questions must be very carefully worded to yield the relatively low within variability desirable as an index of homogeneity.

Conclusion

I have purposely ranged far and wide in this chapter, attempting to cover several issues regarding the conceptualization, measurement, and application of the climate construct. My conceptualization of climate is firmly grounded in a strategic model, emphasizing as it does a focus for the routines and rewards that constitute the data employees (and customers) use to reach a conclusion about the imperatives of the setting. For measurement, I have proposed a strategic focus as well. Thus, I have argued that the items in a survey and/or the questions in an interview should emphasize the issues in the setting that inhibit or facilitate the strategic focus of interest. Finally, I have noted the utility of an open-systems perspective for change when moving an organization from one strategic focus to another. This open-systems model permits identification of the broadest range of issues that might promote the strategic focus.

Throughout the chapter I used service as a convenient foil for demonstrating how one can think about, assess, and change climate. I happen to believe that a focus on service is important in and of itself, but others may disagree, preferring to emphasize the climate for safety or innovation or sales. Service is a useful foil, because the attributes of service make it imperative that organizations find a substitute for close and immediate supervision. The suggestion provided here emphasizes the creation of a climate through the routines and rewards of organization.

References

Albrecht, K., & Zemke, R. (1985). *Service America: Doing business in the new economy*. Homewood, IL: Dow Jones–Irwin.

Alderfer, C. P., & Brown, L. D. (1972). Designing an "empathic questionnaire" for organizational research. *Journal of Applied Psychology*, *56*, 456–460.

Aldrich, H. E. (1979). *Organizations and environments*. Englewood Cliffs, NJ: Prentice-Hall.

Argyris, C. (1958). Some problems in conceptualizing organizational climate: A case study of a bank. *Administrative Science Quarterly*, *2*, 501–520.

Banas, P. A. (1988). Employee involvement: A sustained labor/management initiative at the Ford Motor Company. In J. P. Campbell, R. J. Campbell, & Associates, *Productivity in organizations: New perspectives from industrial and organizational psychology*. San Francisco: Jossey-Bass.

Barnard, C. I. (1948). *Organization and management*. Cambridge, MA: Harvard University Press.

Bateson, J.E.G. (1977). Do we need service marketing? In *Marketing consumer services: New insights* (Report No. 77-115). Cambridge, MA: Marketing Science Institute.

Berry, L. L. (1980, May-June). Service marketing is different. *Business*, pp. 24–29.

Bowen, D. E. (1983). *Customers as substitutes for leadership in service organizations*. Unpublished doctoral dissertation, Michigan State University.

Bowen, D. E., & Schneider, B. (1983). Toward understanding

boundary roles in service organizations: Some research findings and future directions. In J. A. Czepiel, M. R. Solomon, & C. Suprenant (Eds.), *The service encounter*. Lexington, MA: Lexington Books.

Bowen, D. E., & Schneider, B. (1988). Services marketing and management: Implications for organizational behavior. In B. M. Staw & L. L. Cummings (Eds.), *Research in organizational behavior* (Vol. 10). Greenwich, CT: JAI Press.

Brown, K. A., & Mitchell, T. R. (1988). *Employee performance obstacles in retail banking: Attitudes and outcomes* (unpublished paper). Seattle: Seattle University, School of Business.

Chase, R. B. (1978). Where does the customer fit in a service operation? *Harvard Business Review, 56*, 137–142.

Chase, R. B. (1981). The customer contact approach to services: Theoretical bases and practical extensions. *Operations Research, 29*, 698–706.

Chase, R. B., & Tansik, D. A. (1983). The customer contact model for organization design. *Management Science, 49*, 1037–1050.

Czepiel, J. A., Solomon, M. R., & Suprenant, C. F. (Eds.) (1985). *The service encounter*. Lexington, MA: Lexington Books.

Delbecq, A. L., & Mills, P. K. (1985). Managerial practices that enhance innovation. *Organizational Dynamics, 14*, 24–34.

Eiglier, P., & Langeard, E. (1977). A new approach to service marketing. In *Marketing consumer services: New insights* (Report No. 77-115). Cambridge, MA: Marketing Science Institute.

Fleishman, E. A. (1953). Leadership climate, human relations training, and supervisory behavior. *Personnel Psychology, 6*, 205–222.

Forum Corporation. (1988). *Customer focus research*. Boston: Author.

Grönroos, C. (1990). *Service management and marketing: Managing the moment of truth in service competition*. Lexington, MA: Lexington Books.

Guion, R. M. (1973). A note on organizational climate. *Organizational Behavior and Human Performance, 9*, 120–125.

Gunnarson, S. A. (1989). *Some organizational correlates of employees' agreement with customers' perceptions of service quality*. Unpublished master's thesis, Department of Psychology, University of Maryland, College Park.

Hall, D. T. (1971). A theoretical model of career subidentity development in organizational settings. *Organizational Behavior and Human Performance, 6,* 50–76.

Hall, D. T., & Schneider, B. (1973). *Organizational climates and careers: The work lives of priests.* New York: Academic Press.

Hogan, J., Hogan, R., & Busch, C. M. (1984). How to measure service orientation. *Journal of Applied Psychology, 69,* 167–173.

James, L. R., & Jones, A. P. (1974). Organizational climate: A review of theory and research. *Psychological Bulletin, 81,* 1096–1112.

James, L. R., Joyce, W. F., & Slocum, J. W., Jr. (1988). Comment: Organizations do not cognize. *Academy of Management Review, 13,* 129–132.

Jones, A. P., & James, L. R. (1979). Psychological climate: Dimensions and relationships of individual and aggregated work environment perceptions. *Organizational Behavior and Human Performance, 23,* 201–250.

Joyce, W. F., & Slocum, J. W. (1982). Climate discrepancy: Refining the concept of psychological and organizational climate. *Human Relations, 35,* 951–972.

Katz, D., & Kahn, R. L. (1978). *The social psychology of organizations* (2nd ed.). New York: Wiley.

Kerr, S., & Jermier, J. M. (1978). Substitutes for leadership: Their meaning and measurement. *Organizational Behavior and Human Performance, 22,* 375–403.

Levitt, T. (1972). Production line approach to services. *Harvard Business Review, 50,* 802–810.

Lewin, K., Lippitt, R., & White, R. K. (1939). Patterns of aggressive behavior in experimentally created "social climates." *Journal of Social Psychology, 10,* 271–299.

Likert, R. (1967). *The human organization: Its management and values.* New York: McGraw-Hill.

Litwin, G. H., & Stringer, R. A. (1968). *Motivation and organizational climate.* Cambridge, MA: Harvard University, Graduate School of Business Administration, Division of Research.

Lovelock, C. H. (1981). Why marketing management needs to be different for services. In J. H. Donnelly & W. R. George (Eds.), *Marketing of services*. Chicago: American Marketing Association.

Lovelock, C. H. (1988). *Managing Services: Marketing, operations, and human resources*. Englewood Cliffs, NJ: Prentice-Hall.

Lovelock, C. H., & Young, R. F. (1979). Look to customers to increase productivity. *Harvard Business Review, 57*, 168–178.

McGregor, D. M. (1960). *The human side of enterprise*. New York: McGraw-Hill.

Mills, P. K. (1985). The control mechanisms of employees at the encounter of service organizations. In J. A. Czepiel, M. R. Solomon, & C. F. Suprenant (Eds.), *The service encounter* (pp. 163–177). Lexington, MA: Heath.

Moeller, A., Schneider, B., Schoorman, D., & Berney, E. (1988). Development of the Work Facilitation Diagnostic. In D. Schoorman & B. Schneider (Eds.), *Facilitating work effectiveness*. Lexington, MA: Lexington Books.

Normann, R. (1984). *Service management: Strategy and leadership in service business*. New York: Wiley.

Nunnally, J. C. (1978). *Psychometric theory* (2nd ed.). New York: McGraw-Hill.

Parasuraman, A., Zeithaml, V. A., & Berry, L. L. (1985). A conceptual model of service quality and its implications for future research. *Journal of Marketing, 49*, 41–50.

Parasuraman, A., Zeithaml, V. A., & Berry, L. L. (1988). SERV-QUAL: A multiple item scale for measuring consumer perceptions of service quality. *Journal of Retailing, 64*, 12–40.

Parkington, J. P., & Schneider, B. (1979). Some correlates of experienced job stress: A boundary role study. *Academy of Management Journal, 22*, 270–281.

Pennings, J. M., & Associates. (1985). *Organizational strategy and change: New views on formulating and implementing strategic decisions*. San Francisco: Jossey-Bass.

Peters, T. J. (1987). *Thriving on chaos*. New York: Knopf.

Peters, T. J., & Waterman, R. H., Jr. (1982). *In search of excellence: Lessons from America's best-run companies*. New York: Harper & Row.

Pettigrew, A. M. (Ed.). (1987). *The management of strategic change.* Oxford: Blackwell.

Powell, G. N., & Butterfield, D. A. (1978). The case for subsystem climates in organizations. *Academy of Management Review, 3,* 151–157.

Roberts, K. H., Hulin, C. L., & Rousseau, D. M. (1978). *Developing an interdisciplinary science of organizations.* San Francisco: Jossey-Bass.

Roberts, K. H., & Sloane, S. B. (1988). An aggregation problem and organizational effectiveness. In F. D. Schoorman & B. Schneider (Eds.), *Facilitating work effectiveness.* Lexington, MA: Lexington Books.

Rousseau, D. M. (1985). Issues of level in organizational research: Multi-level and cross-level perspectives. In L. L. Cummings & B. M. Staw (Eds.), *Research in organizational behavior* (Vol. 7). Greenwich, CT: JAI Press.

Schneider, R. (1973). The perception of organizational climate: The customer's view. *Journal of Applied Psychology, 57,* 248–256.

Schneider, B. (1975). Organizational climates: An essay. *Personnel Psychology, 28,* 447–479.

Schneider, B. (1980). The service organization: Climate is crucial. *Organizational Dynamics, 9,* 52–65.

Schneider, B. (1985). Organizational behavior. *Annual Review of Psychology, 36,* 573–611.

Schneider, B. (1987). Imperatives for the design of service organizations. In C. Suprenant (Ed.), *Add value to your service.* Chicago: American Marketing Association.

Schneider, B. (1990a). Applied psychology in business: A multilevel overview. In J. W. Jones, B. D. Steffey, & D. Bray (Eds.), *Applying psychology in business: The manager's handbook.* Lexington, MA: Lexington Books.

Schneider, B. (1990b). Creating service-oriented organizations: Simultaneous and sequential models for change. In D. E. Bowen, R. B. Chase, & T. G. Cummings, & Associates, *Service management effectiveness: Balancing strategy, organization and human resources, operations, and marketing.* San Francisco: Jossey-Bass.

Schneider, B., & Bartlett, C. J. (1968). Individual differences and organizational climate, I: The research plan and questionnaire development. *Personnel Psychology, 21*, 323-333.

Schneider, B., & Bartlett, C. J. (1970). Individual differences and organizational climate, II: Measurement of organizational climate by the multitrait-multirater matrix. *Personnel Psychology, 23*, 493-512.

Schneider, B., & Bowen, D. E. (1985). Employee and customer perceptions of service in banks: Replication and extension. *Journal of Applied Psychology, 70*, 423-433.

Schneider, B., & Gunnarson, S. (1990). Organizational climate and culture: The psychology of the workplace. In J. W. Jones, B. D. Steffey, & D. Bray (Eds.), *Applying psychology in business: The manager's handbook*. Lexington, MA: Lexington Books.

Schneider, B., Parkington, J. J., & Buxton, V. M. (1980). Employee and customer perceptions of service in banks. *Administrative Science Quarterly, 25*, 252-267.

Schneider, B., & Schechter, D. (1990). Development of a personnel selection system for service jobs. In S. Brown, E. Gummesson, B. Edvardsson, & B. Gustavsson (Eds.), *Service quality*. Lexington, MA: Lexington Books.

Schneider, B., & Snyder, R. A. (1975). Some relationships between job satisfaction and organizational climate. *Journal of Applied Psychology, 60*, 318-328.

Shostack, G. L. (1977a). Banks sell services—not things. *Bankers Magazine, 32*, 40-45.

Shostack, G. L. (1977b). Breaking free from product marketing. *Journal of Marketing, 41*, 73-80.

Stern, G. G. (1970). *People in context*. New York: Wiley.

Thompson, J. D. (1967). *Organizations in action*. New York: McGraw-Hill.

Weick, K. E. (1979). *The social psychology of organizing* (2nd ed.). Reading, MA: Addison-Wesley.

Woodman, R. W., & King, D. C. (1978). Organizational climate: Science as folklore. *Academy of Management Review, 3*, 816-826.

Zemke, R., & Schaff, D. (1989). *The service edge: 101 companies that profit from customer care*. New York: New American Library.

Zohar, D. (1980). Safety climate in industrial organizations: Theoretical and applied implications. *Journal of Applied Psychology, 65*, 96-102.

Conclusion

Andrew M. Pettigrew

Organizational Climate and Culture: Two Constructs in Search of a Role

Knowledge development in the social sciences is like adding pieces to a complex mosaic. Precisely because the social science mosaic is so untidy and complex, it is important from time to time to stop and review the pieces and ask awkward questions about additiveness and distinctiveness. Are these glass towers of dazzling logical integrity really so dazzling? Have the foundations of the towers in the empirical world become more and more precarious as they rose higher and higher? Of course, the problem of assessing additiveness and distinctiveness in the social sciences is made worse by our tendency to claim that progress has been made when new words enter the analytical vocabulary. Social scientists are inveterate wordsmiths. Neologisms abound. Obscurity, not clear progress, is often the result.

Doubts about the veracity of progress in knowledge development make periodic reviews and syntheses of parts of the field important. Such critical reflections are especially significant in an area such as organizational culture that has burgeoned so quickly and been used by practitioners so readily, and whose development has been distorted by the lack of empirical inquiry. When assessment in one subfield can occur simultaneously with

413

review in a related area, the possibility of simplifying the whole mosaic may even exist. In reviewing research on organizational climate and culture, this book therefore offers the reader a double benefit.

This brief and final chapter to the book has three sections. The first draws on the material in the book to discuss the similarities and differences between the two fields of study, climate and culture. This section also pulls together what the previous authors may have communicated by way of pessimism and optimism about progress in the related fields of study. The second and third sections express a personal view of two aspects of using culture in future organizational analysis. Both ways forward involve linking culture to related themes or forms of analysis. Thus I propose the virtues of studying organizations as political and cultural systems, and I argue the case for studying culture as part of a holistic, temporal, and contextual analysis of major issues such as competitiveness and strategic change.

Organizational Climate and Culture

What have the authors of this book said about the similarities and differences of these two fields of inquiry? Both have had definitional problems. This has been true of culture from the outset, perhaps because there has been a history of confusion about the concept from its origins in social anthropology. The definitional debates about organizational culture in the 1980s are reminiscent of Winston Churchill's comment about the Soviet colossus in the early 1950s as "a riddle wrapped in a mystery wrapped in an enigma." Part of the problem with culture is that it is not just a concept but the source of a family of concepts (Pettigrew, 1979), and it is not just a family of concepts but also a frame of reference or root metaphor for organizational analysis (Pettigrew, 1979; Smircich, 1983; Morgan, 1986). However, some progress has been made, and most scholars would now agree that organizational culture is a phenomenon that involves beliefs and behavior; exists at a variety of different levels in organizations; and manifests itself in a wide range of features of organizational life such as structures, control and reward systems, symbols, myths, and human resource practices.

With climate, the definitional problems and level-of-analysis issues arose after and not before empirical inquiry. Industrial psychologists are a much more pragmatic group than the often curious band of settlers who gathered around the camp fire to endlessly discuss the meaning of life and culture. The early climate researchers were not comfortable wringing their hands and biting the carpet over definitional issues. They were more likely to be driven by the maxim "if you can't measure it, it doesn't exist." So off they went to measure, and the same definitional and level-of-analysis issues emerged for them when they had to make sense of the mass of data collected in such an atheoretical fashion.

Interestingly, both culture and climate have been treated as independent and intervening variables linked to dependent variables such as financial performance and productivity. Chapters Seven and Eight in this volume leave one skeptical about such simple, linear thinking, and I will return to this issue later.

Not surprisingly, both climate and culture have largely been studied through cross-sectional research designs. In this respect, the study of climate and culture merely reflects the biases inherent in the social sciences generally and in the study of organizations in particular. As Thompson and Luthans, Mirvis and Sales, and Schneider in this volume remind us, we still know relatively little about the what, why, and how of climate and culture change. This is especially worrying in the culture area, since academic consultants and major consulting firms have rushed into producing culture change packages and programs before we even have a critical mass of high-quality case studies about how culture change processes occur.

A conclusion to be drawn from this book is that climate and culture share features of complexity and multidimensionality. They are also multilevel constructs. I will argue shortly that these features direct research naturally toward incorporating climate and culture in holistic, temporal, and contextual analyses of organizational life.

But what are some of the obvious and important differences between climate and culture raised by the authors in this volume? Culture certainly comes across as the more inclusive concept. Thus Schneider and Reichers conclude Chapter One by arguing that "culture exists at a higher level of abstraction than climate, and climate is a manifestation of culture." The disciplinary roots of culture in social anthropology and sociology are much wider and older than those for organizational climate, and culture is capable of being treated as a generic form of analysis, while organizational climate can be restricted to the status of a variable. Crucially, organizational culture deals with beliefs, perceptions, and behavior, whereas organizational climate has been built up from measures or qualitative assessments of individual perception. The chapters in this book create the impression that climate studies have been boxed in, even marginalized by the appearance in the nest of this rather overnourished, noisy, and enigmatic cuckoo called organizational culture. This pressure from an interloper may, however, be energizing climate researchers to rethink the role of climate studies, and one important benefit of this has been the important work by Schneider and his colleagues on the nature and creation of service climates (see Chapter Eleven in this volume as well as Schneider, 1980; Bowen & Schneider, 1988).

This book has both a pessimistic and an optimistic tone. The pessimism comes on the one hand from Dansereau and Alutto's well-judged piece on levels of analysis (see Chapter Six), and on the other from the rightly skeptical writing of Siehl and Martin on culture as a determinant and consequence of financial performance (see Chapter Seven). The definitional and conceptual ambiguities of culture (especially) but also of climate are brought up by nearly all the authors. The deeper concerns in the culture area are brought out with great intellectual surefootedness by Rousseau and by Siehl and Martin. Thus we are told about the uneven quality of case study work on culture, which is of no surprise given the amount of superficial "smash and grab" research that goes on under the banner of case study work. We are reminded of the limited quantitative work on organizational culture, but more interestingly, we discover that findings on culture may be method-bound. Qualitative studies tend to portray culture in terms of uniformity and mutuality, while more quantitative studies tap into diversity and variability of subculture (Rousseau). There are also soapbox cries that culture may already have been hijacked for managerial purposes, having been appropriated for their own purposes by executives and consultants. But the most serious cause for concern is the lack of empirical study of organizational culture in the 1980s. Here Chapters Five and Seven not only discuss the empirical intractability of examining the relationship between culture and performance, but also convey a deeper worry about the sheer difficulty of empirically studying culture in organizational settings. Is this pessimism justified?

Leaving aside for the moment critical matters such as the alternative research strategies and forms of data collection necessary to study culture in organizations, there are seven analytical issues that make culture difficult to study and indeed change. These are the

1. Levels issue
2. Pervasiveness issue
3. Implicitness issue
4. Imprinting issue
5. Political issue
6. Plurality issue
7. Interdependency issue

Briefly put, the *levels issue* arises because organizational culture exists at a variety of different levels in the firm. Thus at the deepest level it refers to the beliefs and assumptions of people inside the organization both about the internal workings of the organization and the way the organization faces its external environment. It is rather more difficult to study and change the core beliefs and assumptions within the organization than it is to identify some of the manifestations of culture in, for example, the organization's structure and systems.

Chapter Six in this volume is strikingly clear in exposing the level-of-analysis issues in climate and culture research. Dansereau and Alutto posit four approaches: single-level and multiple-level analysis, multiple-variable analysis, and finally multiple-relationship analysis. In terms of the practice of research they make two essential points about levels of analysis. In the formulation of theory and analysis of data about climate and culture, researchers should be explicit about choices of levels of analysis; second, researchers should expose and test conclusions from their preferred level of analysis to conclusions that emerge from studies using alternative levels of analysis. Although logically valid, I suspect their second requirement may be a bridge too far for most if not all climate and culture researchers. However, new standards in linking a theoretical approach to empirical patterns will result just from following Dansereau and Alutto's first suggestion of a more explicit choice of levels of analysis. This alone will tighten up research designs and limit claims for empirical progress from such analyses of climate and culture.

The *pervasiveness issue* is a corollary of the points made about different levels of culture. Culture is not only deep; it is also broad. Thus organizational culture not only encompasses people and their relationships and beliefs but also their views about company products, structures, systems, corporate purpose, and modes of recruitment, socialization, and reward. Recognizing that culture is identifiable at the level of the organization, the industry sector, and the national level only adds to complications about pervasiveness (Whipp, Rosenfeld, & Pettigrew, 1989).

In this volume a number of authors take up the issue of pervasiveness. Thus Schneider recognizes that "some dependent variable or strategic focus of interest has, mostly implicitly, driven research on the climate construct." He goes on to emphasize the extent to which his strategic focus in climate research (service climate) is dependent not just on human resource practices but on many facets of the organization functioning optimally. Hence service climate must not only be broadly studied through multiple dimensions and levels of analysis, but any practical theory of service climate change would have to involve interventions of a systemic character.

In a much less accessible but nevertheless instructive

chapter—Chapter Two—James, James, and Ashe recognize the systemic and therefore pervasive nature of the culture construct, but then seem to put an unnecessarily tight boundary around culture by characterizing it as "a group-level construct, a product of social interactions among group members." Group is fine as long as it is inclusive of departmental groups in the firm, sector cultures that can emerge between key groupings of firms in an industry or service sector, or even national cultures which can impact on culture development at firm and sector levels. But culture is pervasive, and therefore its study requires a conceptual approach and sources of data that are sensitive to the breadth and depth of culture expression. Later in this chapter I describe a form of holistic, temporal, and contextual analysis capable of capturing the pervasiveness of culture.

The *implicitness issue* pertains to the fact that much of organizational culture is taken for granted. It is remarkably difficult to study and change things that are implicitly part of people's thinking and behavior and that are rarely brought out explicitly for consideration.

The *imprinting issue* evokes the deep historical roots of much of organizational culture. History weighs a very heavy hand in the present and future operation of most corporations. James, James, and Ashe usefully recognize the importance of historical imprinting on attributed meanings in work environments. Thus individuals are not portrayed as entering new work environments with their minds blank waiting to be filled with new beliefs, meanings, and practices. Part of the tension around the acquisition of new meaning occurs because over time individuals acquire underlying belief systems that then need to accommodate to current work environments. Louis's chapter also acknowledges the power of history, this time by recognizing the role of "trustworthy recipes" in acculturation processes. However, it is Mirvis and Sales, with their ten-year analysis of culture change, who most powerfully bring home the heavy hand of history and its impact on cultural change processes (see Chapter Ten).

The *political issue* refers to the connections between culture and the power distribution in the firm, an analytical

connection I will develop shortly. Certain power groups in the
organization have a vested interest in the beliefs and assumptions that may have primacy at any point in time in the firm's
development. Those power groups are unlikely to be willing to
discard those beliefs and assumptions without persistent and
consistent challenge.

The *plurality issue* is a close cousin of politics and culture.
Most firms do not just have a single culture but at any point in
time may have a variety of different sets of beliefs and assumptions — in effect a series of subcultures. Tension about the future
development of the organization is often expressed in terms of
the language and political positioning of these different
subcultures.

In her perceptive and lucid chapter (Chapter Five), Rousseau points to the implicit character of culture and its pluralism.
Crucially, she argues that different layers of culture are amenable to different research methods. Thus the more explicit and
observable manifestations of culture can be studied by means of
structured and quantitative methods, while the more implicit
and taken-for-granted features of culture are only likely to be
penetrated by deep immersion in the social processes of field
research situations.

Rousseau also acknowledges that organizations may have
strong subcultures, although she recognizes that cultural pluralism will vary from organization to organization. The interesting question, then, is why? Why do some organizations have
strong and uniform corporate cultures, while others appear
more like a fragmented set of tribes? I recognize that there may
be some truth in her generalization that qualitative research
methods tend to end up portraying uniformity and mutuality in
organizations, and quantitative methods catch diversity, but a
glance at Pettigrew (1985a) and Pettigrew, McKee, and Ferlie
(1988) will also reveal plenty of evidence of cultural pluralism
and conflict in studies using so-called qualitative research
methods.

Finally, the *interdependency issue* focuses on the fact that
culture is interconnected not only with the politics of the firm,
but also with the structure, systems, people, and priorities of the

firm, and, of course, with the many environments linked to the organization.

But lest the reader take pessimism as an excuse for inactivity, where do the contributors to this book signal ways forward for climate and culture research? Where are the optimistic signs and signals? When and where can organizational climate and culture be used with the greatest analytical and empirical effectiveness? What role in organizational analysis can climate and culture studies play in the future?

The clear message from this book is that climate and culture are complex, multidimensional, and multilevel constructs. They are systemic constructs that come alive when they are studied in a holistic fashion and when they are linked to key themes or problems of organizational functioning. It is one thing to produce a multidimensional analysis of organizational climate across a sample of thirty organizations; it is quite another to link such an analysis to the service, safety, or innovation capability of those organizations. Equally well, organizational culture can be studied atomistically and descriptively through and within case or comparative analysis of, for example, top-management belief systems or symbols and rituals, or it can be studied more thematically by linking variability in organizational culture to the rate and pace of strategic change in a number of organizations. Louis with her theme of acculturation; Joyce and Slocum linking climate to business strategy; Kopelman, Brief, and Guzzo trying to connect climate and culture to productivity; and Schneider establishing a link between service organization and climate — all of these authors begin to make use of climate and culture in a systemic and thematic fashion.

The leading question, of course, is how is this thematic work to be done? Not, I would suggest, by treating organizational climate or culture as an independent or intervening variable somehow linearly "associated" with a theme of study (or focus of interest, to use Schneider's words), such as service quality, productivity, or performance. All of the authors in this book who take the argument this far end up concluding that variability in their focus of interest cannot be explained just by reference to one variable. Thus Schneider reports in Chapter Eleven that "service climate is dependent on many facets of the organization functioning optimally, not just the human resource practices." And Siehl and Martin contend in Chapter Seven that any future research attempting to link culture to performance should minimally examine that link through broader organizational processes of learning and change. The conclusion I would draw from this is that if one way forward is to link climate and culture to key themes or foci of interest, then the systemic quality of such linkages should be studied holistically. In the final section of this chapter I will exemplify such a holistic analysis by drawing on recent research at the Centre for Corporate Strategy and Change, University of Warwick (Whipp, Rosenfeld, & Pettigrew, 1989; Pettigrew & Whipp, 1990).

But before I do that I wish to return to amplify a theme explicit in my 1979 paper on organization culture, the role of culture as a frame of reference for organizational analysis.

Organizations as Cultural and Political Systems

The purpose of my 1979 paper on organizational culture was to help integrate concepts familiar to social anthropologists with the analytical vocabulary of organizational behavior. Behind this was a belief that the study of processes of leadership, commitment building, and change could be enriched through an analysis of the more cultural and expressive aspects of organizational life. Since 1979 I have pursued a number of empirical inquiries of links between culture and strategic change (Pettigrew, 1985a, 1987; Pettigrew, McKee, & Ferlie, 1988; Pettigrew, Hendry, & Sparrow, 1989; Whipp, Rosenfeld, & Pettigrew, 1989), as well as trying to develop the epistemological and methodological bases for such inquiries (Pettigrew, 1985b, 1990). Meanwhile other colleagues have made strides in developing culture as a root metaphor and image for organizational analysis (for example, Smircich, 1983; Morgan, 1986).

I wish now to signal again the important theoretical role of culture in organizational analysis, but this time to connect both cultural and political ideas to the study of change processes. In making this explicit connection between culture and politics I recognize the long tradition of thinking in this area, particularly by Edelman (1964), but also more recent writing on organizational analysis by Riley (1983) and Lucas (1987).

The starting point for this analysis of strategic change is the notion that formulating the *content* of any change inevitably entails managing its *context* and *process*. Outer context refers to the social, economic, political, and competitive environment in which the firm operates. Inner context refers to the structure, organizational cultures, and political context within the firm through which ideas for change have to proceed. Content refers to the particular areas of change under examination. Thus the firm may be seeking to change technology, employees, products, geographical positioning, or indeed organizational culture. The process of change refers to the actions, reactions, and interactions from the various interested parties as they seek to move the firm from its present to its future state. Thus the "what" of change is encapsulated under the label *content*, much of the "why" of change is derived from an analysis of inner and outer context, and the "how" of change can be understood from an analysis of process.

What are the implications of studying change through a political and cultural frame of reference? First, there is no pretense to see strategic change as a rational analytical process of analyzing environments, resources, and gaps, revealing and assessing strategic alternatives and choosing and implementing carefully analyzed and well-thought-through outcomes (Andrews, 1971; King & Cleland, 1978). Rather, in the manner of Bower (1970), Mintzberg (1978), and Burgelman (1983), the transformation of the firm is seen as an iterative, multilevel process, with outcomes emerging not merely as a product of rational or boundedly rational debates, but also shaped by the interests and commitments of individuals and groups, the forces of bureaucratic momentum, gross changes in the environment, and the manipulation of the structural context around decisions. Taking this view, the focus of attention is on seeing change as a multilevel and continuous process in context, where leadership is expressed through understanding and tactical skill as

well as through the purposive force of mobilizing often im-
precise and inarticulate visions, which are used to challenge
dominating beliefs and institutional arrangements. In this contextualist view of strategic change the analyst has a choice of
alternative process modes. Although on the surface the custom
and practice of persuasion may dictate that initiatives for
change are publicly justified on the weight of technical evidence
and analysis, or more narrowly in terms of managerial drives for
efficiency and effectiveness, it is too narrow to see change just as
a rational, linear problem-solving process. Explanations of
change have to be able to deal with continuity and change,
actions and structures, and endogenous and exogenous factors,
as well as with the role of chance and surprise. Although there is
force in Poggi's (1965, p. 284) stricture that "a way of seeing is a
way of not seeing," there is also a trap in trying to be overly
eclectic, trying to see everything and thus to see nothing. In this
author's view, and indeed in the theoretical writing and empirical research of others (Greenwood & Hinings, 1986; Hardy,
1985; Johnson, 1987; Normann, 1977; Pfeffer, 1981), a view of
process combining political and cultural elements evidently has
real power in explaining continuity and change.

The interest in culture directs attention to sources of
coherence and consistency in organizational life, to the dominating beliefs or ideologies that provide the systems of meaning
and interpretation that filter in and filter out environmental
and intraorganizational signals. The recognition that culture
can shape and not merely reflect organizational power relationships directs attention both to the ground rules that structure the character of political processes in the firm, and to the
assumptions and interests that powerful groups shield and
lesser groups may only with fortitude challenge.

The acts and processes associated with politics as the
management of meaning represent conceptually the overlap
between a concern with the political and cultural analyses of
organizations. A central concept linking political and cultural
analyses essential to the understanding of continuity and
change is legitimacy. The management of meaning refers to a
process of symbol construction and value use designed to create

legitimacy for one's ideas, actions, and demands, and to delegitimate the demands of one's opponents. If one sees strategic change processes at least partially as a contest about ideas and rationalities between individuals and groups, then the mechanisms used to legitimate and delegitimate particular ideas or broader ideologies are obviously critical in such an analysis. Equally well, the resolution of such contests about ideas needs to be sensitive to questions of power and control in the firm.

Building on Lukes (1974) and Pfeffer (1981), Hardy (1985) has argued that a concern with power and control as explanations of strategic choice and change processes would in effect correspond to two uses of power: power used to defeat competition in a choice or change process, and power used to prevent competition in a choice or change process. In both of these processes there would be an explanatory role for unobtrusive systems of power derived from the generation and manipulation of symbols, language, belief, and ideology—that is, from culture creation—and from the more public face of power expressed through the possession, control, and tactical use of overt sources of power such as position, rewards or sanctions, or expertise.

There are two further essential points to derive from the above way of thinking about process. The first is that structures, cultures, and strategies are not just being treated here as neutral, functional constructs connectable to some system need such as efficiency or adaptability; those constructs are viewed as capable of serving to protect the interests of dominant groups. Thus the biases existing in structures and cultures can protect dominant groups by reducing the chances of challenge, and features of inner and outer context can be mobilized by dominant or aspiring groups to legitimate the existing order, or indeed to help create a new order. These points are as pertinent to understanding processes of strategic change as they are to achieving practical outcomes in strategic change. As Normann (1977, p. 161) has so aptly put it, "the only way to bring about lasting change and to foster an ability to deal with new situations is by influencing the conditions that determine the interpretation of situations and the regulation of ideas."

The above political and cultural view of process gives a central place to the processes and mechanisms through which strategic changes are legitimated or delegitimated. The content of strategic change is thus ultimately a product of a legitimation process shaped by political/cultural considerations, though often expressed in rational/analytical terms. This recognition that transformation in the firm may involve a challenge for the dominating ideology, cultures, systems of meaning, and power relationships in the organization makes it clear why and how the processes of sensing, justifying, and creating change can be so tortuous and long.

The author's longitudinal study of strategic change in Imperial Chemical Industries (ICI) illustrates how much the formulation of the content of strategic change is dependent on managing its context and process (Pettigrew, 1985a). The process skills at the most general level involve the legitimation of the content of strategy in the evolving inner and outer context of the firm. The ICI data illustrate the deep-seated organizational cultural and political roots of strategy, and the existence of dominating rationalities or core beliefs inside the firm that provide the frame of reference by which individuals and groups make sense of changing features of their inner and outer context. The case also points to the enormous difficulties in breaking down such core beliefs once a particular marriage of content, context, and process has become established. The breaking down of such core beliefs is reported as a long-term conditioning process—a political learning process, influenced by the interest and, above all, the persistence of visionary leaders, the changing pattern of competition between individuals and groups representing different rationalities, the massive enabling opportunity created by changes in outer context, and ultimately a subtle process of connecting what are perceived to be coherent solutions at particular points in time to legitimate problems. Thus a political and cultural view of change directs attention to uniformity and diversity in organizations, to context and action, and to expressive and instrumental behavior; most important, it ties any explanation of change into longer-term processes of continuity.

The Contextual Analysis of Competitiveness and Change

Siehl and Martin conclude Chapter Seven in this volume by exclaiming that "the concept of culture holds too much promise to be sold short as just another intervening variable in existing models of the determinants of organizational performance." In Chapter Eight, Kopelman, Brief, and Guzzo draw a similar conclusion, this time about "a long and tenuous link between culture and productivity." The broader analytical conclusion I have drawn from these and related arguments is that organizational culture and climate will be most profitably researched in a holistic and temporal manner. Only this way will the systemic character of culture be adequately linked to key features of organizational life such as service quality, strategic change, productivity, or competitive performance. In what follows, I briefly describe the contextualist character of such research, and then illustrate its use in a study of competitiveness and strategic change.

Elsewhere I have described the ahistorical, aprocessual, and acontextual weaknesses of research on change in organizations (Pettigrew, 1985a, 1987). Chapters Five and Seven of the present volume also describe the contextual and processual weakness of research on culture. In addition, we know that much research on climate is atemporal (see Chapter Two). But what are the key features of a contextualist analysis of change? A contextualist analysis of a process such as change draws on phenomena at vertical and horizontal levels of analysis and on the interconnections between those levels through time. The vertical level refers to the interdependencies between one or more levels of analysis upon phenomena to be explained at some further level — for example, the impact of changing socioeconomic context on features of organizational culture and power. The horizontal level refers to the sequential interconnectedness among phenomena in historical, present and future time. An approach that offers both multilevel or vertical analysis and processual, or horizontal, analysis is said to be contextualist in character.

In summary, the key points to emphasize in analyzing

change in a contextualist mode are first the importance of embeddedness, implying the need to study change in the context of interconnected levels of analysis. Second, the importance of temporal interconnectedness — the need to locate change in past, present, and future time — should be stressed. Third, the need to explore context and action (how context is a product of action and vice versa) is crucial. Finally, the central assumption about causation in this kind of holistic analysis is that causation of change is neither linear or singular — the search for a simple and singular grand theory of change is unlikely to bear fruit. Arguments over the true or single source of change, while interesting and worthwhile in the sharpening of academic minds and egos, are ultimately pointless. For the analyst interested in the theory and practice of changing, the task is to identify the variety and mixture of causes of change and to explore through time some of the conditions and contexts under which these mixtures occur.

The first assumption of contextualism is that target changes should be studied in the context of change at other levels of analysis. Thus explanations for the fluctuations in the relative competitive performance of firms should be linked to sector and economic change (Pettigrew & Whipp, 1990). A source of change is the asymmetries between levels of context, where processes at different levels of analysis are often observed to have their own momentum, rates, pace, and trajectory. Thus the rate and trajectory of change in an industrial sector characterized by significant boundary changes may be much faster than the sensing and adjustment pathways of individual firms to the regrouping of the sector. The relative slowness of the sensing and adjustment process of firms, and their failure to recognize that the bases of competition may have changed in that sector, is a key factor explaining their loss of competitive performance (Pettigrew & Whipp, 1990). Equally well, the analyst of change has to recognize that activities at some levels of context may be more visible and rapid than at other levels, and thus in the short term sources of change may appear unidirectional, while in the longer term a multidirectional pattern may appear.

The second background assumption about contextualism

is the importance of revealing temporal interconnectedness. The need arises to catch reality in flight. Antecedent conditions shape the present and the emerging future. The human resource inheritance of many firms may affect the rate and pace of business strategy change if the business change requires significant adjustments in the knowledge base of the firm (Pettigrew, Hendry, & Sparrow, 1989). Thus history is not just an event in the past but is alive in the present and may shape the future. However, history is to be understood not just as events and chronology; there may be deeper pathways if the analyst searches for structures and underlying logics. But in the search for deeper structures, beware of the dangers of determinism. No assumptions are made about predetermined timetables — that is, about ordered and inevitable sequences or stages. Trajectories of change are probabilistic and uncertain because of changing contexts.

The third background assumption relates to the role of context and action. Here the key starting point is that it is not a question of nature or nurture, or context or action, but of context *and* action. Context is not just a stimulus environment but a nested arrangement of structures and processes where the subjective interpretations of actors perceiving, comprehending, learning, and remembering help shape process. Thus processes are both constrained by contexts and shape contexts, either in the direction of preserving or altering them. In the past, structural analyses emphasizing abstract dimensions and contextual constraints have been regarded as incompatible with processual analyses stressing action and strategic conduct. Here an attempt is being made to combine these two forms of description and analysis. This is done first by conceptualizing structure and context not just as a barrier to action but as essentially involved in its production (Giddens, 1979; Ranson, Hinings, & Greenwood, 1980), and second by demonstrating how aspects of structure and context (including culture) are mobilized by actors and groups as they seek to obtain outcomes important to them (Pettigrew, 1985a; Pettigrew, McKee, & Ferlie, 1988; Ferlie & Pettigrew, 1990).

Finally, this holistic and multifaceted treatment of change

makes certain causal assumptions. Causation is neither linear nor singular. There is no attempt to search for the illusory single grand theory of change, or indeed of how and why a single independent variable causes or even impacts on a dependent or outcome variable. Changes have multiple causes and are to be explained more by loops than lines — "the shifting interconnectedness of fused strands," as Mancuso and Ceely (1980, p. 15) put it. Thus in Pettigrew and Whipp (1990), five key features distinguish our high-performing automobile, investment banking, insurance, and book publishing firms from their less successful competitors: environmental assessment, human resources as assets and liabilities, linking strategic and operational change, leading change, and coherence. But the real explanation for relative competitive performance was not found in these five features but in isolation from each other, the convergent interactions and interconnected loops among the features in each firm over time.

As in Siehl and Martin's review in Chapter Seven, Pettigrew and Whipp (1990) concluded our research study by arguing that culture does not provide a direct explanation of performance; it is only one component of a much more complex set of relationships that the process of competition contains. Our contextualist and processual understanding of competition, combined with an in-depth analysis of more and less successful firms in four sectors over twenty plus years, allowed us to isolate the five core features represented in Figure C.1. The interested reader may wish to consult Pettigrew and Whipp (1990) for a fuller treatment of our findings linking cultural change within the firm to competitive performance. The picture of the relationships is a rich and complex one. Thus in Jaguar Cars the interlocking causes extended from new senior management and their radically altered business strategy and values, to the impact of exchange ratios, to the shift in the cooperative/competitive balance within the sector, to the host of changes in the company and parent corporate cultures.

If a firm's competitive position rests on such a range of bases that are changing across time, then culture is only one paradoxical yet critical factor among them. Culture is akin to a

Figure C.1. Managing Change for Competitive Success: Five Factors.

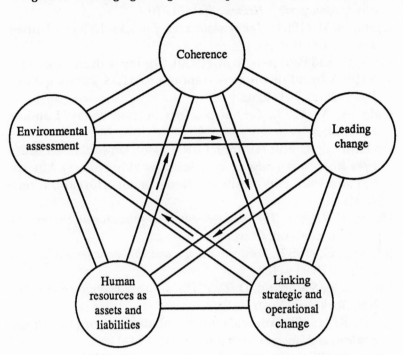

Pandora's box. Academics and practitioners should not make any easy assumptions about their control of the contents.

References

Andrews, K. (1971). *The concept of corporate strategy*. Homewood, IL: Irwin.

Bowen, D. E., and Schneider, B. (1988). Services marketing and management: Implications for organizational behavior. In B. M. Staw and L. L. Cummings (Eds.), *Research in organizational behavior* (Vol. 10). Greenwich, CT: JAI Press.

Bower, J. L. (1970). *Managing the resource allocation process*. Cambridge, MA: Harvard University Press.

Burgelman, R. A. (1983). A model of the interaction of strategic behavior, corporate context, and the concept of strategy. *Academy of Management Review, 8*(1), 61–70.

Edelman, M. (1964). *The symbolic uses of politics*. Urbana: University of Illinois Press.

Ferlie, E., and Pettigrew, A. M. (1990). Coping with change in the NHS: A frontline district's response to AIDS. *Journal of Social Policy, 19*(2), 191–220.

Giddens, A. (1979). *Central problems in social theory*. London: Macmillan.

Greenwood, R., and Hinings, C. R. (1986). *Organizational design types, tracks, and the dynamics of change* (working paper). Alberta, Canada: University of Alberta, Department of Organizational Analysis.

Hardy, C. (1985). *The management of organisational closure*. Aldershot, England: Gower Press.

Johnson, G. (1987). *Strategic change and the management process*. Oxford: Blackwell.

King, W. R., & Cleland, D. T. (1978). *Strategic planning and policy*. New York: Van Nostrand.

Lucas, R. (1987). Political-cultural analysis of organizations. *Academy of Management Journal, 12*(1), 144–156.

Lukes, S. (1974). *Power: A radical view*. London: Macmillan.

Mancuso, J. C., & Ceely, S. G. (1980). The self as memory processing. *Cognitive Therapy and Research, 4*(1), 1–25.

Mintzberg, H. (1978). Patterns of strategy formation. *Management Science, 24*(9), 934–948.

Morgan, G. (1986). *Images of organization*. Newbury Park, CA: Sage.

Normann, R. (1977). *Management for growth*. London: Wiley.

Pettigrew, A. M. (1979). On studying organizational cultures. *Administrative Science Quarterly, 24*(4), 570–581.

Pettigrew, A. M. (1985a). *The awakening giant: Continuity and change in ICI*. Oxford: Blackwell.

Pettigrew, A. M. (1985b). Contextualist research: A natural way to link theory and practice. In E. E. Lawler, III, A. M. Mohrman, Jr., S. A. Mohrman, G. E. Ledford, Jr., T. G. Cummings, & Associates, *Doing research that is useful for theory and practice*. San Francisco: Jossey-Bass.

Pettigrew, A. M. (1987). Context and action in the transformation of the firm. *Journal of Management Studies, 24*(6), 649–670.

Pettigrew, A. M. (1990). Longitudinal field research on change: Theory and practice. *Organizational Science, 1*(3).

Pettigrew, A. M., Hendry, C., & Sparrow, P. R. (1989). *Training in Britain: Employers' perspectives on human resources.* London: Her Majesty's Stationery Office.

Pettigrew, A. M., McKee, L., & Ferlie, E. (1988). Understanding change in the NHS. *Public Administration, 66,* 297–317.

Pettigrew, A. M., & Whipp, R. (1990). *Managing change for competitive success.* Oxford: Blackwell.

Pfeffer, J. (1981). *Power in organizations.* Marshfield, MA: Pitman.

Poggi, G. (1965). A main theme of contemporary sociological analysis: Achievements and eliminations. *British Journal of Sociology, 16,* 283–294.

Ranson, S., Hinings, C. R., & Greenwood, R. (1980). The structuring of organization structures. *Administrative Science Quarterly, 25*(1), 1–18.

Riley, P. A. (1983). A structurationist account of political culture. *Administrative Science Quarterly, 28,* 414–437.

Schneider, B. (1980). The service organization: Climate is crucial. *Organizational Dynamics, 9,* 52–65.

Smircich, L. (1983). Concepts of culture and organizational analysis. *Administrative Science Quarterly, 28,* 339–358.

Whipp, R., Rosenfeld, R., and Pettigrew, A. M. (1989). Culture and competitiveness: Evidence from two mature UK industries. *Journal of Management Studies, 26*(6), 561–585.

Name Index

Subject Index